WESTERN EUROPEAN PAINTING
IN THE HERMITAGE

Raphael's Loggias

WESTERN EUROPEAN PAINTING
IN THE HERMITAGE

Harry N. Abrams, Inc., Publishers, New York

INTRODUCTION BY ACADEMICIAN *BORIS PIOTROVSKY*

TRANSLATED BY *YURY NEMETSKY*

LAYOUT BY *GENNADY GUBANOV* AND *VIACHESLAV BAKHTIN*

LIBRARY OF CONGRESS CATALOGUE CARD NUMBER: 78-58588

INTERNATIONAL STANDARD BOOK NUMBER: 0-8109-1751-3

COPYRIGHT © 1978 BY AURORA ART PUBLISHERS, LENINGRAD

PUBLISHED IN 1978 BY HARRY N. ABRAMS, INCORPORATED, NEW YORK

PRINTED AND BOUND IN THE USSR

THE HERMITAGE, one of the largest and oldest museums in the world, has come a long way from its position as a "place of seclusion" (the French *ermitage*, whence its name) in the palace of the Russian Empress to its present-day standing as an immensely popular national museum. Though in 1778, referring to the Hermitage treasures in a letter to a French correspondent, Catherine II could say: "The only ones to admire all this are the mice and me," and even after it became a "public" museum in 1852 the far from numerous visitors could get admission tickets only from the court office, today the Hermitage is visited annually by over three and a half million people.

At the present time the museum occupies five buildings, each an architectural masterpiece. Four of these are stretched out in a line on the left bank of the Neva in the centre of Leningrad: the Winter Palace, built in 1762 by Rastrelli, the Small Hermitage, designed by Vallin de la Mothe in 1769, the Big Hermitage, designed by Velten and completed in 1784, and the Hermitage Theatre, built by Quarenghi and linked to the Big Hermitage by an arched bridge over the Winter Canal. The façade of the fifth building, the New Hermitage, put up in 1851 from a design by Klenze, fronts Khalturin (formerly Millionnaya) Street, which runs parallel to the Neva. The portico of the New Hermitage is adorned by ten huge figures of atlantes hewn out of granite by Russian craftsmen under the supervision of Terebenev.

The Hermitage today is virtually a museum of the history of culture — from its very dawn, the Stone Age, to modern times. It consists of six major departments which have on display relics of prehistoric culture (for the most part archaeological finds discovered in the territory of the Soviet Union), the culture of antiquity (including treasures coming from excavations of ancient Greek and Roman settlements on the Northern Black Sea coast), the culture of the peoples of the East (beginning with the ancient civilizations of Egypt and Mesopotamia), Russian culture, Western European art (painting, drawing, sculpture and applied art), and numismatics (coins, medals and orders). The entire exposition is housed in 353 rooms. Each year the Hermitage stages no less than twenty temporary exhibitions drawn from its own limitless stocks or loaned by foreign museums.

The Hermitage collection of Western European painting enjoys world renown. Most richly represented are the French, Italian, Flemish and Dutch schools, which were especially popular in Russia in the eighteenth and nineteenth centuries, the period when the collection was being assembled.

Pictures by famous European masters had graced the residences of Russian emperors beginning with the early eighteenth century. In 1716, for example, Peter the Great purchased in Amsterdam for his Peterhof palace a number of works by Dutch artists, including Rembrandt's *David's Farewell to Jonathan*. A rich collection of European paintings was housed also in the Catherine Palace erected in 1756 in Tsarskoye Selo (now the town of Pushkin).

The history of the Hermitage picture gallery begins with the year 1764, when 225 canvases bought a year earlier by Catherine II from the German merchant Johann Ernest Gotzkowsky were delivered to the Winter Palace. This collection consisted for the most part of works by Flemish and Dutch artists and included such famous pieces as Hals's *Portrait of a Young Man Holding a Glove*, Steen's *The Revellers* and Goltzius's *The Baptism of Christ*.

This first purchase of pictures was followed by new acquisitions made one after another. Catherine II kept up a regular correspondence with the French encyclopedists Diderot and Grimm, whom she would ask for advice in matters pertaining to the augmentation of her Hermitage collection.

Acting on the Empress's orders, Russian diplomats abroad engaged in the purchase of works of art. In France this assignment fell to the young ambassador Golitsyn, a highly educated man, who was to become an honorary member of the St Petersburg Academy of Sciences. Golitsyn's many personal contacts and his friendship with the progressive-minded public figures and artists of Paris helped him to carry out his mission with success. He was responsible for the purchase in 1766 of such masterpieces as Rembrandt's *The Return of the Prodigal Son* and Poussin's *Tancred and Erminia*. This was followed by the acquisition, also in Paris, of entire collections — Jean de Julienne's, which chiefly included pictures of the Dutch school, in 1767, and Nicolas Gaignat's in 1768. In 1768, also thanks to Golitsyn, the Hermitage acquired for its picture gallery the Hague collection of the Austrian minister Count Cobentzl — forty-six pictures and over four thousand drawings. Two of the pictures from that collection, *The Statue of Ceres* by Rubens and *Portrait of a Lady with Her Daughter* by Bruyn, are reproduced in this album.

In 1769 Prince Beloselsky bought for 90 thousand roubles the large Dresden collection of Count Brühl of Saxony. This minister had been entrusted by the Elector of Saxony with the task of selecting pictures for the Dresden Gallery and had simultaneously put together a sizable collection of his own, preferring works of the Flemish and Dutch schools. Among these were such superb pieces as Wouwerman's *View in the Environs of Haarlem* and Mieris's *Breakfast with Oysters*.

By the end of the 1760s the Hermitage collection of pictures had become too large for the Winter Palace. Additional room for new acquisitions was found in the Small Hermitage, designed by Vallin de la Mothe. This new building consisted of two pavilions (north and south) and a hanging garden between them. Two narrow galleries were added in 1775 by Quarenghi expressly for hanging newly acquired paintings. The north pavilion, which fronts the Neva, was completed in 1769; it was designed to serve as a "place of seclusion", much like the detached garden pavilions, known as "hermitages", of Tsarskoye Selo and Peterhof (in this case, though, the structure had to be placed in direct propinquity to the palace, not in the garden). The walls of the pavilion accommodated 92 pictures.

Catherine II used to refer to the entire collection of pictures, antiquities, porcelain and gems located in different parts of the Winter Palace and in the adjacent structures (23 years in the building, from 1764 to 1787) as the Hermitage, and it is under this name that the museum has been known since.

The acquisition of pictures abroad was not without its mishaps. In 1771, for example, the Brankamp collection, purchased in Genoa, was lost at sea together with the ship carrying it to Russia. This loss was, however, compensated for the very next year when through the good services of Diderot and Tronchin the famous Crozat collection (the Thiers Gallery) was acquired in Paris, in spite of objections from the Parisian public. Crozat's collection included works of different schools selected with sound artistic taste and discretion. Among its masterpieces mention should be made of Giorgione's *Judith*, Raphael's *The Holy Family* (*The Madonna with the Beardless St Joseph*), Titian's *Danaë*, Veronese's *The Adoration of the Magi* and *Pietà*, Van Dyck's *Portrait of a Young Man*, Bourdon's *The Death of Dido* and Watteau's *Actors of the Comédie-Française*. Purchased at the same time was the small but very interesting collection owned by the French foreign minister, the Duke of Choiseul; one of his pictures, Murillo's *Boy with a Dog*, is reproduced in this album.

The provenance of some Hermitage pictures, however, is to this day an unclear point. Between 1764 and 1774 the following masterpieces of world art found their way into the Hermitage: *Family Group* by Van Dyck, *Flora* by Rembrandt, *The Marsh* by Ruisdael, *The Dancer La Camargo* by Lancret and *Grace before Meat* by Chardin.

Some impressions recorded by visitors to the Hermitage in the second half of the eighteenth century have come down to us. Daniel Bernoulli, connected with the St Petersburg Academy of Sciences, mentions a visit to the Hermitage picture gallery in his Russian travel notes of 1777—78. At that time it occupied the Small Hermitage and the two galleries flanking the hanging garden. Bernoulli was dissatisfied with the way the pictures were hung, "without any order or selection, with different schools intermixed haphazardly", but at the same time remarked that "this collection contains some unexpected treasures, some truly priceless pictures". He also reports that visitors were provided with a catalogue issued in 1774 in 60 copies (this first catalogue listed 2,080 works). Another visitor who complained in his diary of 1776 of the indiscriminate way the pictures were arranged and of the cramped and narrow space in the hanging garden's galleries was the French diplomat Corberon.

The Hermitage pictures were further pressed for space in 1779 with the acquisition in London by Count Musin-Pushkin of the greater part of Sir Robert Walpole's collection from Houghton Hall. This was a sensational purchase, so much so that attempts were made to prevent the collection being taken out of the country. Like Crozat's, Walpole's was a diversified collection and thus a welcome acquisition for the Hermitage because of the long-time preponderance in the museum of Flemish and Dutch paintings. Among the many magnificent canvases that came with the Walpole collection were Rubens's *The Carters* and *The Temple of Janus*, Van Dyck's *Portrait of Elizabeth and Philadelphia Wharton*, Lorrain's *The Bay of Baiae*, Kneller's *Portrait of the Wood-carver Grinling Gibbons*, Maratti's *Portrait of Pope Clement IX*, and others. The last major acquisition of the eighteenth century was the purchase in 1781 in Paris of 119 pictures, including nine Rembrandts, from the collection of Count Baudouin.

Another development that contributed to the systematic policy of acquisition at that time was the museum's contacts with contemporaneous European artists; not only were their finished canvases purchased, but new ones commissioned as well. Thus, in 1766 the Hermitage purchased from Greuze his famous canvas *The Paralytic* and in 1785 *The Blacksmith's Shop* from Wright of Derby. Joshua Reynolds, President of Britain's Royal Academy, was commissioned by the Russian Imperial Court in 1785 to paint the canvas *The Infant Hercules Strangling the Serpents*, an allegory of the struggle led by the newly emerging Russian state against her enemies; another Reynolds piece, *Cupid Untying the Zone of Venus*, was sold by the master to the Hermitage in 1786. Most of the orders for pictures were placed with French artists — Van Loo, Chardin and Vigée-Lebrun. Chardin executed for the St Petersburg Academy of Arts the canvas *Still Life with Attributes of the Arts*, which was brought to Russia by the sculptor Falconet and eventually housed in the Hermitage.

In addition to Imperial collections, the eighteenth century also saw the creation of numerous private collections which boasted some truly superb pieces. Among the best known were the Shuvalov, Beloselsky, Stroganov, Yusupov and Sheremetev collections; many works from these, at one time or another, found their way into the Hermitage or other Soviet museums. Thus, *The Madonna from the Annunciation* by Simone Martini, that gem of early Italian painting, and Filippino Lippi's *The Adoration of the Infant Christ* entered the Hermitage in 1911 from the Stroganov collection in Rome.

When Velten completed the Big Hermitage in 1784, its first floor was taken over by the picture gallery, a room-to-room guide to which (with even the number of canvases in each room) is to be found in *A Description of St Petersburg* published in 1794 by N. Gheorghi. According to the author, there was now more system in the hanging of the pictures which had come to occupy the two galleries along the sides of the hanging garden, the north, so-called La Mothe pavilion, and two suites of rooms in the new building. They were hung so close to each other as to cover the entire surface of the wall; located separately were portraits of members of the Imperial family of the Romanovs and "pictures for copying".

In the same period, two suites of rooms for large-size pictures were added to the southeast corner of the Big (or Old) Hermitage, as well as a special gallery which was to be a complete reproduction of the world-famous Raphael's Loggias, painting and all. Catherine II wrote to Grimm in Paris: "I vow to St Raphael to build a gallery of his loggias, come what may." The copies of the frescoes were commissioned to Christopher Unterberger, and the erection of the gallery to Quarenghi, who completed the Hermitage Theatre in 1785. The entire project took ten years to carry out, and it was only in 1788 that the copies were finally mounted. Of course, from our point of view the work of Unterberger and his assistants cannot be termed an exact copy because they freely filled in the missing parts of the original painting, but even so this was definitely a major event in the cultural life of eighteenth century Russia.

The Hermitage interiors as they were in the late eighteenth century and as they remained right up to the building of the New Hermitage, have come down to us in sketches made by Julius Friedenreich between 1839 and 1841. His drawings are arid and formal, but undoubtedly factual.

Information on the growth of the picture gallery in the second half of the eighteenth century can also be gleaned from its catalogues. As mentioned above, the first printed catalogue in French, published in 1774, listed 2,080 canvases. There is a second, manuscript, catalogue in the archives of the Hermitage, which was put out in 1783 and which carries the titles of 2,658 works. By 1797 the number of pictures in all the Imperial palaces reached 3,996. This figure is taken from an inventory drawn up by a special committee appointed after Catherine II's death to determine the number of art works in her Petersburg and suburban residences. Under Paul I some of the Hermitage canvases were moved to the Mikhailovsky (Engineers') Castle in St Petersburg and to the palaces in Pavlovsk and Gatchina. Later they were all returned to the Hermitage.

In the last decade of the eighteenth and in the early nineteenth century there were only occasional acquisitions, some of them true masterpieces, for example *The Union of Earth and Water* by Rubens.

At the end of the eighteenth century it became necessary to appoint a custodian. The first man to hold the position was Lucas Pfandzelt. He was succeeded in 1797 by Franz Labensky, who occupied the post for over fifty years. Labensky not only acted as keeper, describing and attributing the pictures, but took an active part in replenishing the gallery's stocks. During a trip to Paris in 1808 he bought the famous Caravaggio canvas *The Lute Player* from the Giustiniani gallery, and in 1810 De Hooch's *Mistress and Maid* from the Paris antique dealer La Fontaine. Credit for some of the acquisitions must go to the Director of the Louvre Vivant Denon, whose co-operation was fully in keeping with the traditional ties that existed between the Hermitage and the French capital.

At the beginning of the nineteenth century certain alterations were made in the layout of the Hermitage's rooms. The first "Statute" of the museum was drawn up whereby it was divided into five departments, second in the list being "the picture gallery, the chamber of rarities, the bronzes and marbles". A restorers' school was set up in the museum where four artists studied the trade under Andrei Mitrokhin, a Labensky appointee (before that the restoration of pictures had been a matter of experimentation, and not always successful at that).

The normal life of the Hermitage was interrupted by the War of 1812. In the September following Napoleon's invasion of Russia the Hermitage was instructed to dispatch all its treasures by "secret expedition". This order was carried out in the strictest secrecy. Only the record books of the court office contain information on the removal of the Hermitage collections and their return in 1813.

Major acquisitions were made after the war. In 1814 the Hermitage purchased 118 pictures from the Malmaison Palace of the Empress Josephine, the first wife of Napoleon. Among them were magnificent works by Flemish, Dutch and French artists, some of which had been seized as booty by Napoleon in other countries. Such works as *The Guard-room* by Teniers, Potter's *The Farm* and Ter Borch's brilliant canvas, *A Glass of Lemonade*, came to the

Hermitage with this collection. In 1829 several more pictures of the Malmaison gallery were purchased from Josephine's daughter, Countess of Saint-Leu.

Another event that led to a significant enlargement of the museum's Spanish section was the purchase in 1814—15 in Amsterdam of a number of pictures from the Coesevelt collection. These included *Portrait of Count Olivares* by Velázquez, *Portrait of Don Diego Villamayor* by Pantoja de la Cruz and *Still Life* by Pereda. This nucleus was further enriched in 1834 with the entry of several Spanish canvases from the collections of Gessler, the Russian consul-general in Cadiz, and Paez de la Cadeña, the Spanish ambassador in St Petersburg.

To commemorate Russia's victory in the War of 1812 a special gallery designed by Carlo Rossi was set aside in the Winter Palace to house portraits of the officers who distinguished themselves in that war, much like the gallery in Windsor Castle with its portraits by Lawrence of those who fought in the battle of Waterloo. The Winter Palace portraits were commissioned to the English painter George Dawe. In all, Dawe and his assistants, the Russian artists Golike and Poliakov, executed 329 portraits of generals which were subsequently hung in the gallery.

The Hermitage had by then become an important element of Russian culture. Many outstanding artists of the first half of the nineteenth century — Fiodor Tolstoi, Karl Briullov, Alexei Venetsianov, Pavel Fedotov and others — came here to study and copy the works of the Old Masters. However, access to the Imperial museum was still very limited.

In 1837 a great fire destroyed the Winter Palace. It was only at the price of titanic efforts, such as dismantling the passageways and sealing up the door and window apertures with brickwork, that the museum escaped a similar fate. The Winter Palace was rebuilt in a very short space of time, but the reconstruction temporarily diverted the court administration's attention from the Hermitage, which was suffering from an insufficiency of space for its collections: in 1828 the ground floor of the Big Hermitage had been handed over to the State Council and the Committee of Ministers (these premises were reassigned to the museum only in 1855). It now became evident that the construction of a new building for the museum could no longer be postponed.

The edifice was commissioned to Leo Klenze, the architect who had built the Pinakothek in Munich; the site chosen was the territory between the Winter Canal and the Small Hermitage facing Millionnaya Street plus the courtyards behind the Velten building. Klenze's plan was approved in 1839; the actual construction took about ten years. A special committee whose leading members were the Russian architects Vasily Stasov and Nikolai Yefimov was set up to oversee the implementation of the project. The New Hermitage was from the beginning conceived as a museum building whose prime function was to house all the Hermitage collections. The aspect of its halls has been preserved for posterity in the extremely accurate water-colours executed between 1852 and 1860 by Eduard Hau and Lodovico Premazzi.

The pictures were selected and their hanging supervised by a committee chaired by Fiodor Bruni, Keeper of the Hermitage gallery since 1849. All canvases were divided into three groups: for display, for transference to other Imperial residences and for sale. As a result 1,219 works were auctioned off. It should be noted that similar sales occur in the history of other European museums — the Dresden Gallery and the Munich Pinakothek. Years later, some of the canvases sold in 1854, Chardin's *Still Life with Attributes of the Arts*, to cite an example, found their way back into the Hermitage.

On the other hand, important acquisitions continued to be made. Several Titians were bought in Venice in 1850, among them two magnificent canvases, *St Mary Magdalene in Penitence* and *St Sebastian*. That same year Bruni purchased several interesting pictures at the auction sale of the collection owned by Willem II of the Netherlands, among them Guido Reni's *St Joseph and the Infant Christ*. At a Paris auction in 1852 Bruni bought Zurbarán's *St Lawrence*, which came from Marshal Soult's collection.

The New Hermitage, proclaimed a "public museum", was opened on February 5, 1852, but a year later the Emperor decreed that "the issue of admission tickets to the Imperial

Hermitage and the galleries thereof be entrusted to the Court Office, not to the keepers of the Hermitage departments". The names of all visitors were to be recorded in a special book.

After the new building of the museum was completed, reconstruction began of the Old (Big) Hermitage. The austere interiors created by Quarenghi were redesigned by Stackenschneider as additional palace premises. The reconstruction also took in the La Mothe Pavilion, where an impressive but somewhat eclectic hall overlooking the hanging garden was built to replace Catherine's Hermitage.

Twenty-one rooms on the first floor of the New Hermitage were allotted to the picture gallery. The canvases were arranged mainly according to national school, but without any strict system. The last Hermitage catalogue before the transference of the collection to the new building was compiled by Labensky in French in 1838 and contained notes on 1,683 pictures then on display. With the opening of a new exposition the need arose for a new catalogue and a thorough systematization of all the stocks. An inventory completed in 1859 became the main document listing the Hermitage pictures and recording all subsequent acquisitions. Some valuable advice concerning the study of the collection and the layout of the exhibits was offered by Gustav Friedrich Waagen, Director of the Berlin Museum's picture gallery, who had been invited for the purpose by the Hermitage authorities. The hanging of the pictures was completed in 1860—61 and by and large remained unchanged up to World War I.

In addition to the spacious halls given over to the works of Rembrandt, Rubens and Van Dyck, and to the extensive collections of national schools (for example, the Dutch in the Tent Hall), canvases were also hung in the modest-size rooms adjoining these halls. Displayed in a separate hall were works by Russian artists, among them Briullov's *The Last Day of Pompeii* and Bruni's *The Brass Serpent*, to name a few. In 1898 all 72 pictures of the Russian school were handed over to the Russian Museum.

Though still subordinated to the palace administration, the Hermitage was gradually assuming the character of a *bona fide* museum. One of the factors that indubitably contributed to this was the sizable distance separating the exposition from the royal quarters; another was the fact that the personal tastes of the reigning monarch no longer influenced the selection of pictures. In 1863, ninety-nine years after the inauguration of the picture gallery, the first Director of the Hermitage was nominated. He was Stepan Gedeonov, Head of the Archaeological Commission in Rome prior to his new appointment. Gedeonov greatly eased the restrictions that barred public access to the Hermitage and rescinded the rule whereby only persons in full regimental uniform or tail-coats were admitted to the museum. In 1865 he reported to the palace administration that "steps taken over the past eighteen months to facilitate public access to the Imperial Museum, new acquisitions of important art collections, the issue of catalogues and other like measures had as their consequence an unending flow of visitors to the Hermitage".

The Hermitage came to play a major role in the history of Russian culture. It was repeatedly visited by the new generation of artists — Perov, Kramskoi, Surikov, Repin — and served as an invaluable school for art historians. However, many of the barriers hindering free access to the museum were still in force. The art critic Vladimir Stasov (son of the architect who built the New Hermitage) expressed the opinion that the museum was not fulfilling its true function. The Hermitage was deprived of all initiative by its subordination to the Court Office and by a total lack of funds of its own for the purchase of new pictures. Still, thanks to Gedeonov's untiring energy, Leonardo da Vinci's *Madonna and Child* was purchased in 1866 from the Duke of Litta's gallery in Milan; and in 1870 Raphael's early canvas *Madonna and Child*, painted in 1500 for Count Alfano di Diamante, was acquired in Perugia from Count Conestabile. This masterpiece was at first housed in the Winter Palace, but in 1881 was handed over to the Hermitage picture gallery.

Alexander Vasilchikov, who succeeded Gedeonov as Director of the Gallery, also had difficulties in obtaining funds for the purchase of pictures. Nevertheless, in 1882 he managed to acquire in Florence Fra Beato Angelico's fresco *Madonna and Child with St Dominic and St Thomas of Aquinas*, which previously adorned the refectory of the Monastery of San Domenico in Fiesole.

In 1882 the picture collection was enriched by the transfer to the Hermitage of canvases from Peterhof and Gatchina. Among these were Rembrandt's *David's Farewell to Jonathan*, Van Goyen's *Landscape with an Oak*, Van Ostade's *The Scuffle*, Crespi's *Scene in a Cellar*, Bellotto's *New Market Place in Dresden* and Tiepolo's *Maecenas Presenting the Liberal Arts to Augustus*. In 1886, 73 pictures from the Golitsyn gallery in Moscow, amassed in the second half of the eighteenth century, entered the Hermitage.

The beginning of a serious study of the Hermitage collections is linked with the name of Andrei Somov, Keeper of the Picture Gallery from 1885 to 1909. A prominent art historian and an outstanding connoisseur of painting, he devoted much of his activities to the compiling of *catalogues raisonnés* and to the popularization of the Hermitage treasures, even though the board of directors was opposed to the idea of using the Hermitage for educational purposes. Somov invited two more art experts, Ernest Liphart and James Schmidt, to work in the museum; these latter were especially successful in matters of attribution and in improving the exposition. Liphart, for example, proved that *Madonna with a Flower*, which entered the Hermitage in 1914 from the Benois collection, was a Leonardo da Vinci work.

Among the significant acquisitions made prior to World War I especially worthy of mention is the large collection of Flemish and Dutch paintings put together by the famous Russian geographer and traveller Semionov-Tian-Shansky, which was purchased in 1910 and brought to the Hermitage in 1915. Of primary importance was the Khitrovo collection of English paintings, bequeathed to the Hermitage by its owner. Its most interesting pieces are portraits by such well-known English artists as Gainsborough (*Portrait of the Duchess of Beaufort*), Romney (*Portrait of Mrs Greer*) and Lawrence (*Portrait of Lady Raglan*).

On the eve of World War I the number of visitors to the museum amounted to almost 180 thousand a year. The Hermitage of that period was brilliantly described by Alexander Benois in his *Guide to the Picture Gallery of the Imperial Hermitage* published in 1910. This was a comprehensive assessment of the collection, although the author pointed out that the museum could not be regarded as a manual of the history of culture: certain schools and epochs were well and in many cases superbly represented, but there were also a number of lacunae. In spite of the rearrangement the exposition still had its drawbacks, and its overall character had not changed much in the sixty years of the museum's existence.

The October Revolution made the Hermitage into a state institution which eventually became a museum of the history of world culture. New departments were set up (in particular the Department of the East), but the picture gallery of Western European art lost none of its significance: in fact, it was greatly expanded by the inclusion not only of nineteenth, but of early twentieth century works as well. Prior to October 1917 the museum had been an annex, as it were, of the Winter Palace; after the revolution it was the Winter Palace that was, at first partially, later entirely, incorporated into the museum as an outstanding architectural and historic monument.

On October 5, 1918 the Council of People's Commissars issued a decree on the itemization and preservation of historical and artistic monuments. From the very first days of Soviet power Lenin repeatedly pointed out that the creation of a new, socialist, culture could be based only on the achievements of world culture, which in the past belonged to the ruling classes. The preservation of art works of museum value was entrusted to the State Museum Fund, which had its headquarters in the Winter Palace. This body's function was to assemble works of art and distribute them among the country's museums. As a result, a number of canvases from nationalized private collections entered the Hermitage, filling in many of the gaps in its stocks, especially as regards nineteenth century art: *Sappho and Phaon* by David, *Napoleon at Arcole* by Gros, *Portrait of Josephine* by Gérard, *Portrait of Count Guryev* by Ingres, and others. In 1922 the Academy of Arts turned over to the

Hermitage the so-called Kushelev gallery, a collection built up by Count Kushelev-Bezborodkoin the 1860s and 1870s. This included Jordaens's *Feast of the King of Beans*, Delacroix's *Lion Hunt in Morocco* and *Arab Saddling His Horse*, Troyon's *On the Way to the Market*, Millet's *Peasant Women Carrying Firewood*, Courbet's *Landscape with a Dead Horse* and other superb canvases which enabled the museum to have nineteenth century Western European painting, a very interesting and important chapter in the history of world art, amply represented in its exposition.

In 1930—31 all the work of the Hermitage was put on a new footing: the museum's pattern of organization was altered, the exposition rearranged so as to stress art's links with history, the picture gallery was provided with additional space in the Winter Palace. The systematic study and detailed enumeration of the collections were begun. The volume of restoration work was significantly increased. A fruitful period of exchange and co-operation between the Hermitage and European museums began.

These activities were interrupted by the War of 1941—45. The Hermitage collections were taken out of the besieged city and dispatched to Sverdlovsk, deep in the hinterland. The museum staff who travelled with the collections continued their research work even there. Those that stayed behind undertook, under very harsh conditions, the conservation of the remaining collections and the museum building itself.

In October 1945 all the evacuated treasures were returned to the Hermitage intact and there began the revival and expansion of its exposition, including the picture gallery, which was allotted several more rooms.

The Hermitage collection was significantly enlarged with the transfer to it in 1948 of many canvases from the Moscow Museum of Modern Western Art. The nucleus of this museum had been composed of two famous private collections, chiefly of late nineteenth and early twentieth century French painting, built up by Sergei Shchukin and Ivan Morozov (several pictures from the museum had come into the Hermitage in 1930 and 1931). It is this transfer that enriched the Hermitage collection with canvases by Monet, Sisley, Renoir, Pissarro, Degas, Cézanne, Van Gogh, Gauguin, Bonnard, Matisse, Marquet, Derain and Picasso.

In 1958 a two-volume catalogue of Western European painting in the Hermitage was published listing over 4,000 canvases (that is, all the pictures on display plus the finest of the reserve stocks). The catalogue was compiled by the eminent Soviet art historian Vladimir Loewinson-Lessing.

In 1964 the Hermitage celebrated its bicentenary. The museum was awarded the Order of Lenin for its contribution to the aesthetic education of the Soviet people.

The staff of the museum continues to do research on the paintings, compile catalogues of pictures of all schools and publish albums, scientific papers and guide-books. The scope of restoration work has markedly increased, with new methods being used that yield stunning results. For example, an X-ray investigation of the canvas *The Adoration of the Magi*, earlier thought to be a copy of the Rembrandt original in the Göteborg museum (Sweden), revealed the presence of substantial compositional alterations by the author. This allowed the Hermitage canvas to be recognized as the original and the Göteborg piece a copy done by one of the master's pupils. X-ray photography likewise revealed that in *Danaë* Rembrandt removed some of the woman's ornaments to enhance the effect of the golden light emanating from the depths of the picture. It was also discovered that Van Dyck's *Portrait of a Man* was painted over a sketch of Cardinal Guido Bentivoglio, that the French artist Lafosse painted his *Hagar in the Desert* on a canvas that carried a finished male portrait by another artist, and that other monarchs were later depicted over the portrait of Louis XIV in the medallion of *The Allegory of Rule* by the Italian painter Solimena.

The removal of old varnish layers presented some well-known paintings in an entirely new light. The colour scheme of Giorgione's famous *Judith*, for example, underwent a complete transformation after the removal of a layer of dark varnish laid on by antiquarians, and of later overpaintings.

The growth of the museum's collections is a never-ending process. In the last few years the Hermitage has acquired works by French and Italian artists, for example, Bellange, Drouet, Troyon, Boudin, Dufy, Vlaminck, Matisse, Stazione, and Guttuso. The Flemish and Dutch sections were enriched by the entry of Teniers and Ostade canvases, the German — by the works of Friedrich and Hans Grundig. The collection of Rockwell Kent's pictures, the artist's gift to the Soviet people, laid the beginnings of the Hermitage's collection of American painting. In 1972 the American collector Armand Hammer presented to the Hermitage *The Portrait of the Actress Antonia Zárate* by Goya, a great master until then not represented in the museum. The Hermitage also continues to receive pictures by modern Polish, Hungarian, Rumanian and German artists.

In recent years the Hermitage has hosted many first-class exhibitions of works from the museums of France, Italy, Great Britain, Holland, the USA, Poland, Hungary, Czechoslovakia, Rumania, the German Democratic Republic, Bulgaria, Japan and other countries, thereby acquainting its visitors with a wide range of outstanding works of world art. On the other hand, exhibitions of Hermitage masterpieces in many countries of Europe, Asia and America invariably elicit great interest on the part of art lovers and enjoy wide popularity.

BORIS PIOTROVSKY,
Academician, Director General of the Hermitage

The main staircase in the Winter Palace

Room of Early Italian Art

The Leonardo Room

1   *SIMONE MARTINI. The Madonna from the Annunciation*

ANTONIO DA FIRENZE. Madonna and Child with Saints

3   *ANTONIO DA FIRENZE. Madonna and Child with Saints. Detail*

4   *FRA BEATO ANGELICO DA FIESOLE. Madonna and Child with Angels*

5   *FRA BEATO ANGELICO DA FIESOLE. Madonna and Child with Angels. Detail*

6 *FRA BEATO ANGELICO DA FIESOLE. Madonna and Child with St Dominic and St Thomas of Aquinas*

FRA FILIPPO LIPPI. The Vision of St Augustine

CIMA DA CONEGLIANO. The Annunciation

9   *FILIPPINO LIPPI. The Adoration of the Infant Christ*

10   *LEONARDO DA VINCI. Madonna and Child (The Litta Madonna)*

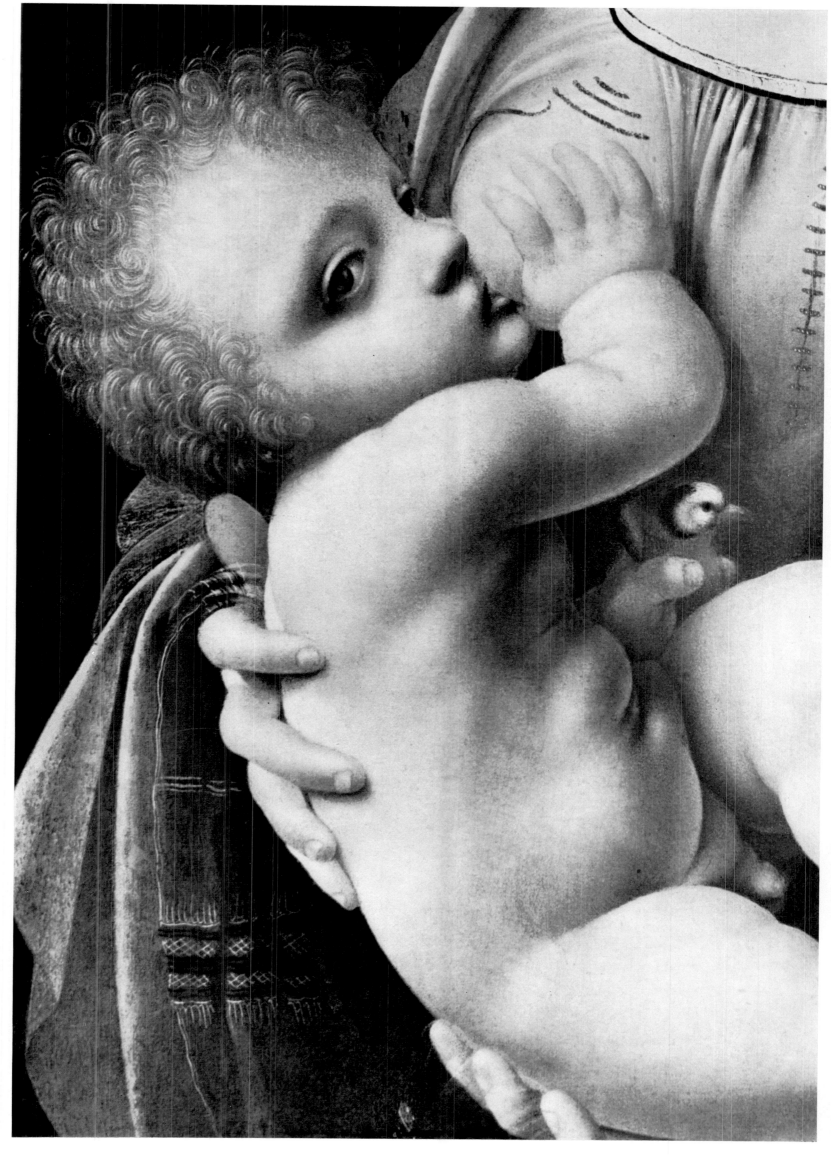

11   *LEONARDO DA VINCI. Madonna and Child (The Litta Madonna). Detail*

RAPHAEL. Madonna with the Beardless St Joseph

13   *RAPHAEL. Madonna and Child (The Conestabile Madonna)*

ROGIER VAN DER WEYDEN. St Luke Drawing a Portrait of the Virgin. Detail

15   *ROGIER VAN DER WEYDEN. St Luke Drawing a Portrait of the Virgin*

16   *ROBERT CAMPIN. The Virgin and Child before the Fireplace*

17   *UNKNOWN SPANISH ARTIST OF THE SECOND HALF OF THE 15TH CENTURY.*
The Meeting of St Joachim and St Anne at the Golden Gate

18   *CATALAN PAINTER OF THE LATE 15TH CENTURY. St Sebastian and St Fabian. Detail*

19   *CATALAN PAINTER OF THE LATE 15TH CENTURY. St Sebastian and St Fabian*

20   *MASTER OF THE THUISON ALTARPIECE.*
The Entry into Jerusalem

21—23   *MASTER OF THE THUISON ALTARPIECE. The Entry into Jerusalem. Details*

HERRI MET DE BLES. Landscape with the Flight into Egypt

25   *HERRI MET DE BLES. Landscape with the Flight into Egypt. Detail*

PIETER BREUGHEL THE ELDER. *The Fair*

29   *PIETER BREUGHEL THE ELDER. The Fair. Detail*

30   *GIORGIONE. Judith*

31   *GIORGIONE. Judith. Detail*

TITIAN. The Flight into Egypt

33　　　　　　　　　　　　　　*TITIAN. St Mary Magdalene in Penitence. Detail*

TITIANVS. P.

34   *TITIAN. St Mary Magdalene in Penitence*

TITIAN. St Sebastian

36   *TITIAN. Portrait of a Young Woman*

TINTORETTO. The Birth of St John the Baptist

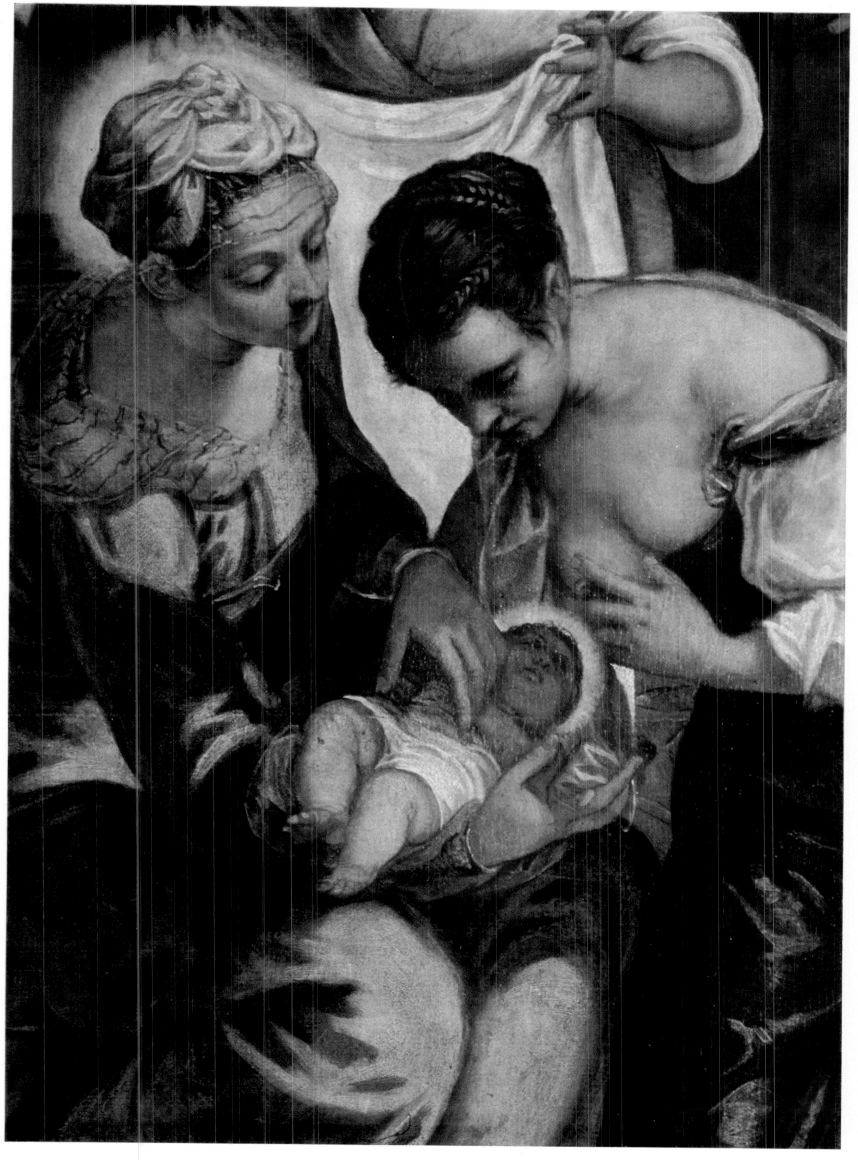

TINTORETTO. The Birth of St John the Baptist. Detail

CORREGGIO. Portrait of a Woman

VERONESE. Pietà

41   *VERONESE. The Adoration of the Magi*

DOMENICO CAPRIOLA. *Portrait of a Man*

43   *AMBROSIUS HOLBEIN. Portrait of a Young Man*

44   LUCAS CRANACH THE ELDER. *Portrait of a Woman*

45   *LUCAS CRANACH THE ELDER. The Virgin and Child under the Apple-tree. Detail*

LUCAS CRANACH THE ELDER. The Virgin and Child under the Apple-tree

PELLE · CVPIDINEOS · TOTO   CONAMINE · LVXVS
NE · TVA · POSSIDEAT   PECTORA · CECA · VENVS

47   *LUCAS CRANACH THE ELDER. Venus and Cupid*

LUCAS CRANACH THE ELDER. Venus and Cupid. Detail

49   *CHRISTOPH AMBERGER. Portrait of a Young Man with a Fur Collar*

BARTHOLOMMÄUS BRUYN. Portrait of a Lady with Her Daughter

EL GRECO. *St Peter and St Paul. Detail*

EL GRECO. St Peter and St Paul

JUAN PANTOJA DE LA CRUZ. *Portrait of Diego de Villamayor*

54   *UNKNOWN FRENCH ARTIST OF THE 16TH CENTURY. Portrait of an Unknown Man*

ABRAHAM BLOEMAERT. Landscape with Tobias and the Angel

56   *GIJSBRECHT LIJTENS. Winter Landscape*

PIETER CLAESZ. Breakfast with Ham

58   FRANS HALS. *Portrait of a Young Man Holding a Glove*

59   *WILLEM CLAESZ HEDA. Breakfast with Lobster. Detail*

WILLEM CLAESZ HEDA. Breakfast with Lobster

FRANS VAN MIERIS THE ELDER. Breakfast with Oysters

PIETER DE HOOCH. Mistress and Maid

GERARD TER BORCH. Portrait of a Woman

GERARD TER BORCH. A Glass of Lemonade

JAN STEEN. *The Revellers*

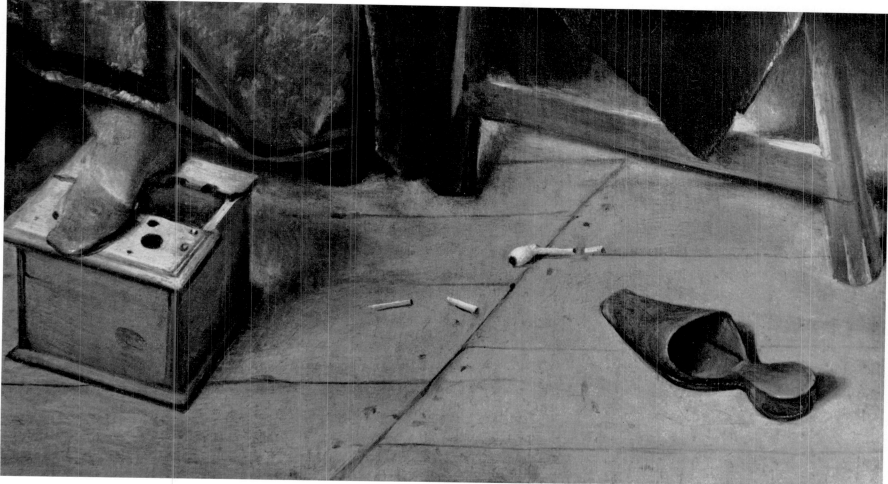

JAN STEEN. The Revellers. Details

PAULUS POTTER. *The Farm. Detail*

PAULUS POTTER. *The Farm*

71

JACOB VAN RUISDAEL. The Marsh

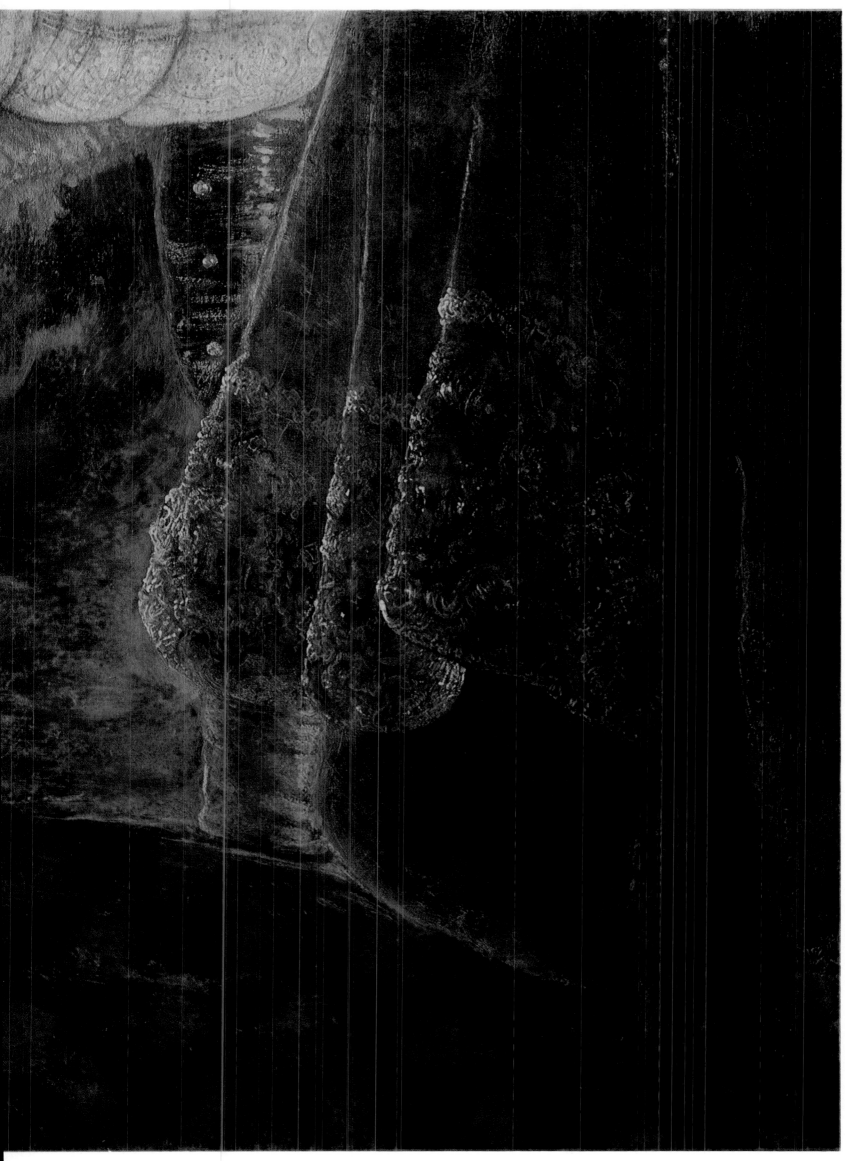

REMBRANDT. *Danaë. Detail*

82   REMBRANDT. *Portrait of Jeremias de Decker*

REMBRANDT. *The Return of the Prodigal Son*

PETER PAUL RUBENS. Statue of Ceres

PETER PAUL RUBENS. *The Coronation of Marie de' Medici*

PETER PAUL RUBENS. *Perseus and Andromeda*

87   *PETER PAUL RUBENS. The Union of Earth and Water*

PETER PAUL RUBENS. *The Union of Earth and Water. Detail*

PETER PAUL RUBENS. The Carters

PETER PAUL RUBENS. *The Carters. Detail*

ANTHONIS VAN DYCK. Portrait of Sir Thomas Chaloner

ANTHONIS VAN DYCK. *Family Group*

93   *ANTHONIS VAN DYCK. Portrait of Elizabeth and Philadelphia Wharton*

JACOB JORDAENS. Feast of the King of Beans

DAVID TENIERS THE YOUNGER. Landscape with Cows

DAVID TENIERS THE YOUNGER. The Guard-room

ADRIAEN BROUWER. A Village Quack

ADRIAEN VAN OSTADE. *The Scuffle*

99 *FRANS SNYDERS. Bowl of Fruit on a Red Table-cloth*

100 *JAN FYT. Still Life with Fruit and Parrot*

JAN VAN HUYSUM. Flowers

DIEGO VELÁZQUEZ. Luncheon

DIEGO VELÁZQUEZ. Luncheon. Detail

104   *DIEGO VELÁZQUEZ. Portrait of Count Olivares*

FRANCISCO DE ZURBARÁN. St Lawrence

106 *JOSÉ RIBERA. Clio*

ANTONIO PEREDA. *Still Life*

BARTOLOMÉ ESTEBAN MURILLO. Boy with a Dog

BARTOLOMÉ ESTEBAN MURILLO. The Ascension

110   *CARAVAGGIO. The Lute Player*

CARAVAGGIO. The Lute Player. Detail

· *ANNIBALE CARRACCI. The Three Marys at the Sepulchre*

113   *DOMENICO FETTI. Portrait of an Actor*

CUIDO RENI. St Joseph with the Infant Christ

CARLO MARATTI. Portrait of Pope Clement IX

BERNARDO STROZZI. *Allegory of the Arts*

GIUSEPPE MARIA CRESPI. *Self-portrait*

LOUIS LE NAIN. A Visit to Grandmother

LOUIS LE NAIN. The Milkmaid's Family

NICOLAS POUSSIN. Tancred and Erminia

121   *NICOLAS POUSSIN. Tancred and Erminia. Detail*

NICOLAS POUSSIN. Landscape with Polyphemus. Detail

123   *NICOLAS POUSSIN. Landscape with Polyphemus*

124

CLAUDE LORRAIN. *Midday*

CLAUDE LORRAIN. *The Bay of Baiae. Detail*

126 *CLAUDE LORRAIN. The Bay of Baiae*

SÉBASTIEN BOURDON. The Death of Dido

LAURENT DE LA HYRE. Mercury Entrusting the Infant Bacchus to the Nymphs

129 *PIERRE MIGNARD (?). Portrait of Hortense Mancini (?)*

NVLLVM
NVMEN ABEST

SIMON VOUET. *Minerva*

JAN WEENIX. Trophies of the Chase

GEORG FLEGEL. *Still Life with Flowers and Refreshments*

JOHANN HEINRICH SCHÖNFELDT. The Rape of the Sabines

134   *FRANZ ANTON MAULPERTSCH. The Baptism of the Eunuch*

135   *THOMAS GAINSBOROUGH. Portrait of the Duchess of Beaufort (?)*

JOSHUA REYNOLDS. Cupid Untying the Zone of Venus

JOSEPH WRIGHT OF DERBY. The Blacksmith's Shop

GEORGE MORLAND. *Approaching Storm*

139   *BERNARDO BELLOTTO. New Market Place in Dresden*

140   *ALESSANDRO MAGNASCO. Bacchanalian Scene*

141   *GIOVANNI BATTISTA TIEPOLO. Fabius Maximus Quintus in the Senate at Carthage*

GIOVANNI BATTISTA TIEPOLO. Maecenas Presenting the Liberal Arts to Augustus

GIOVANNI BATTISTA TIEPOLO. Maecenas Presenting the Liberal Arts to Augustus. Detail

FRANCESCO GUARDI. *Landscape*

145   *FRANCESCO GUARDI. View of a Town*

146—148 *CANALETTO. Reception of the French Ambassador at Venice. Details*

CANALETTO. Reception of the French Ambassador at Venice

150   *ANTOINE WATTEAU. Savoyard with His Marmot*

ANTOINE WATTEAU. Actors of the Comédie-Française

ANTOINE WATTEAU. An Embarrassing Proposal. Detail

ANTOINE WATTEAU. An Embarrassing Proposal

154   ANTOINE WATTEAU. *The Capricious Girl*

NICOLAS LANCRET. *The Dancer La Camargo*

FRANÇOIS BOUCHER. Landscape near Beauvais

157   *FRANÇOIS BOUCHER. Pastoral Scene*

158   *JEAN-BAPTISTE GREUZE. The Spoilt Child*

159   *JEAN-BAPTISTE PERRONNEAU. Boy with a Book*

JEAN-BAPTISTE SIMÉON CHARDIN. Still Life with Attributes of the Arts

161   *JEAN-BAPTISTE SIMÉON CHARDIN. Still Life with Attributes of the Arts. Detail*

162   *JEAN-BAPTISTE SIMÉON CHARDIN. Grace before Meat. Detail*

163   *JEAN-BAPTISTE SIMÉON CHARDIN. Grace before Meat*

JEAN-HONORÉ FRAGONARD. The Snatched Kiss. Detail

JEAN-HONORÉ FRAGONARD. *The Snatched Kiss*

166   *FRANCISCO GOYA. Portrait of the Actress Antonia Zárate*

ANTOINE-JEAN GROS. Napoleon at Arcole

MARGUERITE GÉRARD. *The First Steps*

FRANÇOIS GÉRARD. Portrait of Josephine

PIERRE-PAUL PRUD'HON, CONSTANCE MAYER. Innocence Preferring Love to Wealth

PIERRE GUÉRIN. *Morpheus and Iris*

JACQUES LOUIS DAVID. Sappho and Phaon. Detail

JACQUES LOUIS DAVID. Sappho and Phaon

174   *THOMAS LAWRENCE. Portrait of Lady Raglan*

JEAN AUGUSTE DOMINIQUE INGRES. Portrait of Count Guryev

THÉODORE ROUSSEAU. Market Place in Normandy

177   *RICHARD PARKES BONINGTON. Boats by the Shore*

CASPAR DAVID FRIEDRICH. *Riesengebirge*

179   *CASPAR DAVID FRIEDRICH. On a Sailing Boat*

FERDINAND GEORG WALDMÜLLER. Children

181   *THOMAS COUTURE. The Little Bather*

THÉODORE GUDIN. The Body of Napoleon Being Shipped to France from the Island of St Helena

183   *ALFRED RETHEL. Nemesis*

ALEXANDRE GABRIEL DECAMPS. *Self-portrait*

JEAN LOUIS ERNEST MEISSONIER. The Musketeer

ALFRED DE DREUX. *A Ride*

189   *EUGÈNE DELACROIX. Lion Hunt in Morocco*

NARCISSE DÍAZ DE LA PEÑA. A Road in the Forest

JULES DUPRÉ. Autumn Landscape

CAMILLE COROT. Peasant Woman Pasturing a Cow on the Edge of a Wood

193   *CAMILLE COROT. Landscape with Cows*

194

CAMILLE COROT. *Trees in a Marsh*

195   *GUSTAVE COURBET. Landscape with a Dead Horse*

196   *JEAN-FRANÇOIS MILLET. Peasant Women Carrying Firewood*

CONSTANT TROYON. On the Way to the Market

CHARLES FRANÇOIS DAUBIGNY. The Banks of the Oise

199 *HANS VON MARÉES. Courtyard of the Royal Residence in Munich*

　　　　　HENRI FANTIN-LATOUR. Vase of Roses and Nasturtiums

CLAUDE MONET. Lady in the Garden at Sainte-Adresse

CLAUDE MONET. *Corner of the Garden at Montgeron*

CLAUDE MONET. *Poppy Field*

CLAUDE MONET. Poppy Field. Detail

ALFRED SISLEY . Village on the Seine (Villeneuve-la-Garenne)

ALFRED SISLEY. *River Banks at Saint-Mammès*

CAMILLE PISSARRO. *Place du Théâtre-Français*

CAMILLE PISSARRO. Place du Théâtre-Français. Detail

CAMILLE PISSARRO. *Boulevard Montmartre*

210   *PIERRE AUGUSTE RENOIR. Child with a Whip*

211   *PIERRE AUGUSTE RENOIR. Girl with a Fan*

PIERRE AUGUSTE RENOIR. Lady in Black

213 *PIERRE AUGUSTE RENOIR. Portrait of the Actress Jeanne Samary*

PAUL CÉZANNE. *Vase of Flowers*

217   *PAUL CÉZANNE. Girl at the Piano (Overture to* Tannhäuser*)*

218   *PAUL CÉZANNE. Pine Tree near Aix*

PAUL CÉZANNE. *The Banks of the Marne*

220

PAUL CÉZANNE. *Still Life with Drapery*

221   *PAUL CÉZANNE. Portrait of the Artist in a Peaked Cap*

PAUL CÉZANNE. *The Smoker*

VINCENT VAN GOGH. Ladies of Arles (Memory of the Garden at Etten)

VINCENT VAN GOGH. Ladies of Arles (Memory of the Garden at Etten). Detail

VINCENT VAN GOGH. *Thatched Cottages*

VINCENT VAN GOGH. *Lilac Bush*

PAUL GAUGUIN. Tahitian Pastoral Scenes

228   *PAUL GAUGUIN. Woman Holding a Fruit*

PAUL GAUGUIN. Sacred Spring (Sweet Dreams). Detail

PAUL GAUGUIN. Sacred Spring (Sweet Dreams)

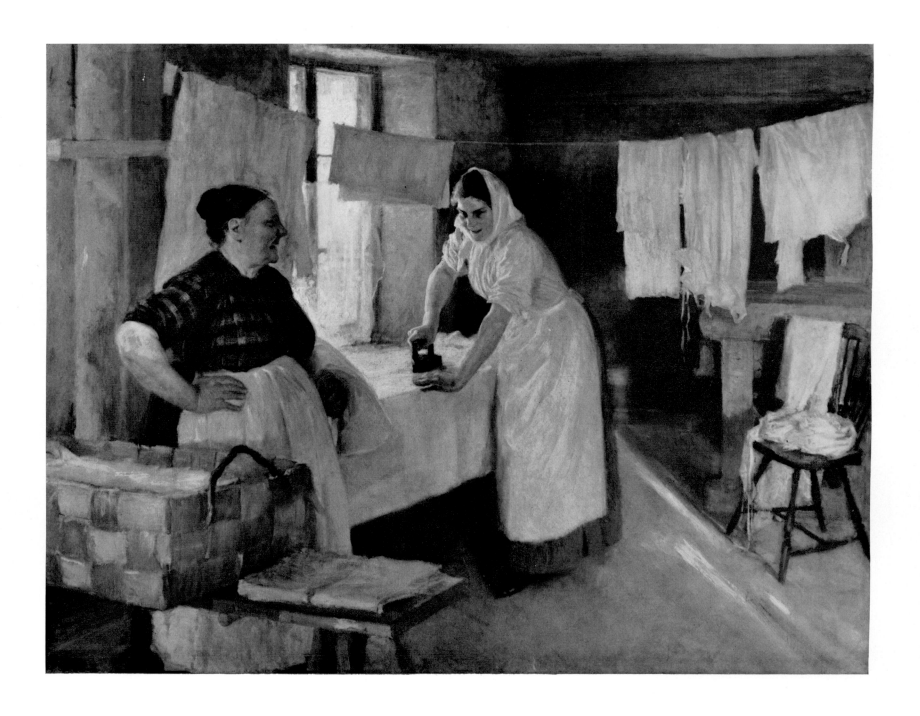

ALBERT EDELFELT. Washer women

MAX LIEBERMANN. Girl in a Field

FRITS THAULOW. At Night

IGNACIO ZULOAGA. *Gregorio the Dwarf*

235   *FRANK BRANGWYN. Charity*

HENRI MANGUIN. Morning (Lady Sitting on the Shore of Cavalière Bay)

HENRI CROSS (DELACROIX). View of the Church of Santa Maria degli Angeli near Assisi

240   *PAUL SIGNAC. Harbour at Marseilles*

241   *HENRI ROUSSEAU. In a Tropical Forest. Battle between the Tiger and the Bull*

HENRI ROUSSEAU. The Luxembourg Gardens. Monument to Chopin

PIERRE BONNARD. Early Spring (Little Fauns)

244　　　　　　　　　　　　*PIERRE BONNARD. Landscape with a Goods Train*

245   *PIERRE BONNARD. Morning in Paris*

246   *PIERRE BONNARD. Evening in Paris*

PIERRE BONNARD. Evening in Paris. Detail

PIERRE BONNARD. The Mediterranean. Detail

PIERRE BONNARD. *The Mediterranean*

250   *ALBERT MARQUET. Place de la Trinité in Paris*

HENRI MATISSE. The Artist's Family

HENRI MATISSE. The Red Room (La Desserte. Harmony in Red)

MAURICE VLAMINCK. View of the Seine. Detail

258   *MAURICE VLAMINCK. View of the Seine*

GEORGES ROUAULT. Spring

KEES VAN DONGEN. Woman in a Black Hat

ANDRÉ DERAIN. *Road in the Mountains. Cassis*

262   *ANDRÉ DERAIN. Harbour in Provence (Martigues)*

ANDRÉ DERAIN. Portrait of an Unknown Man with a Newspaper (Chevalier X)

ANDRÉ DERAIN. *Table and Chairs*

265 *PABLO PICASSO. Portrait of Soler*

PABLO PICASSO. Woman Drinking Absinth

267   *PABLO PICASSO. Flowers in a Grey Jug with Wine-glass and Spoon*

PABLO PICASSO. *Musical Instruments*

HENRI LE FAUCONNIER. *The Signal*

HEINRICH EHMSEN. *The Execution*

273   *ANDRÉ FOUGERON. Chad-fishers*

274   *RENATO GUTTUSO. Rocco and His Son*

The Matisse Room

CATALOGUE

1. SIMONE MARTINI. *C.* 1284—1344
Italian School
The Madonna from the Annunciation
Tempera on panel. 30.5 × 21.5 *

2, 3. ANTONIO DA FIRENZE. Active in the
first half of the 15th century
Italian School
Madonna and Child with Saints
Tempera on panel. 151.5 × 84.5
Signed below middle: *Antonius. De Florentia*

4, 5. FRA BEATO ANGELICO DA FIESOLE.
C. 1400—1455
Italian School
Madonna and Child with Angels. *C.* 1425
Tempera on panel. 80 × 51

6. FRA BEATO ANGELICO DA FIESOLE.
C. 1400—1455
Italian School
Madonna and Child with St Dominic and
St Thomas of Aquinas. 1424—30
Fresco. 196 × 187

7. FRA FILIPPO LIPPI. *C.* 1406—1469
Italian School
The Vision of St Augustine
Oil and tempera on panel. 29 × 51.5

8. CIMA DA CONEGLIANO. 1459—1517
Italian School
The Annunciation
Oil and tempera on canvas (transferred from a pan-
el). 136.5 × 107
Signed and dated on the sheet of paper: *1495. Juan
Baptista da Conegliano f...* (the rest of the in-
scription is difficult to decipher)

9. FILIPPINO LIPPI. *C.* 1457—1504
Italian School
The Adoration of the Infant Christ
Oil and tempera on copper plate (transferred from
a panel). Diam. 53

10, 11. LEONARDO DA VINCI. 1452—1519
Italian School
Madonna and Child (The Litta Madonna)
Tempera on canvas (transferred from a panel).
42 × 33

12. RAPHAEL. 1483—1520
Italian School
Madonna with the Beardless St Joseph. 1506
Tempera on canvas (transferred from a panel).
72.5 × 57

13. RAPHAEL. 1483—1520
Italian School
Madonna and Child (The Conestabile Madonna).
1502—3
Tempera on canvas (transferred from a panel).
17.5 × 18

14, 15. ROGIER VAN DER WEYDEN.
C. 1400—1464
Netherlandish School
St Luke Drawing a Portrait of the Virgin.
C. 1435—40
Oil on canvas (transferred from a panel).
102 × 108.5

16. ROBERT CAMPIN. *C.* 1380—1444
Netherlandish School
The Virgin and Child before the Fireplace (part of
a diptych). 1430s
Oil on panel. 34.3 × 24.3

17. UNKNOWN ARTIST OF THE SECOND HALF
OF THE 15TH CENTURY
Spanish School
The Meeting of St Joachim and St Anne at the
Golden Gate
Tempera on panel. 167.5 × 88.5

18, 19. CATALAN PAINTER OF THE LATE 15TH
CENTURY
Spanish School
St Sebastian and St Fabian
Tempera and oil on panel. 141.4 × 89.5

20—23. MASTER OF THE THUISON ALTARPIECE.
Second half of the 15th century
French School
The Entry into Jerusalem
Oil on panel. 116.5 × 51

24, 25. HERRI MET DE BLES. Second half
of the 16th century
Netherlandish School
Landscape with the Flight into Egypt
Oil on panel. 33 × 59.7

26, 27. MASTER OF THE FEMALE HALF-
LENGTHS. 16th century
Netherlandish School
The Virgin and Child
Oil on panel. 41 × 29

28, 29. PIETER BRFUGHEL THE ELDER.
1525/30—1569
Netherlandish School
The Fair. 1562
Oil on panel. 111 × 164.5

30, 31. GIORGIONE. *C.* 1478—1510
Italian School
Judith
Oil on canvas (transferred from a panel).
144 × 66.5

32. TITIAN. 1485/90—1576
Italian School
The Flight into Egypt. *C.* 1508
Oil on canvas. 206 × 336

33, 34. TITIAN. 1485/90—1576
Italian School
St Mary Magdalene in Penitence. 1560s
Oil on canvas. 118 × 97
Signed left, on the rock: *Titianus p.*

35. TITIAN. 1485/90—1576
Italian School
St Sebastian. *C.* 1570
Oil on canvas. 210 × 115

36. TITIAN. 1485/90—1576
Italian School
Portrait of a Young Woman. 1530s
Oil on canvas. 96 × 75

37, 38. TINTORETTO. 1518—1594
Italian School
The Birth of St John the Baptist. *C.* 1550
Oil on canvas. 181 × 266

39. CORREGGIO. 1489—1534
Italian School
Portrait of a Woman
Oil on canvas. 103 × 87.5
Signed left, on the tree-trunk: *Anton Laet*

---

* All measurements are given in centimetres.

40. VERONESE. 1528—1588
   Italian School
Pietà. Between 1576 and 1582
Oil on canvas. 147 × 111.5

41. VERONESE. 1528—1588
   Italian School
The Adoration of the Magi
Oil on copper plate. 45 × 34.5

42. DOMENICO CAPRIOLA. 1494—1528
   Italian School
Portrait of a Man. 1512
Oil on canvas. 117 × 85
Signed and dated below right, on the medal:
MD X 1 Dominicus A XXV

43. AMBROSIUS HOLBEIN. *C.* 1495—*c.* 1520
   German School
Portrait of a Young Man. 1518
Oil on panel. 44 × 32.5
Right, in the medallion, the monogram *AHB.* Left,
in the cartouche: *Ætatis suae XX MDXVIII*

44. LUCAS CRANACH THE ELDER. 1472—1553
   German School
Portrait of a Woman
Oil on panel. 88.5 × 58.6
Signed with a monogram and dated middle left:
LC 1526

45, 46. LUCAS CRANACH THE ELDER. 1472—1553
   German School
The Virgin and Child under the Apple-tree. *C.* 1525
Oil on canvas (transferred from a panel). 87 × 59
Signed with a monogram middle left: *LC*

47, 48. LUCAS CRANACH THE ELDER.
   1472—1553
   German School
Venus and Cupid
Oil on canvas (transferred from a panel). 213 × 102
Signed with a monogram and dated: *LC 1509*

49. CHRISTOPH AMBERGER. After 1500—*c.* 1561
   German School
Portrait of a Young Man with a Fur Collar
Oil on panel. 50.5 × 42.5

50. BARTHOLOMMÄUS BRUYN. 1493—1555
   German School
Portrait of a Lady with Her Daughter
Oil on canvas (transferred from a panel). 75.5 × 46

51, 52. EL GRECO. 1541—1614
   Spanish School
St Peter and St Paul. 1587—92
Oil on canvas. 121.5 × 105
Signed in Greek below right: *Domenikos Theoto-
kopoulos epoiei*

53. JUAN PANTOJA DE LA CRUZ. 1551—1609
   Spanish School
Portrait of Diego de Villamayor
Oil on canvas. 89 × 71
Signed and dated below: *Ju. . .es Pantoja de la +
Faciebat 1605*

54. UNKNOWN ARTIST OF THE 16TH CENTURY
   French School
Portrait of an Unknown Man
Oil on panel. 48.5 × 32

55. ABRAHAM BLOEMAERT. 1564—1651
   Dutch School
Landscape with Tobias and the Angel
Oil on canvas. 139 × 107.5

56. GIJSBRECHT LIJTENS. *C.* 1586—after 1643
   Netherlandish School
Winter Landscape
Oil on panel. 71.5 × 89

57. PIETER CLAESZ. 1596/97—1661
   Dutch School
Breakfast with Ham
Oil on panel. 40 × 61
Signed with a monogram and dated: *16 PCH 47*

58. FRANS HALS. 1581/85—1666
   Dutch School
Portrait of a Young Man Holding a Glove. *C.* 1640
Oil on canvas. 80 × 68.5
Signed with a monogram, right: *FH*

59, 60. WILLEM CLAESZ HEDA. 1594—1680/88
   Dutch School
Breakfast with Lobster
Oil on canvas. 118 × 118
Signed and dated on the table-cloth: *Heda 1648*

61. FRANS VAN MIERIS THE ELDER. 1635—1681
   Dutch School
Breakfast with Oysters
Oil on panel. 44.5 × 34.5
Signed and dated right, above the door: *F. van.
Mieris A 1659*

62. PIETER DE HOOCH. 1629 — after 1684
   Dutch School
Mistress and Maid. *C.* 1657
Oil on canvas. 53 × 42

63. GERARD TER BORCH. 1617—1661
   Dutch School
Portrait of a Woman
Oil on canvas. 80 × 59

64. GERARD TER BORCH. 1617—1661
   Dutch School
A Glass of Lemonade. 1663—64
Oil on canvas (transferred from a panel). 67 × 54

65—68. JAN STEEN. 1626—1679
   Dutch School
The Revellers. *C.* 1660
Oil on panel. 39 × 30
Signed above right: *J. Steen*

69, 70. PAULUS POTTER. 1625—1654
   Dutch School
The Farm
Oil on panel. 81 × 115.5
Signed and dated below right: *Paulus Potter 1649*

71. JACOB VAN RUISDAEL. 1628/29—1682
   Dutch School
The Marsh
Oil on canvas. 72.5 × 99
Signed below left: *J 1 Ruisdael*

72. SIMON DE VLIEGER. 1601—1653
   Dutch School
Rough Sea with Sailing Vessels
Oil on canvas. 30 × 46 (oval)
Signed with a monogram and dated left, on the
broken mast: *SV 1624*

73. WILLEM VAN DE VELDE THE YOUNGER.
   1633—1707
   Dutch School
Ships in the Roadstead
Oil on canvas. 42 × 48
Signed and dated below right: *W. v. Velde 1653*

74. AELBERT CUYP. 1620—1691
   Dutch School
Sunset on the River
Oil on panel. 77 × 107.5
Signed below right: *A. Cuyp*

75. PHILIPS WOUWERMAN. 1619—1668
   Dutch School
View in the Environs of Haarlem
Oil on canvas. 76 × 67
Signed with a monogram below left: *PHLS W.*

76. JAN VAN GOYEN. 1596—1656
   Dutch School
Landscape with an Oak
Oil on canvas. 87 × 105
Signed and dated middle right: *V Goyen 1634*

77. REMBRANDT. 1606—1669
   Dutch School
Flora
Oil on canvas. 125 × 101
Signed and dated below left: *Rembrandt. f. 1634*

78. REMBRANDT. 1606—1669
   Dutch School
David's Farewell to Jonathan
Oil on panel. 73 × 61.5
Signed and dated below middle: *Rembrandt f. 1642*

79. REMBRANDT. 1606—1669
   Dutch School
The Holy Family
Oil on canvas. 117 × 91
Signed and dated below left: *Rembrandt. f. 1645*

80, 81. REMBRANDT. 1606—1669
   Dutch School
Danaë. 1636
Oil on canvas. 185 × 203
Signed and dated below left: *Rembrandt. f. . . .6. . .6*

82. REMBRANDT. 1606—1669
Dutch School
Portrait of Jeremias de Decker
Oil on panel. 71 × 56
Signed and dated below right, on the background:
Rembrandt 1666

83. REMBRANDT. 1606—1669
Dutch School
The Return of the Prodigal Son. C. 1668—69
Oil on canvas. 262 × 205

84. PETER PAUL RUBENS. 1577—1640
Flemish School
Statue of Ceres. C. 1615
Oil on panel. 90.5 × 65.5

85. PETER PAUL RUBENS. 1577—1640
Flemish School
The Coronation of Marie de' Medici
Oil on panel. 49 × 63

86. PETER PAUL RUBENS. 1577—1640
Flemish School
Perseus and Andromeda. 1620—21
Oil on canvas (transferred from a panel).
99.5 × 139

87, 88. PETER PAUL RUBENS. 1577—1640
Flemish School
The Union of Earth and Water. C. 1618
Oil on canvas. 225 × 180.5

89, 90. PETER PAUL RUBENS. 1577—1640
Flemish School
The Carters. C. 1620
Oil on canvas (transferred from a panel). 87 × 129

91. ANTHONIS VAN DYCK. 1599—1641
Flemish School
Portrait of Sir Thomas Chaloner. 1630s
Oil on canvas. 104 × 81.5

92. ANTHONIS VAN DYCK. 1599—1641
Flemish School
Family Group. C. 1621
Oil on canvas. 113.5 × 93.5

93. ANTHONIS VAN DYCK. 1599—1641
Flemish School
Portrait of Elizabeth and Philadelphia Wharton.
1635—40
Oil on canvas. 162 × 130

94. JACOB JORDAENS. 1593—1678
Flemish School
Feast of the King of Beans. C. 1638
Oil on canvas. 160 × 213

95. DAVID TENIERS THE YOUNGER.
1610—1690
Flemish School
Landscape with Cows
Oil on copper plate. Diam. 40.5

96. DAVID TENIERS THE YOUNGER. 1610—1690
Flemish School
The Guard-room
Oil on panel. 69 × 103
Signed and dated below left: *David Teniers F. 1642*

97. ADRIAEN BROUWER. C. 1606—1638
Flemish School
A Village Quack. C. 1625
Oil on panel. 25 × 18

98. ADRIAEN VAN OSTADE. 1610—1685
Dutch School
The Scuffle
Oil on panel. 25 × 33.5
Signed and dated below right: *A. V. Ostade fe
1637*

99. FRANS SNYDERS. 1579—1657
Flemish School
Bowl of Fruit on a Red Table-cloth
Oil on canvas (transferred from a panel).
59.5 × 90.5

100. JAN FYT. 1611—1661
Flemish School
Still Life with Fruit and Parrot
Oil on canvas (transferred from a panel). 58 × 90
Signed and dated right, on the edge of the table:
Joannes Fyt 1645

101. JAN VAN HUYSUM. 1682—1749
Dutch School
Flowers
Oil on canvas (transferred from a panel). 79 × 60
Signed and dated below, on the edge of the table:
Jan Van Huysum Fecit 1722

102, 103. DIEGO VELÁZQUEZ. 1599—1660
Spanish School
Luncheon. C. 1617
Oil on canvas. 107 × 101

104. DIEGO VELÁZQUEZ. 1599—1660
Spanish School
Portrait of Count Olivares. C. 1638
Oil on canvas. 67 × 54.5

105. FRANCISCO DE ZURBARÁN. 1598—1664
Spanish School
St Lawrence
Oil on canvas. 292 × 225.5
Signed and dated below right, on the gridiron:
F de Zurbaran facie 1636

106. JOSÉ RIBERA. 1591—1652
Spanish School
Clio
Oil on canvas. 113 × 81
Signed with a monogram below right: *JR*

107. ANTONIO PEREDA. 1608—1678
Spanish School
Still Life. 1652
Oil on canvas. 80 × 94
Signed middle, on a box-lid: *Pereda f*

108. BARTOLOMÉ ESTEBAN MURILLO.
1618—1682
Spanish School
Boy with a Dog. 1650s
Oil on canvas. 77.5 × 61.5

109. BARTOLOMÉ ESTEBAN MURILLO. 1618—1682
Spanish school
The Ascension
Oil on canvas. 195.6 × 145

110, 111. CARAVAGGIO. 1571—1610
Italian School
The Lute Player. 1595
Oil on canvas. 94 × 119

112. ANNIBALE CARRACCI. 1560—1609
Italian School
The Three Marys at the Sepulchre. C. 1605
Oil on canvas. 121 × 145.5

113. DOMENICO FETTI. 1589—1624
Italian School
Portrait of an Actor. Early 1620s
Oil on canvas. 105.5 × 81

114. GUIDO RENI. 1575—1642
Italian School
St Joseph with the Infant Christ. 1620s
Oil on canvas. 126 × 101

115. CARLO MARATTI. 1627—1713
Italian School
Portrait of Pope Clement IX
Oil on canvas. 158 × 118.5
Signed and inscribed right, on the folded sheet
of paper on the table: *Alla Santita di N. Sig.re
Clemente IX Per Carlo Maratti*

116. BERNARDO STROZZI. 1581—1644
Italian School
Allegory of the Arts. C. 1640
Oil on canvas. 153 × 140

117. GIUSEPPE MARIA CRESPI. 1665—1747
Italian School
Self-portrait. C. 1700
Oil on canvas. 60.5 × 50 (oval)

118. LOUIS LE NAIN. 1593—1648
French School
A Visit to Grandmother. 1640s
Oil on canvas. 58 × 73

119. LOUIS LE NAIN. 1593—1648
French School
The Milkmaid's Family. 1640s
Oil on canvas. 51 × 59

120, 121. NICOLAS POUSSIN. 1594—1665
French School
Tancred and Erminia. C. 1631—33
Oil on canvas. 98 × 147

122, 123. NICOLAS POUSSIN. 1594 — 1665
French School
Landscape with Polyphemus. 1649
Oil on canvas. 150 × 198

124. CLAUDE LORRAIN. 1600—1682
French School
Midday
Oil on canvas. 113 × 157

125, 126. CLAUDE LORRAIN. 1600—1682
French School
The Bay of Baiae. C. 1646—47
Oil on canvas. 99.5 × 125

127. SÉBASTIEN BOURDON. 1616—1671
French School
The Death of Dido
Oil on canvas. 158.5 × 136.5

128. LAURENT DE LA HYRE. 1606—1656
French School
Mercury Entrusting the Infant Bacchus to the
Nymphs
Oil on canvas. 125 × 133
Signed and dated below left: *L. de La Hyre
m. X. F. 1638*

129. PIERRE MIGNARD (?). 1612—1695
French School
Portrait of Hortense Mancini (?)
Oil on canvas. 76 × 62 (oval)

130. SIMON VOUET. 1590—1649
French School
Minerva
Oil on canvas. 202 × 172

131. JAN WEENIX. 1640—1719
Dutch School
Trophies of the Chase
Oil on canvas. 100 × 82

132. GEORG FLEGEL. 1566—1638
German School
Still Life with Flowers and Refreshments
Oil on panel. 52.5 × 41
Signed with a monogram middle right: *G. F.*

133. JOHANN HEINRICH SCHÖNFELDT.
1609—1682/83
German School
The Rape of the Sabines
Oil on canvas. 98.5 × 134

134. FRANZ ANTON MAULPERTSCH. 1724—1796
Austrian School
The Baptism of the Eunuch
Oil on canvas. 50.5 × 34.5

135. THOMAS GAINSBOROUGH. 1727—1788
English School
Portrait of the Duchess of Beaufort (?). Late 1770s
Oil on canvas. 76 × 64

136. JOSHUA REYNOLDS. 1723—1792
English School
Cupid Untying the Zone of Venus. *C.* 1788
Oil on canvas. 127.5 × 101

137. JOSEPH WRIGHT OF DERBY. 1734—1797
English School
The Blacksmith's Shop
Oil on canvas. 105 × 140
Signed and dated below, on the hammer:
J. Wright pinxit 1773

138. GEORGE MORLAND. 1763—1804
English School
Approaching Storm
Oil on canvas. 85 × 117
Signed and dated below right, on the bole of the
fallen tree: *G. Morland 1791*

139. BERNARDO BELLOTTO. 1720—1780
Italian School
New Market Place in Dresden
Oil on canvas. 134 × 236

140. ALESSANDRO MAGNASCO. 1667—1749
Italian School
Bacchanalian Scene. 1710s
Oil on canvas. 110.5 × 167.5

141. GIOVANNI BATTISTA TIEPOLO. 1696—1770
Italian School
Fabius Maximus Quintus in the Senate at
Carthage. *C.* 1725
Oil on canvas. 387 × 224

142, 143. GIOVANNI BATTISTA TIEPOLO.
1696—1770
Italian School
Maecenas Presenting the Liberal Arts to Augustus.
1743
Oil on canvas. 69 × 89

144. FRANCESCO GUARDI. 1712—1793
Italian School
Landscape
Oil on canvas. 120 × 152

145. FRANCESCO GUARDI. 1712—1793
Italian School
View of a Town
Oil on panel. 52 × 34.5

146—149. CANALETTO. 1697—1768
Italian School
Reception of the French Ambassador at Venice.
1740s
Oil on canvas. 181 × 259.5

150. ANTOINE WATTEAU. 1684—1721
French School
Savoyard with His Marmot. 1716
Oil on canvas. 40.5 × 32.5

151. ANTOINE WATTEAU. 1684—1721
French School
Actors of the Comédie-Française. *C.* 1711
Oil on panel. 20 × 25

152, 153. ANTOINE WATTEAU. 1684—1721
French School
An Embarrassing Proposal. *C.* 1716
Oil on canvas. 65 × 84.5

154. ANTOINE WATTEAU. 1684—1721
French School
The Capricious Girl. *C.* 1718
Oil on canvas. 42 × 34

155. NICOLAS LANCRET. 1690—1743
French School
The Dancer La Camargo. *C.* 1730
Oil on canvas. 45 × 55

156. FRANÇOIS BOUCHER. 1703—1770
French School
Landscape near Beauvais. Early 1740s
Oil on canvas. 49 × 58
Signed below right, on a stone: *F Boucher*

157. FRANÇOIS BOUCHER. 1703—1770
French School
Pastoral Scene. 1740s
Oil on canvas. 61 × 75 (oval)
Signed below, on a stone: *F Boucher*

158. JEAN-BAPTISTE GREUZE. 1725—1805
French School
The Spoilt Child. Early 1760s
Oil on canvas. 66.6 × 56

159. JEAN-BAPTISTE PERRONNEAU. 1715—1783
French School
Boy with a Book. *C.* 1745—46
Oil on canvas. 63 × 52

160, 161. JEAN-BAPTISTE SIMÉON CHARDIN.
1699—1779
French School
Still Life with Attributes of the Arts
Oil on canvas. 112 × 140.5
Signed and dated below left, on the table:
Chardin 1766

162, 163. JEAN-BAPTISTE SIMÉON CHARDIN.
1699—1779
French School
Grace before Meat
Oil on canvas. 49.5 × 38.4
Signed and dated below left, on the background:
Chardin 1744

164, 165. JEAN-HONORÉ FRAGONARD.
1732—1806
French School
The Snatched Kiss. 1780s
Oil on canvas. 45 × 55

166. FRANCISCO GOYA. 1746—1828
Spanish School
Portrait of the Actress Antonia Zárate. *C.* 1811
Oil on canvas. 71 × 58

167. ANTOINE-JEAN GROS. 1771—1835
French School
Napoleon at Arcole
Oil on canvas. 134 × 104

168. MARGUERITE GÉRARD. 1761—1837
French School
The First Steps
Oil on canvas. 45.5 × 55

169. FRANÇOIS GÉRARD. 1770—1837
French School
Portrait of Josephine. 1801
Oil on canvas. 178 × 174

170. PIERRE PAUL PRUD'HON. 1758—1823
CONSTANCE MAYER. 1778—1821
French School
Innocence Preferring Love to Wealth
Oil on canvas. 243 × 194
Signed and dated below left: *Const^{ce} Mayer. pinxit.
1804*

171. PIERRE GUÉRIN. 1774—1833
French School
Morpheus and Iris
Oil on canvas. 251 × 178
Signed and dated below right: *P. Guerin 1811*

172, 173. JACQUES LOUIS DAVID. 1748—1825
French School
Sappho and Phaon
Oil on canvas. 225 × 262
Signed and dated below left: *L. David 1809*

174. THOMAS LAWRENCE. 1769—1830
English School
Portrait of Lady Raglan. *C. 1815*
Oil on panel. 76 × 63

175. JEAN AUGUSTE DOMINIQUE INGRES.
1780—1867
French School
Portrait of Count Guryev
Oil on canvas. 107 × 86
Signed and dated below left: *Ingres Flor 1821*

176. THÉODORE ROUSSEAU. 1812—1867
French School
Market Place in Normandy
Oil on panel. 29.5 × 38
Signed below right: *T. Rousseau*

177. RICHARD PARKES BONINGTON. 1802—1828
English School
Boats by the Shore. *C. 1825*
Oil on canvas. 35.5 × 46

178. CASPAR DAVID FRIEDRICH. 1774—1840
German School
Riesengebirge. 1835
Oil on canvas. 73.5 × 102.5

179. CASPAR DAVID FRIEDRICH. 1774—1840
German School
On a Sailing Boat. 1818—19
Oil on canvas. 71 × 56

180. FERDINAND GEORG WALDMÜLLER.
1793—1865
Austrian School
Children
Oil on panel. 25 × 31
Signed and dated middle right: *Waldmüller 1834*

181. THOMAS COUTURE. 1815—1879
French School
The Little Bather
Oil on canvas. 117 × 90
Signed and dated below left: *T. C. 1849*

182. THÉODORE GUDIN. 1802—1880
French School
The Body of Napoleon Being Shipped to France
from the Island of St Helena
Oil on canvas. 42 × 65
Signed and dated below right: *T. Gudin Peterhoff
24. Juin 1841*; below left: *T Gudin. Peterhoff 24.
Juillet 1841*

183. ALFRED RETHEL. 1816—1859
German School
Nemesis
Oil on canvas. 95 × 48
Signed and dated below left: *A. Rethel 1837*

184. ALEXANDRE GABRIEL DECAMPS.
1803—1860
French School
Self-portrait
Oil on canvas. 32.5 × 24.5

185. JEAN LOUIS ERNEST MEISSONIER.
1815—1891
French School
The Musketeer
Oil on panel. 24.5 × 15
Signed and dated below right: *E. Meissonier 1870*

186. ALFRED DE DREUX. 1810—1860
French School
A Ride
Oil on canvas. 24 × 32
Signed below left: *Alfred D. D.*

187. CHRISTINA ROBERTSON. Active between
1830 and 1860
English School
Children with a Parrot
Oil on canvas. 112 × 104
Signed and dated above left: *C. Robertson pinxit
1856* [1850?]

188. EUGÈNE DELACROIX. 1798—1863
French School
Arab Saddling His Horse
Oil on canvas. 56 × 47
Signed and dated below right: *Eug. Delacroix 1855*

189. EUGÈNE DELACROIX. 1798—1863
French School
Lion Hunt in Morocco
Oil on canvas. 74 × 92
Signed and dated below right: *Eug. Delacroix 1854*

190. NARCISSE DÍAZ DE LA PEÑA. 1808—1876
French School
A Road in the Forest
Oil on panel. 29 × 35
Signed right: *N Diaz*

191. JULES DUPRÉ. 1811—1889
French School
Autumn Landscape
Oil on canvas. 51 × 46
Signed below right: *Jules Dupré*

192. CAMILLE COROT. 1796—1875
French School
Peasant Woman Pasturing a Cow on the Edge of
a Wood. 1865—70
Oil on canvas. 47.5 × 35
Signed below right: *Corot*

193. CAMILLE COROT. 1796—1875
French School
Landscape with Cows. 1865—75
Oil on canvas. 22 × 17
Signed left: *Corot*

194. CAMILLE COROT. 1796—1875
French School
Trees in a Marsh. 1855—60
Oil on canvas. 25.5 × 38
Signed below right: *Corot*

195. GUSTAVE COURBET. 1819—1877
French School
Landscape with a Dead Horse. 1855—60
Oil on canvas. 46 × 56
Signed below left: *G Courbet*

196. JEAN-FRANÇOIS MILLET. 1814—1875
French School
Peasant Women Carrying Firewood. *C. 1858*
Oil on canvas. 37.5 × 29.5
Signed below right: *J. F. Millet*

197. CONSTANT TROYON. 1810—1865
French School
On the Way to the Market
Oil on canvas. 260.5 × 211
Signed and dated below left: *C. Troyon 1859*

198. CHARLES FRANÇOIS DAUBIGNY.
1817—1878
French School
The Banks of the Oise
Oil on canvas. 25.5 × 41
Signed below left: *Ch. Daubigny*

199. HANS VON MARÉES. 1837—1887
German School
Courtyard of the Royal Residence in Munich.
C. 1862—63
Oil on canvas. 242 × 162

200. HENRI FANTIN-LATOUR. 1836—1904
French School
Vase of Roses and Nasturtiums
Oil on canvas. 28 × 36
Signed and dated below right: *Fantin. 83*

201. CLAUDE MONET. 1840—1926
French School
Lady in the Garden at Sainte-Adresse. 1867
Oil on canvas. 80 × 99
Signed below left: *Claude Monet*

202. CLAUDE MONET. 1840—1926
French School
Corner of the Garden at Montgeron. *C. 1876—77*
Oil on canvas. 172 × 193
Signed below right: *Cl. M.*

203, 204. CLAUDE MONET. 1840—1926
French School
Poppy Field. Late 1880s
Oil on canvas. 59 × 90
Signed below right: *Claude Monet*

205. ALFRED SISLEY. 1839—1899
French School
Village on the Seine (Villeneuve-la-Garenne)
Oil on canvas. 59 × 80.5
Signed and dated below left: *Sisley 1872*

206. ALFRED SISLEY. 1839—1899
French School
River Banks at Saint-Mammès
Oil on canvas. 50 × 65
Signed and dated below left: *Sisley. 84*

207, 208. CAMILLE PISSARRO. 1830—1903
French School
Place du Théâtre-Français
Oil on canvas. 65.5 × 81.5
Signed and dated below right: *C. Pissarro 98*

209. CAMILLE PISSARRO. 1830—1903
French School
Boulevard Montmartre
Oil on canvas. 73 × 92
Signed and dated below right: *C. Pissarro 97*

210. PIERRE AUGUSTE RENOIR. 1841—1919
French School
Child with a Whip
Oil on canvas. 105 × 75
Signed and dated below right: *Renoir. 85*

211. PIERRE AUGUSTE RENOIR. 1841—1919
French School
Girl with a Fan. 1881
Oil on canvas. 65 × 50
Signed above right: *Renoir*

212. PIERRE AUGUSTE RENOIR. 1841—1919
French School
Lady in Black. *C.* 1876
Oil on canvas. 63 × 53
Signed middle right: *A. Renoir*

213. PIERRE AUGUSTE RENOIR. 1841—1919
French School
Portrait of the Actress Jeanne Samary
Oil on canvas. 173 × 103
Signed and dated below left: *Renoir. 78*

214. EDGAR DEGAS. 1834—1917
French School
Woman Combing Her Hair. 1886
Pastel on cardboard. 53 × 52
Signed above right: *Degas*

215. EDGAR DEGAS. 1834—1917
French School
After the Bath. Mid-1890s
Pastel, gouache with traces of charcoal and varnish
on three horizontal strips of grey paper, mounted
on cardboard. 82.5 × 72
Signed above right: *Degas*

216. PAUL CÉZANNE. 1839—1906
French School
Vase of Flowers. *C.* 1873—75
Oil on canvas. 56 × 46
Signed below left: *P. Cézanne*

217. PAUL CÉZANNE. 1839—1906
French School
Girl at the Piano (Overture to *Tannhäuser*).
C. 1868—69
Oil on canvas. 57 × 92

218. PAUL CÉZANNE. 1839—1906
French School
Pine Tree near Aix. Late 1890s
Oil on canvas. 72 × 91

219. PAUL CÉZANNE. 1839—1906
French School
The Banks of the Marne. 1888
Oil on canvas. 65 × 81

220. PAUL CÉZANNE. 1839—1906
French School
Still Life with Drapery. *C.* 1899
Oil on canvas. 53 × 72

221. PAUL CÉZANNE. 1839—1906
French School
Portrait of the Artist in a Peaked Cap. *C.* 1873—75
Oil on canvas. 53 × 38

222. PAUL CÉZANNE. 1839—1906
French School
The Smoker. *C.* 1895
Oil on canvas. 91 × 72

223, 224. VINCENT VAN GOGH. 1853—1890
Dutch School
Ladies of Arles (Memory of the Garden at Etten).
1888
Oil on canvas. 73 × 92

225. VINCENT VAN GOGH. 1853—1890
Dutch School
Thatched Cottages. 1890
Oil on canvas. 60 × 73

226. VINCENT VAN GOGH. 1853—1890
Dutch School
Lilac Bush. 1889
Oil on canvas. 73 × 92
Signed below left: *Vincent*

227. PAUL GAUGUIN. 1848—1903
French School
Tahitian Pastoral Scenes
Oil on canvas. 86 × 113
Below right: *Pastorales Tahitiennes 1893 Paul
Gauguin*

228. PAUL GAUGUIN. 1848—1903
French School
Woman Holding a Fruit
Oil on canvas. 92 × 73
Below left: *P Gauguin. 93 Eu haere ia oe*

229, 230. PAUL GAUGUIN. 1848—1903
French School
Sacred Spring (Sweet Dreams)
Oil on canvas. 73 × 98
Below left: *Nave nave moe P. Gauguin 94*

231. ALBERT EDELFELT. 1854—1905
Finnish School
Washerwomen
Oil on canvas. 97 × 128
Signed and dated below left: *A. Edelfelt 1893*

232. MAX LIEBERMANN. 1847—1935
German School
Girl in a Field
Pastel on paper. 54 × 79
Signed below right: *M. Liebermann*

233. FRITS THAULOW. 1847—1906
Norwegian School
At Night
Oil on canvas. 61 × 82
Signed and dated below right: *Frits Thaulow*

234. IGNACIO ZULOAGA. 1870—1945
Spanish School
Gregorio the Dwarf. 1908
Oil on canvas. 187 × 154
Signed below left: *I. Zuloaga*

235. FRANK BRANGWYN. 1867—1956
English School
Charity
Oil on canvas. 94 × 91
Signed with a monogram and dated below right:
F.B. 90

236. HENRI MANGUIN. 1874—1949
French School
Morning (Lady Sitting on the Shore of Cavalière
Bay). 1906
Oil on canvas. 81.5 × 64.5
Signed below right: *Manguin*

237. MAURICE DENIS. 1870—1943
French School
Female Figures in a Spring Landscape (Sacred
Grove)
Oil on canvas. 157 × 179
Signed with a monogram and dated on the tree-
trunk: *MAUD 97*

238. MAURICE DENIS. 1870—1943
French School
The Flying Eros Is Struck by the Beauty of Psyche.
From *The Story of Psyche* series (eleven decorative
panels). 1908—9
Oil on canvas. 394 × 269

239. HENRI CROSS (DELACROIX). 1856—1910
French School
View of the Church of Santa Maria degli Angeli
near Assisi
Oil on canvas. 74 × 92
Signed and dated below right: *Henri Edmond Cross 09*

240. PAUL SIGNAC. 1863—1935
French School
Harbour at Marseilles. 1906
Oil on canvas. 46 × 55
Signed below left: *P. Signac*

241. HENRI ROUSSEAU. 1844—1910
French School
In a Tropical Forest. Battle between the Tiger and
the Bull
Oil on canvas. 46 × 55
Signed and dated below left: *Henri Rousseau 1908* (?)

242. HENRI ROUSSEAU. 1844—1910
French School
The Luxembourg Gardens. Monument to Chopin
Oil on canvas. 38 × 47
Signed and dated below right: *H. Rousseau 1909*

243. PIERRE BONNARD. 1867—1947
French School
Early Spring (Little Fauns). 1909
Oil on canvas. 102.5 × 125
Signed below right: *Bonnard*

244. PIERRE BONNARD. 1867—1947
French School
Landscape with a Goods Train. 1909
Oil on canvas. 77 × 108
Signed below right: *Bonnard*

245. PIERRE BONNARD. 1867—1947
French School
Morning in Paris
Oil on canvas. 76.5 × 122
Signed below right: *Bonnard*

246, 247. PIERRE BONNARD. 1867—1947
French School
Evening in Paris. 1911
Oil on canvas. 76 × 121
Signed below right: *Bonnard*

248, 249. PIERRE BONNARD. 1867—1947
French School
The Mediterranean. Triptych
Oil on canvas. Central panel, 407 × 152; side
panels, 407 × 149
Signed and dated below middle (right panel):
Bonnard 1911

250. ALBERT MARQUET. 1875—1947
French School
Place de la Trinité in Paris. 1911
Oil on canvas. 81.5 × 65
Signed below right: *Marquet*

251. ALBERT MARQUET. 1875—1947
French School
Marine (Naples)
Oil on canvas. 61.5 × 80
Signed and dated below right: *Marquet 1909*

252. HENRI MATISSE. 1869—1954
French School
View of Collioure. 1906
Oil on canvas. 59.5 × 73
Signed below left: *H. Matisse*

253. HENRI MATISSE. 1869—1954
French School
The Artist's Family
Oil on canvas. 143 × 194
Signed and dated on the subframe: *Henri Matisse
1911*

254. HENRI MATISSE. 1869—1954
French School
The Dance
Oil on canvas. 260 × 391
Signed and dated below right: *Henri Matisse 1910*

255. HENRI MATISSE. 1869—1954
French School
Portrait of the Artist's Wife. 1913
Oil on canvas. 145 × 97
Signed below right: *Henri Matisse*

256. HENRI MATISSE. 1869—1954
French School
The Red Room (La Desserte. Harmony in Red)
Oil on canvas. 180 × 220
Signed and dated below left: *Henri Matisse 1908*

257, 258. MAURICE VLAMINCK. 1876—1958
French School
View of the Seine. *C.* 1905—6
Oil on canvas. 54 × 64.5
Signed below right: *Vlaminck*

259. GEORGES ROUAULT. 1871—1958
French School
Spring
Water-colour and pastel on paper. 55 × 52 (oval)
Signed and dated below right: *1911 G. Rouault*

260. KEES VAN DONGEN. 1877—1968
French School
Woman in a Black Hat. *C.* 1908
Oil on canvas. 100 × 81
Signed below right: *Van Dongen*

261. ANDRÉ DERAIN. 1880—1954
French School
Road in the Mountains. Cassis. 1907
Oil on canvas. 80.5 × 99

262. ANDRÉ DERAIN. 1880—1954
French School
Harbour in Provence (Martigues). 1913
Oil on canvas. 140 × 89
Signed on the back: *a derain*

263. ANDRÉ DERAIN. 1880—1954
French School
Portrait of an Unknown Man with a Newspaper
(Chevalier X). 1914
Oil on canvas. 160.5 × 96
Signed on the back: *a derain*

264. ANDRÉ DERAIN. 1880—1954
French School
Table and Chairs. *C.* 1912
Oil on canvas. 87 × 85.5
Signed on the back: *a derain*

265. PABLO PICASSO. 1881—1973
French School
Portrait of Soler
Oil on canvas. 100 × 70
Signed and dated above left: *Picasso 1903*

266. PABLO PICASSO. 1881—1973
French School
Woman Drinking Absinth. 1901
Oil on canvas. 73 × 54
Signed above right: *— Picasso —*

267. PABLO PICASSO. 1881—1973
French School
Flowers in a Grey Jug with Wine-glass and Spoon.
1908
Oil on canvas. 81 × 65
Signed on the back, above left: *Picasso*

268. PABLO PICASSO. 1881—1973
French School
Musical Instruments. 1912
Oil on canvas. 98 × 80 (oval)
Signed on the back: *Picasso*

269. GIORGIO MORANDI. 1890—1964
Italian School
Still Life
Oil on canvas. 51 × 57.5
Signed above middle: *Morandi*

270. FILIPPO DE PISIS. 1896—1956
Italian School
Flowers
Oil on canvas. 64.5 × 46
Signed and dated below right: *De Pisis 28*

271. HENRI LE FAUCONNIER. 1881—1946
French School
The Signal. 1915
Oil on canvas. 80 × 90

272. HEINRICH EHMSEN. 1886—1963
German School
The Execution
Oil on canvas. 109.5 × 135
Signed and dated below right: *Ehmsen 1919*

273. ANDRÉ FOUGERON. Born 1913
French School
Chad-fishers. 1964
Oil on canvas. 146 × 114
Signed above right: *a fougeron*

274. RENATO GUTTUSO. Born 1912
Italian School
Rocco and His Son. 1960
Oil on canvas. 136 × 113
Signed below right: *Guttuso*

ЗАПАДНОЕВРОПЕЙСКАЯ ЖИВОПИСЬ
В ЭРМИТАЖЕ

ИЗДАТЕЛЬСТВО «АВРОРА», ЛЕНИНГРАД

RESEARCH AND TECHNOLOGY BUILDINGS – A DESIGN MANUAL

A DESIGN MANUAL

Research and Technology Buildings

Hardo Braun

Dieter Grömling

Contributions by

Helmut Bleher

Hannelore Deubzer

Jürgen Eichler

Oswald W. Grube

Gerhard Hausladen and Hana Meindl

Manfred Hegger

Gunter Henn

Hans-U. Jaeger

Svante Pääbo

Kai L. Simons

Birkhäuser – Publishers for Architecture
Basel · Berlin · Boston

Project management, image and information research: Sieglinde Kermer, Munich

Translation: Jörn Frenzel, Berlin (edited by Caroline Behlen, Berlin)

Layout and cover design: Oliver Kleinschmidt, Berlin

Cover photograph: Manfred Seidl, Vienna

Lithography: Licht & Tiefe, Berlin

Printing: Medialis, Berlin

This book is also available in a German language edition
(ISBN-13: 978-3-7643-2173-4, ISBN-10: 3-7643-2173-3)

Bibliographic information published by Die Deutsche Bibliothek
Die Deutsche Bibliothek lists this publication in the Deutsche Nationalbibliografie; detailed
bibliographic data is available in the Internet at http://dnb.ddb.de.

A CIP catalogue record for this book is available from the Library of Congress,
Washington D.C., USA

© 2005 Birkhäuser – Publishers for Architecture, P.O.Box 133, CH-4010 Basel, Switzerland
Part of Springer Science+Business Media

Printed on acid-free paper produced from chlorine-free pulp. TCF ∞

Printed in Germany
ISBN-13: 978-3-7643-2174-1
ISBN-10: 3-7643-2174-1

www.birkhauser.ch

9 8 7 6 5 4 3 2 1

Principles of
Research and Technology Buildings

Selection of Projects

Context

Access Systems

SCIENCE CAMPUS

66
Maersk McKinney Møller Institute
for Production Technologies
Henning Larsens Tegnestue A/S

68
Bourns Hall, Engineering Science
Building, University of California
Anshen + Allen

70
Institute of Physics,
Humboldt University of Berlin,
Adlershof Campus
Augustin und Frank Architekten

72
Max Planck Campus Tübingen
Fritsch + Tschaidse Architekten

74
Institutes and Lecture Hall
for Biology and Chemistry,
University of Rostock
Volker Staab Architekten

76
Fred Hutchinson
Cancer Research Center
Zimmer Gunsul Frasca Partnership

78
Belfer Building for Molecular
Genetics and Cancer Research,
Weizmann Campus
Moshe Zur Architects Urbanists
& Town Planners

82
Laboratory Building
of Cologne University Hospital
Heinrich Wörner + stegepartner

84
Centre for Cellular
and Biomolecular Research
Behnisch, Behnisch & Partner Architekten
with architectsAlliance

URBAN LANDMARKS

86
Male Urological Cancer
Research Centre
Copping Lindsay Architects

88
Biosciences Building,
University of Liverpool
David Morley Architects

90
Life Sciences Complex,
Ben Gurion University
Ada Karmi-Melamede & Partners

92
Centre for Information and Media
Technology, Adlershof Science and
Technology Park
Architectenbureau cepezed b.v.

94
Parque Tecnológico IMPIVA
Carlos Ferrater, Carlos Bento,
Jaime Sanahuja

96
Center for Biotechnology
and Bioengineering
Bohlin Cywinski Jackson

98
Max Bergmann Centre of Biomaterials
Brenner & Partner
Architekten und Ingenieure
Brenner-Hammes-Krause

100
Max Planck Institute
for Evolutionary Anthropology
SSP Architekten
Schmidt-Schicketanz und Partner GmbH

102
Max Planck Institute for
Infection Biology and
German Arthritis Research Centre
Deubzer König Architekten

104
Barcelona Botanical Institute
Carlos Ferrater, Joan Guibernau,
Elena Mateu

LARGE STRUCTURES

108
Computer Science and
Electrical Engineering Institutes,
Graz University of Technology
Riegler Riewe Architekten ZT-Ges.m.b.H.

112
Saitama Prefectural University
Riken Yamamoto

114
Technology Centre,
Rhine-Elbe Science Park
Kiessler + Partner Architekten GmbH

116
La Ruche, Technocentre Renault
Valode & Pistre Architectes

COMB-LIKE SYSTEMS

120
Headquarters of NeuroSearch A/S
Henning Larsens Tegnestue A/S

122
Institute for Chemistry and Lecture
Building for Chemistry and Physics,
Humboldt University of Berlin,
Adlershof Campus
Volker Staab Architekten

124
Sciences Institute
Heinle, Wischer und Partner
Freie Architekten
Krebs und Kiefer International

126
Nokia Research Center
Tuomo Siitonen and Esko Valkama,
Helin & Siitonen Architects

DOUBLE-LOADED SYSTEMS

128
State Office
for Chemical Investigations
Dipl.-Ing. Michael Weindel
Freier Architekt

130
Max Planck Institute of Biophysics
Auer + Weber + Architekten

134
Fraunhofer Institute
for Manufacturing
and Advanced Materials
Brenner & Partner
Architekten und Ingenieure
Brenner-Hammes-Krause

136
Center of Advanced European Studies
and Research (CAESAR)
BMBW Architekten + Partner

140
Fraunhofer Institute
for Applied Polymer Research
Brenner & Partner
Architekten und Ingenieure
Brenner-Hammes-Krause

142
Pharmacological Research Building,
Boehringer Ingelheim Pharma KG
sauerbruch hutton architekten

Principles
of Research
and Technology
Buildings

SVANTE PÄÄBO

What is research?

Research is more lifestyle than work. It is a lifestyle that tends to form a large part of a researcher's life. Particularly if belonging to the biomedical research community, researchers will spend much time in the laboratory, in front of computer screens, or talking to colleagues. They experience recognition of their achievements both through the joy of covering new ground as well as through the feedback of their colleagues. They feel strongly attached to their work and therefore are inclined to experience mood swings according to the results of their research projects.

Research is teamwork. Teams are composed of scientists and technical assistants; however, the members of a team might be pronounced individualists. Every scientist deals with projects partly alone, partly in collaboration with others. This conflict between the team and the individual is a constant source of stress even if its disturbing effects can be reduced to a minimum, as is the case in well-functioning teams.

Research is a global phenomenon. The fruit of this work – knowledge – is common property basically accessible to everyone on the planet. It is expected of scientists in most research fields not only to change jobs during their career but also countries to gain international experience. Young ambitious scientists and the established elite alike are extremely mobile and regard the entire industrialised world as their potential job market.

Research is also competition. This fact sometimes leads to a frantic run to be the first to discover or publish results. One can look at global research today as a Darwinist process: Those who find solutions to the most important issues using the fastest and most efficient methods are the ones who are really successful. However, fair competition between individual research teams is healthy and governed by professional respect.

What characterises the most successful research teams that are setting the benchmark in this process? They succeed in recruiting the best talents among students and on the international job market. They are able to mobilise creativity and enthusiasm to get the best out of a team.

What are the crucial preconditions needed to achieve this? Beyond obvious attractors such as the significance of a research project and a sound financial base, the most important factor for successful teamwork is social interaction. The social structure of a team can either boost or hamper its creativity and enthusiasm. The architecture of a research building potentially plays a positive and stimulating role in achieving this.

Almost all scientific ideas are born out of communication between research colleagues. The exchange of ideas is also indispensable for recognising the most viable and visionary ones among the many ideas that form the "raw material" of progress in a research team. Criticism and revision of scientific goals and strategies ensure that dead-ends are identified and abandoned quickly. In this process social interaction between all members of the team is essential. Communication – whether it happens among few or many persons, or whether it is organised less or more formally – is the focal point of social life in a research team. Hence, a research building has to provide ample spaces for conversations and meetings on all levels of communication. This, for example, concerns "open" seminar and meeting rooms that are situated next to circulation routes in an institute or department. Accidental passers-by may get involved into conversations and share unexpected or novel points of view. Open plan office layouts encourage communication and are flexible enough to accommodate changing work procedures. Nonetheless, as in many other areas of life, a mixed strategy is also desirable in this case: individual office cells – in combination with open areas – provide a spatial or even intellectual enclosure that might be helpful for some employees or research tasks.

Research challenges established knowledge. Taken in this sense, the nature of research is anti-authoritarian. Hierarchic structures have to be avoided since they hamper creativity and keep doctrines from being questioned. For example, research buildings should not suggest or even stipulate hierarchic structures by providing remote executive offices that can only be reached through an outer office.

It is just as vital to create an atmosphere of openness and trust. People will only voice daring, unusual or even crazy ideas when they feel secure – and it is only in this way that the entirely new and unexpected can be born. The building should therefore be associated with warmth and security rather than impersonal technocratic monumentality lacking human scale. The building design can make use of a rich repertoire of solutions to achieve this: a meeting room that also serves as a kitchen may create a private ambient; warm colours and materials like timber can enhance interior qualities etc.

Since scientists spend a great deal of their lifetime in a research institute – both physically and emotionally – it is important to provide opportunities for relaxation and communication that extend beyond the professional realm. Lively social interaction is also crucial as foreign employees from all parts of the world are separated from their friends and family for a couple of years. Social activities should cater for a broad range of interests: squash, yoga, music, dancing, table tennis and the like. A research building should at least offer space for such activities.

Scientists usually do not work from nine to five. Hence, a cafeteria offering breakfast, lunch, and dinner allows individual working hours and encourages employees to linger and spend some time with colleagues – provided the food is good enough. Researchers are often on a lower salary than other professions whose academic education took a similar amount of time. However, they are privileged as they have an interesting and fulfilling job. If they are able to pursue this job in a pleasant and functional research facility that recognises the communicative and playful aspects of research they can count themselves among the happiest professions within our society.

Research today

Research and technology buildings represent the growing importance of knowledge-intensive occupations in our industrial society. Today, more than 50 % of all occupations are rated as particularly knowledge-intensive – and this figure is rising. At the beginning of the 20th century only approx. 15 % were rated as such. Even in the industrial sector, knowledge-intensive occupations, for example construction, analysis, or service are more critical than the actual production.

Research is demanding and expensive. Because of this, corporations and research facilities have to deal with a number of conflicting goals. An increase of efficiency is commonly associated with standardisation and simplification of complex processes and occupations. Yet innovation is only possible if people have insight into processes or organisational structures as a whole – if they possess knowledge and have access to its resources. To make their knowledge-based potential unfold, companies have to foster freedom of team-work, increase the density of information and communication within the firm, and go public.

The design of research environments is based on fundamental changes of time and space frameworks. The dynamics and qualities of these frameworks are no longer tied to traditional ordering systems. The world as we know it consists of places of stay which are more or less linked by a communication network. Global media and transportation networks increasingly function independently of "real" places and structure the world. At certain points, these networks form nodes that in turn may assume the stability of actual places of stay. Architecture and space have to react to these new ways of defining place or communication nodes respectively. In this context architecture will continue to create order, even if under new conditions and in consideration of new technologies.

Requirements made of research buildings for universities and the industry vary. The primary task of universities and other research facilities is to generate and develop knowledge, to strive for cognition, to conduct basic research, and share information. The main objective of companies is the generation of new innovative products in short intervals. Their knowledge-intensive potential mainly resides in the fields of research and development (R & D), and application. In the Project Building of the BMW Research and Innovation Centre (FIZ) in Munich about 2,000 engineers and technicians work in a real-time process. The decisive factor in this process is the pace at which knowledge is converted into added value. Within an organisation, the best indicators for an efficient use of its store of knowledge ultimately are the pace and flow of the "knowledge turnover".

These factors have an impact on time and space of communication which, just like the various technological preconditions, have to be considered by the architect. For example the planning of laboratories, clean rooms, and work processes generating emissions have to follow very specific standards. The goal is to embed this high-tech working environment into a communicative layout. After all, research and technology buildings act as information systems that need to redefine their internal and external permeability; yet they also act as "immune systems" that serve an environment, allowing for concentration and focussing on a certain subject. How different the individual strategies of information transfer may be – at the end of the day they have to improve communication between the employees, how they join a conversation and how they listen to each other. In a knowledge-oriented enterprise, talking is part of the working process. The required "culture of knowledge" is characterised by trust, openness, creativity, and a constructive handling of mistakes; hereby, unknown factors are always considered a chance. Just as important for a "culture of knowledge" is team spirit and the identification of the employees with similar goals and values. "Culture of knowledge" is "culture of communication".

Consequently, challenges when planning a research or technology building are the selection of an appropriate site for such a knowledge-intensive organisation as well as the design of places that lend themselves to communication and social interaction. It is essential to connect these buildings with the process-oriented dynamics taking place within. More than ever, modern research buildings call for places that not only allow self-organisation of the users but provoke it. The strictly functional organisation of space has to be replaced by the principle of networking, in other words a circulation system that facilitates communication. This kind of architecture initiates and encourages people to co-operate.

Contemporary global research, particularly within the realm of natural science, is a highly dynamic sector subject to fierce competition. The most successful institutes are able to publish their results quickly and efficiently. Hence, research is reliant on exchange of information at the shortest intervals and must adapt new working methods and application processes as fast as possible. Of increasing importance are synergies with other universities, the industry, and the public. For example, the Max Planck Institute for Molecular Cell Biology and Genetics in Dresden, Germany, is part of the local research environment "Biopolis". It maintains close links to the Technical University Dresden with its key disciplines biology, medicine, and engineering. At the same time, the project is embedded into a local business context including innovative newcomers as well as established large corporations. Moreover, the building's central location in the city of Dresden encourages a closer interaction with the public.

Platforms for the exchange of knowledge are important. Unrestricted, global access to knowledge and the fact that scientists need time to absorb knowledge and to experiment with it lead to new design approaches. This applies to external relations as well as to the quality of internal work and communication processes. Architecture must stand the test of time by providing flexible layouts.

New solutions are not to be found through separation of disciplines anymore but increasingly arise from a trans-disciplinary approach. This involves the combination of different or even disciplines that are considered contrary as well as the bridging of the gap between universities and the industry. Volkswagen's MobileLifeCampus AutoUni in Wolfsburg, Germany, stands at the forefront of this trend. The campus offers management training in which executives learn that innovative sustainable strategies often emerge from informal, self-organised networks within a corporation. Casual encounters and communication improve the creative environment that leads to new ideas. The generation of knowledge in this way is an independent process that has to be cultivated. The AutoUni architecturally expresses these dynamic clusters of knowledge. Its conceptual design is based on a double-folded five-storey ribbon. The resulting building typology is the compressed three-dimensional image of the street and the marketplace, this way establishing the base for a communicative campus whose fourth dimension is the potential generation of knowledge.

Not least, investors and scientists measure a company's or an institution's attractiveness against the architectural quality it offers. Therefore, research and technology buildings rank among the most enduring building tasks of our times.

Project design building of BMW AG, Munich, Germany; architects: Henn Architekten

For the first time, the new Project Building of the BMW Research and Innovation Centre (FIZ) in Munich enables a new kind of teamwork in the product development process through a particular spatial layout. The central atrium space of the 100 x 100 m building accommodates the glazed pod structure of the studio workshop. On different floor levels, design stages of projects in progress are visualised in full-scale models using the Rapid Prototyping Process.

The areas are fully transparent towards the surrounding areas assigned to specific projects. This opens up new paths of communication and workflow: every designer can visually compare the computer model on his screen with the workshop model in real time. The centrally positioned full-scale model provides a vivid attractor that brings together all persons involved (collective intelligence) in the right moment (real time).

KAI L. SIMONS

Research and research buildings: the example of Life Sciences

The image of the distracted professor working isolated in his study is a thing of the past. Scientific research is still carried out by individuals, but the achievements of somebody like Mendel who conducted his experiments in the seclusion of a monastery garden and created a new scientific discipline are inconceivable today. Contemporary molecular life sciences bring together such an enormous amount of information that one scientist by himself would not have a chance of making a significant discovery.

The groundbreaking discoveries of modern biology were still based on creative simplification. Research results of many scientists – for instance, the decodification of DNA by Crick and Watson – count as masterpieces of genetics. Databases of modern biology ultimately are the result of brilliant reduction: Biochemists and genetic scientists split life into its smallest particles, identified, and described genes and proteins. A molecular biologist was able to gain a global reputation with the discovery of a single gene or protein.

These times are over. Human and other genomes have been completely decodified; now, biologists have to put the pieces of the puzzle together – a task that requires multi-disciplinary co-operation. We are trying to understand how hundreds of genes and proteins work together. We need to analyse how different processes of life function, not only in the test-tube, but also (and primarily) under natural conditions. What does exactly happen when a hormone like insulin docks onto its cell receptor? What processes take place in a cell and what are the effects of this on the entire organism? When answering these questions, traditional boundaries between disciplines like biochemistry, genetics, cellular biology, endocrinology, and physiology increasingly blur and even vanish altogether. That is why in a modern molecular life sciences institute scientists with very different expert knowledge work together. Yesterday's hierarchic and non-flexible research structures would obstruct inter-disciplinary co-operation; therefore, the organisation of an institute has to be highly flexible and transparent.

It is not sufficient anymore that biologists and physicians work in a team. When analysing the mechanisms of life processes in their context, physicists, chemists, and information technologists are involved. The cells within our bodies are marvels of nanotechnology. "Nano-machines" produce energy and a great variety of chemical substances. Internal circulation systems working like high-speed train networks distribute proteins from their "manufacturing plants" via many intermediate stations to their locations in a cell. Without "wiring", inter-cellular communication functions just by means of chemical sensors. Nowadays, nano-video systems are in place to scrutinise life in "cell city". Chemical probes enable the analysis of cellular mechanisms and the surveying of individual chemical reactions. To put together thousands of puzzle pieces of genes and proteins, the scientist also needs the help of information technologists. These bio-technologists work on new algorithms to filter crucial information from genomes and other data sources. Another challenge of this biological discipline is to exercise an influence on entire systems of life processes, which gives rise to a new integrated discipline called systems biology.

The Max Planck Institute for Molecular Cell Biology and Genetics (MPI-CBG) in Dresden, Germany, is an example of a research institute for molecular life sciences. Within one faculty, roughly 25 independent research teams work together at the time of writing. The projects of the groups overlap and support each other. A broad range of professionally organised and managed service facilities is available. In order to efficiently use synergy effects, frequent work steps like DANN-sequencing, protein expression, mass spectrometry, bio-IT, and light and electron microscopy are centralised as services available to all research teams and labs. The conceptual idea of the building is to create a "communicative building" that maximises social interaction between employees and scientists. An atrium forms the heart of the five-storey building; it contains an extraordinary spiral stair – the institute's communication axis – which links to seminar rooms and a "piazzetta" on all levels; here, more platforms for the exchange of ideas and discussion are provided. Within the atrium and adjacent to the auditorium and library, a canteen and a cafeteria are located. Since the main entrance provides the only access to the institute, the atrium is the focal point of social life. Weekly internal seminars held in the auditorium encourage the exchange of ideas on current projects. Just before the seminar begins, music selected by the respective speaker can be heard throughout the building, inviting everybody to attend. Afterwards, staff can enjoy casual drinks in the atrium. The atrium also serves as a platform for public events communicating scientific issues and functioning as a meeting place for Dresden's general public.

Laboratories are located on four storeys on either side of the atrium. Each wing houses four research teams which form clusters that collaborate even closer than usual. Every research cluster is called a home base and comprises service rooms and equipment pools at its centre. To enhance communication, individual teams of a home base share one corridor. The writing desks in the laboratories are arranged along the windows and are separated from the lab benches with glazed partitions. Throughout the building, the use of glass provides transparency.

Max Planck Institute for Molecular Cell Biology and Genetics (MPI-CBG), Dresden, Germany; architects: Heikkinen-Komonen Architects with Henn Architekten, 2002

First floor plan of laboratory building

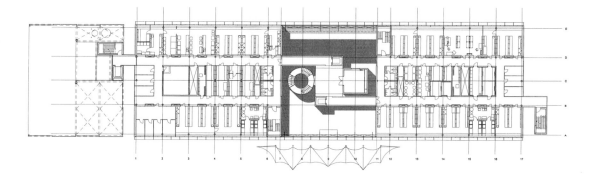

Discussion in the atrium

Cafeteria

The offices of the five directors are glazed and directly attached to the laboratories of their units to facilitate spontaneous conversations. The same principle of openness applies to the administrative offices on the ground floor. If scientists need a space for concentrated work they have access to individual writing cells in the library.

Every home base offers bridges and visual connections to the piazzetta and the atrium. This kind of architecture has stood the test and helped to create a communicative atmosphere within the house. The institute's attractiveness is proven by more than 330 applications for the doctoral program which came from more than 30 countries in the year 2004 (two years after its inauguration). In the same year, the building was the only European laboratory building to be featured in "The Scientist" in an article on "scientific temples" alongside the famous Salk Institute by Louis I. Kahn. An international profile encourages multi-disciplinary co-operation. The corridors, the spiral stair, the cafeteria, or the canteen set the stage not only for a multitude of voices in different mother tongues, but also for a vivid discourse between different disciplines. If we also switch from reductionism to more tranquillity in the natural sciences, a better understanding of life's complexities may be born.

Salk Institute for Biological Studies,
La Jolla/San Diego, California, USA;
architect: Louis I. Kahn, 1959-1967.
Central court facing the sea

Building culture: magic and identity of place

Great space has no corners.
Great form has no contour.[1]

The document of a historical place: the Boulevard du Temple in Paris, photographed by one of the ingenious technical pioneers of the 19th century. The painter Louis Daguerre states that on that day in 1838, the boulevard was "filled by a busy crowd" yet the photograph does not show any sign of this. Because the inventor of the "light-stylus art" had to expose his glass plate for minutes, only entirely still objects would be fixed: chimneys, houses, trees. The mobile parts of the scenery – the smoke above the roofs, the pedestrians, the horses and carriages – have left no trace on the image, with one exception: In the bottom left corner, bathed in sunlight, a small figure is standing on the pavement, his right foot on the ground, the left foot on the stool of a shoeblack. Out of the many fleeting incidents of this day and place, solely this scene alone has been captured – a shadowy message of long gone times, the only witness of a moment that made history.

Louis Daguerre, The Boulevard du Temple in Paris, France, 1838

Architect, painter and poet Louis Kahn wrote about the magic of a quiet place lost in dreams: "Let us go back in time to the building of the pyramids. Hear the din of industry in a cloud of dust marking their place. Now we see the pyramids in full presence. There prevails the feeling of Silence, in which is felt man's desire to express. This existed before the first stone was laid. (...) When its use is spent and it becomes a ruin, the wonder of its beginning appears again. It feels good to have itself entwined in foliage, once more high in spirit and free of servitude."[2]

Kahn conjures up the quality and energy of the origin's spirit that is independent of the particular circumstances of the emergence of a structure, its use and its purpose. This energy transcends all practical and functional intentions. Instead, much like a poem, it carries a subtext or immaterial content between the lines, connotations that go beyond the story, the pure facts, and gives it meaning and universal range. Places that radiate and house such energy cannot be clearly localised in space and form, cannot be precisely sized or measured. It is hard to attribute clearly specified characteristics to them since they do not have a secured identity. In this sense, they are like quanta – the smallest energetic particles in physics – whose discovery marked the introduction of coincidence, or, in other words, the "magic moment" to the realm of natural science. Magic and identity originate from entirely different spheres, sources, and intentions. Identity is associated with recognition, relief, satisfaction, and limitation. Magic, on the other hand, sparks man's inspiration and taps the vast, unlimited reservoir of origin. Where this spark is missing, there "may fly words", but the thoughts remain below: words without thoughts never to heaven go.[3] Where this sense is missing, one believes oneself to be "close to heaven" while actually just stacking storey upon storey.

Great architects have always been aware of this. When Le Corbusier built the chapel of Ronchamp he attached great value on mathematics, physics, and acoustics. In this question he was "inexorable" as is noted in his biography. However, when he handed the building over to the Bishop of Besançon he found quite different words: "I envisaged this chapel as a place of quietude, of prayer, of peace and inner joy. A sense of sacredness inspired our efforts."[4] Calculation and reflection, action and contemplation, to deal with all aspects and not give preference to either, that could be the first essential in the design of a place by means of architecture. To start with, such a place would have to be patiently "sounded" and questioned, – just like Auguste Rodin did before he went took hammer and chisel: he walked around the stone for a long time, looking at it, tapping it, and asking: What is this stone? What does it require?

Chapel Notre-Dame-du-Haut, Ronchamp; architect: Le Corbusier, 1950-1954

In architecture, every project that respects the magic of its genius loci as much as its measurable coordinates should pose these questions: What is this place? What does it require? Oswald Mathias Ungers' answer reads as follows:

"If architecture deals with reality then it is also the result of a dialectic process between the given conditions and its derived ideal vision. The term contextualism is called to mind, which means nothing else but architecture that is derived from its local context... Architecture means vitally fathoming the multi-layered, mysterious, grown, and imprinted environment. The creative objective of architecture is to visualise the task, to integrate itself into the context, to accentuate and enhance the qualities of the site. Over and over again architecture is the recognition of the genius loci it arises from."[5]

A good example for the successful merging of architecture and place is situated in La Jolla on the Californian coast. In 1960, physician Jonas Salk, who discovered the vaccine against polio, resolved to build a bacteriological institute. He was so involved with the project that he personally supervised design and construction. Salk did not simply leave this task to one of his employees or some architectural practice, but managed to win Louis Kahn for the project. Both personalities – one more difficult and adamant than the other – engaged in an intensive discussion. For Salk it was not enough that the institute worked properly; it rather had to be the material expression of an idea, a conviction: instead of writing a book, he had chosen to voice his opinion architecturally, Salk would later say about the project.[6]

Kahn understood: He could visually imagine what scientists were missing, what they were only too prepared to ban from their world. The architect or the architecture respectively, was to replace the missing link with its own means – at least it should try. "The scientist," Kahn writes, "snugly isolated from other mentalities, needed more than anything the presence of the unmeasurable, which is the realm of the artist." Besides spaces, which should be flexible, there are also some which should be completely inflexible. "They should be sheer inspiration... just the place to be, the place which does not change, except for the people who go in and out. It is the kind of place that you enter many times."[6] A place providing architectural quality is a complex situation that is not simply created by putting individual elements together in a refined and logic manner. A car or a plane will not create such a place, how impressive they may be.

In La Jolla, within the load-bearing structure of the Vierendeel girders, technical facilities are housed; the open plan research laboratories are accommodated below and are in turn linked to small private studies. An ingenious and clearly structured system of stairs and bridges links all areas together. This layout respects the general purpose of the building and at the same time provides private space for individual study and therefore "free" research. Kahn's proposal shows the relationship between the institute's employees and their work places in an exemplary way and simultaneously transcends it.

Yet La Jolla's main feature is the large courtyard between the two institute wings. It is a plaza, a free open space with a narrow watercourse running in the middle of the paving and flowing into a little well at the end of the courtyard. Beyond, there is nothing but the unobstructed view to the west, across the Pacific.

If architecture would be reduced to its pure content of function and information, on its obvious aspects, if one was to seek its essence by analysing, explaining, and understanding its components and relationships – architecture would become rough, massive, and soulless. "... architecture weakens and turns into mere visual fabrication and rhetoric when it loosens its connections with the arts, on the one hand, and loses the existential and mythical ground of dwelling, on the other," writes Finnish art historian Juhani Pallasmaa. "Architecture, like all arts, is simultaneously autonomous and culture-bound. It is bound to its era in the sense that tradition and the cultural context provide the basis for individual creativity, and it is autonomous in the sense that an authentic expression is never simply a response to prescribed expectations or definitions. A fundamental existential mystery is at the core of architecture, and the confrontation of this mystery is always unique and autonomous, totally independent of the specifications of the 'social commission'."[7]

In such self-forgetting moments far from any object, fear, and ambition, any creative work becomes its own end. Philosopher Ludwig Wittgenstein who started out as a teacher and also worked as an architect for a couple of years in Vienna and certainly cannot be suspected of mystical sentimentality, said about architecture that it compels and glorifies, that architecture cannot exist where there is nothing to be glorified.[8] This would constitute its splendour and freedom, but also its limitations and endangerment. Yet it would not to be obtained for less either.

Salk Institute for Biological Studies,
La Jolla/San Diego, California, USA;
architect: Louis I. Kahn, 1959-1967
Fountain, closing off the central court space

Notes

1
Laotse, Tao Te King 41

2
Louis I. Kahn, Writings, Lectures, Interviews,
edited by Alessandra Latour, New York 1991, p. 248

3
William Shakespeare, Hamlet, 3rd act, 3rd scene

4
Le Corbusier, Le livre de Ronchamp, Paris 1961, p. 21

5
Oswald Matthias Ungers, "Wir brauchen keine neuen Utopien
sondern Erinnerungen", in: Die Welt, February 20, 1979

6
Louis I. Kahn, Writings, Lectures, Interviews,
edited by Alessandra Latour, New York 1991, p. 163 ff.

7
Juhani Pallasmaa, "The Art of Reason", in: Gentle Bridges,
Basel, Berlin, Boston 2002, pp. 24-33

8
Ludwig Wittgenstein, "Vermischte Bemerkungen 548",
in: Works vol. 1, Frankfurt/Main 1984

Styling Group, General Motors Technical Center, Warren, Michigan, USA;
architect: Eero Saarinen, completed 1956

OSWALD W. GRUBE

The birth of the modern
research building in the USA

Laboratory Tower of Johnson Wax Co.,
Racine, Wisconsin, USA;
architect: Frank Lloyd Wright, 1950

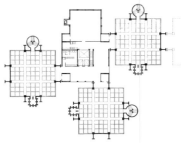

Richards Medical Research Building at the
University of Pennsylvania, Philadelphia, USA;
architect: Louis I. Kahn, 1957-1961.
Connection of two laboratory buildings

American post-war architecture was largely determined by the enormous economic resources of a nation which had become a dominating world power. Fleeing from persecution and repression, many European (primarily German) visionaries of Modernism had taken refuge in the United States. In the New World, their ideas fell on fertile soil and in co-operation with young American architects they set the stage for a new development that would dominate global architecture for decades to come. The building-up of a powerful war industry to defeat the fascist dictatorships in Europe and Asia culminated in the construction of the first nuclear bomb; it was developed in the Manhattan Project at the University of Chicago. Since the forties, new research facilities were set up mainly along the east coast at an awesome pace. Subsequently, some of these institutions became architectural prototypes for the further development of research buildings.

Similar to the industrial buildings of the thirties, laboratory and research buildings at that time took on a pioneer role in American Modernism. Both building types were and still are essentially governed by similar planning principles. Typical features of modern architecture such as large flexible open-plan spaces with separate office and service zones won undisputed recognition; they were first realised in industrial buildings, later in administrative buildings, and then in laboratory buildings. The best architects of this era attended to planning research facilities: Louis I. Kahn, Philip Johnson, Walter Gropius with his TAC practice, Frank Lloyd Wright, and I. M. Pei among others conceived research buildings that became icons of 20th-century architecture and are works of reference for this building type to the present day.

Landmark buildings

Planned by Frank Lloyd Wright, the headquarters of Johnson Wax Co. in Racine, Wisconsin, were inaugurated in 1939. The famous laboratory tower, an addition to this complex, was completed in 1950. Together, the administration building of the first phase and the slender research structure with its rounded corners form an impressive ensemble. All vertical elements are located at the core of the tower. The streamlined façade to a large extent consists of glass tubes and provides ample natural light for the laboratory floors that alternate with mezzanine floors. The building is reminiscent of factory laboratories of the thirties; it represents an independent approach of a great individualist of the 20th century.

The laboratory towers of the Richards Medical Research Building at the University of Pennsylvania in Philadelphia, erected from 1957 to 1961 and planned by Louis I. Kahn, were a globally acclaimed radical experiment with prefabricated concrete elements. Square work towers, alternately used as offices or laboratories, are grouped around a central service tower containing general facilities. The square zones are free of columns and do not contain any other vertical elements either; all "serving" elements, articulated as variations of a theme, are positioned around the perimeter and brace the structure. The slender concrete structure determines ceiling spans and the shape of the towers as well as the façades. The fully flexible primary floor area is strictly separated from all vertical elements. In doing so, the building's typology follows the floor plan layout of Skidmore, Owings and Merrill's (SOM) administrative buildings of the same time for Inland Steel Co. in Chicago and for Crown Zellerbach Co. in San Francisco.

With hindsight, however, the importance of Kahn's laboratory towers lies in their ingenious architectural language rather than in their function as laboratory buildings. This is because such a precisely crafted "clockwork" made of prefabricated concrete elements has never been economical in the United States. Also, the stacked, relatively small office areas are not suitable for many large-scale research projects. In Germany, however, Kahn's design became an example for type schemes of educational facilities of the sixties. His idea to position all vertical ventilation and air-conditioning shafts along the exterior walls also set standards for the further development of research buildings in the USA. Various laboratory towers show this arrangement: for instance, the Kline Biology Tower at Yale University in New Haven, Connecticut (1966), by Philip Johnson; in modified form, the Earth Sciences Tower by I. M. Pei at the MIT in Cambridge, Massachusetts (1964), or, also in Cambridge, the five-storey Hoffman Laboratory at Harvard University designed by Walter Gropius and his TAC practice as far back as in 1960. In contrast to the uncompromising clarity of Kahn's and SOM's designs, these buildings contain a rather conventional middle zone. Except for individual peripheral shafts, this zone accommodates all service and circulation cores and thus forms a considerable barrier to a flexible plan layout.

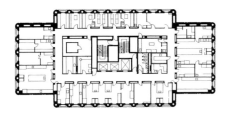

Kline Biology Tower of Yale University, New Haven, Connecticut, USA; architects: Philip Johnson and Richard Foster Architects, 1966. Ground floor plan

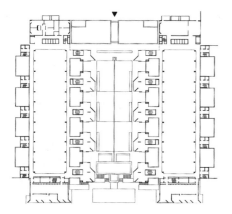

Salk Institute for Biological Studies, La Jolla/ San Diego, California, USA; architect: Louis I. Kahn, 1959-67. Ground floor plan

National Center for Atmospheric Research, Boulder, Colorado, USA; architect: I. M. Pei, 1961-67

The other laboratory building by Louis I. Kahn, the Salk Institute for Biological Studies in La Jolla near San Diego, California, completed in 1965, is considered to be one of the masterpieces of 20th century architecture. Kahn made use of the spectacular setting on a cliff above the Pacific Ocean to create a holistic work of art embracing the landscape, self-confident architectural volumes, and awesome views. Although the unique character of this research building is mainly based on its location, its design concept still comprises some groundbreaking ideas. The client, microbiologist Dr. Jonas Salk, made a major contribution to the design. The complex consists of two parallel building wings separated by a court featuring a narrow canal, pools, and sea views. In-situ concrete Vierendeel girders span the entire floor width of the building volumes. As in the Richards Medical Research building, all vertical elements are integrated into the perimeter of the lab floors. Horizontal ducts run in interstitial floors. In contrast to the Richards building, there are fewer storeys, and the laboratory zones are rectangular and much larger. Facing the court, small individual cells for concentrated study are attached to the open lab floors. Offices and libraries are positioned at the gable ends of both wings. Kahn succeeded in creating a human working environment by contrasting the exposed in-situ concrete with untreated timber elements and careful detailing. The floor plan layout of the complex became a reference for many laboratory buildings to come, particularly in the highly equipped chemical, biological, and pharmaceutical sector.

Between 1961 and 1967, the practice of I. M. Pei had the opportunity to design a research building in similarly breathtaking countryside. The National Center for Atmospheric Research was to be planned in the virgin mountain scenery of a mesa in the Rocky Mountains near Boulder, Colorado. At an altitude of 2000 m, the institute of scientist Walter O. Roberts was to give a number of selected scientists from different American universities a base for creative work outside the big cities. The complex consists of two groups of six-storey towers about 33 m in height resting on a two-storey pedestal. One of the groups accommodates laboratories, the other houses offices. The base contains an entrance hall, conference rooms, a canteen, and a library. The original plans proposed a third cluster of towers at the southern edge of the mesa, which would have rounded off the architectural composition – unfortunately it was never built. Roberts had envisaged a research complex that would encourage the intensive exchange of ideas between scientists. He did not want any narrow corridors, but instead opted for intimate clusters of spaces for meetings and social interaction. At the same time, the building had to be as flexible as possible to cater for the frequently changing requirements of scientific work. Pei translated this brief into an extremely small-scale layout providing many spatial interrelations between open plan areas (laboratories) and single rooms (offices) linked by mobile partitions. As it turned out, since the building's inauguration nearly every room has been changed at least once.

Out of respect for the location, Pei refrained from designing monumental axes but leads the visitor to the complex on a narrow, twisted mountain road. The prevailing building material is porous, hammered in-situ concrete containing red aggregates from the surrounding mountains. The roofs of the laboratory towers are shaped like fume hoods. Due to the harsh climate only 15 % of the exterior received continuous vertical glazed slots. The location is also crucial for this project: one could call it a high-tech monastery in the wilderness. The small-scale interior interrelations have set an example for many other research buildings mainly in the field of arts.

A new architecture for industrial research

However, possibly the most interesting and groundbreaking development took place independently from these unique architectural achievements in the Midwest and the suburban periphery of New York City. In the fifties, these areas saw the emergence of a new industrial research architecture that was closely related to the fundamental economical and social changes of the era. In his book *The Organizational Complex – Architecture, Media and Corporate Space* (MIT Press, 2003), Reinhold Martin, professor at Columbia University, New York, analysed the foundations of American commercial architecture right after the war by detecting and re-evaluating original sources and linking them to social sciences. His analysis puts corporate architecture into the context of structures of a so-called "organisational complex". World War II and the pace at which economical interdependences within the new market created organisational structures for the leading corporations. They called for schematic and modular design patterns that were to be transformed into three-dimensional structures. This development must be seen against the technological, aesthetical and social background of the forties, fifties, and early sixties in the USA. Also, the reception and transformation of the modern architectural movement in America has to be taken into consideration. Later, this development was to take effect in post-war Europe as well.

The ideals of Modernism were transformed fundamentally by the accelerated commercialisation of the times. In America, the non-bearing glass curtain wall was invented. Its grid-like structure reflected the upcoming serial production of consumer goods in the thirties, with the automobile production of Ford as its most prominent example. From now on, the entire architectural vocabulary was subjected to standardised formats and modular dimensions. This allowed flexible organisational structures following the requirements of the "organisational complex" to be accommodated within its grids. In form, the repetitive patterns of curtain walls on all sides of a building created a "floating" architecture. The huge, low-rise buildings by Eero Saarinen are particularly prominent examples of this approach. In trying to explain this formal aspect, Martin reverts to the writings of Gyorgy Kepes who describes the translation of Bauhaus principles into the realm of cybernetics.

Saarinen and contemporary architects such as Gordon Bunshaft or Walter Netsch who worked in the design sections of large architectural and engineering practices (for example Skidmore, Owings and Merrill) that were organised like business corporations, themselves understood the corporate client's requirements, and they knew best how to deliver. In merging the ideals of the European avant-garde and the interests of capital, they managed to launch Modernism into the second half of the 20th century. But it would be unfair to claim that these architects betrayed Modernism, an opinion held by some critics. The emergence of the "corporate image" irrevocably demanded new solutions that went far beyond one-dimensional façade patterns reminiscent of IBM punch cards. Saarinen and SOM were in the vanguard of a large number of architectural practices – among them Mies van der Rohe with his later works – that succeeded in reconciling their architectural designs with the new "corporate ethos" of their clients. The list of Eero Saarinen's clients in the fifties reads like a who-is-who of the American "military-industrial complex" on the verge of cold war: General Motors, International Business Machines (IBM), and Bell Telephone. This architecture cannot be understood without its historical context. The avant-garde had started its march through the ranks of big business.

Eero Saarinen and General Motors

When Eero Saarinen started designing the General Motors Technical Center in Warren, Michigan (near Detroit), in 1945 he still worked in his father's, Eliel Saarinen, practice that he soon took over. Prefabricated building elements were already commonly used for industrial facilities. Just like in the car production, this type of architecture allowed a number of variations within system limits. GMC's own development reflected this aspect of industrial fabrication. After World War II, military production was switched to civil goods again. With an annual production of ten million automobiles General Motors subsequently became the most successful industrial corporation in the world. GMC sold a range of different models which were, however, all based on a small number of basic modules.

Even in post-war terms the extent of Saarinen's commission was gigantic: the brief called for 25 buildings on a 130 ha site. The final scheme proposed five groups of buildings adjoining a 9 ha artificial lake and linked together by almost 18 km of roads. Parking lots took up 35 ha. At the time of its enthusiastic inauguration in 1956, about 5,000 scientists, engineers, technologists, and designers were employed.

Although the site plan of the realised scheme bears strong resemblance to the IIT campus in Chicago designed by Mies van der Rohe in the beginning of the forties, it would be unfair to call Saarinen a disciple of Mies (who shared this view). Among other things, Saarinen had worked on the Futurama Pavilion of the New York World Fair in 1939/40 and was strongly influenced by streamline design and Norman Bel Geddes.

For the individualised consumer culture emerging in America, car production was more than simple mass production of equal products. The industry rather produced branded images that were revised and updated every year. GMC's Technical Center became the birthplace of countless new stylings. Saarinen's client was the glamour designer Harley J. Earl from Hollywood, who translated streamline design into extra-long automobiles with low silhouettes that seemed to follow fashion rather than the laws of aerodynamics. With the Technical Center, Saarinen had broken free from Mies' strict functionalism. Instead,

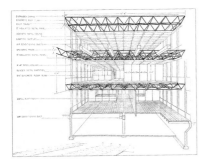

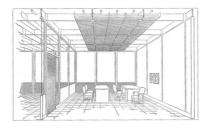

Styling Group, General Motors Technical Center,
Warren, Michigan, USA; architect: Eero Saarinen,
completed 1956. Perspectives

Styling Group, General Motors Technical Center,
Warren, Michigan, USA; architect: Eero Saarinen,
completed 1956.

the flat and long building volumes with their endless façade patterns strongly echoed the ideas of his client. In the Technical Center, product designers, engineers, and management jointly developed every new model. All of them were branded to cater for individual groups of clients. Only production and sales took place separately in other building complexes. The project was an enormous logistic challenge that Saarinen also managed to handle through his experience in the US army.

Saarinen's first proposal from 1945 pictured a streamlined campus and an organically shaped artificial lake. This scheme reflects the early ideas of organic urban design by Eliel Saarinen. At that time, this type of campus was believed to be a universal solution for the design of suburban development areas. During further work on the scheme, Saarinen kept the basic layout. The lake now became a rectangle and the surrounding buildings were subdivided into groups for service, research and development, engineering, and design. Furthermore, the scheme comprised two centrally located buildings on stilts in the lake housing administration and a canteen. From that stage on, the architectural language displays the influence of Albert Kahn and undoubtedly also Mies van der Rohe. But Saarinen felt closer to the vocabulary of Mies' Lake Shore Drive Apartments than to his IIT buildings. Due to organisational changes at GMC the administration building was not built. The engineering complex was the first building to be erected. It is based on a 5 ft grid and comprises a structure with large ceiling spans and curtain walling. The building itself became a testing laboratory for new building technologies and materials: Saarinen used enamel-coated spandrel panels, tinted solar glazing, luminous ceilings, glazed bricks, and mobile partitions. Other innovations like glazing set into neoprene gaskets reflect technologies that were used in car production.

The gigantic dimensions of the campus, highlighted by the long, regularly structured façades, appear like a single introverted organisational and formal unit. At that, it created an unprecedented spatial experience. The scale reflects the dynamic perception of the complex from an automobile in motion. The landscaping scheme and the large lake tie the complex together; the most elegantly detailed group of buildings is the design complex. Generally, only the entrance halls of the individual buildings and their prominent canopies act as identifying elements. Landmarks of the complex are the steel water tower rising from the lake and the almost 20 m high aluminium-clad steel dome with a diameter of 57 m which serves as a show room for new GMC models. The dome's skin reflects the surrounding landscape and passing automobiles.

Altogether, the General Motors Technical Center appears as an integral corporate organisational structure which is also typical for other SOM projects of the same period, for example the Connecticut General Life Insurance headquarters (1956/57) or the US Air Force Academy (1954). The boundaries between military, commercial, and academic use became increasingly blurred.

Eero Saarinen and IBM

In the mid-fifties, a fascination for shapes of the first computers and their product patterns, the IBM punch cards, evolved. People who could read and understand these signals counted themselves members of a new era. From now on, the lives of people were embossed into the modular system of the punch cards – like in the matrices of the modularly structured sheathing of the facilities they were made in. In 1956, Eero Saarinen had been commissioned to design the new IBM Manufacturing and Training Facility in Rochester, Minnesota. This factory, which also included administration, was to stand at the forefront of a new series of IBM production buildings displaying the company's corporate image. The extensive low-rise complex received a curtain wall made of extremely thin tinted neoprene glazing with different shades of colour based on a 4 ft grid. The wafer-thin glass skin makes the building appear abstract and dematerialised; it is a telling expression of the precision of the IBM machines manufactured inside. The blue shades of the façade colour scheme also hint at the IBM nickname "Big Blue". (Just like Olivetti, IBM was in the process of creating a new corporate logo). The individual wings containing the production halls are connected to a central shared area accommodating the canteen, lounge and visitor areas. Instead of designing a conventional lavish entrance lobby Saarinen concentrated his attention on creating a good working environment. Differences in the appearance of production and administration facilities were abolished as far as possible in order to tear down traditional hierarchies and differences between workers and employees. To express this equality, both areas are indiscriminately sheathed with the same façade pattern. In the following, IBM went on building further factories across the US modelled on the Minnesota facilities.

The IBM plant in Rochester was a precursor for Saarinen's next commission, the Thomas J. Watson Research Center in Yorktown Heights, New York (completed in 1961). The centre was to provide facilities for the development of a new "intelligent" computer generation.

During World War II a new type of large research laboratory for the private industry had emerged based on a diffuse affiliation of military and university research. Academic research hereby grew increasingly dependent on private foundations which in turn were governed by large companies. In addition, the government co-ordinated military projects during the war, thus taking a leading role in this field of research. This development continued during the cold war and led to the formation of the National Science Foundation (NSF) in 1950. In the following years, this affiliation became known as the "military-industrial-academic complex". The new research facilities needed for this purpose were separated from production and obtained their own corporate image.

When Saarinen was commissioned to design the IBM Yorktown Heights centre IBM had entertained close links with Harvard University for years. At the same time, it handled public contracts in the military sector. This close connection between military and university research also existed in another project by Saarinen which he carried out in two phases for Bell Telephone Laboratories in Holmdel, New Jersey between 1957 and 1966. Both projects have to be considered together since their planning was carried out almost at the same time. Furthermore, both projects had to provide maximum flexibility because the outcome of the respective research projects they were to house could not be foreseen. While the IBM facilities in Yorktown Heights contained six departments for multi-disciplinary computer sciences, the Bell complex in Holmdel comprised research and product development. It maintained close links with universities and was designed particularly for research in the fields of circuits, data transmission, quality control, and network design.

Saarinen's first proposal for the IBM project envisaged a campus consisting of low-rise, interconnected buildings with double-loaded corridors, grouped around a large courtyard and nestling in the hilly terrain. In contrast, the design proposal for Bell was based from the beginning on an introverted compact massing of the building volume. Saarinen's starting point for both projects was a remarkably progressive research complex completed in 1941 – the Bell Telephone Laboratories in Murray Hill, New Jersey. Yet in developing the scheme, Saarinen turned conventional day-lit areas with workplaces on the building perimeter into centrally located deep work zones which were air-conditioned and artificially lit. This tendency had become apparent in office and laboratory buildings throughout the USA, but Saarinen pursued this idea more radically. Whereas in his preliminary design sketches at least offices were positioned along the façades, ultimately all offices and laboratories were allocated in central zones accessed by peripheral corridors. The completed scheme drastically broke with the ideals of European Modernism which had postulated a strong doctrine in the twenties with its call for light and air for apartments and workplaces. From now on, the public and circulation areas around the perimeter set the stage for sweeping views of the landscape or into inner courtyards; relationships between interior and exterior space could only be experienced in a controlled manner during periodical breaks and were to take place along the building's curtain walls.

It is interesting to compare Saarinen's project with Kahn's Salk Institute in La Jolla, built approximately at the same time (1959-1965): Kahn's offices were day-lit and naturally ventilated "thinking cells" with adjoining loggias; they were located in front of the inner laboratory zones.

The Thomas J. Watson Research Center for IBM was one of the first large research complexes to be linked to new highways, thereby changing the bucolic landscape of the Hudson Valley south of New York City. Initially, Saarinen had envisaged natural lighting for the laboratories via courtyards and for the offices via exterior façades respectively. Yet eventually he opted for a compact three-storey building volume based in plan on a 4 ft x 6 ft grid. Each floor plan comprises funnel-shaped cores and corridors along the façades. The open plan spaces are column-free. 24 ft deep rows of laboratories are arranged back to back along narrow service corridors perpendicular to the façades. Alternately, 12 ft deep office rows are also arranged back to back along central rows of fitted cabinets. Both zones are accessed via transverse corridors. The sweeping lightweight façades of the building are juxtaposed by massive natu-

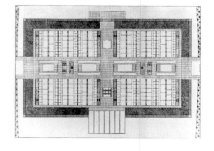

Bell Telephone Laboratories, Holmdel, New Jersey, USA; architect: Eero Saarinen, 1962 (1st building phase), 1966 (2nd building phase). Floor plan

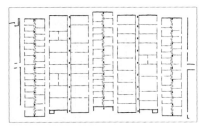

IBM Thomas J. Watson Research Laboratory,
Yorktown Heights, New York, USA;
architect: Eero Saarinen, 1961.

ral stonewalls facing the peripheral corridors on their inner side. The rocks were gathered locally. Individual rocks have been marked with the coordinates of their original position within the landscape. The corridors afford generous views of the surroundings. The staggering of the natural stonewalls supports the contrast between the orthogonal workspaces and the sweeping shape of the glazed exterior membrane – at that time, this was an extraordinary composition! Just how groundbreaking this scheme really was became apparent 40 years later when Sir Norman Foster adapted it for his McLaren Technology Centre in Woking, Surrey, England, in a striking way.

While the concave façade of the IBM building consists of natural stone and glazed panels, the convex main façade received a full height curtain wall made of dark tinted glass. It is based on a 4 ft grid and bears no relation to the 6 ft interior grid. All interior partitions are modular steel-and-glass elements. The interior grid manifests itself in prefabricated wall and cabinet elements consisting of modular panels in two different widths in dark and light colours. This differentiated interior scheme is reminiscent of the façades of the IBM factory in Rochester; it facilitates orientation in the highly repetitive circulation system.

Walter Gropius and his TAC practice were also commissioned in 1962 by IBM to design a large research centre for the development of computer systems for the Federal Government. Gropius' proposal for the IBM Federal Systems Division Facility in Gaithersburg, Maryland, was a clear layout comprising linked rectangular rows of laboratories. In an alternative scheme he proposed square building volumes with inner courtyards. Unfortunately, the interesting schemes were never realised.

Saarinen's final design for the Bell Laboratories is based on a monolithic, introverted block structure with very deep inner zones and a row of small courtyards. The basement houses the IT control rooms; also, an auditorium and a canteen are located here.

The Bell Laboratories are characterised by the strict correspondence of the square 6 ft ceiling grid, the transparent glazed interior partitions, and the grid of the continuous curtain walls. Although the building volume is embedded in a generous baroque elliptical layout of roads and green spaces, in reality the complex appears just as neutral as the grid of the interior partitions (their only variation being different shades of grey). The neutral appearance is reinforced by the sheer endless and repetitive veneer of the light reflective glazing supported by a delicate 3 ft grid of metal profiles. In the two-dimensional, graphic system, the floor levels are no longer visible. With a length of more than 400 m it was the longest "mirror" that had ever been built. This achievement was also revolutionary in terms of building technology. Saarinen had brought together the transparency of the interior spaces with a reflective exterior skin. Solar heat gains were reduced and with it energy consumption for the air-conditioning of the exterior corridors by approximately 70 %. At that time, the Architectural Forum called this an "inside-out" air-conditioning.

Paradoxically, the huge reflective façade does not reflect much; the flat landscape and the huge parking lots do not produce images that could be mirrored. Yet this effect was fully intended: Saarinen and his client wanted to express IBM's corporate image with an impersonalised, incomprehensible façade – a mirroring computer screen that in its way was to become a symbol for the "military-industrial complex" of the time.

The visions, wealth of ideas, and architectural potency of the portrayed American research buildings of the post-war era between 1945 and 1965 are the key to a better understanding of an important period of architectural history of the 20th century. After the end of Postmodernism and the rediscovery and resumption of Modernism, the echo of these projects can be heard. This is true for today's laboratory and research buildings and many other building types.

MANFRED HEGGER

Architecture and technical service systems: requirements for research buildings

Research buildings are highly complex structures. Hardly any other building type has to fulfil such a vast range of functional, technical, economical and legal requirements. Hence, these structures are expensive to build and operate. They represent a means of innovative production – and as such they are exposed to rapid modifications . New regulations and standards, in addition to innovative technologies and modes of operation, personnel modifications, and new research projects represent constantly changing challenges for a laboratory building.

All eventualities that may occur over the entire life span of a building can hardly be predicted for ordinary buildings – let alone for research buildings that stand at the forefront of defining our future. However, systematic analysis of the major developments in contemporary laboratory research reveals tendencies towards certain layouts. The most important one among these tendencies is the emergence of more flexible open plan arrangements as these layouts provide the greatest flexibility for unpredictable future developments.

The following tabulation particularly identifies the assumed effects on architectural features and technical service systems of contemporary research tendencies on the arrangement of spaces. Indirectly, it also shows that the design is not merely affected by new architectural and technical requirements, but also by necessary changes in the planning process itself. However, due to lack of space this publication will not discuss this issue in greater detail.

This chart highlights a number of interesting aspects. Different tendencies in research development apparently have identical architectural and technical effects. This is also true for tendencies in the mechanical and electrical engineering of research buildings. They seem to represent reliable developments of pivotal importance for future research building. Even if individual predicted developments should not materialise this does not disturb the overall picture.

Changed density of lab work

Automation, miniaturisation, and rationalisation lead to a more efficient use of laboratory spaces and consequently a higher density. This may or may not entail a decrease in the available working area per employee. Highly automated processes require less manpower, whereas in the event of more manual work the opposite is the case. An increased number of employees per lab unit evokes a greater sense of safety, social control, and communication. The reverse case will happen if numbers decrease.

These two tendencies can occur simultaneously within the same research discipline. Universal automation of research processes is not to be expected. At the same time, more efficient use of laboratory space has become a general priority. These developments call for larger and flexible spatial arrangements, which suit both automated processes (large space requirements, low manpower) and manual processes that concentrate a large number of employees.

Larger spatial units

Larger spatial units can adapt more easily to unpredictable developments than smaller cellular arrangements. For legal and security reasons more than one employee should be present in the laboratory at any time. This requirement can actually only be met with larger units. They also boost social interaction and the exchange of ideas. Also the often-feared anonymity of open plan workspaces is not necessarily an issue. Quite the reverse is true: a skilful and differentiated interior layout provides bright and lofty spaces that support teamwork, yet manages to preserve privacy. Small spaces will only continue to prevail in a few cases. This involves areas where toxic substances are handled or cross contamination poses a potential risk.

Proximity of office and laboratory spaces

Flat office hierarchies support team spirit and creativity. As office and laboratory work are merging, new communicative structures arise. Another trend pointing in the same direction is the convergence of manual and intellectual work through the use of computers, which calls for a close proximity of lab bench and office desk.

Therefore, the integration of desks for analysis and offices into laboratory wings has become more common. This way, office spaces are in close contact with the laboratory processes, yet benefit from

Assumed tendencies	Requirements for architecture	Requirements for technical building service systems
Flatter organisational structures, teamwork	Close proximity of laboratories and office-type work spaces	
Miniaturisation of experimental equipment	Higher density of lab work	Increased sensitivity to environmental factors, lower air change rates
Experiments in micro-environments	Higher density of lab work	Increased demands on conditioning of the micro-environment, lower demands on conditioning of labs, lower air change rates
Progressing automation of all processes	Lower density of lab work, flexible floor plans suitable for automats and robot use	High demands on flexibility in technological upgrading
Growing importance of IT in scientific research	Close proximity of laboratories and office-type work spaces, integrated "thinking cells" within laboratories	Increasing wire interconnections or stable LAN network
Modelling partly replaces analytical wet chemistry experiments	Convertibility of laboratories into offices, reduced building depth	Potentially, this will reduce the amount of required services
Individualised medical treatment replaces standard medications	Intensification and decentralisation of lab work, if necessary, public access to patient/probationer rooms	
Higher security standards	Larger, clearer layouts, more transparency, improved internal communication	Proliferation of sensor technology for technical building service systems and equipment
Increased competition on all levels (international, national, institutional)	Rapid adaptability to new spatial requirements of the research market	
Increased formal and informal communication	Larger, open-plan laboratory units, improved interrelation between lab and office-type work, spaces for social interaction, informal meeting points and *joker spaces*	Video-conferencing, wireless and wired connections
Increased cost effectiveness of research	Low investment costs for buildings, high flexibility and low running costs, prefabricated lab units	Low running costs for low-maintenance systems, automated facility and chemicals management
Increased sustainability and energy efficiency	Durability/flexibility/structural adaptability/low-energy building materials	Efficient facility management, intelligent control of technical building service systems, application of low-tech where possible
Competition for the best talents, long-term liaisons with employees	Strong corporate identity, sense of place, attractive working environment	

natural ventilation. Offices allocated to lab spaces can be smaller and also reduce circulation areas. Consequently, they improve the ratio of net floor area to circulation area.

Small building depths

To the present day, many laboratory buildings are very deep. Triple-loaded systems with a central dark zone and a building depth of 20 m to 25 m frequently occur. These buildings may serve their purpose well – however, often they lack flexibility. Load-bearing central cores limit free circulation; several rows of columns and decentralised service shaft systems lead to further restrictions. The great depth of the buildings hampers penetration of daylight and internal communication.

In connection with open plan structures, smaller building depths can overcome these disadvantages. The result is lofty premises which also allows for another option: building depths between 13.50 m and 17.00 m allow the conversion into offices, e.g. for computer modelling or entirely different uses at a later stage.

Spatial structures supporting communication

Good communication in a laboratory has to be encouraged by appropriate architectural scenarios that create opportunities for social interaction. In this context, additional areas are not required, but skilfully arranged working environments that boost identity, team spirit, and eventually success.

Working groups, which are usually composed of several teams, need areas both for informal and formal communication. Generously dimensioned, attractive circulation routes and stairs provide informal meeting points, meeting rooms with multi-media equipment serve formal communication; "coffee points" provide opportunities for both kinds of interaction. A holistic building organism should additionally provide a cafeteria or casino as well as conference spaces where exchange between working groups can take place.

Sustainability

So far the topic of sustainability has not been a priority in research buildings. Over the next years, increasingly sparse resources and legal requirements, however, are bound to put this issue in the centre of interest when planning and constructing buildings. Apart from being an ethical priority, sustainability is increasingly becoming an ecological, economical, and cultural factor that amplifies the durability of a building. The different aspects and resulting requirements form a complex system.

Sustainability in this sense can be illustrated here only by few examples: The above mentioned economical use of space helps to save building costs, building material, running costs and – if employed correctly – potentially improves working and corporate culture. High flexibility enhances the utility value of a building and increases its life span. This is important particularly in view of the fact that most changes or developments cannot be predicted precisely. Pleasant interior and working environments call for carefully selected materials, reduce the number of employees on sick leave and decrease maintenance costs. The use of recyclable materials helps to resolve disposal issues when buildings are refurbished and anticipates sustainable recycling policies. Energy efficient building and appropriate technical installations reduce investment and running costs; ideally, users should be able to control the room climate individually.

Architectural quality

The attributes of research buildings mentioned can help to secure high-class functional and spatial qualities of great innovative potential. However, users and passers-by will primarily relate to the architectural qualities of a project. A careful and holistic design approach down to the last detail gives architects the opportunity to create functional and sustainable buildings, which offer spatial qualities that support identification and a lasting sense of place.

High-quality innovative architecture can inspire its users; this is even more true and desirable in the realm of research. It creates a sense of individual and corporate identity. Last not least, a successful building is more likely to establish close links between employees and employers and the architectural environment. In the long run, such "soft" factors can turn into concrete "hard" advantages in the global competition for the best talents.

HARDO BRAUN

Laboratories in research buildings: main features and developments

Research institutes of largely varying size, layout, and purpose are places dedicated to the quest for cognition. As such, they are no invention of our times but have always been forward-looking institutions accompanying and dependent on the further development of the disciplines and of knowledge. New issues lead to new architectural solutions for the individual laboratory as well as for complex institute buildings.

The schools of the ancient world, for example the Museion at Alexandria, the Atheneum at Athens, the Medrese in Cordoba, Toledo, Syracuse, Baghdad, Damascus, or Samarkand – even though teaching medicine, mathematics, and astronomy – did not comprise laboratories. At the beginning of occidental history, the preparation of remedies was carried out in a manual non-scientific way on the basis of tradition and empirical experience.

In the Occident, reading The Book of Nature meant looking at Creation and was an act of worship; again, research of natural correlations was a secondary issue here. In the 10th and 11th century, when the first European universities in Bologna, Paris, and Oxford had not yet been established, students from Andalusia, France, and even England came to study at Fez's Kairouine University together with students from Tunisia, Tripoli, and Egypt. The centrally located university equally served as caravanserai, library, and mosque. Despite natural scientific activities and growing observation of and regard for nature, this university did not encompass laboratories.

At the turn of the 13th century so-called "universitates magistrorum et scholarum" where established in Italy, France, and England in cities with a venerable scholar tradition like Bologna, Paris, and Oxford. The replacement of the traditional knowledge of scholasticism with rational thinking (ratio) significantly enhanced intellectual life and encouraged the formation of new intellectual topics and methods. Now, experiments became a crucial aid for those striving for cognition and enlightenment in the field of natural sciences. This gave a substantial impulse to the historical development of research buildings.

The beginnings of the laboratory building are closely connected to the emergence of pharmacies from the 13th century onwards. As a result of the Constitutions of Melfi and the first basic medical regulations the professions of doctor and pharmacist were separated. Pharmacy-like establishments came into being. However, at the end of the Middle Ages above all kitchens of alchemists and furnaces of steelworks attained importance. These facilities contained early types of tools such as retorts and mortars, which were essential for the work in chemical laboratories, and are still used today in a more sophisticated form. Chemical stoves with exhaust hoods became precursors of today's fume cupboards. They became a trademark of "distillation places" as pictured by scientist and doctor Georg Bauer, also known as Agricola (1494–1555), or as used by natural philosopher, doctor, and chemist Paracelsus (1493–1541) in Basle. It was mainly Paracelsus who fought against the scholastic tradition of the times and rated knowledge derived from scientific experiment higher than traditional knowledge from books.

It was only in the 17th century that the separation of manual craft and science began to materialise. In the field of physics, mechanics formed a central part of practical life at that time. However, neither Galileo Galilei (1564–1642) nor Isaac Newton (1642–1727) required a special laboratory for their theoretical work which was carried out in study rooms. In the field of medicine, on the contrary, the beginnings of scientific pharmaceutics called for a change of programme: the "offizin" for sales and dispensing, an additional storage room for materials and herbs, the laboratory, and a cool storage for medications in the basement became one functional unit.

By the end of the 17th century, mining research, for instance in the field of silver mining, looked closer into mineralogical and chemical phenomena related to increasingly injurious effects during the melting process. In mining, the workshops of early experimentalists and clerks started to resemble simple laboratories. The "Royal Swedish Laboratory" established in 1686 is an example for a chemical laboratory in the proper sense; it was used for the examination of ores, minerals, and chemical products. In the 18th century it was also Sweden which became the centre of mineral and metal analysis. The scientific impulses of this research discipline triggered Sweden's significant and highly developed ore mining and processing industry.

If one looks at images of "witches' kitchens" and early laboratories it is striking that these were also places for intellectual exchange of ideas and scientific discussion. The schemes and realised visions extend from notions of ascetic solitariness in monasteries (separation) to the development of ideas in a social academic environment and inspiring atmosphere (communication) following the model of classical antiquity. Libavius (1540–1616) even incorporated arcades, baths, and taverns into his laboratory schemes. Giovanni Battista Piranesi's utopian design for an ideal university complex including all kinds of facilities, housing etc. within its walls, drafted at the height of European enlightenment in 1750, takes this idea to the extreme.

A sound foundation for scientific knowledge soon became a public priority. While powerful kings like Augustus the Strong, who in 1701 funded Johann Friedrich Böttger's laboratory in Dresden in his pursuit to transform metals into gold, displayed a strong "private" interest. The public interest in scientific research also grew and expressed the need to make knowledge commonly accessible and usable. Thus, demands on sciences increased. The steam engine soon became the heart of production in England and then France. The required raw materials were no longer precious metals, but iron, coal, and steel; hence, every aspect of theoretical and practical research focussed on these materials. No longer did merely large quantities of chemical substances count, but also their purity. New analytical methods, particularly wet chemical research procedures, were required. In 1774, Karl Wilhelm Scheele and – simultaneously yet independently – Joseph Priestley discovered oxygen. By doing so, they contributed substantially to the explanation of combustion processes and gas analysis. Lavoisier for the first time made a distinction between the actual chemical elements – he classified them into metals and non-metals – and chemical compounds. Between 1760 and 1830, chemistry as well as electrical and mechanical engineering entered the work and production processes. Thus, requirements of chemistry became a decisive factor for the equipment of modern laboratories for research and applied sciences.

Over the last 200 years, a broad range of research disciplines creating new knowledge has evolved. In the 19th century, government and industry erected research institutes that often supplemented each other. The chemical-analytical laboratory of Justus von Liebig at Gießen University, which he started to equip in 1824, became a model for almost all German universities and colleges. At that time, famous scientists all over Europe maintained more or less personal contact – just like the worldwide elite today. Hence the laboratories that were built were almost identical.

After 1870, laboratories and research institutes of the industry could be found at paint and chemical producers BASF, Hoechst, Bayer, and Agfa, and at large companies, for example Krupp (from 1863 on) and Siemens (after 1905). In 1928, AEG began building one of the most modern industrial research institutes, but also Schering, Zeiss, Schott, and many other firms recognised the necessity of research for their entrepreneurial future. Over time, the new institutes for chemistry, pharmacy, astronomy, physics, etc. developed specific requirements in terms of natural lighting and vibration control. They started to be a nuisance for others and it became impossible to share facilities with the humanities. This marked the beginning of specialised laboratory planning which focussed on the optimisation of lighting and ventilation of working spaces. From now on, ventilation and natural lighting became major factors for the usability of experimental spaces: air ducts supplying cool air from the basement, thrust ventilation, filters, heat coils to pre-heat air, moisturisers (moisture towels), and, a little later, exhaust pipes, were incorporated.

The single and double-loaded layouts of the beginning were soon followed by more complex solutions such as arrangements with two double-loaded corridors enclosing a central dark zone. Here, special rooms such as weigh rooms, equipment rooms, incubators, cool storage, and rooms with constant temperature were located. Building sections reveal horizontal and vertical installation ducts. The differentiation of building's spaces evolved in accordance with the principle of zoning of areas and disentanglement of mechanical services – encompassing office and study zones with natural daylight and ordinary building service systems, day-lit zones with individual or central shafts containing complex laboratory service systems, and central dark, highly equipped service zones for special purposes.

In the mid-sixties, apart from research standards and types of research, the coordination of structural and interior dimensions and the proliferation of rationalised grids and modules to shorten planning and construction periods became major factors of the progressing standardisation. Often, the entire design of large and highly complex volumes was determined by these industrial standards. The modular

Grid and modular system:
The "Marburg System." University buildings on
Lahnberge, Germany; architects: State University
Building Department, Marburg, 1967-1970

Coordination of
measurements

Suspended ceiling

Façade

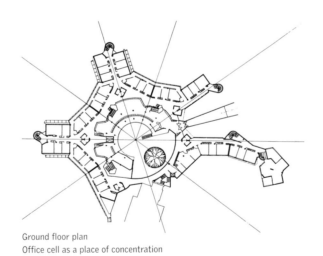

Organically shaped buildings:
Max Planck Institute for Astrophysics, Garching,
Germany; architects: Fehling und Gogel, 1979

Ground floor plan
Office cell as a place of concentration

Hall and stair – places of communication and
social interaction

Exterior view

vertical and horizontal structure of a building manifested itself down to laboratory desks which for the first time became truly prefabricated flexible elements.

Yet only a few years later diversified, individual, sometimes organically shaped buildings emerged that were based on the idea of communication. They provided places for social interaction and identification of the users with their built environment. Once again, it had to have a human scale. The typical architectural feature for social interaction and scientific debate was the central atrium. The many variations of this building type became flagships of a new communicative architecture that was to encourage the generation of new ideas as a result of face-to-face contacts.

Today, education and lifelong qualification have become a priority. The innovative potential of the teamwork-based, pluralist, and ever more global research and science sector needs to be backed up by suitable measures – among them the architectural design – that foster flexibility and competition.

Apart from life sciences in the broadest sense, new important inter- and trans-disciplinary research fields emerged: nanotechnology, merging electronic and biological systems, new hard- and software systems and their multimedia applications, and the development of new sustainable products and methods. In view of global demographic developments, the humanities have also gained importance for the evaluation and understanding of human cultural heritage and the bridging of the gap between natural sciences and man. Last but not least, the use of computers is now no longer limited to IT but has also spread to the humanities, who have begun conducting computer-supported experiments in laboratories.

1
Based on the research of Bonsal, according to
H. Eggert, C. Junk et al.

2
According to L. Boehm and R. A. Müller, the university
of the Middle Ages arose out of the formation of professional associations of teachers and scholars motivated by social and scientific commitment.

3
The Constitutions of Melfi, initiated 1231 in Capua,
put a stop to the power of territorial lords and the
games of quack doctors and charlatans.

Literature

H. Eggert, C. Junk, C. Körner, E. Schmidt, Gebäude
für Erziehung, Wissenschaft und Kunst; Handbuch
der Architektur, vol. IV, part 6, issue 2.a., 1905

Laetitia Boehm, Rainer A. Müller, Hermes Handlexikon
– Universitäten und Hochschulen in Deutschland,
Österreich und der Schweiz, Düsseldorf 1983

Eberhard Horst, Friedrich der Staufer,
Düsseldorf 1976

Hardo Braun, Die Entwicklung des Institutsbaus,
doctoral thesis 1987

Max-Planck-Gesellschaft zur Förderung der Wissenschaften e.V., "Bauten der Max-Planck-Gesellschaft",
series, edited by the General Administration in Munich

Hardo Braun, Dieter Grömling, Carl-Egon Heintz,
Alfred Schmucker, Building for Science,
Basel, Berlin, Boston 1999

DIETER GRÖMLING

Design parameters:
location, use and typology

The design parameters for a scientific laboratory and research facility of average size can be used as a guideline when planning research and technology buildings. It goes without saying that simply ticking off basic design parameters will not necessarily point the way to architectural quality. To achieve this, a creative design process which also considers all specific site conditions has to drive the urban and architectural scheme. However, paying little or no regard to the basic parameters discussed here will not lead to an overall sound research building. It would be a mistake to assume that only architects are involved in the design of research buildings – quite the opposite is true. Hence, practical basic knowledge is required more than ever for creating research buildings that will see future users fit for global competition and have their very own sense of identity and place.

A | URBAN DESIGN AND SITE FACTORS

The individual process that will lead to the choice of a particular site depends on numerous criteria, which may vary with regard to the client (industrial or business client, government) or the specific goals of the project (basic research or applied sciences). The following factors incorporate the most important site-related design parameters:

Professional scientific context
- Co-operation with related facilities, formation of scientific clusters
- Interdisciplinary co-operation
- Promotion of junior talents (students, graduates, doctoral candidates)

General site criteria
- Close proximity to other research facilities
- Good public and local transport connections
- International networking; good national and international infrastructure (airport, train station with inter-city connections)
- Quality of the urban context (strengthening corporate identity)

Technical criteria
- Size of the plot; potential for expansion
- Public planning regulations
- Technical infrastructure/services: heating, water, data, power, fire access etc.
- Specific equipment requirements regarding seismic vibrations, electromagnetic fields, acoustics etc.
- Building ground: load-bearing capacity, contaminations, previous land-refill, existing service systems

Until the seventies, research facilities – single academic institutes, research centres or industrial facilities alike – were mainly developed on detached suburban sites to prevent dangerous effects of toxic emissions and public nuisances such as noise from machinery or traffic. However, with increased regulations for emissions that contemporary buildings have to comply with these restrictions are now superseded. Furthermore, laboratory use of toxic substances could be reduced drastically through methods of measuring that are more precise today than it was ever imagined. Many dangerous substances are replaced by less toxic chemicals; in some cases, laboratory experiments are completely replaced by computer simulations. Hence, integration of industrial and scientific facilities into the urban context has become a reality.

However, recent scientific developments in the fields of nanotechnology have given rise to a whole new generation of machinery and equipment (microscopes, tomography, work benches etc.) that is highly sensitive to electromagnetic, seismic or acoustic influences. These influences have to be thoroughly considered, analysed and incorporated into the planning process on a case-to-case basis. They may even include unobtrusive factors such as rivers (low frequency noise of ships' bows or screws), distant tramlines (vibrations depending on the rail construction and building ground, or potential electromagnetic fields). Such factors may lead to an overall revision of the choice of location or specific on-site measures concerning foundation work or screening. To address these issues, architects may turn to historical

Hidden networks
Section through a *pinus contorta* seedling with distinctive *mycorrhizal* growth; the seedling sticks approx. 4 cm out of the ground

examples, and house special equipment in separate metal-free structures (for example made of timber). Today, the rule is: proximity is possible, provided the neighbouring buildings don't disturb!

B | CLIENTS AND BUILDING USE

Other crucial factors for the design of research buildings are the nature of the client, the mode of building use, and the point of time the client starts to participate in the planning process.

Client
- Architectural background (architects or engineers)
- No architectural background (scientists, businessmen, lawyers)
- Public client
- Private client

Mode of building use
- Teaching or scientific research (public or private)
- Particular requirements stipulated in the brief
- General distribution of floor area in multi-purpose research facilities
- Future use through the client himself
- Market analysis with a view to future rentals/sales

Point of client participation
- During stipulation of the programme
- At planning/construction stage
- After completion

Fundamentally, all these scenarios follow the typological and technical design and construction parameters for research buildings lined out in this chapter. Differentiation results from the specific type of use and research equipment needed. If no specific requirements were specified, the resulting building would simply provide variable open plan floor arrangements with flexible service installations. Costs for construction and operation of this kind of building would be relatively low. With the increasing complexity and individuality of research buildings the programmes and architectural design of the facilities will also become more complicated, which in turn increases costs. A high percentage of teaching areas and spaces for serial research operations leads to simpler layouts and reduces costs. However, usually these spaces will only represent a fragment of the required programme.

Experienced clients with a relevant professional background may be able to advance the quality of a research building, but may also hamper the creativity of the architect. The issue is to compromise without ruining architectural visions. Scientists are often inclined to repeat tested-and-tried layouts in new buildings; hence, innovative design solutions will need a great deal of convincing and competence.

Public and private research facilities are governed by fundamentally different criteria that are not limited to practical training halls for university institutes or special laboratories for mass analysis in industrial research buildings:

Public research – "personal focus"
- Directors, the majority of scientists and staff are usually long-term employees and tend to identify with the architecture
- Spaces become a personalised environment; relatively small standard sizes have been imposed on laboratory units (20 to 40 m² net floor area).
- As maximum salaries in the public sector are clearly restricted, employees set greater value upon their working environment, the architecture, furnishings and equipment. This has given rise to a particular public building culture distinguished from private institute buildings.
- As a rule, publicly funded research buildings contain many functions under one roof and constitute self-contained units.

Industrial research – "material focus"

• Executives and employees tend to move on in their career after a period of time. They feel less attached to their workspaces.

• Size and layout of the spaces follow practical requirements; open plan laboratories frequently occur.

• Corporate research departments form homogenous units within larger facilities. Due to security considerations, they often take a backseat on the company premises. Entrance buildings or other general facilities fulfil representative functions.

C | BUILDING TYPOLOGY

C1 Scientific laboratories – chemistry/biology/physics

The most important part of a research building is the experimental scientific workspace – the laboratory. Laboratories as we know them today – basically they resemble high-tech kitchens – have been around for more than a hundred years. Now, what does a scientist do in a laboratory? He collects, analyses, construes and summarises information in writing. Goals and work results are discussed in small circles or larger groups. These procedures presuppose a certain critical mass of people and work processes. Architects require the following information to design satisfactory research buildings:

• Type and frequency of work processes
• Length and equipment of work desks
• Media supply
• Number of persons working in a laboratory
• Supplementary equipment, on and between work desks
• Daylight/artificial lighting
• Air-conditioning and ventilation requirements
• Fume boards/exhausts for toxic substances
• Number of desks for writing and analysis
• Number of computer workstations
• Layout and planning of service supply

The following graphics show essential design criteria for standard laboratories (approx. 40 m² net floor area) in the three main natural science research fields chemistry, biology and physics. Shown are:

• Work areas
• Fixtures, furnishings and equipment (FF&E)
• Grids
• Structural and fit-out considerations
• Zoning and required areas for apparatuses and technical equipment

Layout of writing desk areas

"Classical" layout parallel to windows (not suitable for computer work stations)

Layout of desks perpendicular to windows; writing desks directly attached to lab desk

Layout of desks perpendicular to windows; corridor between laboratory and writing area

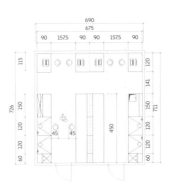
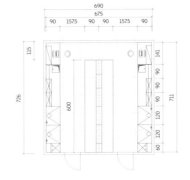
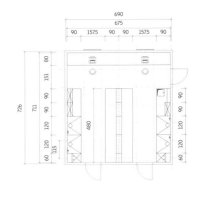

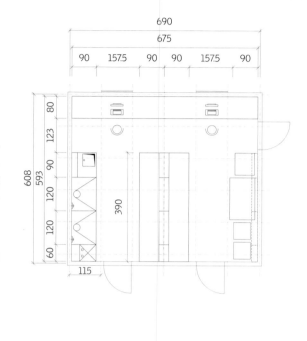

Molecular biological laboratory

Working areas:
Small area for dangerous substances (wet area)
Dry area (small equipment)
Large equipment/possibly wet area
Writing desk

FF&E:
Working desks with stoneware or melamine tops
Laboratory sink
Tall laboratory cupboard
Space for equipment

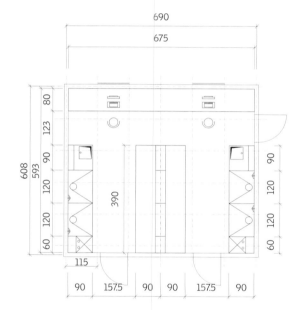

Chemical laboratory

Working areas:
Dangerous substances/wet area
Dry area (equipment/preparation)
Writing desk

FF&E:
Fume cupboard, point air exhaust
Cabinet for dangerous substances
Cabinet for chemicals
Working desks with stoneware/ceramic tops
Laboratory sink
Incubator/dryer
Refrigerator/freezer

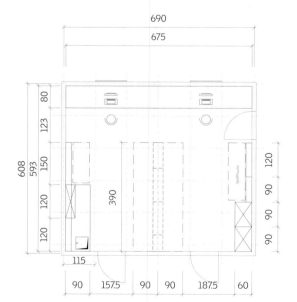

Physical laboratory

Working areas:
Small area for dangerous substances (wet area)
Dry area (small equipment)
Large equipment/possibly wet area
Writing desk

FF&E:
Working desks (with stoneware or melamine tops) or equipment
Laboratory sink
Tall laboratory cupboard
Space for equipment

A general trend is the direct integration of computer workstations into laboratories. An increasing number of computer workstations will determine future lab layouts. It will change the office ratio in research buildings as well as within laboratories with regard to their quantity, FF&E, the working environment and architectural design. This issue will be discussed in greater detail under the headline Open plan laboratory layouts.

The specific design of laboratories as a modular unit within research buildings follows certain organisational principles. These principles include differentiation, distribution of technical services, variability, flexibility, disentanglement, and the vertical and horizontal arrangement (zoning/stacking) of laboratory spaces.

C2 Concentration of similar units – zoning/stacking

Fundamentally, the design of research buildings is the result of complex and interconnected processes. As a first step, the general typological and functional approach to this complicated issue needs to be defined:

"Research buildings: Combining spaces with different requirements"

Every research project consists of a certain number of different types of spaces with individual characteristics in terms of architectural quality and building service systems. The most common room types are laboratories and offices. The main difference between both types – apart from their function – is the amount of required services and the resulting characteristic interior design. Offices require heating, lighting and electrical high and low voltage power supply and a relatively basic range of furniture. Scientific laboratories, in contrast, may require a high or even extreme amount of technical services. Above all, the ventilation and air-conditioning systems and the specific FF&E schedule require entirely different room dimensions and ceiling heights.

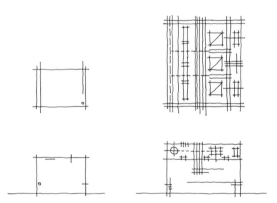

Installation densities
in the office space (left) and in the laboratory (right),
each represented in schematic floor plan and section

A purely arbitrary or organisation-oriented allocation of offices and laboratories would lead to extremely inefficient research buildings. Therefore, the design has to ensure that spaces with comparable technical requirements form groups or clusters. In this respect, two terms are used: horizontal arrangement – zoning – and vertical arrangement – stacking – of spaces.

Zoning denotes the horizontal arrangement of similar spaces along one or several interior access corridors. The length of sequence depends on room dimensions, an economical layout of service ducts and pipes, and local planning requirements (fire regulations, escape routes, industrial trade control). The following design parameters apply:
- Site dimensions and geometry, legal requirements, location
- Distances between spaces, access system
- Organisation of the institute/company
- Requirements of the brief; functional units

- Spatial requirements resulting from preventive fire regulations:
  - Length of escape route or distance between workplaces and required fire stair (according to local building codes; approx. 25 m)
  - Fire compartments (according to local building codes; up to 1,600 m² floor area)
  - Too large distances or areas entail costlier installations and supplementary fire protection devices (fire dampers, barriers etc.)
- Grey water and sewage pipes require a fall of two percent: from a certain length this affects the ceiling height.
- It must be ensured that practical installation sections can be shut off for revision and maintenance.
- If services run in central shafts, required diameters of ventilation ducts determine the economical maximal lengths of horizontal service runs.

Stacking denotes the vertical arrangement of identical or similar spaces on several floors. This involves urban planning issues as well as the positioning of service cores. Design parameters are:
- Site occupancy, urban density
- Programme, interior distances, means of vertical access
- Optimised mechanical engineering, shaft layout
- Construction, structure, wind loads, effective lengths
- Maintenance/cleaning, safety

From experience, units with lengths of approx. 25 to 30 m and three to four storeys plus basement and technical equipment on the roof level are considered to be economically viable.

C3 The programme

The total floor area stipulated in a programme is primarily based on the required staff capacity and the whole of scientific apparatuses and equipment. The budget of the project will be mainly measured against these issues. Just as the programme drives the architectural design, results of the planning process may also alter the nature and extent of the programme. Especially in public building, the net floor area is the most important planning criterion. Usually, laboratories are based on an area of 10 to 15 m² per workplace (for standard laboratories with 20 to 30 or 40 to 60 m² respectively). For offices, 6 m² per workplace is standard (for offices of 12, 18, 24 m² etc.). Apart from the number of workplaces sizes of laboratories are more and more determined by the number of writing desks and computer work-stations. Additional areas for service and equipment may further increase lab space requirements. Depending on the number of access corridors, layout of service shafts, and the fire protection scheme, room depths can range from 6 to 10 m.

How efficient the room programme is in the long run largely depends on the careful appraisal of the strategic brief. In view of current changes in laboratory design, an initial programming phase with strong participation of scientists, clients and architects alike is very helpful and saves all parties a lot of potential hassle.

As shown in the organisation chart (opposite page), a research building comprises different functional areas such as
- Scientific departments; junior teams
- Shared areas, lecture hall, seminar rooms, library, cafeteria/restaurant
- Administration, computer rooms, workshops, storage
- Special facilities like testing halls, animal enclosures, greenhouses

From a strictly functional point of view, laboratory and office units would be arranged in mixed units.

There is a fundamental conflict between scientific interests and the optimisation of mechanical engineering. If a research building were to follow exclusively scientific requirements it would ensure that the largest possible number of experiments could be conducted in the most efficient way. All required room types – laboratories, offices, test rooms, storage, seminar rooms, administration etc. – would be arranged in mixed units at close range. On the contrary, in a research building primarily following concerns of mechanical engineering, the length of service ducts would be minimised and similar room types would be arranged in clusters according to the amount of required services. All participants of the planning process should work closely together and seek a sensible compromise to avoid these extreme scenarios. The goal would rather be a building that can be constructed and maintained economically and affords spatial and design qualities at the same time.

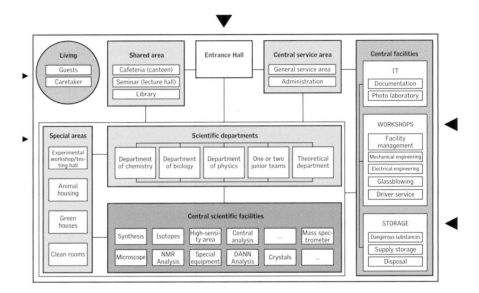

Organisation chart of an institute

As a first design step, the programme has to be ordered in three groups with specific characteristics:
- Rooms with daylight for concentrated theoretical research
  (low level of mechanical services; office spaces)
- Rooms with daylight and accessible/adaptable services/gear for experimental research
  (high level of mechanical services; laboratories)
- Rooms without daylight and with accessible/adaptable services for laboratory equipment and special use
  (high level of mechanical services; dark rooms)

From a functional point of view, the scheme also needs to define a hierarchy of the functional areas with primary and secondary areas being the more relevant ones:
- Primary area:
  - Theoretical and experimental research
- Secondary area:
  - Information, communication (internal, external)
  - Administration
  - Supply (energy, material, service sector)
- Tertiary area:
  - social activities
  - housing and leisure facilities for employees and visitors

In the first instance, the ordering of spaces within the primary area into lab spaces and office spaces is important. Also, the relation of primary area (offices and laboratories) and secondary area (supply and support) is significant and opens up new paths in research building design (refer to: C7 Open plan laboratory layouts). A research institute is reminiscent of a living organism with active and passive elements. Apart from the mentioned "active zones" – the net floor areas – the building also comprises "passive" areas consisting of secondary spaces that support the main areas. They include circulation, secondary, service and technical areas. The latter are of particular importance (refer to: C5 Technical services).

All spatial requirements of the primary and secondary areas combined determine the typological design approach as to the number of storeys and the number of access corridors per floor (refer to: C6 Plan layout)

C4 Building structure – Service cores and shafts/dimensioning/building physics

Contemporary research buildings are mostly framed reinforced concrete structures with flat slabs without binding beams. The separation of load-bearing structure and building envelope enables a modular layout, fully glazed façades and high general flexibility. Practical disadvantages of these structures such as low thermal mass or sensitivity to vibrations tend to be easily accepted or underestimated. In the future, these potential problems will be addressed more thoroughly. Massive structures will serve more and more as models for the building structures to be used.

Shaft layout

The choice of shaft layout and the dimensioning of shafts bear a strong impact on the path and length of services, ceiling heights, the fire protection strategy, and ultimately on the general building design. The main shaft types are service cores (as part of building cores or located on the outside of buildings) and individual service shafts, or a combination of the two systems.

- Advantages of service cores:
  - Few fire dampers, consistent supply, relatively small plant rooms
- Disadvantages of service cores:
  - Horizontal service ducts crossing other rooms; service dimensions may affect the ceiling height;
  - other rooms might be affected by leakages
- Advantages of individual service shafts:
  - Minimal structural ceiling height, short horizontal ducts and a relatively low amount of services in the respective laboratories
  - Individual supply; services can be individually turned off for maintenance
  - Sewage pipes do not entail floor slab penetrations
- Disadvantages of individual service shafts:
  - Relatively high consumption of floor area; increased number of fire barriers
  - Increased floor slab reinforcement required (frequent slab penetrations)
  - Limited number of storeys

A generally tried-and-tested scenario is the use of both central cores and individual shafts with a separate allocation of air-exhaust, air-supply and other services. Individual shafts should be chosen if legal, site-related or economical requirements stipulate limited ceiling heights. Central cores are needed for high air quantities (high number of fume cupboards, high air exchange rates). Increased hygienic requirements call for individual shafts (although they are only economically viable up to a maximum of four floors).

Where possible, horizontal service ducts should not be concealed by suspended ceilings. This way, concrete ceiling slabs can function as valuable thermal mass. Exposed services require coordinated planning, which is advantageous in terms of revisions, maintenance, and cleaning.

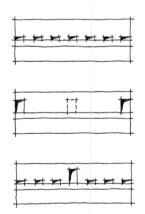

Shaft concepts
Individual shafts
Service cores
Mix of individual shafts and service cores

Building structures
L - Laboratory
O - Office
D - Dark zone
B - Building service complex
A - Atrium or open space
* - Office space floor hight not adapted
  to laboratory space floor hight

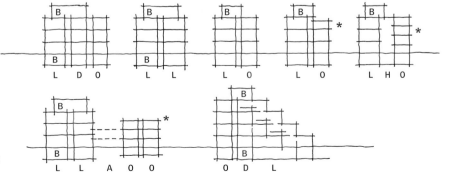

Dimensioning/grid

The width of lab spaces is determined by functional considerations, whereas the depth follows the dimensions of laboratory furnishings.

Convenient grid dimensions for the width of lab spaces were found to be 1.15 m for the interior fit-out and 6.90 m on centre for the bearing structure. This structural grid provides the most efficient spacing of laboratory workbenches and corridors. It is also in tune with building regulations for laboratory buildings and prevents excessive spare areas. The interior fit-out grid ranges between 1.05 and 1.30 m. The classic interior works dimension is the 1.20 m "Euro-grid", which can be reduced to 1.05 m to minimise the cubic content of the building. As common laboratory furnishings are based on 0.6 m / 1.2 m modules, these dimensions also determine the depth of laboratory spaces. Common structural grid dimensions for the depth of spaces, therefore, range between 6.90 m and 7.20 m. Whether architects opt for square or rectangular lab spaces depends on the particular design.

Appropriate laboratory floor-to-floor heights range from 3.80 m to 4.10 m; for offices they range between 2.90 m and 3.40 m. As a rule of thumb, a laboratory height of 4.00 m can be generally assumed as suitable. This dimension can be reduced to 3.80 m if individual shafts are used and only small air quantities have to be handled (one or two fume cupboards per standard lab).

By and large, suspended ceilings should be avoided except for particular cases such as high safety requirements, clean room conditions, or to achieve high air-exchange rates by means of a ventilated ceiling. Office spaces should have a minimum floor height of 3.00 m to obtain pleasant room proportions and enable future changes. Depending on local building regulations, minimum clear ceiling heights are required from certain room areas on.

Office spaces adjacent to laboratories often have the same ceiling heights as the lab spaces. This may entail problems with regard to the acoustics and proportions of these spaces. To solve this problem, offices and laboratories may be built with different ceiling heights. However, this will lead to greater interior distances and constitutes a major design factor that needs to be addressed at the earliest planning stage.

Building physics/indoor climate

Previous projects have shown that circulation areas and studies/offices of research buildings (especially if these buildings contain laboratories) are subject to increased room temperatures (internal heat loads). Especially during summer, users often find the indoor climate unpleasant. Design and planning have to take account of the following:

- As a rule, façades have to be fully protected by exterior solar shading devices, if necessary also in north-northeast and north-northwest facing directions. Solar protection has to be power-operated and provide optional central and individual control.
- Usage of thermal mass principles: solid interior walls, exposed concrete ceiling soffits etc.
- The design has to ensure night-cooling by means of underground channels or other measures controllable and in accordance with safety and fire regulations.

C5 Technical service systems – Air-conditioning and ventilation/other building service systems/data and electrical services

From the earliest stage on, it is absolutely essential for architects to have a firm grip on the type and standard of all technical services and their relevance for the architectural design. Ideally, architects will recognise the creative potential of the services to become an integral part of the architectural design that, much like an organism, reflects all dynamic movements within the building. Technical supply and its architectural implementation are guided by the principle of separation or disentanglement. This means that horizontal distribution of services should run on different levels that do not cross each other.

The provision of technical building service systems should be discussed in detail with the users. By all means, arbitrary estimates and excessive installation should be avoided. Instead, binding standards should be agreed on to keep costs at bay. Air-conditioning and ventilation systems require large shaft diameters. Other services like cooling, water, gas and electrical power have to be based on an intelligent, disentangled horizontal and vertical layout. If architects fail to comply with these basic demands they will jeopardize even the most creative design. Technical services will consume about fifty percent of the total building cost of modern research buildings. Therefore, the optimal and coordinated planning and installation of the technical services has a strong influence on initial building expenditures and especially on running costs. It needs to be identified as the key to an economically viable building and as an opportunity to enhance the interior and exterior architectural quality.

Technical equipment has a visual impact on research buildings. This fact is not recognised by many conceptual designs and competition entries, although it becomes fundamental in the later stages of a project. After all, a research building is nothing short of an industrial building with a delivery area, material supply problems and large technical facilities. Thus, from an early stage on architects should observe the following aspects with regard to their design impact. For the different technical building service systems these are:

Ventilation and air-conditioning

- Ventilation and air-conditioning systems in research buildings usually only include air exhausts and supply ducts with three different kinds of air-treatment (filtering, heating, cooling). As desiccant and moisturising treatment is not included, these systems are not air-conditioning systems in the classic sense.
- Most primary floor areas in research buildings – except offices, circulation areas, entrance halls and general areas – are ventilated or "air-conditioned". This mainly concerns rooms with a high thermal output, rooms located in central zones and all laboratories.
- Of all trades of the technical services, ventilation and air-conditioning systems have the largest impact on planning and design: positioning of the air handling units, the layout of the vertical and horizontal service ducts, impact on the building volume, the number of storeys and the façade design.
- Ideally, an air intake unit is placed in the basement and an exhaust unit on the roof. Such a configuration can achieve savings in material, shaft dimensions, and energy.
- Air supply in laboratories functions via ducts and nozzles; the air is drawn off via ducts or fume cupboards. The installation has to comply with acoustic and fire regulations.
- Air exhausts and supply openings have to maintain a certain distance to avoid short cuts; they have an impact on the appearance of a building.
- Flaps or openings for maintenance and revisions should be provided.

Other building service systems
Cooling/water cooling

- A cooling system should only be installed if cooling cannot be provided externally (this is generally less expensive and easier to build).
- Cooling is required for ventilation and air-conditioning, but also for process and airflow cooling of scientific experiments with high thermal output. In both cases vertical and horizontal supply is required.
- If supplementary airflow cooling units are needed, the design has to take account of their large dimensions and unpleasant drafts.
- Cooling units are placed in the basement and in roof plant rooms.
- Heat exchangers as part of cooling units are often positioned at roof level. Exterior appearance, noise and formation of steam may lead to legal conflicts with neighbours or could impair the architectural design even if the facilities, strictly speaking, comply with building standards.
- Cooling capacity for laboratory buildings is now of greater importance than ever. In this context, the growing amount of technical equipment with increased thermal output and glazing ratios of façades are crucial factors.
- Potential acoustic and vibration issues arising from the use of heat exchangers or cooling units have to be addressed at an early stage.
- Flaps or openings for maintenance and revisions should be provided.
- The cooling capacity has to be established at an early stage.

Water and sewage
- Water supply: drinking water, grey water, demineralised water
- Usually, laboratory buildings should be equipped with two separate systems for sanitary and laboratory sewage.
- Rainwater drainage and fire fighting facilities (ponds, drainage trenches) may affect the landscaping design.

Heating
- From a technical and ecological point of view, the building should rather receive its energy from the public system than from an individual heating station. This centralised form of energy supply is also less expensive.

Gases and chemical substances
- The fundamental question is: centralised or decentralised supply? This will affect the layout of utility lines and floor plan layout. Utility lines for potential supplementary media should be provided.
- There are three options for storage: central storage, secondary storage (for instance per floor), or storage in bottles within laboratories (this solution has to comply with fire and ventilation requirements).
- Nitrogen supply has to be addressed at an early planning stage: Usually, it involves the construction of a separate large tank with attached delivery zone (turning circles of lorries and accessibility are the decisive criteria here).

Electrical services
- To date, electrical services (high and low voltage) consume almost half of the initial building budget for technical building service systems.
- The development of computer technology and increasing technical equipment make it necessary to plan these services at an early stage. Electrical engineering needs to take account of a clean layout that provides the opportunity to integrate further services at a later stage.
- Since the installation of electrical services in access corridors has to meet higher fire protection standards, they mainly run inside rooms.
- In terms of lighting, general light levels and light levels at the individual work places have to be addressed.
- Usually, emergency power supply has to be provided by means of diesel units (note: potential noise and vibrations). Means of charging and required capacity have to be carefully resolved.
- Computer networks usually require a combination of optical wires in certain areas and copper mains for floor distribution. Generally, the data network has to be addressed early on since it bears a certain impact on utility lines and the interior design.

C6 Floor plan layout – Number of access corridors/circulation systems/building typology

Apart from the urban and architectural design strategy the floor plan layout is a crucial factor for the building. Architects should try to achieve compact buildings with well-considered façade areas and floor-to-floor heights as well as acceptable ratios of total floor area to net floor area and total cubic content to net floor area.

Circulation areas facilitate movement, social interaction and transport/supply within a building. Increasingly, the classic lab space is opened up and lab "cells" are abandoned. Instead, circulation areas are integrated into general open plan or mixed laboratory areas with writing zones, equipment and service pools. Hence, the ratio of circulation areas within buildings will decrease.

Floor plan layouts also have to enable supplementary installation of services and equipment and provide sufficient flexibility to accommodate future changes of technical building standards that cannot be foreseen.

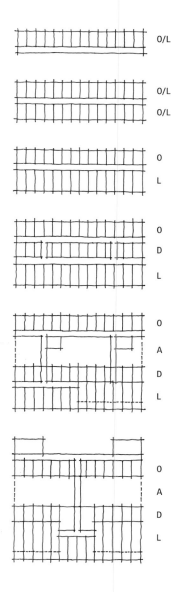

Access systems

Single-loaded access system

Double-loaded access system

Double-loaded access system

Triple-loaded access system

Single- and double-loaded system
(left double-loaded with dark area and laboratory, right combi lab)

Single loaded system
(open lab structure dark area/combi lab with
service zone, lab workplaces and writing zone)

(For key of letter codes refer to page 43)

At the preliminary design stage, a comb-shaped layout of the programme might provide initial guidance. The further development of the design depends on the particular site, the basic architectural idea etc. Comb-shaped layouts or T, U and H-shaped variations are appropriate when particular groups of rooms have to meet increased security requirements (for instance biological and genetic laboratories). The spatial separation provided by these figures may also be desirable for individual companies as is the case in business parks. The optimal number of storeys ranges between three and four: less or more storeys generally lead to less economical solutions in terms of the horizontal and vertical floor arrangement and service layout. Today, it is generally agreed on that the air intake plant of a research building with full basement floor should be positioned in the basement and the air exhaust plant should be positioned on the roof; their position should be in vertical line with the highly equipped laboratory areas.

Circulation systems

Distances between laboratories and offices have a large impact on the layout of research buildings. Although the separation of the two room types in individual wings would make economical sense, usually such a scenario is not desirable because it entails long distances between spaces. Architects can choose from various circulation systems and design options:

- Frequently, offices and laboratories are arranged under one roof and on the same floor.
- The arrangement of offices and laboratories in separate building parts linked by bridges etc. open up the opportunity for greater variety in the architectural design, different ceiling heights etc.
- Ultimately, separate buildings – office buildings with standard technical building service systems and highly equipped laboratory buildings – could be erected. This, however, is likely to hamper social interaction and teamwork.

Number of access corridors

The number of access corridors per floor in research buildings varies greatly from single-loaded corridors to two or more access corridors. The classic layout is a double-loaded access corridor with laboratories and offices opposite each other. As a first design step, laboratories, offices, and service rooms arranged along corridors as well as entrance halls or exterior spaces etc. have to be classified and have to be brought into relation to each other. The following charts also highlight the increasing tendency towards open plan spaces and the combination of offices and laboratories. Individual research disciplines are associated with particular layout types (regarding the number of corridors):

- Contemporary chemical laboratories (wet or dry) usually lead to double-loaded corridors. They are equipped with a high number of fume cupboards (two to six per lab); two access corridors per floor are only required if a separate service zone for secondary spaces and equipment and measuring rooms is needed.
- Wet or dry biological, biochemical or molecular biological laboratories can be designed as double-loaded corridor layouts. Yet often, triple-loaded systems are chosen to accommodate the large number of service spaces (equipment, constant-temperature rooms, cool storage, freezing storage, incubators etc.) in central dark zones. The number of fume cupboards is smaller compared to chemical laboratories (one to two per 40 m² standard lab).
- Physical laboratories rather resemble experimental workshops than classic chemical or biological laboratories. There are no or few fume cupboards; laboratory furnishings are only required along the side partitions to make room for experimental installations and apparatuses. State-of-the-art facilities will require racks with integrated sensor measuring and computer equipment and a complex data cable network. Usually, physical laboratories are accessed with double-loaded corridors. Apart from offices and laboratories, frequently experimental halls or large high-tech spaces (for instance microscopy or clean rooms) are needed.

Building typology

Based on the aforementioned parameters, there are three main types of research buildings:

- **Linear systems**
- **Comb-like systems**
- **Central or core systems**

Each system has a variety of sub-types; yet each building is derived from one of the basic types or, for complex buildings, a combination of them. The right choice of layout and circulation system depends on various factors:

- General factors
  - Site, legal and planning requirements, urban design
  - Programme/brief
  - Type and number of workplaces
  - Technical services
  - Cubic content; economical viability

C7 Open plan laboratory layouts – Combi lab

Especially molecular biological and biochemical laboratories increasingly call for flexible and variable open plan layouts. This development has to be put in context with the current understanding of teaching and research in natural sciences. Although specialised knowledge in the core disciplines of biology, chemistry and physics is still essential, teaching is increasingly based on a multi-disciplinary approach. The same is true for industrial research: working methods of different disciplines converge; pure biological or chemical institutes are a thing of the past. Modern research buildings rather call for a mix of specific programmes and room equipment. Also in this respect, a certain convergence of laboratory types and equipment has to be conceded.

Standard laboratories of 20 to 40 m² with allocated offices and service areas – a layout, which has been common especially in public buildings – are being replaced by open plan arrangements along the lines of mixed-use or Combi lab or "lab scapes". Such an open plan arrangement consists of the following areas:

- Circulation areas
- Service areas
- Studies, offices
- Special rooms
  - Dark rooms, (cool) storage
  - Special laboratories (possibly with noise or toxic emissions)
  - Special laboratories for "copyright" products: cell cultures (biology) or laser products (physics)
- Combi labs comprising
  - Individual laboratory work desks
  - Service facilities: fume cupboards, washing basins, lockers
  - Writing desks

The general revision of laboratory design was brought about by a number of particular factors:

- The overall multi-disciplinary character of contemporary research
- Systematic multi-disciplinary co-operation boosts innovation
- Provision of non-pyramidal, flexible (temporary) work environments
- Economical concerns; cost-benefit analysis

Open plan arrangements provide the following architectural benefits:

- Communicative working environment
- Direct and short distances
- Reduction of circulation areas/corridors (gain in open plan lab floor area)
- Gained areas can be used for storage, lockers, refrigerators etc.

Typology of building layouts
Arrows indicate differenciation
and combination of systems

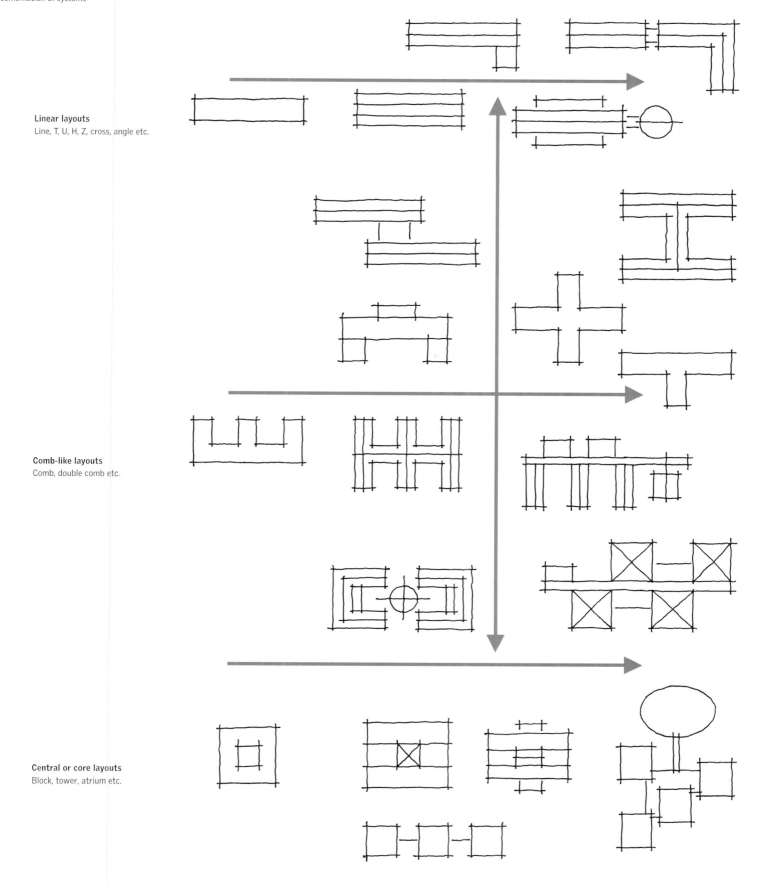

Linear layouts
Line, T, U, H, Z, cross, angle etc.

Comb-like layouts
Comb, double comb etc.

Central or core layouts
Block, tower, atrium etc.

• Simplification of building standards, cost reduction through
  - Dispensing with fire safety requirements:
    • Simpler layouts of service ducts: ducts can cross without additional fire barriers and encasements
    • No fire loads in corridors or escape routes; better storage
  - Simpler structure, less walls and doors
• Flexible areas and desk layout for varying organisational scenarios
• Common use of equipment and facilities will create synergy effects among users.

However, open plan layouts also have disadvantages:
• Increase of net floor area
  - This theoretical increase has an impact on the evaluation of the building cost per cubic metre
  - However, reduced circulation areas will partly compensate for this increase in net floor area. It can be expected that over time cost evaluations will acknowledge the development towards open layouts.
• Sound insulation
  - Laboratories pose potential acoustic problems, especially when large spaces are concerned. Acoustic insulation is obligatory.
• Anonymous working environment
  - Motivation and work results of employees can suffer if open plan working areas are too large.
  - Separation of individual areas and variations in the layout can compensate this problem.

All in all, the benefits of mixed open plan office environments clearly outnumber the disadvantages. The initially mentioned conflict between functional considerations and technical issues concerning the mechanical engineering is gradually taken over by the events and has become a "win-win situation. The current development is moving in the direction of an intelligent mix of open and flexible spaces with a number of economical and architectural benefits that also appeal to the up-and-coming generation of scientists. It is to be expected that the general tendency towards open plan arrangements will continue and eventually prevail both in new projects and conversions (for example, in refurbished institute buildings of the seventies, circulation areas were reduced).

Literature

Werner Schramm, Physikalische und technologische Laboratorien, Planung-Bau-Einrichtung, Weinheim 1962

Werner Schramm, Chemische und biologische Laboratorien, Planung-Bau-Einrichtung, Weinheim 1969

Bruno Krekler, Hentrich-Petschnigg & Partner, Laboratorien für Forschung, Anwendungstechnik und Überwachung, Munich 1977

Hardo Braun, Die Entwicklung des Institutsbaus, doctoral thesis 1987

Ernst Neufert, Bauentwurfslehre, Wiesbaden, numerous editions

Hardo Braun, Dieter Grömling, Carl-Egon Heintz, Alfred Schmucker, Building for Science, Architecture of the Max Planck Institutes, Basel, Berlin, Boston 1999

Dieter Grömling, Materialien zur Vorlesung Forschungsbau, Munich Technical University, Lehrstuhl für Entwerfen und Raumgestaltung, Prof. H. Deubzer, spring/summer 1999

Georg Kuchenbecker, Schering AG, Technik Berlin, "Labor der Zukunft", 2001

Standard laboratories with 40 m² net floor area

left
Max Planck Institute for Chemical Ecology, Jena,
Germany, 2001

right
Max Planck Institute for Evolutionary Anthropology, Leipzig,
Germany, 2003

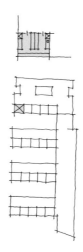

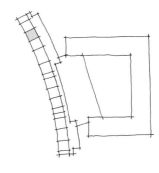

Open "lab scape" in conversions

left
Max Planck Institute on the Martinsried campus,
Munich, Germany; star-layout with two double-loaded
corridors; left: two existing wings; top right: wing
with larger labs; bottom right: wing with open laboratory plan incorporating former corridor space

right
Max Planck Institute for Biophysical Chemistry,
Göttingen; above: superseded floor plan;
below: revised open floor plan

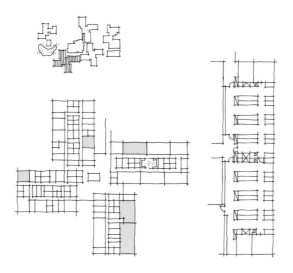

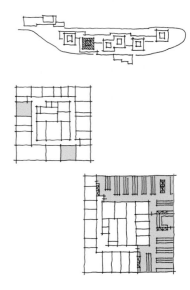

Open "lab scape" in new buildings

left
Max Planck Institute for Heart and Lung Research,
Bad Nauheim, Germany, with open plan laboratories
(under planning)

right
Max Planck Institute for Molecular Biomedicine,
Münster, Germany (under construction)

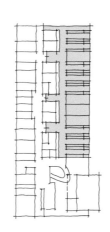

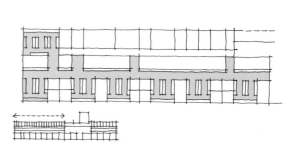

JÜRGEN EICHLER

The laboratory workplace

Systematic scientific research examines the feasibility and verifiability of theoretical propositions and confirms the findings by means of reproduction. The respective workplace requirements are as varied as the possible tasks and processes. Workplaces have to provide the best possible working conditions for individual tasks as well as extensive serial processes. As is the case in most architectural projects the design of laboratories also has to mediate between individual aspirations and a viable general scheme. Ideally, laboratory interiors should be based on a flexible, modular FF&E schedule that enables a great variety of uses and fit-outs.

Today, the fixtures and equipment particularly of chemical/biological/medical laboratories are limited to a small number of components that provide maximum flexibility for a large range of use. These systems are essentially based on the following standardised or prefabricated modules:

Energy block	Providing all required laboratory service systems
Trunking	Screened conduit for high and low voltage High voltage: mains, emergency power, three-phase current, fuses for individual laboratory units, emergency stop Low voltage: IT, telecommunication, house monitor and control system
Laboratory	Work top material (material density) depends on specific use (heat/cold, solvents, hygienic performance): resin, compound materials, polypropylene, ethylene, engineered stone etc.
Shelving	Fixed above the work tops and wall trunking Use: storage of frequently used instruments and equipment, control gear (for measurements, controlling, documentation)
Wall cupboard	Storage of short-term equipment, clipboard, filing, forms/stationary. Recommended material: transparent glazed sliding doors for easy access and orientation
Laboratory sink unit	Size as required, with supplementary rack for wet instruments, eye bath, high-purity water supply if necessary; floor cupboard equipped with first-aid kit, laboratory bin
Fume cupboard	Exhaust of toxic or dangerous substances Isotope fume cupboard/filter etc. if necessary
Writing desk	Near window (glare protection) or integrated into laboratory unit (splash protection); used to write minutes, protocols, log books; Sockets for computer and other electrical equipment Floor units for filing, reference library
Special furniture	Safety cupboard (storage of acid and alkaline solutions, solvents, gas bottles, toxic agents). Cabinet for supplementary equipment etc.

The arrangement of these modules has to follow considerations related to scientific use, technical service supply and cost effectiveness.

Commonly, modules are arranged in rows; wet and dry units alternate and are either fitted or free-standing. Other solutions involve free open plan arrangements of the components or the provision of basic service units or racks without further fixtures or equipment.

The semi-mobile equipment of the workplace is often supplemented by the grouping of standard labs with adjacent secondary spaces, possibly as niches or ante-zones. Here, noise-emitting equipment (centrifuges etc.) or equipment with extreme thermal output (-80° Celsius refrigerators), incubators, cold storage, isotope laboratories, studies etc. are located. The close proximity of laboratories and these secondary spaces creates economical and efficient modular work units with non-pyramidal flat hierarchies for flexible and targeted work.

It is generally desirable to provide additional informal meeting places close to the laboratories that encourage social interaction. These areas sometimes can be integrated into circulation areas.

Easy access to technical building service systems and convenient installation of supplementary services is crucial for an efficient laboratory environment. Maintenance and upgrading must be possible without causing major disruption to laboratory operations. This also extends to facilities and service systems that form part of the safety supply system of the building. Generally, electrical supply shafts and horizontal utility lines should be oversized to allow the installation of supplementary service systems if this should be required.

Access for maintenance work, installation of supplementary service systems and local revisions should largely be provided from outside the laboratories. Shafts for air supply should be arranged close to lab spaces. If the design fails to comply with this requirement horizontal air ducts might, for instance, cross circulation areas. In this case, more complicated fire regulations apply.

The separation of air-conditioning and ventilation and gas/water/sewage shafts is generally accepted as good practice since they have different sizes. The space requirements for electrical and IT service systems are often underrated. However, these service systems need particular attention – particularly their junctions with other service ducts. Service systems that are frequently required in all areas throughout the building (such as water, pressurized air, gases etc.) should be concentrated in central shafts. Service systems for use in certain parts of a building or infrequent use (such as vacuum, special gases etc.) are to be accommodated in individual shafts.

Architects should be aware that well-meaning and painstakingly worked out laboratory arrangements do not automatically pass the test of reality. Building structures and spatial layouts often radically differ from expectations and working methods of creative and absorbed scientists. Hence, all participants have to join forces to define a common language so the building does not end up as an expression of incomprehensible – and therefore impractical – ideas.

Scientists are often "creatures of habit" – that is, they develop certain working styles and habits based on previous workplaces. Architects have to identify the actual need by means of an intensive and persistent dialogue with the users. Even after thorough co-ordination of every single aspect architects should look into building a mock-up laboratory when planning a large facility to finalise all design and service details.

Increasingly, computerised and automated processes join more classical work patterns in the laboratories. Ever more sophisticated experimental processes entail "encapsulated" apparatuses; similar processes used to be carried out openly. This development called for deeper and often larger worktops, storage and shelving, which are now standard. These processes are supervised in detached studies or computer rooms.

The development of more sophisticated equipment and working methods has also brought about exacerbated requirements with regard to the purity and cleanliness of the used chemical substances and the working environment. Here, research requirements and health and safety regulations meet. Increased hygienic standards have found an architectural expression in changing rooms, security gates, air filters, fume cupboards, security zones for genetic research/isotope/hygiene etc. Finishes and all FF&E items must be smooth and without joints so they can be cleaned/disinfected easily. In this context, particular attention should be extended to junctions and joints of different building components. Wall claddings are generally not desirable as concealed cavities increase the risk of microbiological contamination and toxicity. Exposed service lines provide excellent accessibility for cleaning and maintenance and remind users of this necessity as "...what is out of sight is out of mind!". Further potential requirements such as heat resistance, solvent resistance, non-porous solid surface etc. have to be established before planning commences.

In any event, all requirements of the brief should be carefully listed and questioned because either inappropriate expectations of the client or insufficient initial provisions by the planners may entail considerable additional costs.

Energy

Modern laboratory buildings for research institutes have to live up to energy demands of our times. Energy efficient buildings with good facility management can achieve significant savings in runningcosts and are more convenient to use. In view of increasing global energy consumption (Image 1) and the growing exploitation of fossil fuel resources it must be a public priority to plan energy efficient buildings and to use renewable energy.

Laboratory facilities for research or industrial use have to meet different requirements than their office counterparts: primarily they have to ensure a smooth and safe operation of all service systems, constant supply, and a secure and environmentally friendly extraction and disposal of contaminated gaseous, fluid or solid chemical substances of the laboratory and production areas. High air change rates and constant climatic room conditions call for efficient air-conditioning and ventilation systems. Flexible floor plan layouts and technical building service systems are even more important than for office buildings. Laboratory facilities have to be able to accommodate changing research processes and methods, especially if the project is privately funded and tenants will be acquired only after completion. Planning parameters for office spaces in laboratory buildings, however, are the same as for pure office buildings: they have to provide a pleasant room climate for predominantly sedentary occupation, sufficient daylight and technical equipment that is easy to operate.

Planning and operation

All basic parameters for optimal operation and an economically viable building concept are defined at the planning stage. Therefore, the composition of the planning team and the communication between all involved parties is crucial for the success of a project. Often, facility managers join the planning process at an early stage to ensure the efficient operation of the building in co-operation with the architect, mechanical engineer, structural engineer and client. To achieve efficiency, architectural aspects have to be evaluated against the backdrop of technical and financial aspects.

Computer simulations can be useful design tools to estimate the future energy consumption of a building. Strategies worked out at planning stage can be double-checked after completion of the project and improved if required. This involves a detailed track record highlighting the actual energy consumption values that might differ from original estimates. Energy consumption may be recorded in relation to a particular research project or over a certain period of time. Ongoing control and documentation also reduce the risk of failures of the system. Constant improvement of the procedures of use and adjustment to the requirements of the users will enhance the energy performance of the building and make facilities more convenient and easy to use, which helps to avoid handling errors.

Energy concepts

The objective of an energy concept is the saving and efficient supply of energy. A study by Heike Kluttig, Andreas Dirscherl and Hans Erhorn concerned with the energy consumption of Federal German educational buildings found large differences between individual objects. Specifically, the consumption of heating energy and electrical power of various institute buildings were examined. It became obvious that biological, chemical, and pharmaceutical institute buildings had an above-average energy consumption compared to humanities faculties. Energy consumption for heating and power also varied significantly depending on the respective laboratory types and processes.

The high consumption of electrical energy for laboratory processes and cooling energy in research buildings calls for sustainable concepts like combined heat and power systems or desiccative and evaporative cooling systems.

The co-ordination of structure, façade, and technical service systems is essential when planning energy efficient buildings. An important aspect is the energetic evaluation of every individual component of supplied energy and the consideration of hidden potentials for the use of renewable energy sources such as natural daylight, natural ventilation, solar energy, and heat pumps.

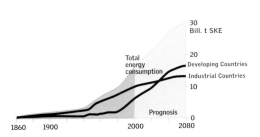

Current and predicted development of world energy consumption

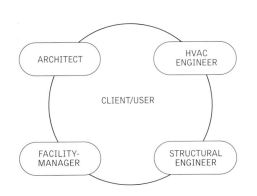

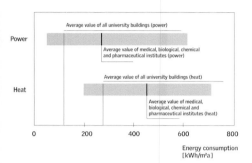

Comparative chart of heating and power consumption of medical, biological, chemical and pharmaceutical university institutes and average consumption of all institutes

A well-insulated building envelope in combination with a heat exchange system can reduce heating energy needs during winter. However, the largest energy consumption factors in laboratory buildings are lighting, refrigeration, and electrical power for lab equipment and air-conditioning. The high electrical energy demand in laboratories and production facilities can be met by combined heat and power plants; they also ensure emergency power supply and can be combined with DEC (desiccative and evaporative cooling) systems to provide power, heat and cooling. In wintertime, excess heat energy produced by electrical plants can be used for heating and changed into cooling energy during summer. Cooling is required to provide constant climatic conditions in research and industrial laboratories. In any event, the integration of heat pumps or solar power stations into the combined heat and cooling system should be considered. Façades offer another great potential for energy savings: sufficient daylight and effective solar protection reduce power consumption for artificial lighting and control solar heat gains. In office spaces in particular, cooling energy consumption can be reduced by passive core cooling ("thermal mass") in conjunction with night-time ventilation . For high air change rates, mechanical ventilation can be used. However, in buildings with average air change rates natural ventilation is desirable as it increases user comfort and does not require power for ventilation and air-conditioning. Also, the general building layout should be integrated into the energy concept – an atrium, for instance, functions as a thermal buffer zone and can provide fresh air for office areas.

Summary

Efficient energy consumption and use of a building have to be based on a thorough planning process. This involves the conscious utilisation of energy and the application of intelligent technology as well as functional, sustainable building and service layouts. Consistent facility management and maintenance during the entire life span of a building ensure that the proposed strategies are put into practice and constantly revised. Employment of recyclable building materials and renewable energy reduce negative impacts onto the environment and enable an ecologically sound demolition and conversion of a building.

HELMUT BLEHER

Electrical power

Technical service systems for research and other technical buildings are to provide a high safety of supply as well as flexibility to be able to adapt to constantly changing requirements of new research processes. Service layout and dimensioning of control rooms have to be based on a thorough evaluation of future electrical energy consumption and the different required mains. The voltages needed follow the brief and local planning requirements.

Close co-operation of all participants of the planning process is required to achieve an optimised service and control room layout. All parameters concerning the position, orientation, extendibility, and modular setting of service areas and electrical control rooms are determined at an early planning stage. The number of central and secondary control areas results from the building geometry, the number of storeys, the total floor area, the particular use of the building, and the related specific energy consumption.

Most research and technological buildings contain individual transformer stations. Required service areas such as medium and low voltage switchgear, transformers, and safety power supply should be arranged next to each other. According to the respective building layout, all issues concerning the ventilation of the spaces, transport of equipment and substances, and maintenance have to be addressed by the building structure – for instance with the position of installation shafts or the plant room. Floor-to-floor heights of service areas have to take account of raised floors.

Despite their high thermal output, in most cases service rooms with optimal, i.e. north orientation and sufficient openings for air-intake and exhaust do not need mechanical ventilation. Such a layout helps to save energy and reduces maintenance costs.

The installation of diesel generators for emergency or safety power supply requires particular care: The generator should be accommodated in a room near the transformer station. The potential impact of exhaust pipes, ventilation, air and structure-borne sound on adjacent spaces has to be carefully studied and co-ordinated with other consultants.

Supplementary service areas for information technology or specific functional requirements consume a considerable amount of additional space.

The layout of electrical plant rooms and distribution of electrical services follows technical and economical parameters. Technical parameters include:
  - A clearly structured service layout
  - Stacking of switch rooms
  - Crossing with other service ducts should be avoided if possible
  - Energy losses within mains should be minimised
  - Supply distances should be short to avoid voltage drops
  - Flexible selection of voltage, circuit, etc.
  - Low-maintenance
  - Accessibility
  - Reliability
  - Long life spans and maximum flexibility in case of changes of use and extensions

Economical parameters are:
  - Low investment costs through specification of non-specific, generic equipment
  - Special solutions should be restricted
  - Short utility lines
  - Short installation periods
  - Low running and follow-up costs

Fire regulations to a large extent determine layout and building standards of electrical plant rooms and service supply. Furthermore, negative electromagnetic influences – particularly of electrical service systems – on highly sensitive measuring and research equipment have to be restricted. When specifying equipment, materials, the strategy for grounding and potential equalisation and service supply, these requirements have to be taken into account.

Due to the fast development of information, computer, communication, security and media technology, central facilities and floor plans should contain buffer zones that can accommodate additional or changed equipment. Installation of supplementary gear, maintenance work or even a replacement of the entire system should be possible without interrupting research operations and without affecting existing systems.

The position and number of switch rooms is influenced by the range of different uses, the architectural design, and the maximum lengths of electrical and IT service lines.

The layout of the horizontal distribution on each floor has to be established in detail with the architect and other engineers and consultants in accordance with the specific architectural and fire protection requirements. Important criteria for the layout include the individual spatial requirements, ventilation and media concepts for laboratories as well as building regulations for electrical service systems, access, and maintenance. Installation of electrical service systems within escape routes is governed by specific building regulations.

Electrical service systems in workspaces run optionally in trunkings, within a raised floor or in underfloor ducts. In laboratories, service systems run almost exclusively in wall trunkings or in conduits within the laboratory furniture. Flexibility and accessibility have to be regarded as important criteria for the specification of distribution systems.

Planning and design of cutting-edge electrical supply systems is not restricted to the initial installation but must be aware of ongoing changes throughout the life of a research building and its technical service systems.

Air

The more complex scientific processes in a research facility are, the more important the mechanical engineering and equipment of the building is. Just how vital the specific air supply for a research or technical building really is can be estimated when air-conditioning and ventilation systems fail. Together with the other technical service systems (heating, cooling, gas, pressurized air and power) it establishes the "bodily functions" of a research building – its circulation, metabolism, and nervous system – which are essential for its proper operation and use.

Air-conditioning and ventilation systems provide the required environmental conditions for laboratory research as well as enabling the reproduction of results. They control temperature and air-humidity and carry off heat and toxic air-borne substances. In certain cases pressurisation (for instance for clean rooms) or suction in spaces with chemical, biological, or radioactive sources of danger are also requisite. Generally, all research buildings have to provide a pleasant working atmosphere and above all protect employees from contaminations through dangerous substances.

In addition to these functions, air-conditioning and ventilation systems enable modular laboratory layouts that can flexibly accommodate various scenarios of use without changing the entire system. This flexibility can be achieved by means of a primary horizontal trunk line that suits the building geometry. The overall energy consumption of the system can be drastically reduced with an operation according to demand, intelligent controlling, and energy recovery systems such as heat exchangers.

According to the individual research disciplines the layout of air-conditioning and ventilation systems focuses on the following functions:

Physical laboratories
Heat exhaust; large amounts of thermal output call for direct water cooling (examples: cooling of electron storage ring, BESSY II; fusion experiment, Max Planck Institute for Plasma Physics, Greifswald)

Chemical, pharmaceutical, and biological laboratories
Exhaust of toxic substances, over/low pressure, clean air (GMP/GLP)

Animal laboratories
Animal protection, sterility, constant temperature and air-humidity, improvement of animal housing

Clean room laboratories
Compliance with specific clean room standards; heat exhaust; constant temperature and air-humidity

Even this rough classification shows the great variety of issues air-conditioning and ventilation systems have to deal with. These issues have direct consequences for the building structure. In order to meet acoustic and energetic requirements, air-conditioning and ventilation ducts have to be relatively large. Furthermore, the air volumes needed for the individual laboratory types vary notably. This fact can be highlighted by two extreme examples:

Biological laboratory
Number of air-changes: 4 to 8 per hour

High-spec clean room (class 10, US standard)
Number of air-changes: approx. 360 per hour

Service areas have to be dimensioned and arranged in accordance with these requirements. If large air volumes have to be transported, air-handling unit and target area should be located next to each other. If air is distributed by means of the mentioned primary horizontal trunk lines, a fair number of risers should be installed to restrict duct dimensions and ensure a flexible and energy sufficient system. Fire protection regulations are also a considerable space factor since shafts connect different fire compartments. Hence, extra space is required for the installation of fire barriers as well as for maintenance and regular revisions.

A sufficiently generous spatial layout is of general importance for all components of the system that are regularly maintained and revised – in particular the central air-handling units. The respective areas for transport of equipment, maintenance works, and installation openings have to be planned carefully. The service layout can also be affected by the fact that maintenance staff may not be entitled to enter particular restricted laboratory or security areas. Based on the brief and the general design strategy it has to be decided at an early design stage whether service ducts should run in central or individual shafts. Crossing ducts should be avoided to restrict floor-to-floor heights to economical dimensions. Generally, there are two supply levels:

Primary supply lines
Primary shafts, electrical and other service supply

Secondary supply lines
Supply lines connecting to individual spaces

Exhaust air should be blown out at roof level to avoid short cuts between air-intake and exhaust and to prevent environmental nuisance. Air-intake should take place at first floor level and not at ground level as this incorporates the risk to suck in contaminated or polluted air.

Air-conditioning and ventilation systems play a fundamental part in the design and layout of a research building. To achieve an optimal result, functional requirements have to be discussed and put into question repeatedly. In order to develop a sustainable and user-friendly solution, all participants in the planning process – from consultants to planning authorities – have to work closely together from an early stage on.

Selection of Projects

In comparison with other pressing social and political issues, investments within the forward-looking realm of research have become a global priority. The resulting high level of building activity necessitates a central and responsible control mechanism, which is by no means self-evident. Acceptance by the user depends on very practical factors such as technical functionality or running costs yet increasingly also calls for exemplary interconnections between culture and science.

The most important criterion for the selection of the 68 projects featured in this section was their overall architectural quality. Moreover, the aim was to represent a certain range in terms of geographic location, typological quality, and field of research.

A general evaluation of all projects led to their division into four sections: Context, Access Systems, Communication, and Form. It goes without saying that the featured structures do not exclusively follow one of these principles, but contain elements of all of them. Any scheme for a research facility is bound to consider communication and zoning issues, for instance. However, the classification seemed appropriate as each category exemplifies a fundamental design principle.

Project design building of BMW AG Munich, Germany;
architects: Henn Architekten

An exposed site or the required programme and floor area of a building may lead to a specific role within the urban context. In this respect buildings for research and technology often gain special significance. Further reasons for implementing a research structure into a wider context may be funding strategies or the public importance of the respective research activity.

All projects featured in this section are specifically related to their context. Some of the selected structures maintain close architectural or functional links with adjacent research institutions and strive to establish clusters and synergies within a research campus. Another group of projects is characterised by its outstanding importance within the urban context that goes beyond scientific interrelations. This may involve the definition of an important public space (e.g. a square or street) or the fact that the project refers to an extraordinary topographic environment.

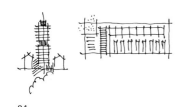

66
Maersk McKinney Møller Institute
for Production Technologies

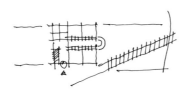

68
Bourns Hall, Engineering Science Building,
University of California

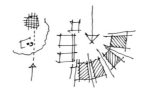

70
Institute of Physics,
Humboldt University of Berlin, Adlershof Campus

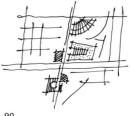

72
Max Planck Campus Tübingen

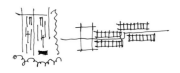

84
Centre for Cellular and Biomolecular Research

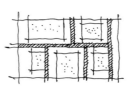

86
Male Urological Cancer Research Centre

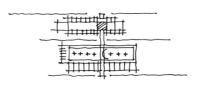

88
Biosciences Building, University of Liverpool

90
Life Sciences Complex, Ben Gurion University

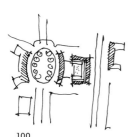

100
Max Planck Institute
for Evolutionary Anthropology

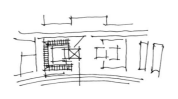

102
Max Planck Institute for Infection Biology and
German Arthritis Research Centre

104
Barcelona Botanical Institute

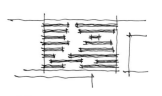

108
Computer Science and Electrical Engineering
Institutes, Graz University of Technology

The sub-section "Large Structures" includes projects that are perceived (by the public and staff alike) as more than a single building. Their overall dimensions and functional/organisational complexity rather suggest an urban scale or else a solitary object.

Context

74
Institutes and Lecture Hall for Biology
and Chemistry, University of Rostock

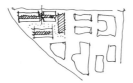

76
Fred Hutchinson Cancer Research Center

78
Belfer Building for Molecular Genetics
and Cancer Research, Weizmann Campus

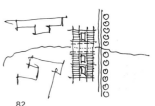

82
Laboratory Building
of Cologne University Hospital

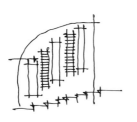

92
Centre for Information and Media Technology,
Adlershof Science and Technology Park

94
Parque Tecnológico IMPIVA

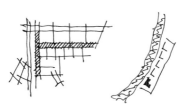

96
Center for Biotechnology
and Bioengineering

98
Max Bergmann Centre of Biomaterials

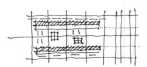

112
Saitama Prefectural University

114
Technology Centre, Rhine-Elbe Science Park

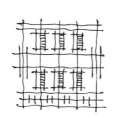

116
La Ruche, Technocentre Renault

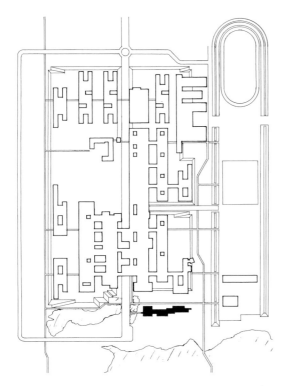

Site plan

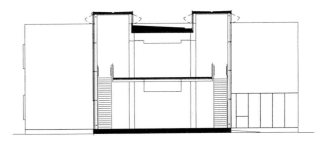

Cross section

from left to right

The south façade is a well-balanced composition of solid and transparent areas | Apart from highlighting the main entrance to the institute the striking longitudinal "bow" also ties the building together resulting in a consistent appearance | The lightweight footbridge structure allows daylight falling in through skylights to reach the ground floor | Above: The workstations in the computer rooms follow the same strict layout that prevails throughout the building | Below: The façade consists of few simple yet effective elements

Maersk McKinney Møller Institute for Production Technologies

Odense, Denmark

Client	Odense University
Architects	Henning Larsens Tegnestue A/S
Construction period	1997-1999
Total floor area	2,500 m²

The institute is situated at the southern end of the Odense University campus on Funen Island, Denmark. In contrast to the existing (exclusively north-south orientated) long buildings on the campus, the new building switches to west-east orientation. The linear layout and lively spatial and functional expression of the volume create a poignant transition from the existing building fabric to the adjacent wooded nature reserve.

The building houses facilities for doctoral candidates and students that are mainly occupied with the development of software for robots. The western wing contains offices, workshops, and laboratories for heavy-duty gear, with further offices located on the

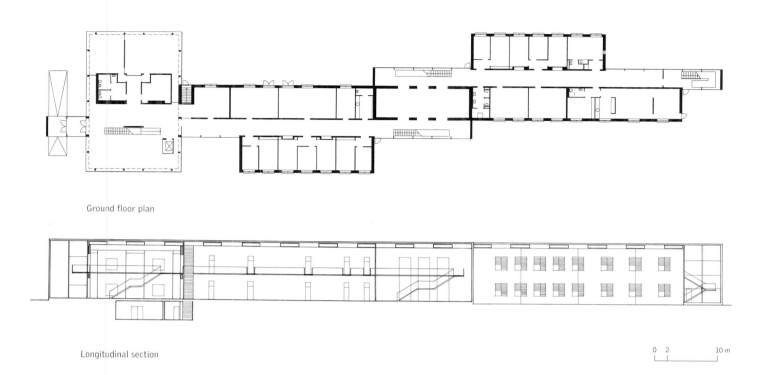

Ground floor plan

Longitudinal section

0 2   10 m

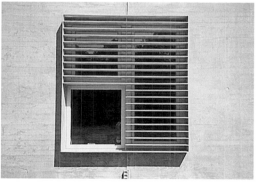

first floor. The eastern wing houses guest apartments, offices, and rooms for teamwork.

One enters the building through a tall glazed entrance situated at the western end. The double height entrance area is also used for exhibitions; an open staircase connects the ground floor with the corridor on the first floor. This 100 m long main passage forms the backbone of the building.

Walking down the main passage the visitor enjoys surprising views and constantly changing light situations. It is designed as a narrow bridge, so that much of the daylight entering through skylights reaches the ground floor. The plan layout of the different functio-

nal areas is a result of the lighting requirements of the respective spaces from relatively dark computer rooms with workstations to bright meeting and training rooms.

In order to avoid long monotonous corridors a transparent space is placed centrally. On the ground floor this space accommodates a common lounge and on the first floor a library. While most spaces receive daylight only from one side, this central space is lit from both sides. Only from here is a complete view through the building possible: onto the other institutes as well as into the forest.

The façade consists of concrete elements produced with a special formwork of slightly sandblasted ash. The window frames are made of anodised aluminium. To minimise glare on the computer screens, sandblasted aluminium louvers are attached in front of the windows; for the ventilation openings below the windows the same material was used. The overall result is a very purist and elegant architecture.

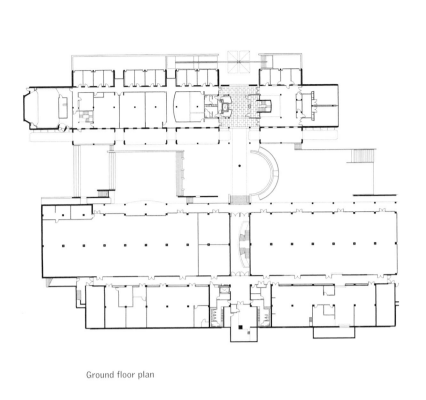

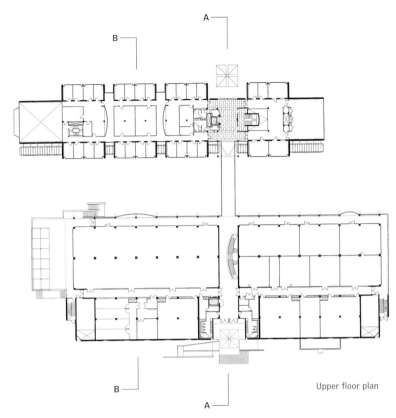

Ground floor plan

B

A

Upper floor plan

from left to right
A well-balanced composition of horizontal and vertical lines emphasises the austere and structured character of the building | The interplay between the glass-and-aluminium façade and the brick walls harmoniously marries heaviness with lightness | Inner courtyard: outdoor space with footbridge | An austere and pure architectural language dominates the interior

Bourns Hall, Engineering Science Building, University of California

Riverside, California, USA

Client	University of California
Architects	Anshen + Allen
Construction period	1995
Total floor area	15,300 m²

The architectural design for Bourns Hall on the University of California Riverside campus physically separates the experimental research area with laboratories and workshops from the scientists' study rooms and administration offices. The differentiated building volume respects the scale of the campus context. At the same time, the building ensemble with its poignant and crisp appearance fosters a strong sense of identity.

The two three-storey volumes enclose two differently designed courtyards: cobblestones give one of them an urban character while the other one rather bears the characteristics of a natural green open space. On the first floor both buildings are linked via a foot-

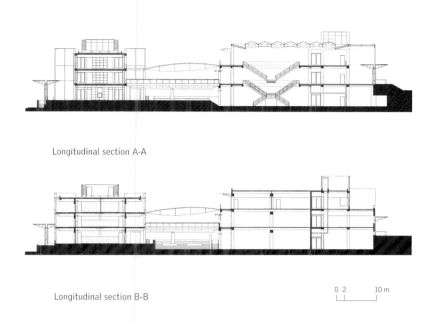

Longitudinal section A-A

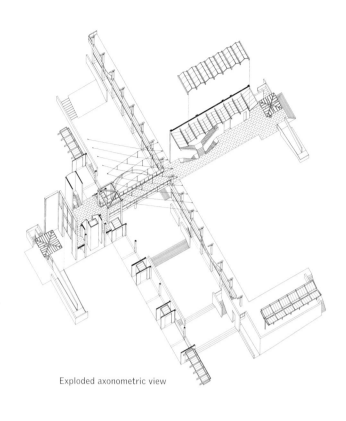

Longitudinal section B-B

0 2   10 m

Exploded axonometric view

bridge that not only serves as an interior circulation route but also as the highly frequented main access to the university campus. The two entrances create a strong architectural feature, which links both volumes and also forms a plausible entrée to the following "grand avenue" connecting the new building with the institutes further south.

As highly sensitive equipment is used in the laboratories, vibration had to be strictly controlled. To ensure vibration-free working conditions, the load-bearing structure is made of in-situ concrete. Furthermore, the building is located in an area threatened by earthquakes, necessitating a rigid floor system for very high rigidity. With a view to constantly changing re-

quirements of scientific research today, the wing containing the laboratories and workshops also had to provide maximum functional and spatial flexibility and convertibility. This has been achieved by means of large continuous spaces, wide spans, double walls for mechanical services, and supplementary secondary and central service cores.

The exposed concrete finishes – thoroughly detailed with horizontal and vertical joints and bands and manufactured with smooth plywood formwork – became an essential architectural element. The reinforced concrete frames and cross-walls received red brick infillings, brick being the predominant building material on the campus. The north and south façades,

in contrast, have curtain walls made of aluminium and glass. Despite its distinctly differentiated architecture the building complex with its clear arrangement of structures and the simple but elegantly and painstakingly crafted details appears rather unobtrusive. The colour scheme mediates and integrates the new buildings into the existing building fabric of the campus.

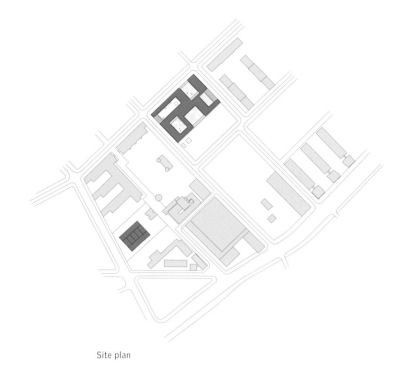

Site plan

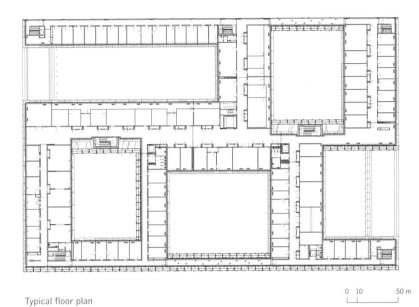

Typical floor plan

0   10   50 m

from left to right
Except for the north side, all façades are equipped with walk-ways on all levels to passively minimise energy consumption |
On the south side, the building received a green façade. In-house physicists will scientifically supervise the vine growing on

bamboo stakes | Due to multiple façade layers, a high glazing ratio, and views into the landscaped courtyards, the building appears transparent and inviting | North-west façade with fig-ured glass

Institute of Physics, Humboldt University of Berlin, Adlershof Campus

Berlin, Germany

Client	Land Berlin; Senatsverwaltung für Wissenschaft, Forschung und Kultur
Architects	Augustin und Frank Architekten
Construction period	1999-2002
Total floor area	20,500 m²
Net floor area	11,000 m²
Cubic content	91,500 m³

On the former airfield in Berlin Johannisthal-Adlershof a new central square came into being as the new heart of the natural science faculty of Humboldt University. The urban layout and architectural design relate to the listed historic building fabric to be found on the site. The test station for airplane engines, a test tower for the spinning of airplanes – the so-called "Trudelturm", – and the wind channel have been turned into sculptural objects on the remodelled square.

The new institute is integrated into the orthogonal urban grid, but remains a solitary building. At this stage, the institute forms the border of the large open space of the former airfield. Its northern façade is of a consistent, smooth appearance with two pre-

Cross section

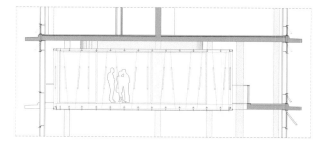

Section/elevation of seminar room

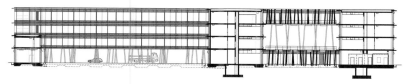

Longitudinal section

cisely cut out openings. A "landscape window" draws views into the landscaped courtyard scenario. With time, the southern façade will overgrow with vine.

The architects refer to their project as a "building experiment": It is a three-dimensional expression of the programme in which plan and elevation entail each other; at the same time, it constitutes an eco- logical experiment. The institute focuses on experi- mental materials science. Apart from standard labo- ratories, offices, and seminar rooms it comprises numerous special laboratories and an experimental lecture hall. Adjacent to the entrance foyer, shared facilities such as a lecture hall, seminar room, and a library are located. On the upper floors, laboratories

and offices are combined in functional units to ensure short distances between spaces for experiments and theoretical analysis.

The plan layout of the four-storey laboratory building constitutes a sophisticated network with double- loaded access corridors that service differentiated areas consisting of laboratories and study rooms. The conceptual variability allows flexibility and adaptabi- lity of the spaces.

To operate ecologically sound, technical equipment as well as maintenance costs were reduced. To achieve this, the architects developed tailored façade systems (double-layered façade, manual ventilation flaps, green

façade) and sustainable engineering solutions such as maximal use of thermal mass and rainwater use.

The green façade uses rainwater for adiabatic cooling in summer. In wintertime, it makes passive use of so- lar energy. The scaffolding for the vine consists of a mixture of steel and bamboo with suspended plant troughs of fibre cement in between. The planting pro- vides heat insulation in summer and passive use of solar energy in winter.

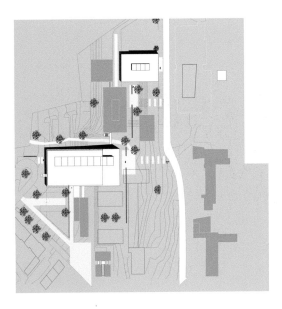

Site plan

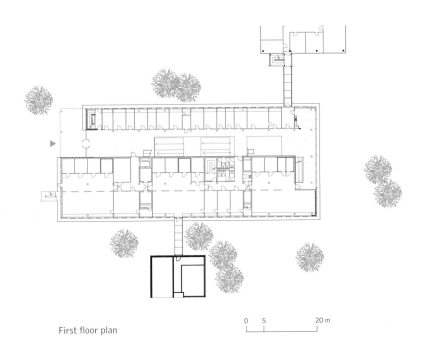

First floor plan

0   5   20 m

from left to right
Max Planck Institute for Developmental Biology under construction | The new campus is embedded harmoniously in its sourroundings | Erection cranes mark the construction site of the new Magnetic Resonance Centre for the Max Planck Institute for Biological Cybernetics | Model photograph showing characteristic wooden louvre structure

Max Planck Campus
Tübingen

Tübingen, Germany

Client	Max-Planck-Gesellschaft zur Förderung der Wissenschaften e.V.
Architects	Fritsch + Tschaidse Architekten
Construction period	2003-2005
Net floor area	4,600 m²
Cubic content	46,200 m³

Changing spatial requirements of two research institutes necessitated a comprehensive and fundamental redevelopment of the existing campus. The some decades old 7 ha campus is situated north of Tübingen's town centre and borders onto residential areas in the south and southwest, a public green space to the northeast (where building is prohibited since it serves as an aisle for fresh air for the town situated in a valley) and the University Observatory and a business park to the west.

The new spatial requirements resulted from current scientific developments at the Max Planck Institutes for Developmental Biology and Biological Cybernetics. Both institutes are extended; an already closed

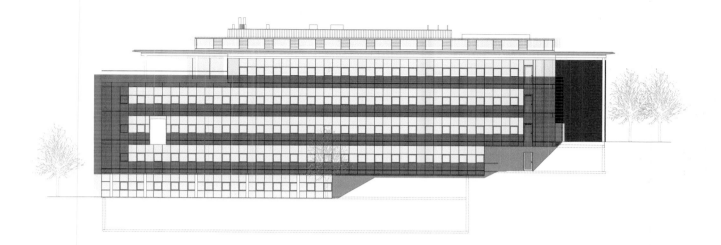

North elevation

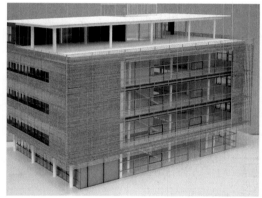

institute and existing buildings of both institutes, which are no longer useful for technical and operational reasons, will be demolished subsequently to open up new opportunities for future development. This may include additional extensions or the construction of further scientific facilities. The creation of such opportunities to promote the formation of scientific clusters and centres of excellence was an essential aspect of the urban redevelopment concept.

The new master plan was derived from the particular topography of the site sloping towards the south as well as the system of paths and the existing buildings. It proposes volumes positioned alternately parallel (existing buildings) and perpendicular (new buildings)

to the slope. This creates a well-proportioned sequence of interspaces between the buildings and makes the contours of the slope readable.

The urban design concept is also reflected by the terraces inside the central entrance hall of the Institute for Developmental Biology. The hall is the major circulation axis connecting different areas within the building and also forming a link to the business park to the west. The Institute for Biological Cybernetics receives two extensions: a laboratory building with a separate technical area for three magnetic resonance scanners and a test hall with large equipment for the simulation of "virtual reality".

The framed reinforced concrete structures have post-and-beam façades with a secondary structure of horizontal timber slats in front. The use of untreated timber and exposed concrete refers to the extensive research field of Life Sciences and the sloped and almost rural context of the campus.

Site plan

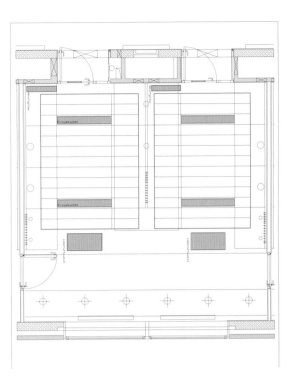

Typical laboratory

from left to right
View from the southwest | The wing on the south campus with central corridor | Glazed corner of entrance to the lecture hall building | Circulation area along the façade linking rooms for practical work

Institutes and Lecture Hall for Biology and Chemistry, University of Rostock

Rostock, Germany

Client	Finanzministerium Mecklenburg-Vorpommern
Architects	Volker Staab Architekten
Construction period	1997-2002
Net floor area	9,000 m²

A new campus site for University of Rostock in the Süd-stadt district is to provide an academic centre for environmental science, engineering, mathematics, and natural science. The particular urban idea for the campus is based on alternating building sites and green spaces. The architects developed a master plan reminiscent of a chessboard. Precisely defined green spaces take turns with staggered building sites.

The institutes for biology and chemistry, first to be built, are almost identical in terms of cubature, plan arrangement, and architectural design. Although both facilities have their main entrances facing Albert-Einstein-Straße, each entrance retains its own presence as a result of the chessboard-pattern.

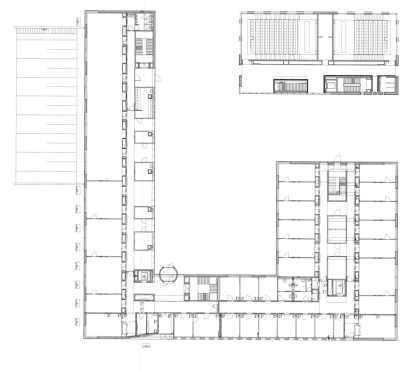

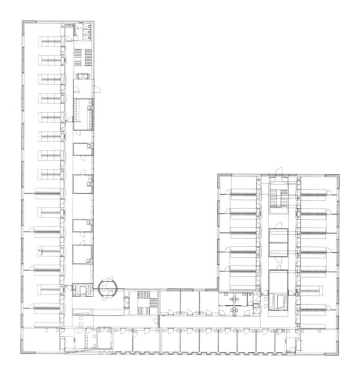

Ground floor plan

First floor plan

0 2   10 m

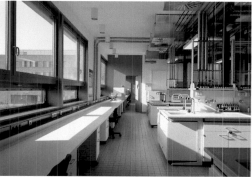

Both institutes show a classic courtyard scheme. The lecture hall buildings supplementing the two U-shaped institute buildings enhance the spatial qualities of the ensemble. These qualities are pronounced by the fact that the buildings' perimeters consistently cover the 60 x 60 m plots.

Due to their particular typology, the new institutes create a clear spatial hierarchy within and outside the complex. Both institutes and lecture hall buildings are accessed via the courtyard. Located in the centre of the buildings, the courtyard becomes the "foyer space" of the complex.

The structured façade composition clearly reveals the position of individual functional areas. Entrance and foyer areas of the buildings housing the lecture halls received full-height glazed corners. These prominent areas form an interesting contrast to the main entrance to the institutes, which lies opposite. The façades of the long laboratory slabs and entrances consist of ventilated facing brick layers and a flush-mounted glass-aluminium structure. Both laboratory wings, which are organised differently, allow for great flexibility in terms of room sizes and uses. The regularly equipped offices connecting the two wings are arranged across the corridor. The long and narrow laboratory wing has a classic central access corridor with laboratories facing west (away from the courtyard); secondary rooms like

storage, cell culture rooms, or air-conditioning rooms face the courtyard. This rhythmically sequenced and fully glazed corridor forms the visual link to the courtyard ("foyer space"). When seen from the courtyard, the frosted glass façade panels of the secondary spaces create an appealing chessboard pattern.

The shorter laboratory wing is based on a layout with two parallel double-loaded corridors. The enclosed central dark zone is penetrated by transverse corridors in order to ensure short distances between the laboratories. The different number of storeys (chemistry: three, biology: four storeys) and a few differences in terms of interior fit-out can be ascribed to the different programmes and the specific user requirements.

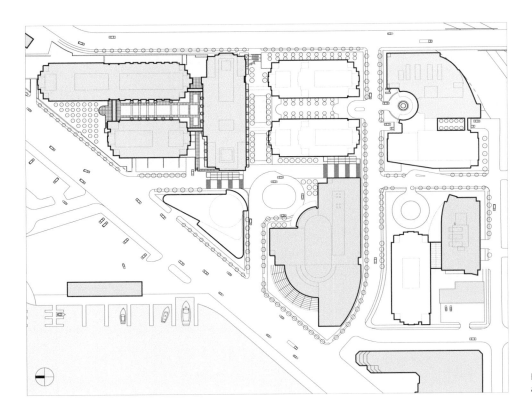

Masterplan: Main research building (phase I) and future buildings

Fred Hutchinson Cancer Research Center

Seattle, Washington, USA

Client	Columbus Center
Architects	Zimmer Gunsul Frasca Partnership
Completion	1994
Base area	6,100 m²

Faced with building restrictions on the former central Seattle location and the undesirable option of moving to the suburbs, scientists of the Cancer Research Center voted for the long-term development of a gradually extendable research campus on a site of more than 4.5 ha at the edge of Seattle's port. At the time of its acquisition, the site at the foot of Capitol Hill – flanked by water to the northwest and the southbound highway, located between the University of Washington campus and Seattle's CBD – was a mix of modest residential buildings and dilapidated industrial premises.

The three departments of the Cancer Research Center were to be realised in four building phases with the option of further extensions. A clearly arranged,

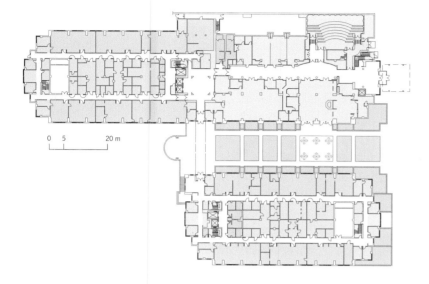

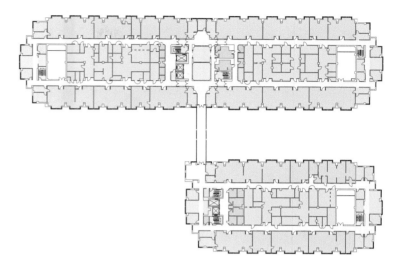

Ground floor plan

Typical floor plan: laboratories, offices, and the central dark zone are accessed with two corridors

from left to right
The new research centre is located at the foot of Capitol Hill in Seattle adjacent to the waterfront | View from the port to the Cancer Research Center | Windows in the laboratories and meeting rooms afford views of the port and the sea | Landscape architect Peter Walker, San Francisco, designed the strictly geometrical interior courtyard

dense and green campus was to be built. The original urban plan envisaged parallel volumes leading down from the hilltop to the waterside like steps of a giant stair. This in terms of urban planning plausible idea turned out to be too expensive. Consequently, the buildings were lined up along the existing roads to enable a partial use of the existing infrastructure.

The completed Basic Research Building for basic research (phase 1) comprises two simple rows of buildings. The urban layout of the premises, – which are located at the northern end of the site, is defined by the pocket-situation between the highway and the waterfront.

Due to the rainy climate a fully glazed steel bridge links both buildings on the first floor. It largely closes the courtyard off the sea, thus compromising the elementary relation to the water.

To allow utmost flexibility, an accessible service mezzanine level was allocated to each floor of the Basic Science Building. Thus, mechanical services of laboratories and other spaces can adapt to future changes at any time and any place. Generous central shafts supplement the mechanical engineering concept. This way, expenditures of time and funds for future redevelopment or refurbishment are to be cut down to less than 50 percent in comparison with conventional laboratory buildings.

The laboratories are embedded into an ordering system of offices, secondary spaces, storage rooms, and service pools. Even though any spot can be serviced, floor plans were strictly zoned. Laboratories are located along the façades to provide a maximum of daylight; spaces for equipment, measuring, and special use are located in the central zone, and offices are situated at the gable ends. From there, the building affords views of the masts of the schooners and yachts, and the sea, or the skyline of the nearby city.

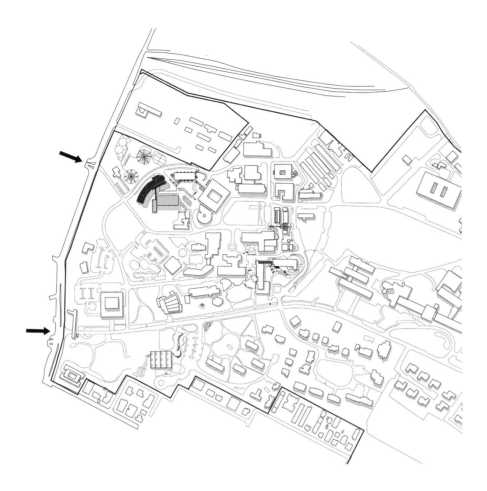

Site plan

from left to right
Along the jutting-out reinforced concrete wall runs the main circulation artery connecting all parts of the building | The western part of the building follows the curved ring road and closes the gap towards the Meyer Building | Curved horizontal lines and a white colouring characterise the design | The galleries in the atrium are to serve as informal meeting points supporting communication

Belfer Building for Molecular Genetics and Cancer Research, Weizmann Campus

Tel Aviv, Israel

Client	Weizmann Institute of Science, Israel
Architects	Moshe Zur Architects Urbanists & Town Planners
Completion	2003
Total floor area	5,000 m²
Laboratory area	2,000 m²

The laboratory building in Rehovot on the venerable campus of the Weizmann Institute supplements and completes the adjacent complex for transgenic research. Currently, the most important focal points of research are molecular genetics and cancer research, which are successfully developed with many international partners. The new building is situated at the main entrance to the campus and is linked to the existing Arnold Meyer Building via a glazed two-storey bridge.

The urban design is dominated by two formal elements: curved horizontal lines and a white colouring reminiscent of Erich Mendelsohn, designer of the Weizmann building on the campus. When seen from

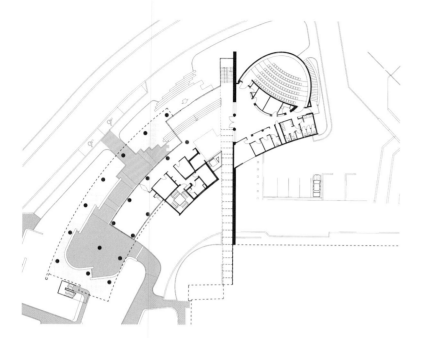

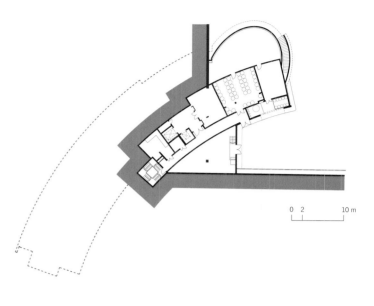

Entrance level plan

Typical floor plan

0 2   10 m

the west, the sweep of the building follows the curve of the ring road around the campus, defines the street space at this point and at the same time effortlessly closes the gap in front of the older Meyer Building. A shared courtyard is created that significantly structures the building ensemble. In order to preserve the visual continuity and the spatial relation to the palm garden surrounding the Meyer Building, the southern end of the new building was raised on stilts allowing the garden to continue underneath the building. The building takes advantage of the descending terrain by allocating extensive service areas for building infrastructure and a secluded delivery yard with parking in the northern part of the building.

The main architectural idea guiding the design is the curved institute building penetrating a slab serving as circulation "backbone". All functional areas of the layout were designed as integrated parts of this sweep.

As a reaction to the functional requirements of the programme the building is split into two main wings linked by a five-storey central entrance hall. It is the "communication hub" of the complex guiding the circulation between the new building and the Meyer building vertically and horizontally. From the atrium one reaches the shared central areas open to the public that are located adjacent to the lobby, e.g. the auditorium, the institute's library as well as the offices on the ground floor, administrative spaces, and the palm

garden. Galleries inside the atrium are designed to provide space for formal and informal meetings. Because of the panoramic views offered through the fully glazed atrium front, the galleries are also popular spots for breaks and recreation. The exposed concrete wall that juts out on both sides way beyond the building volume provides an interior projection area on the southern end of the hall. The full-height wall, which the transparent main staircase leans onto, cuts through the building. It is lit by the top strip of glass of the glazed staircase and in conjunction with steel bridges and galleries of the individual storeys forms the element linking all areas.

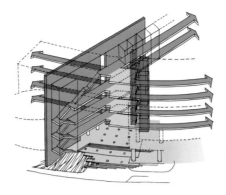

Open main staircase functioning as circulation spine

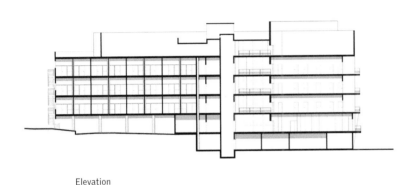

Elevation

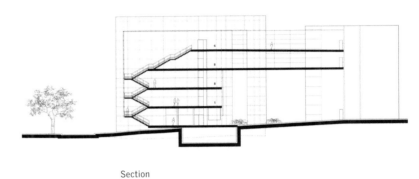

Section

The building consists of a basement, ground floor, three upper floors, and a partially recessed service floor on top, which connects to the shafts. While one wing accommodates the studies for theoretical research, staff offices, and various service and supplementary spaces, the other wing mainly provides laboratories for the different teams, rooms for genetic tissue, and the offices of the heads of team. A typical floor plan contains six laboratory units and eight service rooms. The rooms of the heads of team alternate with genetic tissue stores opposite the laboratories. Connecting doors between the laboratories support interaction between the scientists and allow the formation of research teams of various sizes. They provide for immediate contact and short distances between individual scientists as well as various small research teams and temporarily co-operating teams.

The laboratories are all based on the same modular grid and fitted with largely standardised and identical equipment. According to the work mode of the research teams, every laboratory comprises six work desks, which are well lit by the strip windows facing the ring road. The laboratories provide maximum state-of-the-art flexibility in terms of technical equipment. Every laboratory comprises an air extract connected to the central exhaust system for work with chemicals and solvents and also complies with the GLP guidelines for laboratories regarding air exchange, control of the extract coils, lighting levels,

protection gear, and the dimensions of work and circulation areas. Every floor has been designed as its own fire compartment.

The main building materials of the conventional reinforced concrete skeleton are anodised aluminium cladding (which is mainly used on the front and rear façades) and smooth exposed concrete for the large transverse wall slab, the auditorium, and individual building elements like columns and balustrades. The butt joints of the concrete formwork and the joints of the ventilated aluminium cladding panels are based on exactly the same grid and executed with high precision. The southern and northern gable ends of the building are clad with an aluminium post-and-beam

Concept of spatial relations

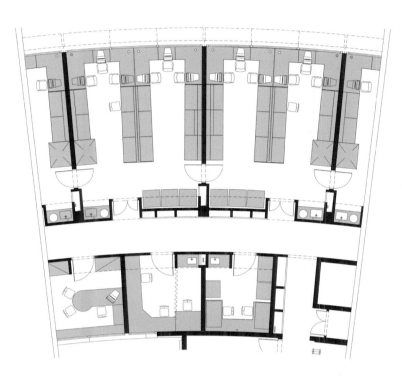

Two laboratory modules

from left to right
The colour scheme and architectural language of the exterior
also dominates the interior | Transparent five-storey central en-
trance hall connecting the research activities with campus life |
The entrance hall serves as a hinge between the two building
parts containing laboratories and offices respectively

structure with obscured glass infillings. The atrium
received a curtain wall with low-energy glazing.

Both the interior and the sculptural exterior have been
formed to support the architectural idea of the building down to the last detail. An abundance of design
elements – the curved main façades, the transverse
wall, the glazed façade of the entrance hall, the circular auditorium – create a holistic architectural composition, whose individual components form a well-
proportioned whole, a special place designed in the
spirit of research that provides a great sense of identity and a stimulating working atmosphere.

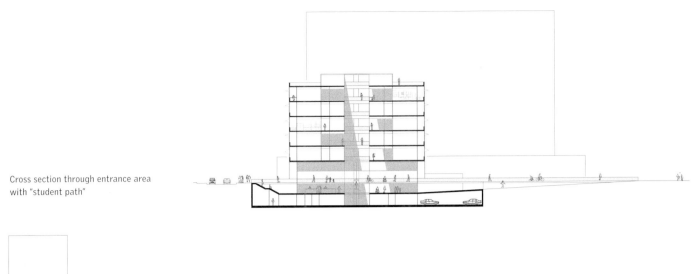

Cross section through entrance area
with "student path"

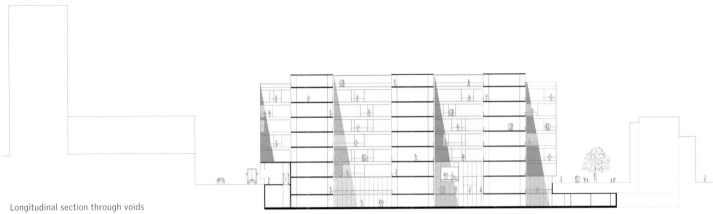

Longitudinal section through voids

from left to right
Entrance area with penetrating "student path" | The perforated
exterior aluminium skin with upward-folding solar blinds creates
a rational and clean façade | The double-height foyer space with
the integrated footpath is conducive to communication | Nine-
storey voids provide daylight

Laboratory Building
of Cologne University
Hospital

Cologne, Germany

Client	Klinikum der Universität zu Köln
Architects	Heinrich Wörner + stegepartner
Completion	2004–2005
Total floor area	21,000 m²
Net floor area	14,500 m²
Cubic content	80,000 m³

The architectural competition for this laboratory building was held by Cologne University Hospital. The urban and functional requirements of the brief posed
special challenges for its design. It accommodates
three research centres under one roof: the Zentrum
für Molekularmedizin Köln (ZMMK), the Zentrum
für Genomforschung (ZFG) – both of them academic
facilities – and the Cell Center Cologne (CCC) as a
private institute.

The site offered relatively little space for the implementation of the required programme. It is bisected
by an important circulation route – the so-called "student path" – which constitutes the main pedestrian
and cycling link between the hospital and the Cologne

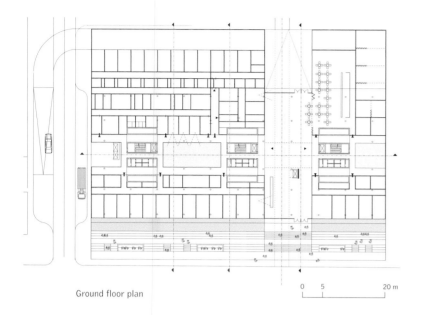

Ground floor plan

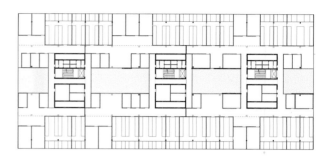

Typical floor plan

0   5   20 m

University campus. As the brief explicitly asked for a common main entrance for the three institutes the design had to ensure that the "student path" would not split the entrance area into two separate zones.

The conceptual design is based on a simple object-type building at the crossing of the street and the "student path". The course of the pedestrian path is elegantly integrated into a two-storey joint foyer space. At the same time, this solution delineates the desired synergetic exchange of private and university based research.

The homogeneous façades consistently reflect the idea of a monolithic solitaire: all sides of the building are

clad with perforated aluminium panels leading to an almost septic technical expression. The upward-folding solar blinds provide for a vivid and suspenseful composition. The extremely compact volume with its highly functional and flexible interior has two access corridors per floor. It is composed of two parallel volumes with an enclosed nine-storey void containing galleries providing areas for communication and exchange of ideas. This space supports the interdisciplinary co-operation and interaction of the different research teams.

Between the three central cores containing vertical circulation, service shafts, and sanitary spaces, dark rooms such as cold-storage rooms, equipment, and

storage rooms are located. Along the main façades, laboratories and their respective working areas and offices alternate. This modular structure allows for flexible management of external lettings and the allocation of variously sized groups of rooms to changing users.

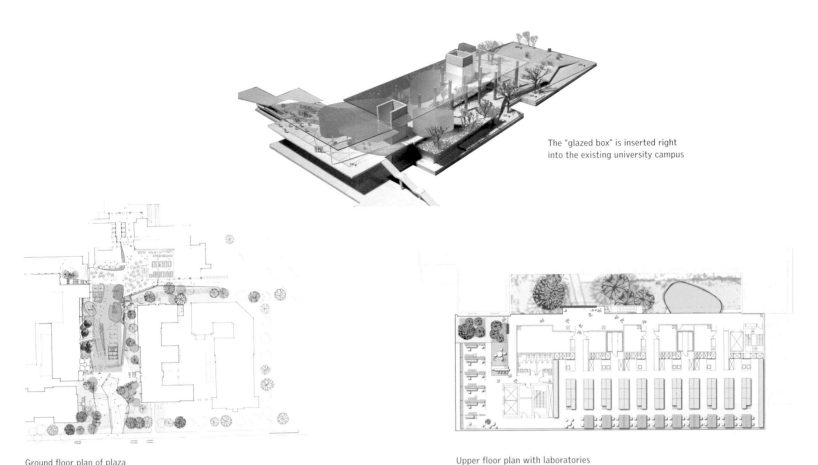

The "glazed box" is inserted right
into the existing university campus

Ground floor plan of plaza

Upper floor plan with laboratories

from left to right
Site plan | On the south side, the new building with its plaza on
the ground floor will provide a bustling link to central Toronto |
The design is based on transparency and openness | The twelve-
storey building is to give a powerful display of the created work
environment and communicate genome research to the public

Centre for Cellular and
Biomolecular Research

Toronto, Canada

Client	University of Toronto
Architects	Behnisch, Behnisch & Partner Architekten architectsAlliance
Completion	2005
Total floor area	20,500 m²

The scientific facilities of University of Toronto are
among the leading institutes in the field of cellular
and biomolecular research. Altogether, 400 scientists
will work there. The main idea of the design concept
refers to a multidisciplinary work philosophy and de-
velops a spatial design under the heading "collaborat-
ing/co-operating/communicating".

The new building will be built at the heart of the
existing campus between King's College and Queen's
Park. It has been designed as a transparent twelve-
storey box floating above a public area. The ground
floor zone, treated differently from the main volume
above, is not governed by technical laboratory requirements but was rather designed according to land-

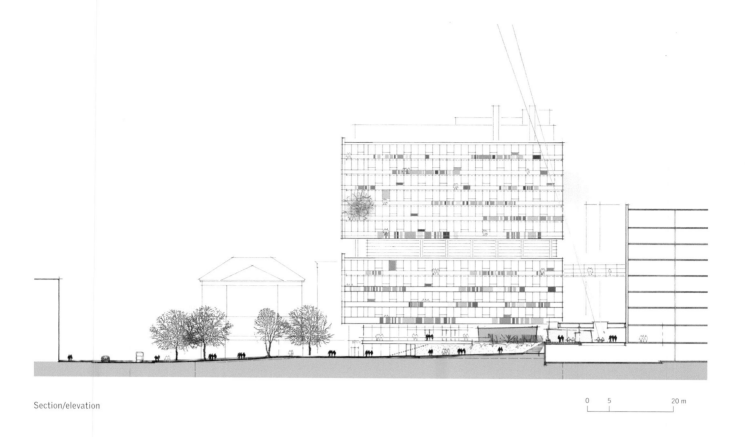

Section/elevation

0 5   20 m

scaping aspects. An essential part of the concept is the idea of preserving the existing public path network which links the campus to the city centre and Queen's Park. The adjacent building to the west is connected to the new institute by a transparent roof, creating a multi-storey green atrium that also joins the open ground floor with the laboratory areas above.

The typical floor plans comprise a core zone with open plan laboratories with work desks allocated behind the façades. To the west, a circulation area with lounge qualities fostering communication is located in front of the service area. The workplaces for theoretical research are arranged at the south

gable end. Multi-storey green spaces add spatial differentiation and support informal interrelations.

The fully glazed façade provides optimal daylight levels for laboratories and offices. It is supplemented by an intelligent daylight control system. In order to handle the varying climatic conditions on the south side and to allow for a partially natural ventilation of the offices allocated here, a glazed double façade was installed. The integrated solar blinds and the interior windows can be controlled and opened by the users themselves.

The technical building infrastructure runs in horizontal ducts starting from two technical floors located

at medium building height and on the roof. Due to their specific technical requirements the laboratory areas receive mechanical ventilation. Depending on the respective technical requirements of the laboratories – for instance the future use as a dry-lab – supplementary natural ventilation is also considered an option.

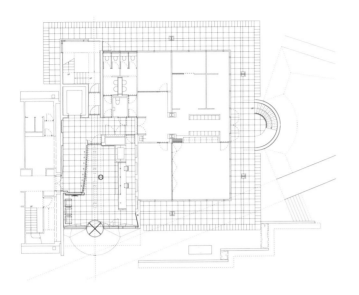

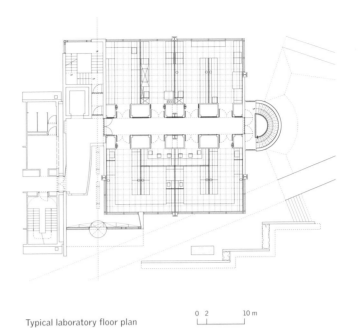

Ground floor plan

Typical laboratory floor plan

0 2   10 m

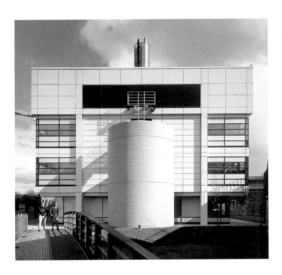

from left to right
In the garden, the main axis leads to a semi-cylindrical structure containing the escape stair | Even the arrangement and design of the cooling and air-handling units on the roof reflect the noble yet simple nature of the building | View from the south: the main wing received a light-grey metal cladding with black joints | White lab volume and atrium | Typical laboratory

Male Urological Cancer Research Centre

Sutton, UK

Client	Institute of Cancer Research
Architects	Copping Lindsay Architects
Completion	2000
Net floor area	800 m²
Cubic content	1,000 m³

The new research centre was built on a tight site in a bland urban context and involved the connection of an adjacent existing building. Its architectural nobility fulfils an important function: While the other buildings on Sutton Campus of Royal Marsden NHS Trust Hospital keep a modest and unspectacular profile, the research centre was funded by a charity organisation via fundraising campaigns. Hence, the donators' commitment is to visibly and physically manifest itself in a respectable, strong, and unique architecture.

As a result of the direct connection of the new building with its adjacent three-storey neighbour a secluded garden could be created. A surprisingly rustic wooden

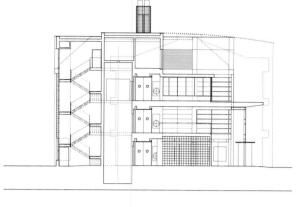

Section

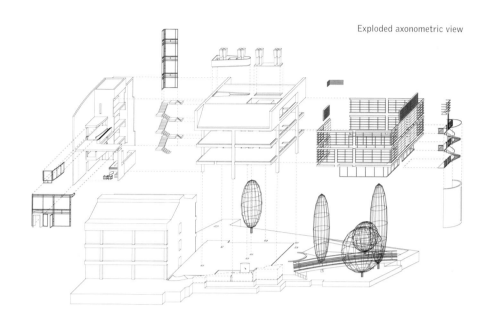

bridge crosses the lawn diagonally and – diving through underneath a recessed building corner – leads to the main entrance. Approaching the building on this path from the garden the onlooker is suddenly confronted with the new building whose materials –light-grey sheet metal cladding with black joints, neatly processed in-situ concrete painted grey, clear and obscured glazing, slender anthracite window profiles – support the elegance and clarity of the design concept.

The complex institute building is heavily equipped with mechanical services. On the two laboratory floors, the functional and technical requirements were met with a consistent plan arrangement of all

facilities on both sides of a central corridor. The laboratories comprise large individual service shafts. Their furnishings follow the clear design of the architecture. The quality of the laboratory environment was improved by the use of translucent glass spandrel panels behind which work desks are situated. The technical control rooms are located on the top floor. On the ground floor, studies for theoretical work with a normal degree of technical services are to be found; it also houses a small double-height entrance hall containing an open gallery with direct access to the adjacent building.

The steel structure of the cubic volume has no corner columns. The horizontal façade pattern supports the volumetric quality of the building, whereas all other elements like the entrance, stairs, and the housing of mechanical services were treated as individual architectural elements enhancing the building's elegance. The entire urban context benefits from the architecture of this building, which prefers thorough elegant detailing to loud and superficial effects.

Ground floor plan

0   5   20 m

from left to right
Terracotta-clad service towers separate the four building volumes of the quarter-circular layout | View of the strictly horizontally structured metal façade | Writing desks allocated to the façades and a glazed curtain wall provide optimal work conditions | Large open plan laboratories have a capacity of approx. 40 work places

Biosciences Building, University of Liverpool

Liverpool, UK

Architects	David Morley Architects
Construction period	2002-2004
Total floor area	14,800 m²

Genetic science increasingly brings together disciplines such as biochemistry, molecular medicine, plant biology, and environmental ecology. This trend manifests itself through the integration of formerly separate sections of the biological faculty within one building.

The site is located at the prominent north-eastern corner of the 2.2 ha university campus. It occupies an important location within the city as it is also situated on a main artery and marks the eastern entrance into Liverpool. A main axis of the campus determines the layout of the access route to the new forecourt. The building consists of four orthogonal and three wedge-shaped volumes with four full storeys and a technical floor each. They are arranged in

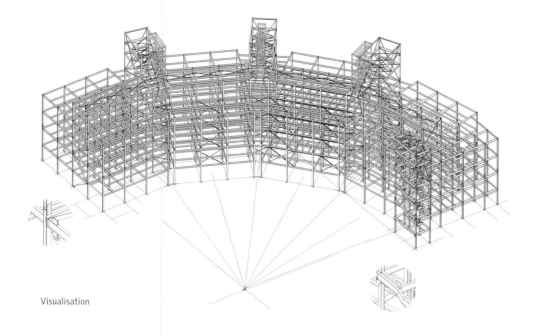

Visualisation

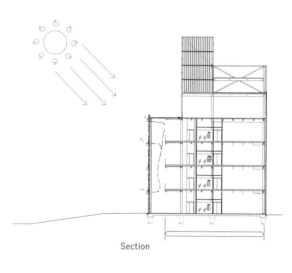

Section

a quarter-circle around the forecourt that is enclosed on three sides. At the north-eastern corner, the new facility is linked to a refurbished teaching building with a "hinge". The overall complex accentuates its location at the campus corner and creates a unique place with a strong sense of identity.

Apart from the spaces for Biosciences (approx. 8,000 m²) the brief also called for an Innovation Centre (Mersey Bio, approx. 1,800 m²). The centre features its own entrance. It occupies the outer building volume with flexible laboratory areas arranged along a double-loaded corridor on the upper floors and office and service areas on the ground floor. The Biosciences area consists of a total of eight (two per

floor) large open plan laboratory zones and four special laboratory zones in the central zone. The large laboratories with a capacity of 40 work places each form the "home base" for every research team; the special laboratories house shared facilities. The large "home bases" with open plan labs flank these shared facilities consisting of special equipment laboratories and secondary spaces. Lifts situated in the wedge-shaped building volumes link all levels and encourage a high degree of social interaction and co-operation. Access areas are under surveillance. A linear technical installation core provides flexible and accessible services. Outside the security area of the laboratories, naturally ventilated offices are orientated towards the courtyard. Little bays near the main entrance of

the central volume as well as little atrium spaces near both main laboratory entrances on all floors further encourage social interaction between scientists.

The framed steel construction with its horizontally structured metal façades makes the individual building volumes readable and highlights the highly equipped character of the building by means of oversized structures for air-intakes and extracts above the wedge-shaped blocks.

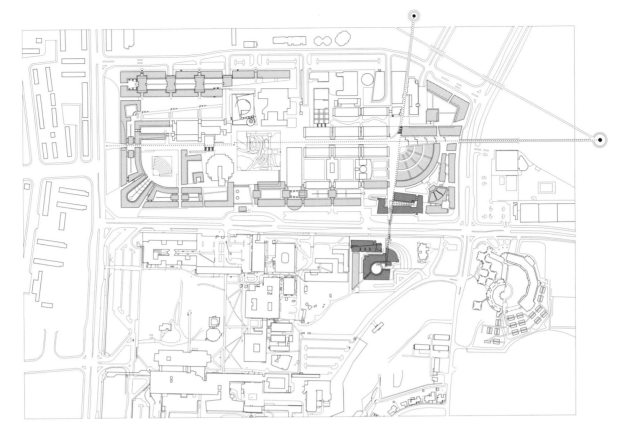

Site plan with dominant lines of reference

Life Sciences Complex, Ben Gurion University

Be'er Sheeva, Negev, Israel

Client	Ben Gurion University
Architects	Ada Karmi-Melamede & Partners
Completion	2001
Total floor area	14,500 m²
Net floor area	7,000 m²

The Life Sciences Complex is located at the fringe of the Negev Desert. The premises are located at the southeastern corner of the main campus; to the west a number of gardens follow at lower levels. To the south, the site is linked to the new Medical School Building via a bridge. To the north, the scheme connects to an access route that grows wider like a funnel. The route defines the position of the individual buildings in relation to each other, forms the base of the urban layout and circulation within the complex.

The three to six-storey complex comprises three closely arranged and connected building volumes grouped around a shared courtyard. Each volume accommodates a different independent institute:

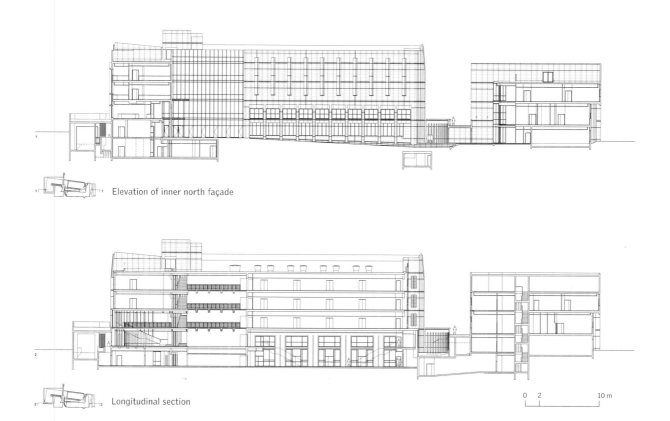

Elevation of inner north façade

Longitudinal section

0 2   10 m

from left to right
Main façade with narrow window slots indicating the laboratories behind | A first view towards the courtyard from the campus square | The strikingly austere, curved shape of the foyer space of the Institute of Applied Biosciences | The generous and light-flooded greenhouse laboratory at roof level | The courtyard offers a quiet, relaxed atmosphere as well as shade and cooling for the adjacent offices

to the north, the University Department of Life Sciences, to the south and east the Institute of Biotech Applied Research, and to the west the Life Sciences Student Laboratories. All three institutes do research in the field of water balance of organisms under desert conditions from a microbiological, physiological, and ecological point of view.

The independent volumes of each facility comprise their own faculty offices, laboratories, and lecture and seminar rooms and share a basement level with facilities used by all institutes. The resulting synergy effects help to reduce costs for expensive scientific apparatuses and considerable maintenance costs. The close proximity of different individual disciplines encourages the efficient exchange of ideas and supports flexible co-operation.

More than the notion of scientific co-operation and communication, the extreme desert climate defines the introverted architectural expression of the complex. In keeping with the functional unity of the building, the consistent pigmented in-situ concrete is to create a monolithic and sculptural appearance. Narrow window slots penetrate the compact building envelope and dim down the light. Hence, the seminar and laboratory spaces – which are lit artificially and hardly require daylight anyway – could be positioned next to the exterior façade. The offices open up towards the courtyard, which provides shade and natural cooling.

The laboratories were designed with particular attention to a modular structure that can be flexibly adapted to future layouts from individual laboratories to open plan spaces.

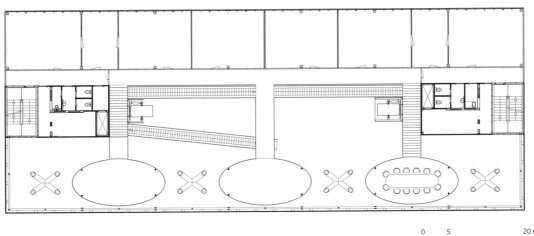

Third floor plan (offices and atrium)

0   5   20 m

from left to right
Einsteinstraße: to the right, the Centre for Information and Media Technology to the left, the administration wing of Bessy II | A generous atrium and strip windows determine the elevation towards Einsteinstraße | The central stair in the atrium leads to the first floor. Glazed lifts are located near the cores | Platforms are suspended between the columns; in conjunction with footbridges they support communication

Centre for Information and Media Technology, Adlershof Science and Technology Park

Berlin, Germany

Client	WISTA-Management GmbH, Berlin
Architects	Architectenbureau cepezed b.v.
Completion	1999
Net floor area	3,200 m²
Cubic content	28,600 m³

After a changeful history, a new "Science Park" was erected in Berlin-Adlershof on the architectural remnants of this research location rich in tradition. Adlershof is supposed to create an urban alternative to the common research, high-tech and business parks at the periphery. The concept comprises a mixture of research, work, living, urban culture, leisure and sports and a landscape park at its centre. The centre does not incorporate any complex production processes. The high-tech building mainly serves as a place for theoretical research. Consequently, the building radiates the abstract character of this type of work. Generous communal areas encourage the individual enterprises to establish synergies and make vital contacts.

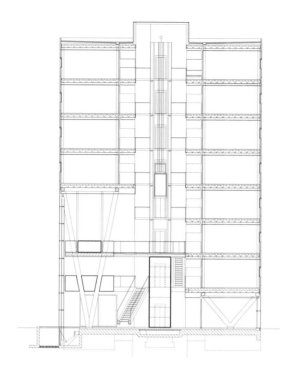

Cross section: the atrium gets narrower on the 4th floor
and splits the Centre into two office wings

The Centre is situated parallel to one of the area's main access routes. As the master plan stipulates a maximum building height of just 14 m, the building was originally to match the height of the office and administration building of Bessy II across the street. Since the resulting cubature would not have provided the required 3,200 m² of net floor area, the architects proposed to raise the office wing facing the street to a 14 m height by putting it on V-shaped steel columns. Thus, height and volume of the resulting hall – or negative volume – corresponded to the dimensions of the opposite Bessy II building. The new research building steps out of the strict alignment of the adjacent buildings. On the other hand, the recessed solid interior façade of the Centre refers to this

alignment and even pronounces its very existence on an urban scale.

The different parts of the edifice can be clearly read. The 14 m atrium forms the heart of the building. At the centre between the two building parts, it rises up to a generous roof light. Both building halves are supported by V-shaped pairs of columns – four storeys high on the side facing the street and one storey high on the northwestern side. This creates the impression of lightweight buildings hovering above the ground, only touching it at eight points.

The first to third storeys can be accessed via single-flight stairs. The offices situated to the rear of the upper floors are accessed via galleries, which are linked to the meeting areas by bridges. Glazed walls create visual connections between the office corridors and the atrium. The top floors provide space for meeting rooms permitting open plan space arrangements.

Site plan

Parque Tecnológico IMPIVA

Castellón, Spain

Client	Regional government of Valencia
Architects	Carlos Ferrater, Carlos Bento, Jaime Sanahuja
Construction period	1993-1995

The project initiated by local Valencia government strives to provide an attractive location for technologically innovative enterprises mainly of the locally important ceramic industry. To solve the task, the design concept had to react to a heterogeneous and varied programme: Laboratories, workshops, experimental hall buildings, offices, sales areas, and meeting rooms had to be arranged in flexible units and equipped with specific mechanical services.

The main challenge of the project was handling the complex functional programme and also the great architectural freedom since the site almost completely lacked any relevant urban and spatial context.

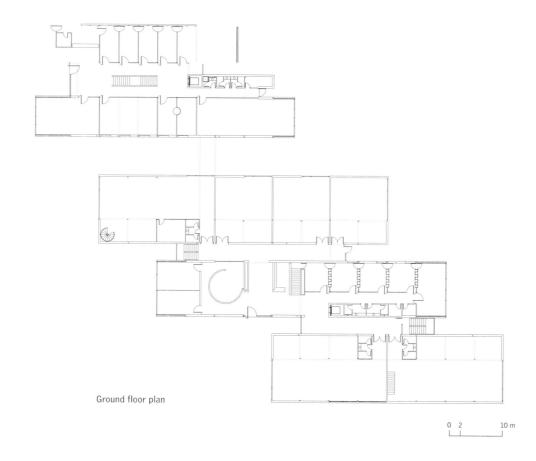

Ground floor plan

0 2 10 m

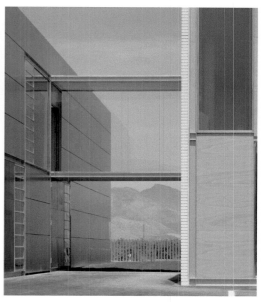

from left to right
Front panorama of the technology park with the stepped arrangement of the cubes | Interior with reception and transition to the adjacent part of the complex | View of glazed light-weight footbridge

The result is a structurally and formally unusual and exciting building. It is located at the crossing of two major roads – the palatial boulevard leading to the port and the ring road to Castellón. A number of building volumes are arranged parallel and shifted successively, poignantly interpreting the urban context and highlighting the street corner.

The architectural solution is unique in separating the required areas from each other and grouping them in a number of individual buildings. The resulting pattern is reminiscent of commercial barcodes. Construction, proportions, and materials used are governed by this basic concept.

The minimal distances between the volumes also order the inside, by enabling natural lighting and strengthening the individuality of each volume by exposing its corners.

The exterior appearance is to reflect the technology-orientated, innovative energies of the young enterprises. Particular façade materials were allocated to particular interior functions: aluminium for the laboratories, experimental hall buildings, and workshops; chessboard-like timber cladding for the office spaces at the gable ends. This use of materials is also followed through on the interior: maple veneered panels dominate the representative rooms; exposed sandlime

brick is used for the industrial areas. The holistic overall appearance of the complex with its individual character is supported by the simplified details of the structure and interior fit-out.

Sketch

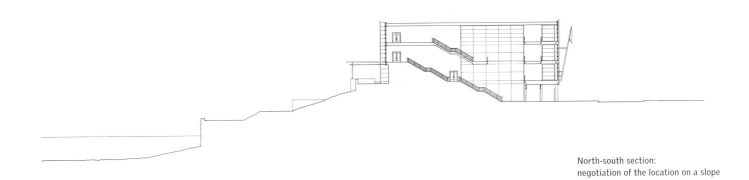

North-south section:
negotiation of the location on a slope

from left to right
At night, the glazed façade areas reveal the functions (laboratories/circulation areas) very clearly through transparent and solid surfaces | The high-tech building affords views of Pittsburgh | East façade dominated by flat and corrugated panels | Yellow steel louvres shade the south-facing offices | The steel-framed light-flooded atrium

Center for Biotechnology and Bioengineering

Pittsburgh, Pennsylvania, USA

Client	State Government of Pennsylvania
Architects	Bohlin Cywinski Jackson
Completion	1993
Total floor area	8,350 m²

The building on the former site of Jones and Laughlin Steel Company sets the stage for a new economical era that is to follow the decline of Pittsburgh's steel industry. It is the first realised scheme out of six proposed research centres designed to attract enterprises of all fields of biomedicine in a medium-term perspective.

The technology park is located on a narrow site between Monogehela River and rail tracks on the outskirts of the city. To the north, the main façades of all buildings are arranged linearly along the same building line. The new facility is the first completed project and forms the entrance to the research park: visitors are guided onto the premises through an arcade par-

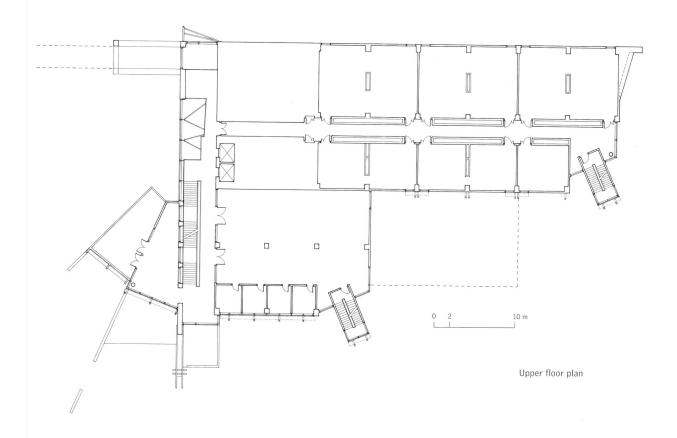

Upper floor plan

allel to the building line. The main entrance to the building itself is located at the northwestern gable end.

The building programme called for an interactive environment supporting the communication between scientists, visitors, and clients. The laboratories were to adapt quickly and flexibly to changing requirements and the needs of different users. The plan layout shows zones of varying size and divisibility that can either be equipped with supplementary services or not. The laboratory wing has a traditional layout with a central corridor and double service walls.

Since the old foundations of the steel plant restricted the depth of the new building's foundations and due

to the extent of the required services, the entire mechanical engineering equipment had to be accommodated on the ground floor. The alternative to put them on the top floor was ruled out because ventilation from bottom to top made more sense and laboratory equipment is sensitive to vibrations.

The various internal uses are reflected in the façades. The laboratory zone in the north presents itself as a largely solid façade with punched windows; the office zone received generous strip windows and solar blinds fixed to exterior steel frames. Silver-blue steel panels protect the building from the elements. The fully glazed and highly transparent entrance atrium with single flight stairs linking all floors forms the joint circula-

tion hub for the various start-up enterprises. At night, the vertical and horizontal linking elements are illuminated and demonstrate openness while the largely solid laboratory façades express the contemplative nature of research.

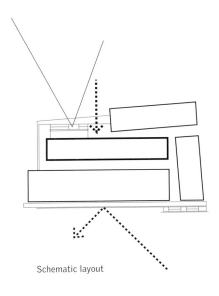

Schematic layout

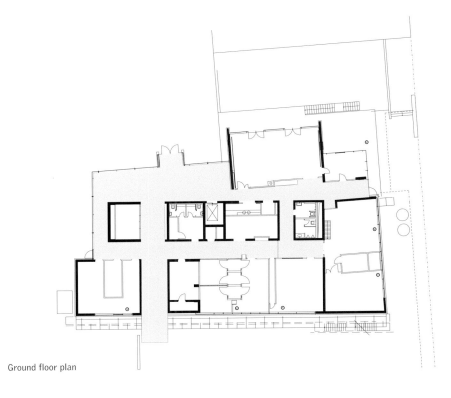

Ground floor plan

from left to right
Transparent façade facing the courtyard | The outer layer of the noise screen towards Budapester Straße consists of glass, the inner of metal mesh | Interior view of laboratory | Gap separating plant room

Max Bergmann Centre of Biomaterials

Dresden, Germany

Client	Institut für Polymerforschung, Dresden
Architects	Brenner & Partner Architekten und Ingenieure, Brenner - Hammes - Krause
Completion	2002
Total floor area	5,000 m²
Net floor area	2,300 m²
Cubic content	19,500 m³

The Max Bergmann Centre is a joint venture of the Institute for Polymer Research Dresden and the Technical University of Dresden. The biochemical, cell biological/microbiological, and physical/chemical laboratories serve the multi-disciplinary co-operation of changing research teams. Apart from the actual research activities carried out on the premises, the centre provides information and educational work and aims to rouse the public's interest in new biomedical technologies, scientific trends, and the latest medical developments.

The differentiated volume with its lively façades render the new building a landmark on this significant inner city site which used to be a gap in the dense

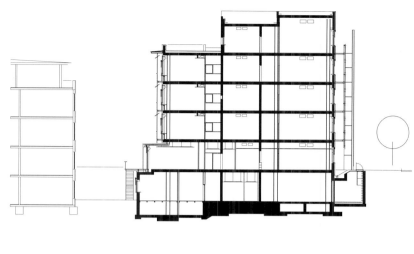

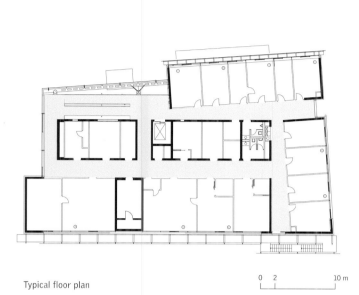

Typical floor plan

0 2   10 m

Cross section

existing building fabric. As an articulate structure full of architectural suspense it reacts to the adjacent context: It defines and supplements the street-space of Budapester Straße with its large-scale façade elements whose layers consist of few elements. The façade layers facing the courtyard consist of smaller and more varied elements. Here, places were created that encourage visitors and users to linger, to "recharge their batteries" and engage in lively exchange.

The urban context, which is reflected in the building's exterior, also finds its expression in the interior layout. The laboratories face northwest, i.e. towards the noisy street. A noise screen in front of the escape walkways also helps to reduce the relatively low remain-

ing solar radiation on this side. The offices and studies for theoretical work face the quiet green courtyard. They received exterior maintenance gangways and exterior solar blinds as shading devices. Also positioned on this side are a seminar room with an attached southern terrace and the full height foyer space with an open stairway. Fully visible from inside and outside, this stairway serves as vertical communication and circulation axis.

The building is a reinforced concrete frame structure with a solid core providing stiffness and thermal mass.

Last not least, the desired transparent, accessible, and inviting atmosphere was achieved by the façade

layers made of different materials such as pre-patinated copper, structural glazing, and weaved metal mesh which change their appearance according to the prevailing light and point of view.

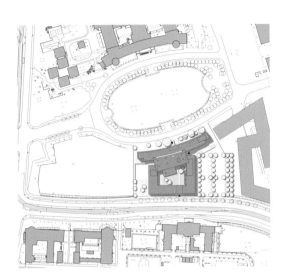

Site plan

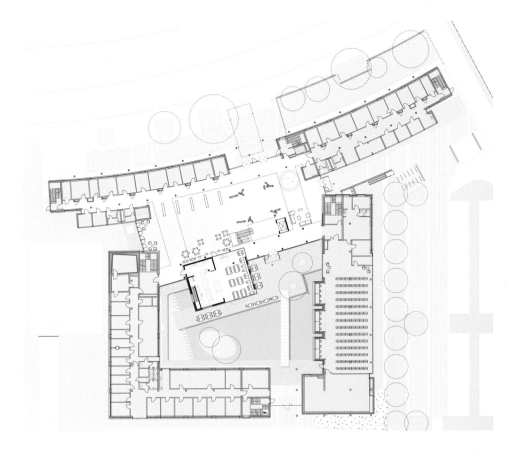

Ground floor plan showing landscaping

from left to right
View from the north with clearly demarcated residential top floor | Façade towards Deutscher Platz with main entrance | Auditorium on stilts within the entrance hall | The communicative and airy ramps of the entrance hall are also used for exhibitions, workshops, and other academic events

Max Planck Institute for Evolutionary Anthropology

Leipzig, Germany

Client	Max-Planck-Gesellschaft zur Förderung der Wissenschaften e.V.
Architects	SSP Architekten Schmidt-Schicketanz und Partner GmbH
Construction period	2000-2003
Net floor area	7,800 m²
Cubic content	83,000 m³

250 scholars, natural and social scientists – mainly molecular biologists, zoologists, psychologists, and linguists – work together in this institute. Co-operating in a unique way, anthropological research is pursued through the analysis of genes, cultures, cognitive abilities, languages, and social systems of human populations and groups of primates closely related to man.

In the new building, three research divisions with a high degree of mechanical services are separated from three study and office divisions that do not require more than average services. The formation of functional units – comparable zones were put together and stacked above each other – enables an economic operation of the complex.

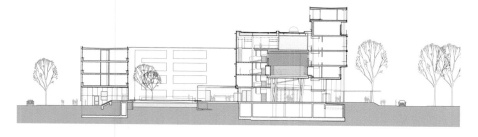

Section

East elevation

The institute's site is dominated by Deutscher Platz, a square important on an urban scale. This public green space marks the entrance to the old trade fair site and is situated exactly on the axis between the New Town Hall in the historical centre and the Völkerschlacht Memorial on the eastern outskirts of Leipzig. A dense row of trees underlines the oval shape. The design of the institute directly relates to this context: to the German Library in the northeast that traces the oval square and to a U-shaped institute building located in the southwest opposite a major thoroughfare.

A curved six-storey volume, containing very diverse functions like laboratories, offices, technical spaces, and apartments faces Deutscher Platz. A three-storey building with reduced ceiling height and a central corridor that accommodates theoretical study rooms was placed facing Zwickauer Straße.

The size and shape of the entrance hall that can be accessed directly from the main entrance at Deutscher Platz was consistently derived from the depth of the site and the geometry of the context. This space is dominated by a freely positioned auditorium raised on stilts, by the slender structure of a ramp system bridging the various levels, and by the views of the water pond in the courtyard. The hall is the building's circulation hub and can be used for multi-functional events or exhibitions on the ground floor.

While the laboratory façade and the crowning residential floor are fully glazed towards Deutscher Platz, the offices received a ventilated aluminium cladding structured by windows. The casement windows of the stucco façades facing the thoroughfare to the southwest received additional glazing for sound protection.

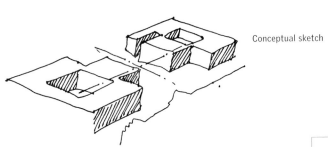
Conceptual sketch

Urban location

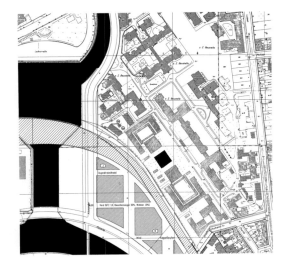

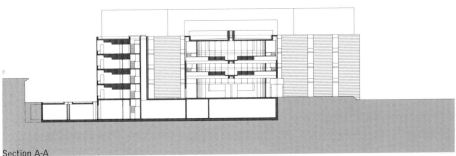
Section A-A

from left to right
View from the hall towards the historic environs | The main entrance façade made of red concrete blocks links the building to the historic context | The library is located in the four-storey entrance cube opposite the central shared facilities | In the hall area, the heaviness associated with stone is opposed by elements that suggest lightweight, volatile qualities | Central aisle of laboratory, with workbenches, worktops on either side, and writing desks next to the façade

Max Planck Institute for Infection Biology und German Arthritis Research Centre

Berlin, Germany

Client	Max-Planck-Gesellschaft zur Förderung der Wissenschaften e.V.
Architects	Deubzer König Architekten
Construction period	1997-2000
Total floor area	21,000 m²
Net floor area	8,000 m²
Cubic content	91,000 m³

Since its inauguration in 1992, the Max Planck Institute for Infection Biology has been committed to basic research in the fields of immunology, molecular and cellular biology. The envisaged co-operation with local universities and hospitals was a major factor for the selection of the site in Berlin's Mitte district. The institute maintains particularly close links to the German Arthritis Research Centre, which occupies about one third of the shared building. The building is located on a prominent plot north of the River Spree that is part of the premises of the Charité – the famous medical faculty of the Humboldt University of Berlin. The architects proposed a dense urban building due to the shortage of space. A compact, nearly square edifice houses an atrium and most of the required

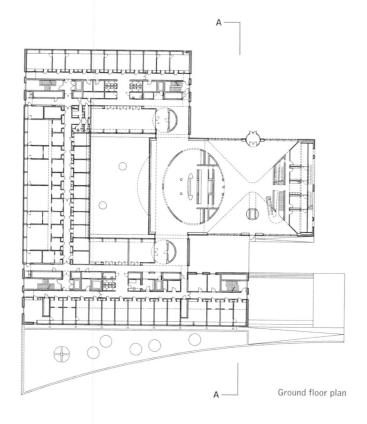

A

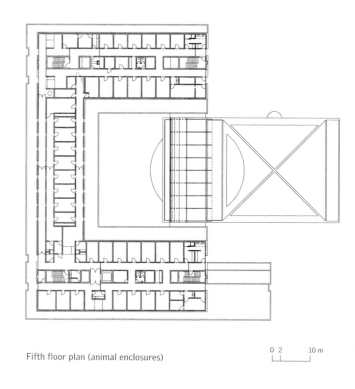

Ground floor plan

Fifth floor plan (animal enclosures)

0 2   10 m

primary floor spaces – above all the highly equipped laboratories and special research areas. The six-storey main building comprises four full storeys plus one service floor and an attic level for animal keeping. The experimental departments of the institute are placed one above the other, each occupying its own floor.

The particular range of research activities in this building called for a special architectural solution. For instance, the areas for research with pathogens have been arranged in an inner high security ring, which can only be accessed via safety gates. In section, the laboratories are designed to permit a maximum of daylight into the spaces. Daylight can penetrate deeply into the laboratories and the exterior fabric is reduced to only a few essential components.

The fully glazed aluminium post-and-beam façade affords generous views from the outside into the modular laboratories and offices. On the other hand, the entrance area and gable façades made of red concrete blocks refer to the architectural character and colours of the surrounding listed historical buildings. This balance with the existing urban fabric is an essential feature of the new research building.

The central entrance cube with its light-flooded sculptural hall supplements the laboratory zones. This core space merges two areas: the central communal facilities facing the inner courtyard and the administrative and library area.

The heaviness of the concrete block of the entrance hall is attenuated by elements that let the visitor associate something "lightweight", "ephemeral": the "closed" research area opens up like a tent towards the main entrance, the communal facilities. Thus, it becomes a linking element between inside and outside – a place of reception and social interaction, for symposiums, discussions and presentations of research results.

Topography

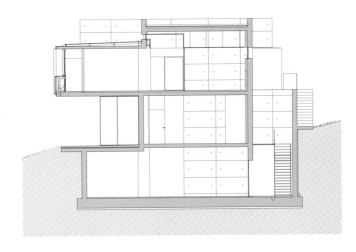

Cross section

Seen from the west, the building shows its harmonious integration into the slope and views of Barcelona.

Barcelona Botanical Institute

Barcelona, Spain

Client	Higher Council for Scientific Research
Architects	Carlos Ferrater, Joan Guibernau, Elena Mateu
Completion	2003
Net floor area	3,800 m²
Cubic content	4,600 m³

The Barcelona Botanical Institute is prominently situated on the highest point of the new Botanical Garden on Mt. Montjuic – 150 m above sea level and far above the city of Barcelona, right on the Olympic Ring.

The long, linear volume cuts into the mountain and forms a conspicuous hinge between the horizontal contour line of the mountain and the sloping topography. It affords spectacular views of Barcelona and establishes a prominent landmark. Despite the reinforced concrete supports and cross walls that rhythmically structure the rigid volume, it appears as if floating above the terrain when seen from the south. This effect is intensified by the recessed ground floor and the change of material. The top floor seems to

South elevation

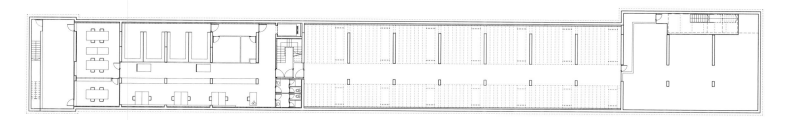

Basement floor plan

The volume suspended between the cross walls seems to hover above the outer lightweight structure of the lower level.

hang between the base rising from the slope and the protruding exposed concrete cross walls and supports. The in-situ concrete, poured with neat joints and smooth formwork, adds to the technically precise architecture that is based on one consistent modular grid. In conjunction with the restricted range of materials – Corten steel and glass – that was also used for most of the other buildings in the Botanical Garden, and were applied with great discipline and in equal sizes, the new building forms a pure and abstract image. Its elegance is underlined by the transparency of the ground floor and the floating transition between the building and the garden.

The sloped site enables the building to be organised round separate, but thematically linked functions with their own respective entrances – both from the street to the rear and the network of paths of the part of the garden dedicated to western Mediterranean and northern African vegetation.

Each level accommodates its own programme. The lowest level, which is fully recessed into the ground, sits in a concrete tank reinforced by massive cross walls and also forms the foundation of the building. Here, the large air-conditioning system, the switch room, and further secondary technical service rooms are located as well as the large herbarium, various preparation rooms, and the bibliographical archive of

the institute containing card indexes of the collection, and conference rooms. These rooms receive daylight from above via narrow light wells.

The very humid climate of Barcelona makes the conservation of the extensive collection of pressed and dried plants particularly difficult. Inspired by the modern herbariums in Geneva and Berlin, a special 500 m² archive was constructed as a waterproof concrete tank in which room temperature and air humidity can be kept constant within small tolerances. The entire building is based on its modular 6 x 6 m grid.

The bays created by the structural cross walls can adapt to room conditions and lighting requirements

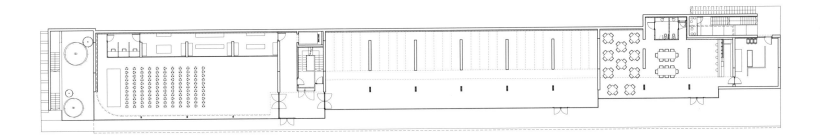

Ground floor plan

The transparency of the multi-functional hall blurs the bound-aries of interior and exterior.

of all sorts. Together the cross-walls, supports, and walls form a three-dimensional composite frame that provides the structural solution for the architectural idea of the detached volume floating above the slope.

The middle level with direct access from the path network of the Botanical Garden is exclusively reserved for public use. On this level, a multi-functional hall, a conference room with state-of-the-art audio-visual equipment, the Salvador Museum, an exhibition area that can be subdivided, and a café-restaurant used by visitors and employees of the institute alike are situated.

Due to the sloping site the non-public top floor has its own entrance. Here, the scientists' individual and

group studies are located as well as the library, various linked laboratories, and the offices for the director, the retired professors, and the administration of the institute. This level affords extensive views over the generous gardens, the Olympic Ring, the city, and the far-away Serralada de Collserola.

The three functional areas herbarium, public zone, and research zone are linked by reinforcing cores that provide vertical access and support communication between the library, the Salvador collection, the café, the herbarium, and the work spaces on the different levels.

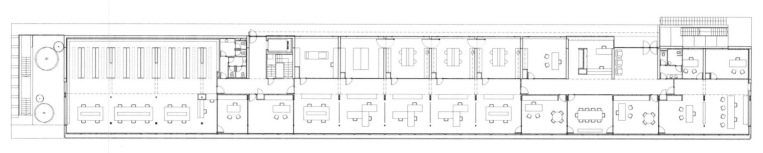

Top floor plan

0 2   10 m

The library located adjacent to the studies on the top floor.

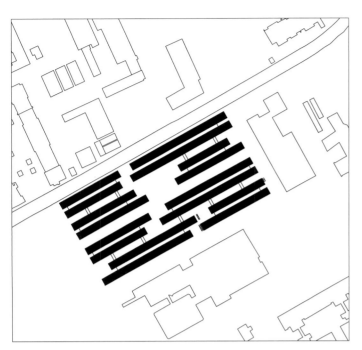

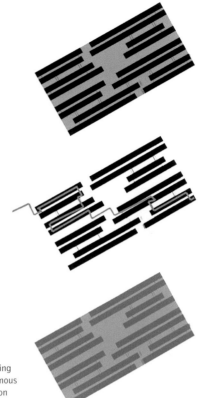

Site plan

Pictograms from top to bottom
Introverted spatial layout | Floating spatial transitions of the autonomous campus | Highly flexible circulation layout

from left to right
The institute can be read in different ways: as parallel pairs of volumes with long or short "legs", as penetrated and shifted rows, or as one building that comprises a number of exterior "corridors" | The "doubled" strip windows of the south façade conceal the height of the floor levels behind | A view into a courtyard shows "shades of grey" | Façades at the gable ends show vertical joints between separately poured concrete panels that are fixed to the framed reinforced concrete structure

Computer Science and Electrical Engineering Institutes, Graz University of Technology

Graz, Austria

Client	Republik Österreich, Bundesministerium für wirtschaftliche Angelegenheiten
Architects	Riegler Riewe Architekten, ZT-Ges. m. b. H.
Construction period	1997-1999 (phase 1) 1998-2000 (phase 2)
Net floor area	8,000 m²
Cubic content	63,800 m³

The building of the Institute for Information Technology and Electrical Engineering represents a building type that is quite average in terms of mechanical engineering and technical infrastructure compared to the facilities of biological/chemical institutes or similar disciplines. Hence, the planning of the extension of the Technical University on a site with no outstanding qualities focussed much more on urban design aspects. Simple residential architecture, a not very sightly high voltage transformer station, and very bland existing university buildings dominate the environment called Inffeldgründe. The architects have responded to this context by concentrating on the building site and a rigid grid – an open urban campus creating its own identity. The buildings have been

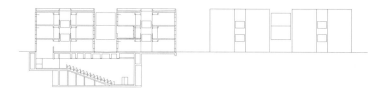

Cross section through two volumes and void

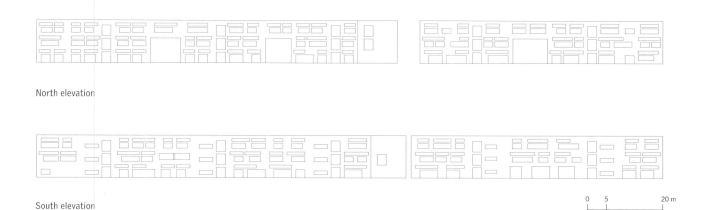

North elevation

South elevation

0 5 20 m

restricted to a height of three storeys, which gives the layout a very human scale.

Based on a strictly orthogonal grid, the buildings generate a city within the city with streets and house fronts, squares and gates, passages and groups of trees. The architecture of the altogether eight exactly parallel volumes is governed by the strict organisation and the openness of the space. The first two of the overall four phases will be completed in 2004 – the completion of the remaining stages is uncertain.

The individual volumes are spaced at regular intervals of 6.00 m in east-west direction. The varying lengths of the individual rows result from the different pro-

grammes of the respective institutes. Every two rows are linked by a void. The offices, galleries, lifts and stairs orientated towards these voids face south; seminar rooms, libraries, and public areas face north. Since the buildings are mostly within the scope of mechanical engineering for normal office buildings (lines for heating and sanitation, electrical and data wiring) the programme does not include zones for technical building services. Supplementary or large central shafts are not required; no vertical or horizontal service lines have to be provided or reserved for future use. The strict layout of the buildings is loosened up by the ubiquitous bridges, corridors, galleries, and openings that link the buildings on all levels and create this interconnected, self-sufficient, and almost

small town-like campus with its varied squares. The permeability of the structure can be felt particularly on the entire ground floor, the "street" level.

The interior and exterior circulation concept sustains an urban structure which at every point reveals the functional and spatial pattern of the "city within the city". While the ground floor features a wide central access corridor, the two upper floors are connected by an atrium. Following the client's explicit request, only the large lecture halls on the basement floor abandon the strict plan layout.

In contrast to many university facilities that accommodate individual institutes in separate buildings or

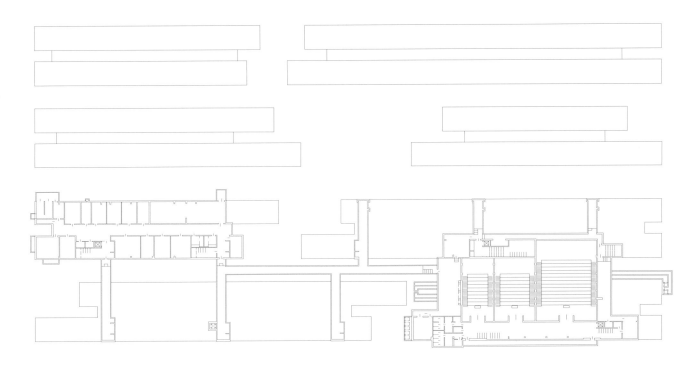

Basement floor plan with auditoriums

from left to right
The austere architectural theme of "shades of grey" also extends
to the interior | The auditoriums are located at basement level |
Footbridges as connective and communicative elements support
the design concept of the "city within the city" | Consistently
rough finishes also dominate the interior

building parts, here a dense yet permeable complex
was built that is linked on all levels. It effortlessly
enables the expansion and reduction of individual
functional units without entailing complicated refurbishment.

Flexibility is also reflected in the structural system
composed of rows of columns behind the external
walls and load-bearing walls in longitudinal and cross
directions. This structural system creates an open plan
providing additional flexibility, as partitions are either
not required or can be installed if needed. However,
the choice of the structural system was mainly steered
by architectural considerations.

The architects considered concrete the ideal material
to link the building parts both structurally and architecturally. The design idea was to highlight the urban
configuration rather than the individual volumes themselves. Therefore, the concrete was designed to appear
as rough as possible to create a consistent finish. To
achieve this finish, recycled formwork boards were
used. Some formwork boards were artificially worn
out since used formwork was not available in sufficient quantities. Black pigments were added to the
grey cement. The intended irregular finish was achieved almost automatically since the in-situ concrete
was poured in three stages and the pigments were
added on site. The interior façades also received the
rough exposed concrete finish – however, without the

black pigments. Consequently, the interior spaces
appear much brighter and therefore more pleasant.

To some degree, the interior appears even more unfinished than the exterior. Austere façades with horizontal strip windows bound the spaces. Little attention
was given to the detailing and materials used – terraz-
zo, concrete, or simple galvanized steel for the doors –
seem unfinished and were put together in a haphazardly to challenge aesthetical conventions.

An essential element of the intended homogeneity
of materials and the characteristic colour scheme of
shades of grey is the treatment of the exterior floor
finishes. The buildings stand in a bed of pebbles, which

Ground floor plan

is to become overgrown with moss at the corners and on the infrequently used areas. Circulation areas and paths can be chosen freely by pedestrians and will form naturally by frequent use and wear. Hence, every space defines a space between, and none is hermetically enclosed. This decomposition is also reflected by the vertical joints at the building edges and the façade pattern with the physical projection of the horizontal strip window. The window openings – two in height per floor – blur the scale of the buildings and conceal the levels behind. Structurally, this is achieved by a reinforced concrete skeleton and a 22 cm strong curtain wall made of concrete; this raw "concrete curtain" disguises the floor levels. Different daylight conditions constantly and subtly change its colour.

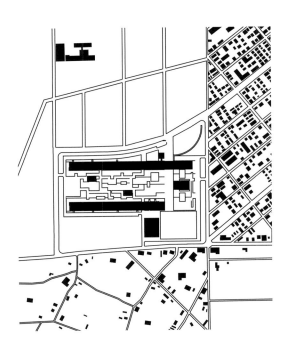

Site plan

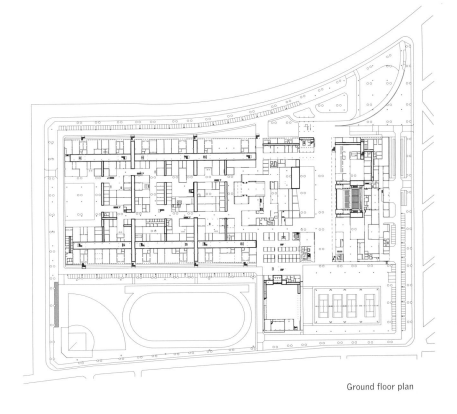

Ground floor plan

from left to right
View from the circulation axis showing the elongated building volume across the park-like campus | The campus forms an elevated plateau organised by an orthogonal grid of paths containing courtyards functioning as light-wells, and lecture halls on stilts | The impressive four-storey zone of the central axis | The laboratories on the ground floor as well as the research rooms and lecture halls on the upper floor are connected to the central axis

Saitama Prefectural University

Saitama, Japan

Client	Saitama Prefecture, Koshigaya
Architects	Riken Yamamoto
Construction period	1997-1999
Total floor area	54,000 m²

According to demographical projections in Japan, in 2025, 70% of the seniors over 65 will live in urban agglomerations. The potential for structural change in these places will possibly be limited, thus jeopardising the existing social structure. Individuals will increasingly have to rely on the resources of society as a whole. Local communities will increasingly replace the traditional role of the family.

The architects based their concept neither on the urban context nor the brief (they were actually entitled to interpret it based on functional considerations). They rather deduced their conceptual idea from the prognosticated social behaviour of the future Japanese population and created a net-like

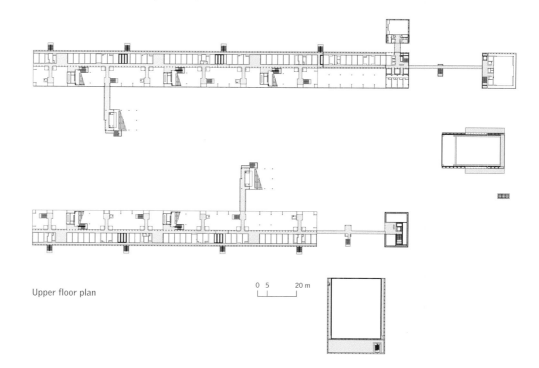

Upper floor plan

0 5   20 m

Cross section

structure that provides varied spaces for spontaneous encounters and generates social patterns resulting from academic everyday life. The design deliberately neglects conventional campus layouts with separate faculties; instead, it links and spatially overlaps them. This blurs the boundaries of the different disciplines and creates "local communities".

The university is situated about 40 km north of Tokyo on a secluded, rectangular and absolutely flat site between rice patties and residential areas. The urban context is very bland: the urban infrastructure is already notably thinned out, yet the natural environment is not highly attractive, either.

Two long volumes to the north and south containing the actual teaching facilities define the space of the complex. The laboratories are located on four levels on the outward-facing sides. They are lined up along an approximately 200 m long light-flooded main circulation axis that also serves as a communication zone and provides space for breaks and recreation.

The central campus is a park-like, raised plateau detached from the ground and situated between the two long volumes. An orthogonal pattern of paths runs through the park. Highly flexible modules of communal facilities are located below plateau level.

These spaces receive daylight via courtyards cut into the plateau. Raised lecture halls, a gymnasium, and an auditorium supplement the campus.

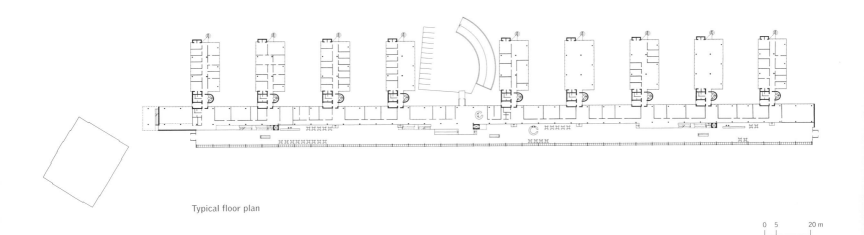

Typical floor plan

0 5   20 m

from left to right
By opening up the lower third of the façade the shopping and restaurant zone turns into a lively boulevard | View across the lake and along the glazed arcade towards the labour court | Entering light and reflections add a lively element to the gallery spaces | At Munscheidstraße, nine three-storey pavilions form a row as part of a comb structure accommodating the institutes and referring to the scale of the opposite residential buildings

Technology Centre, Rhine-Elbe Science Park

Gelsenkirchen, Germany

Client	Land Nordrhein-Westfalen, Vermögensgesellschaft Wissenschaftspark
Architects	Kiessler + Partner Architekten GmbH
Completion	1992-1994/1995
Total floor area	27,200 m²
Net floor area	19,200 m²
Cubic content	104,500 m³

The Science Park Rheinelbe was built as part of the International Building Exhibition Emscher Park to promote structural changes in the Ruhr District. The formation of small, decentralised technology centres was to set the stage for the sustained development of this non-academic and "non-scientific" region, that has been dominated by heavy industries in the past. The altogether 17 technology centres accommodate institutes outsourced by large corporations or associated with academic or non-academic research.

On the 30 ha site of former Thyssen cast steel plant and Zeche Rheinelbe mine the complex forms a new and poignant edge of the city, substantially supporting the redevelopment of the urban fabric destroyed by the

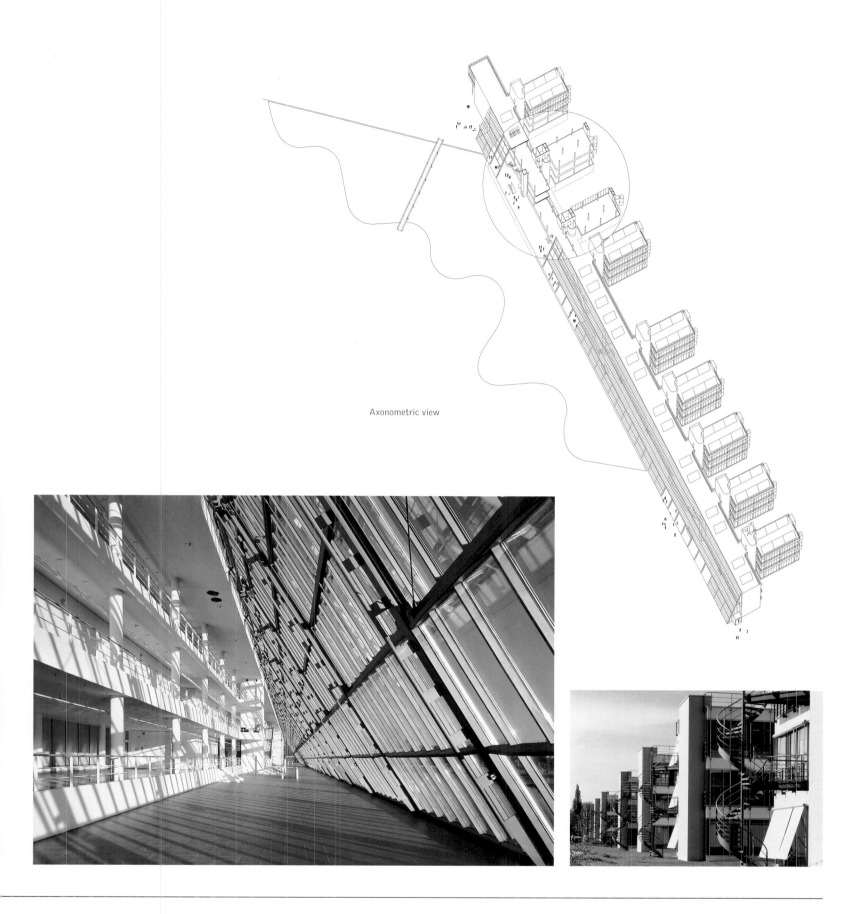

Axonometric view

derelict industrial site. Following the theme "Working in the Park" the buildings are grouped around a new landscaped park including a lake, this way reintroducing a fair bit of nature to the city. The 300 m long glass arcade at the east of the site which runs along the water edge forms the spine of the complex and provides a communicative link between the research and development workshops and the public. It has been conceived as a roofed boulevard with shops and restaurants. The glazed façade elements of the lower third can be electrically moved upwards.

A former administration building which has been converted into a labour court completes the layout at its northern edge, as does a kindergarten in the southeast.

Nine pavilions accommodate administration, solar energy, IT, and medical technology facilities. They are arranged in a comb pattern and accessed from the three-storey arcade building.

The idea of a structural change of the region through the attraction of "soft technologies" does not merely have its expression in the urban design concept. The building itself also marks a technological change from conventional to "intelligent" building technologies. Consequently, its design addresses issues of sustainable energy and climate. The lake, for example, serves as a rain water reservoir and design feature and provides cooling during summer, when the façade is retracted. The shading devices of the glazed façade react to exte-

rior weather conditions and control either solar gain in winter or natural ventilation during summer. The roof was equipped with one of the largest solar power stations at the time of construction.

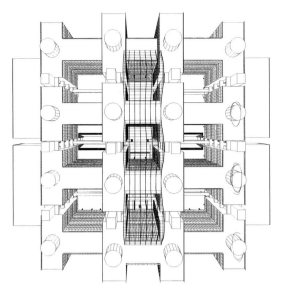

Perspective drawing:
view into light-flooded courtyards

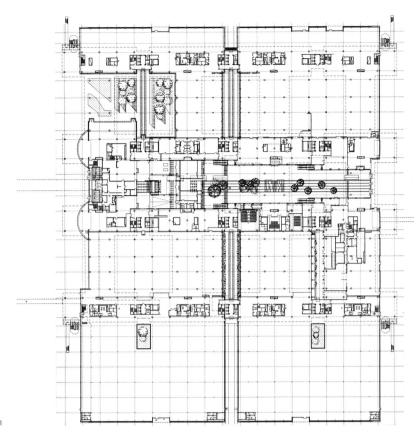

Ground floor plan

from left to right
The metallic-white buildings hover above a grey base made of stone and aluminium | The atriums form a central passage crossed by elevated footbridges | Design rules regulating orientation, colour, and material create homogeneity and a spatial atmosphere

La Ruche,
Technocentre Renault

Guyancourt, France

Client	Renault
Architects	Valode & Pistre Architectes
Construction period	1994-1997
Total floor area	250,000 m²

On the outskirts of Saint-Quentin near Paris, Renault concentrated all facilities for the design of new cars, basic research, development, and production of prototypes in one development centre. On a site with a total area of 150 ha, the centre is to create 8,000 jobs for engineers in an urban context that includes roads, buildings, places for work and communication, parks, and lakes.

The master plan stipulated the orientation of the buildings along an axis between the church bell tower of Guyancourt and the Villaroy Farm. The new complex is embedded into the flat landscape and refers to existing buildings and the natural environment. Situated in the middle of a valley stood with trees and

Longitudinal section through covered internal street

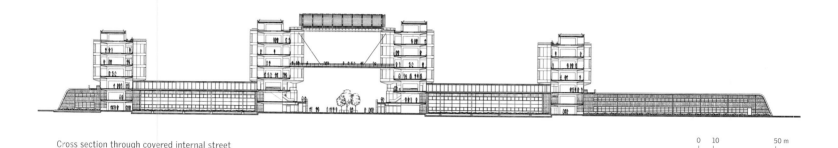

Cross section through covered internal street

0 10 50 m

crossed by a canal it virtually becomes part of the topography.

In contrast with the integration into the landscape a rigid 54 m grid determining the buildings' position was introduced. Based on an associated colour scheme – white stands for research and grey for its materialisation – two building types representing the different development stages of a car have been planned along the main axis.

As one approaches the premises, density and height of the building fabric increase and reach their culmination in the technology centre – the complex where the first design studies come into being. Within the

given framework of the master plan, various architects were to receive a large degree of freedom – yet the architecture was to transport a spatially and formally coherent image of a research city. The centre is functionally highly complex and characterised by high demands on optimal communication.

The multi-layered complex with its crossing network of buildings grouped around inner courtyards is based on a modular grid that keeps a manageable scale. Four metallic white, elongated volumes seem to hover above a base made of stone and aluminium.

The workshops on the ground floor, the public rooms on the mezzanine, and the studios above are strongly

linked by gangways leading to the lifts, stairs, and conference rooms. They provide openness and communication as well as separation and privacy. The transparent corridors and gangways afford views of the surrounding landscape and the inner courtyards. They facilitate orientation and even in the innermost parts of the buildings daytime and seasonal changes can be recognised.

Three atriums serve as meeting and information areas and form the complex' central circulation artery. It is crossed by footbridges and lined with restaurants.

Conceptual ideas for buildings portrayed in this section are derived from typological classifications: Linear layout, comb-like layout, and core layout; in addition, layouts based on the concentration of spaces with similar functions are the basic ordering systems and guide the respective design ideas.

The comb-like structures included are free interpretations of this layout type, ultimately leading to individual solutions. They are based on the arrangement of relatively independent functional units; this approach can be advantageous for the organisation of a facility. The sub-section "Double-Loaded Systems" contains facilities with laboratory and office spaces arranged along a central corridor. Designs in this category show a remarkable creativity and variety of this type of layout. Solutions vary considerably, especially in terms of arrangement and quality of circulation areas and spaces for social interaction.

120
Headquarters of NeuroSearch A/S

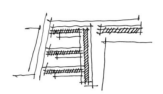

122
Institute for Chemistry and Lecture Building for Chemistry and Physics, Humboldt University of Berlin, Adlershof Campus

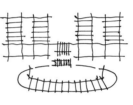

124
Sciences Institute

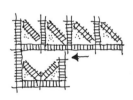

126
Nokia Research Center

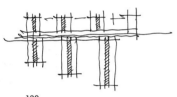

140
Fraunhofer Institute for Applied Polymer Research

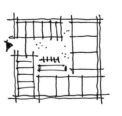

142
Pharmacological Research Building, Boehringer Ingelheim Pharma KG

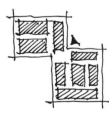

144
Centre for Energy and Technology

146
Molecular Sciences Building

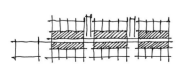

156
Biosciences Building, Bundoora West Campus, RMIT University

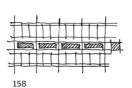

158
BIOSTEIN
Agrobiological Research Centre of Novartis Crop Protection AG

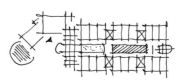

160
Biological Sciences and Bioengineering Building, Indian Institute of Technology

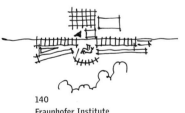

162
Southwest Bio-Tech Intermediate Test Base

In the group "Core Systems" either buildings with a large depth or the requirement to accommodate a high percentage of dark spaces, leading to large inner zones, are presented. These concepts represent functional and formal alternatives to the compact linear triple-loaded layouts.

Access Systems

128
State Office
for Chemical Investigations

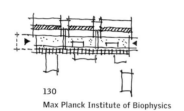

130
Max Planck Institute of Biophysics

134
Fraunhofer Institute
for Manufacturing and Advanced Materials

136
Center of Advanced European Studies
and Research (CAESAR)

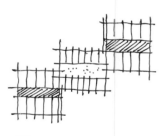

148
CIBA-Geigy Life Sciences Building

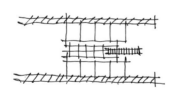

150
Centre for Human Drug Research

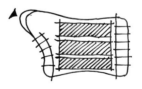

152
Laboratory Building
for Medical Genome Research

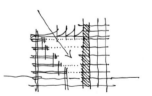

154
Sir Alexander Fleming Building,
Imperial College

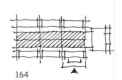

164
Engineering Research Center,
University of Cincinnati

Site plan

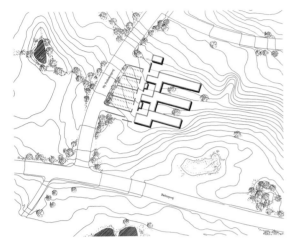

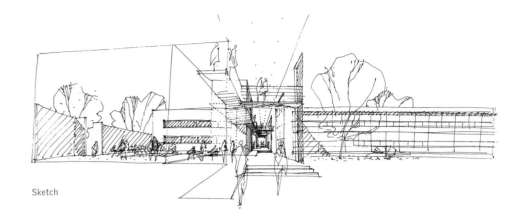

Sketch

Headquarters of NeuroSearch A/S

Ballerup, Denmark

Client	NeuroSearch
Architects	Henning Larsens Tegnestue A/S
Construction period	1997-1999
Total floor area	6,000 m²

The new headquarters of NeuroSearch A/S varies a tried and tested building type and a classical plan arrangement.

Situated in an industrial park of rural appeal, the site is dominated by a slope descending 14 m towards the south. The buildings are located at the highest point of the site. The long wings of the complex are gradually terraced down in east-west direction following the contours of the slope in steps of 80 cm.

The plan of the well-tried comb-shaped structure is organised in such a way that it affords views towards Råmosens Nature Reserve from the canteen, the library, and the spaces on the south side. The three laborato-

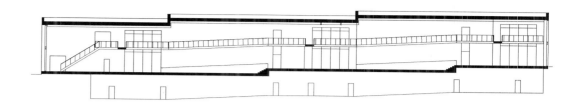

Longitudinal section

Ground floor plan

0   5   20 m

from left to right
Exterior view | Interior view showing circulation area |
View of south façade with solar blinds

ry wings with central access corridors show a classical zoning into spaces with or without supplementary
installation zones; laboratories face north, studies for
theoretical work face south. Hence, undesired solar
gain in the laboratories can be avoided. West of the
main circulation axis, administrative offices are grouped
around little courtyards that are protected from noise
coming from the street and parking lots by secondary
spaces, thus creating introvert and quiet zones.

The two-storey access wing provides spatial and
functional links between the different units. Ramps
and stairs bridge the height difference of 2 m resulting from the sloped terrain. Secondary spaces and
common meeting rooms are located where the main

corridor and the administration wing overlap. The
corridor opens up to the western courtyards with
three foyers. A footbridge on the first floor links the
administrative areas and also connects to the laboratory wings via additional transverse bridges.

At the eastern ends of the laboratory wings the corridors widen into generously glazed spaces; they restore the visual link to the landscape. Like the south
façades of the laboratory wings, the south façade of
the canteen and library wing is dominated by a large
glass-and-aluminium curtain wall. The façades orientated south and west received fixed solar blinds; the
laboratory façades to the north show strip windows
with glazed and solid panels.

All exterior walls are made of load-bearing concrete
elements faced by rendered bricks. The cut-out openings and the flush-mounted window elements give the
geometrical and precise building a sculptural appeal.

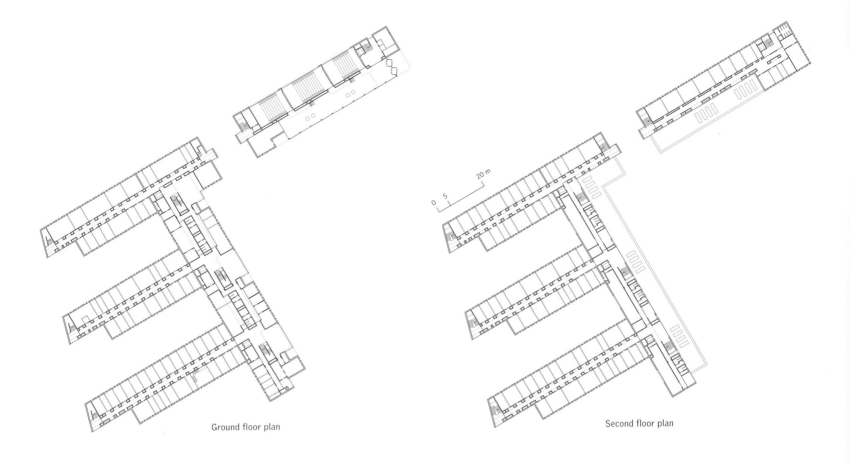

Ground floor plan

20 m

0 5

Second floor plan

from left to right
The required escape stairs form the final elements of the individual "teeth" | Above: The façades clearly show the functions of the spaces behind | Below: The detached lecture building at Abram-Joffe-Straße as seen from the campus | Frontally attached two-storey circulation areas differentiate the building volumes | The internal circulation areas are designed in a purist and geometric manner

Institute for Chemistry and Lecture Building for Chemistry and Physics, Humboldt University of Berlin, Adlershof Campus

Berlin, Germany

Client	Humboldt University of Berlin
Architects	Volker Staab Architekten
Construction period	1999-2001
Total floor area	23,100 m²
Cubic content	93,400 m³

According to urban planning requirements the two new buildings occupy the northern end of the emerging Adlershof campus. The two upper floors of both buildings are recessed to reduce their cubature. The full four-storey height of the volumes refers to the adjacent buildings.

The brief called for an unobtrusive urban layout that was also to reflect and strengthen the identity of the individual units of the institutes. These apparently contradictory requirements could adequately be met with a comb shaped plan. The institute building provides facilities of equal standard for all faculties; each facility has its own address but sustains internal circulation and direct access to commonly used practi-

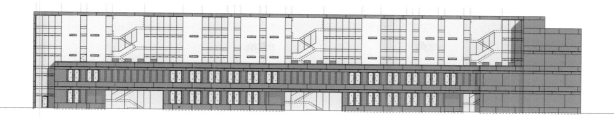

Northeast elevation (Aerodynamic Park)

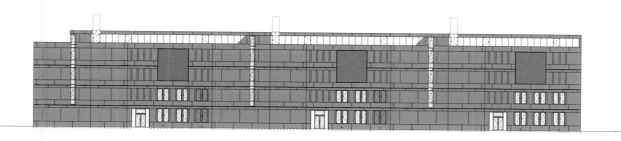

Southwest elevation (Max-Born-Straße)

cal study rooms and workshops. Since all institutes are organized round a square and have mechanical services, communication and circulation paths arranged on this side, large internal circulation areas are avoided. Instead, the outdoor space provides the connecting tissue.

The majority of rooms are to be used as laboratories, which are serviced via individual service shafts. Only a few spaces located at the inner corners facing south contain offices that do not require shafts. On the fourth floor – above the corridors and corezone – mechanical services are located exclusively.

Both buildings are solid structures with load-bearing walls and service shafts made of semi-prefabricated reinforced concrete elements. The double-skin exterior wall consists of load-bearing reinforced concrete, core insulation, and a textured reddish exterior cladding made of prefabricated elements.

The architecture lacks any sculptural quality; instead, generously glazed façade areas hint at the layout behind, making the functional and technical building structure readable: the individual circulation areas of the faculties, the lecture hall, and the technical infrastructure, exemplified by service shafts that can be recognised by recessed façade areas.

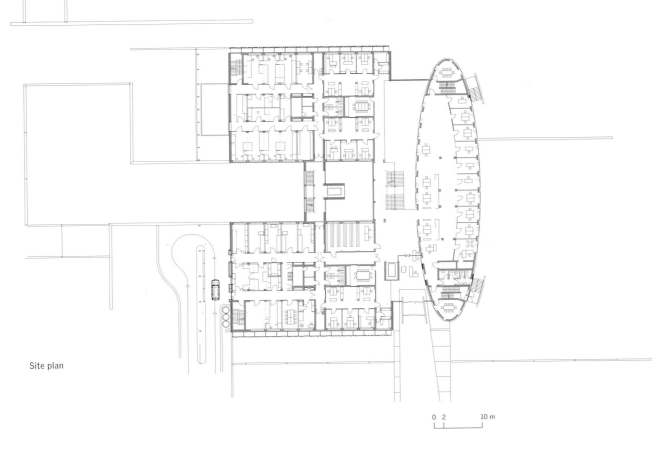

Site plan

0 2   10 m

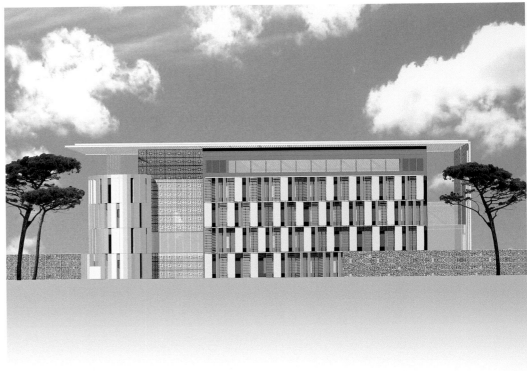

from left to right
Visualisation of the building showing fixed solar blinds made of
vertical metal louvres to the west and east | The slatted sun-
screen roof creates a vivid shade pattern on the south façade |
Stove-enamelled aluminium panels dominate the façade

Sciences Institute

Algier, Algeria

Client	Gendarmerie Nationale
Architects	Heinle, Wischer und Partner Freie Architekten, Krebs und Kiefer International
Completion	2004-2005
Total floor area	ca. 15,000 m²

The Sciences Institute provides Algeria's Gendarmerie Nationale with facilities for forensic research on a high scientific level. The programme for 13 sections and training and administration facilities comprises areas of extremely different uses. These areas were distributed on two orthogonal five-storey volumes. A further elliptical volume contains a lecture hall, seminar rooms, and lounges on the first two levels and, above, rooms for the scientific and administrative management. The central entrance hall is situated between the ellipse and the two orthogonal volumes containing the studies and laboratories. Its corridor, which looks like a mirrored comb, at the same time separates and links the different functional areas.

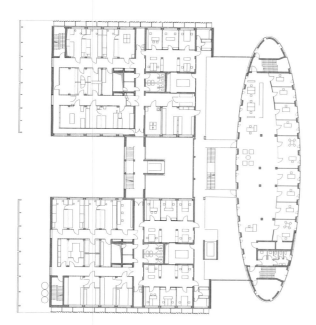

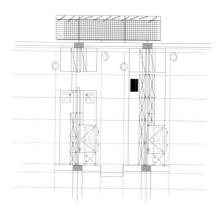

Typical laboratory floor plan
with furniture and technical
equipment

Typical floor plan

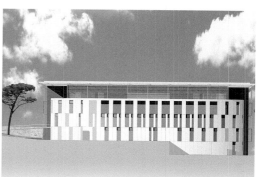

The institute is located on a hill adjacent to one of the main roads leading to Algiers. It is part of a complex of buildings dedicated to forensic tasks that includes residential buildings for the staff, a restaurant, and sports facilities. The main entrance is situated half way up the hill. Due to the topography of the site, the buildings can be serviced on different levels limiting obstructions and security risks to a minimum. Various further requirements had to be incorporated into the design: the building structure had to be earthquake-proof; the forensic analysis required fully air-conditioned laboratories providing constant temperatures; frequent sandstorms had to be considered when planning the air-conditioning system and the exterior building skin.

The central corridors serving three laboratory sections on each level contain a middle zone incorporating central service shafts. Plasterboard partitions provide great flexibility.

The entire building is roofed by a slatted sunscreen shading the rooms facing the courtyard, the south façade, and the façades of the entrance hall. The east and west façades received fixed vertical solar blinds with metal louvers. The insulated and ventilated façade has a cladding of corrosion-proof stove-enamelled aluminium panels. As an architectural symbol for forensic work, the pattern of the solar protection elements is reminiscent of a DNA code.

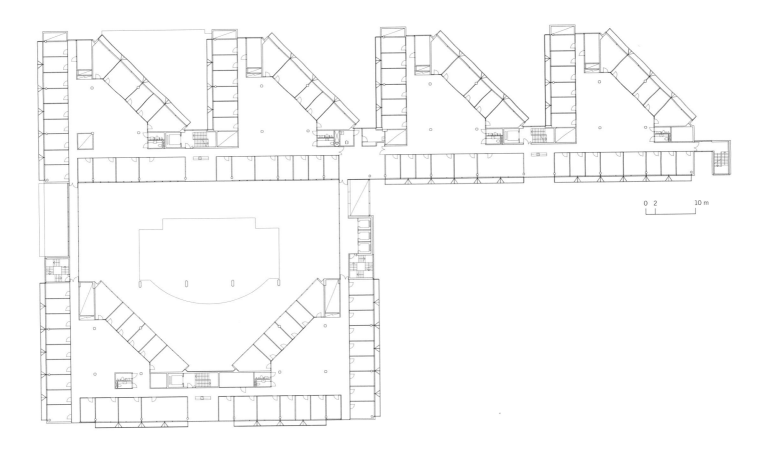

Typical floor plan

from left to right
Main entrance with steel canopy and double-layered façade speak
an equally rigorous architectural language | The north side is char-
acterised by the gable ends of four triangular modules | Transpar-
ent and opaque façade elements reveal the functions of the spaces
behind | The glazed atrium creates light-flooded work spaces | The
conference room, was assigned a strategically propitious position
in the building

Nokia
Research Center

Helsinki, Finland

Client	Nokia
Architects	Tuomo Siitonen and Esko Valkama, Helin & Siitonen Architects
Completion	1999
Net floor area	24,400 m²
Cubic content	166,000 m³

The Finnish telecommunication company built the new
Helsinki research centre to accommodate their R&D
employees that grew by 5,000 persons worldwide
between the years 1998 and 2000. 900 employees
work in the flexible, centrally located building which
is well connected to the circumjacent universities.

The design is based on six and eight-storey triangular
modules that are arranged in a linear row to form
a comb-like structure. The consistent horizontal and
vertical zoning of the functional units results in an
economical structure.

The scheme basically comprises two different room
types: individual study rooms and open plan areas.

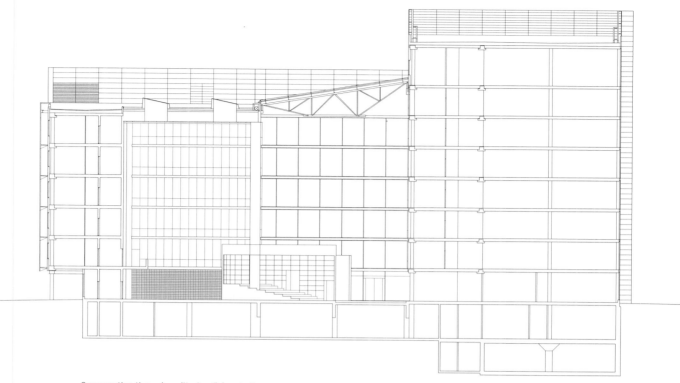

Cross section through auditorium/laboratories

Study rooms for theoretical analysis are highly equipped with data processing technology. Due to high thermal gains in these rooms air-conditioning is required. Designed for individual concentrated work, they are situated around the perimeter of the triangular modules. They enclose semi-public multi-purpose areas, which can be used as mixed office zones, communication zones, or lounge zones. These zones encourage social interaction and informal meetings of the employees in day-to-day work.

The main entrance faces a large forecourt to the east. From here, an interior public route running from east to west links all areas of the building. This route is part of a general public path superimposed by the existing master plan and to be built in due course. Together with modules of the comb structure, two more triangular modules offset to the south and arranged symmetrically enclose a glazed light-flooded atrium. Offices are also orientated towards this atrium. It is the representative heart of the complex providing access and supporting communication and social interaction. A lecture hall is integrated into the atrium as an independent structure; it can be lit artificially or naturally. To the north of the ground floor, a cafeteria and a canteen are located.

The building is a reinforced concrete frame structure with a steel-and-glass curtain wall. The double-layered façade is equipped with adjustable external solar blinds.

Altogether, the research and development centre is a poignant architectural landmark providing high quality interior and exterior spaces.

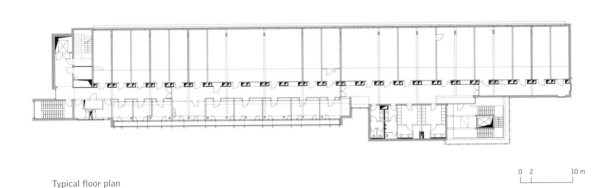

Typical floor plan

0 2   10 m

State Office for
Chemical Investigations

Karlsruhe, Germany

Client	Land Baden-Württemberg
Architects	Dipl.-Ing. Michael Weindel Freier Architekt
Construction period	1996-1999
Total floor area	7,200 m²
Net floor area	3,500 m²
Cubic content	30,300 m³

The building was erected in 1999 as the first phase of a larger project, which had been tendered for in an architectural competition held in 1992. It also comprised additional buildings for the Office of Environmental Protection and shared facilities. The site is a state-owned plot adjacent to an extensive industrial complex of the L'Oreal company.

The design concept was strongly guided by the organisation of the various functional zones of the programme. It was developed, critically analysed, and realised in close co-operation with the users. After thorough analysis of all requirements and definition of relevant standards for the individual room types and after intensive consideration of general and spe-

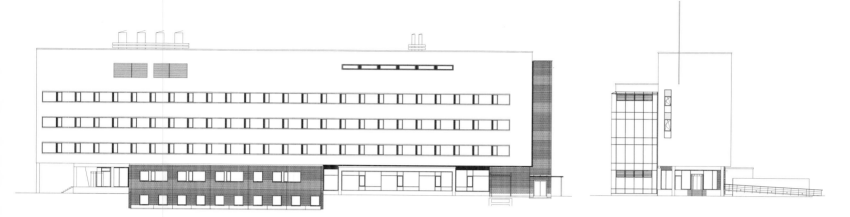

Northeast elevation

Elevation with entrance

from left to right
Laboratories behind strip windows with service floor on top | Offices are located behind a fully glazed façade and service gangways made of steel | Clearly orientated laboratories with allocated writing desks | Teaching area on the ground floor

cific functional procedures, the architects developed a spatial concept, which rigorously concentrates on a few basic modules.

Three functional zones with comparable technical equipment – laboratories/studies/service rooms and circulation zones – were combined. The separation and stacking of these functions generated clearly readable building volumes that have their own character in terms of layout, structure, and choice of materials.

The linear five-storey research building with double-loaded access corridors stands out within a heterogeneous industrial context through its rigorous and

clear design. On top of the northwest-orientated laboratory wing a tall technical service storey covers the entire floor area. This element enhances the physical presence of this highly equipped building, which is the most important part of the institute as for the experimental research conducted there.

The main entrance at the gable end in the northeast leads into an open and communicative foyer space that also provides access to shared facilities like the lecture hall and library. The laboratory levels face northwest and include individual service shafts. The offices facing southeast are located on the same level behind a steel service gangway and a fully glazed façade. The transparency of this façade contrasts

with the horizontally ordered and rather solid façade of the laboratory spaces. The structural system of the building, which is based on a rigorous plan, in combination with the clearly organised layout creates bright and varying public circulation spaces.

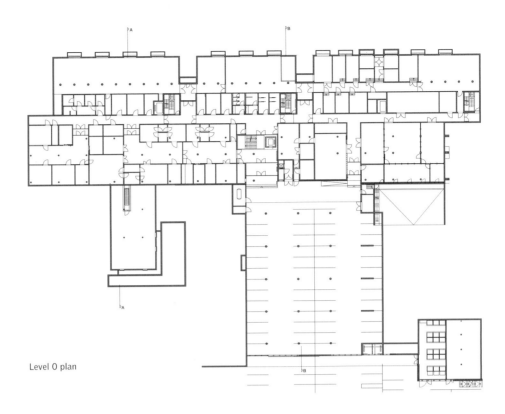

Level 0 plan

from left to right
Entrance to the west with prominent canopy | View from the
north | View from the south: attached transparent library
volume | Atrium linking offices and laboratories

Max Planck Institute
of Biophysics

Frankfurt am Main, Germany

Client	Max-Planck-Gesellschaft zur Förderung der Wissenschaften e.V
Architects	Auer + Weber + Architekten
Construction period	2000 - 2003
Net floor area	5.800 m²
Cubic content	65.000 m³

The new institute building is situated on the natural
science campus of Johann Wolfgang Goethe University at "Niederurseler Hang" adjacent to the faculties of
chemistry, physics and biology as well as further non-
academic research facilities. The building forms the
southern border of the future central campus area
and has been placed parallel to the slope descending
to the south. To the north it follows the proposed main
thoroughfare and to the east it borders onto a north-
south orientated campus axis that will link the proposed campus with the existing institutes.

Using this urban context as a starting point, the architects developed an institute building that consists of

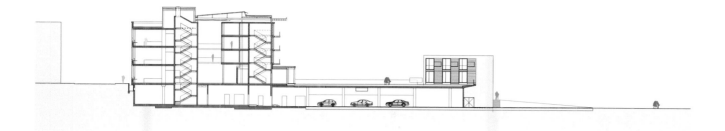

Cross section with guest house

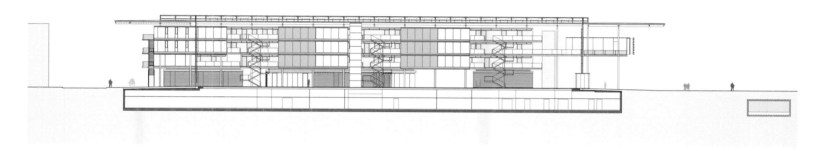

Longitudinal section through hall

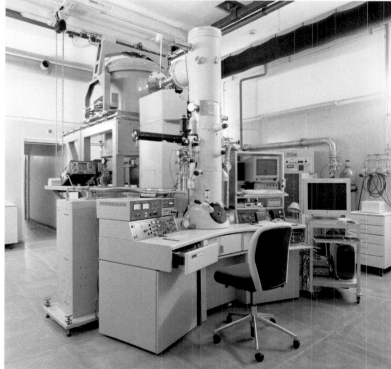

comprises ten guest rooms, communal spaces, and the housekeeper's flat.

The materials and finishes used for the reinforced concrete framed structure support the general conceptual ideas. Exposed concrete and aluminium-glass-façades dominate the outer appearance and render the building a contemporary research facility. The transparent steel-and-glass roof canopy with sun sails on the inside elegantly spans the light-flooded atrium. According to the point of view, season and daytime, it traces changing patterns of shadows onto floors and walls. This effect is supplemented and enhanced by a media/light installation by Dietmar Tanterl.

Section through courtyard and main entrance

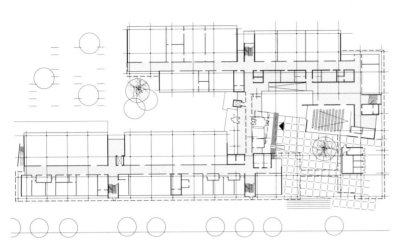

Ground floor plan

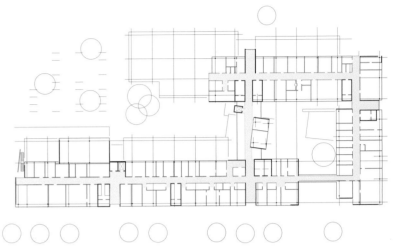

Typical floor plan

0 2 10 m

from left to right
Main entrance with facing brick seen from Wiener Straße |
Access from the green space with utility rooms on both sides |
Teaching room in the courtyard | The spacious technical rooms
lie level with the ground floor and are conveniently accessible
for large equipment

Fraunhofer Institute for Manufacturing and Advanced Materials

Bremen, Germany

Client	Fraunhofer Gesellschaft
Architects	Brenner & Partner Architekten und Ingenieure Brenner-Hammes-Krause
Completion	1999
Net floor area	6,200 m²
Cubic content	48,600 m³

The project is a successful example of highly economical zoning and stacking of functions on up to three
levels, its communicative, impressive, and flexible
architecture being achieved by a thoughtful building
layout. The building located at the border of the University of Bremen campus, adjacent to the Max Planck
Institute for Marine Micro-Biology, brings together
two formerly separated facilities – the Institute for
Bonding Technology and Surfaces and the Institute
for Net-Shape Manufacturing – under one roof.

Based on the master plan and a design statute sti-
pulating block figures and facing brick façades, the
architects developed a building of great character.

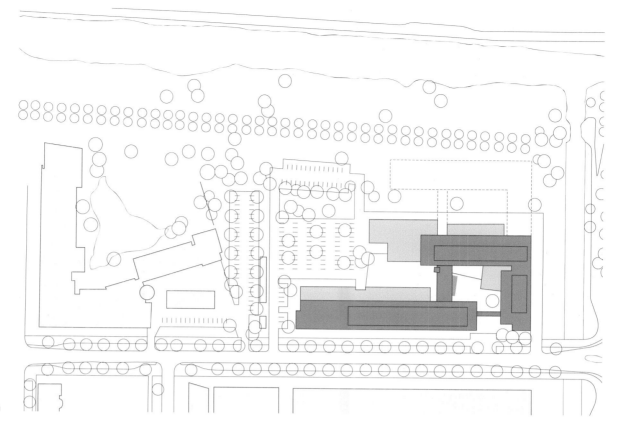

Site plan

were arranged round a courtyard to create a layout that hints at the traditional block type but is at the same time permeable and inviting. Curtain walls consist of brick panels with open cross bond joints, are clearly non-load-bearing and take away the usual heaviness of facing brick façades. The glazed bridge above the main entrance that connects the two building parts is tinted blue on one side and yellow on the other side. When seen from the outside, the two overlapping layers blend into a green tone that is complimentary to the red colour of the facing bricks.

The three-storey building comprises a full basement and includes a supplementary service level above the second floor. The research laboratories and the offi-

ces for theoretical studies are arranged along a double-loaded access corridor; offices face the quiet green space and the courtyard, laboratories face the street. Laboratories and respective offices have been arranged opposite each other to create short distances and enable the constant exchange between experimental work and theoretical analysis.

The services run in a combined system of central and single shafts.

The reinforced concrete structure comprises a range of basic materials that were used in a very disciplined way, clearly preserving their natural qualities and pure finishes. The result is a rational building that suits its

purpose functionally and aesthetically. Apart from exposed concrete, mainly glass was used to symbolise openness and transparency – qualities that were also desired by the scientists. The footbridges linking the two wings in combination with the volumes' differentiation in terms of dimensions and materials create interspaces and visual connections and express the institute's spirit of co-operation.

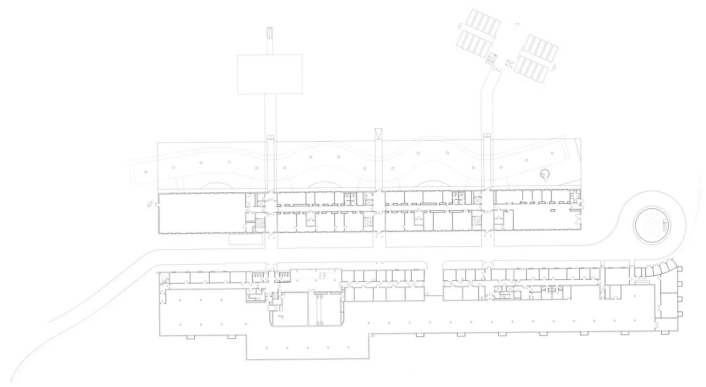

First basement floor plan

Center of Advanced European Studies and Research (CAESAR)

Bonn, Germany

Client	Foundation CAESAR
Architects	BMBW Architekten + Partner
Construction period	2000-2003
Net floor area	14,400 m²
Cubic content	122,500 m³

The foundation of CAESAR in 1995 by initiative of the Federal Republic of Germany and the federal state of North-Rhine-Westphalia was a political signal to strengthen Bonn as a scientific region. This foundation under private law was to compensate the city for the move of the Federal Government to Berlin. CAESAR is not organised in the classical way with a pyramidal personnel structure, but is based on smaller, more flexible work teams of changing size that work on temporary, result-orientated projects.

Research work concentrates on scientific, technological, and social key disciplines of the 21st century. In a strongly multi-disciplinary approach, the centre operates at the overlap of physics, chemistry, biology,

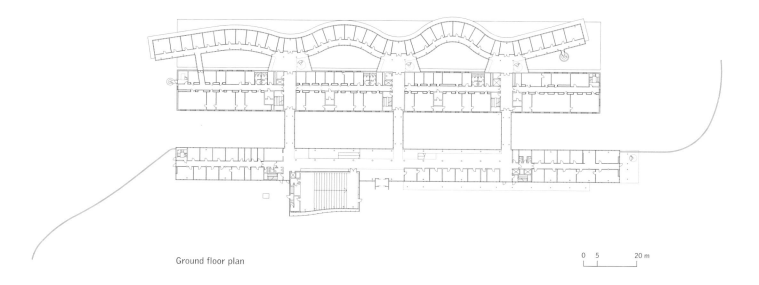

Ground floor plan

0 5   20 m

from left to right
The bird's-eye view shows the strict layout of the building and the connected greenhouse | View from the southwest showing the three separate volumes: the administration wing with the casino and underground parking access, the unostentatious box-shaped laboratory wing, and the wavy office wing | The main entrance with its large forecourt | The main characteristic of the lecture hall and the two-storey library is the double-layered and double-bent point-supported façade

mathematics, medicine, and information and engineering technology. The programme reflects the requirements of such topics as "Nanotechnology – new materials and miniaturising" (work field of experimental physics), "Connection of electronic and biological systems" (work field of experimental biology) and "Communication ergonomics" (work field of data processing, theoretical analysis, and simulation).

The competition-winning design is characterised by a typologically optimised arrangement of the functional units. Three linearly organised volumes are rigorously ordered, zoned, and stacked according to the degree of required mechanical services. The sound building composition is based on these three elements whose

specific outer appearance is derived from their inner functional logic.

The decision for the particular site in the southernmost part of Rheinauen Park in Bonn followed a painstaking search based on thorough consideration of complex criteria. Apart from meeting general requirements like traffic connections, quality of the urban environment, or proximity of other research facilities in the so-called "ABC region" (Aachen, Bonn, Cologne), the design above all had to ensure a smooth operation of the technical equipment. Potential disruptions had to be considered, e.g. electromagnetic fields (for example from railway lines), vibrations caused by heavy-duty trucks, or practically inevitable low fre-

quency vibrations caused by bow waves of ships on the nearby Rhine River. These factors are – apart from other site factors – of essential importance for the inner organisation and the allocation of services, apparatuses, and equipment on the net floor area.

The park, which does not include any other buildings, is the preferred recreational space for the people of Bonn and Bad Godesberg. Therefore, the harmonious integration of the complex into the park context was another fundamental planning criteria. The building is located at the border between Bonn's built-up area and the public park and has not been fenced in to preserve the free circulation of pedestrians and cyclists as far as possible. In contrast to the prominent main

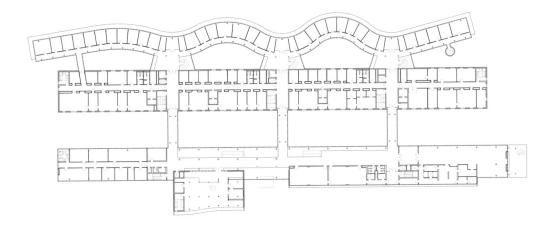

First floor plan

façade facing the city, a wavy office wing faces the park. It is raised on stilts, thus leaving space for a rainwater reservoir underneath. The "wave movement" was motivated by functional considerations; it also creates more floor area. At the same time, it relates the project to the meadows of the Rhine River and provides a smooth spatial transition from the building into the park.

The delivery zone and access route for vehicles make skilful use of the level difference between the main street Ludwig-Erhard-Allee and the lower Rheinauen Park and is discretely placed between the two parallel volumes near the street.

The research centre consists of three volumes serving entirely different functions. Facing the city, the linear, transparent two–storey entrance building houses shared facilities as the lecture hall, library, casino, and generous exhibition spaces. A separate volume dominates the forecourt of the main entrance; its skin of double-bent, point-supported twin glass façade accommodates the lecture hall among other spaces. This part of CAESAR strives to create a public platform for the presentation of research results and exhibitions of related fields. The four-storey building in the middle is also a linear volume. Organised along a central access corridor, it is of great functional and spatial density. Central and single service ducts shafts in conjunction with plant rooms and technical infra-

structure in the basement and on the top floor create ideal work conditions. The wavy three-storey office volume faces east towards the park. It is elevated on stilts and comprises one-sided offices for theoretical research.

In the laboratory and office wings, thematically related areas are positioned face to face. This way, four laboratory units on three levels each are directly linked to the offices. This generates a high flexibility for the allocation of spaces for varying research projects and also reduces the distance between laboratories and studies for analysis. Three bridges on two levels lead from the entrance building to the laboratory wing.

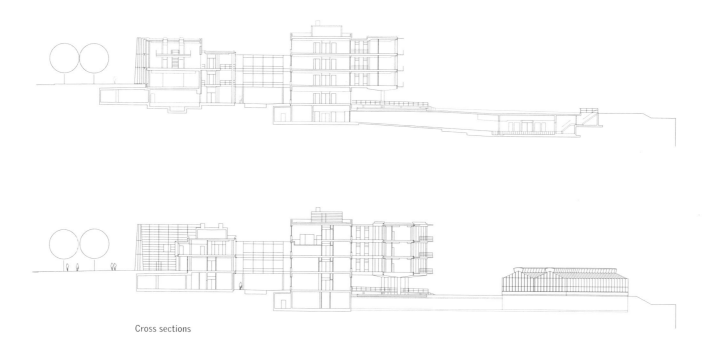

Cross sections

from left to right
View from the Casino onto the solid, rigorous stainless steel cladding of the "laboratory spine" | The linear foyer space provides access to all floors | Meeting points in the foyer

The laboratory wing meets all requirements in terms of functional flexibility. Based on an interior fit-out grid of 1.15 m, a structurally and economically sound reinforced concrete frame building was developed consisting of load-bearing exterior walls, reinforcing cores, and ceilings without joists.

On the basement level of the laboratory wing, central facilities like clean room, analytical laboratories, and scientific workshops are located. A greenhouse laboratory that is connected to the main complex underground was freely placed in the park. On Level –2, next to the greenhouse, high-resolution electron microscopes are positioned. The distance to the main building prevents the influence of electromagnetic

fields and structurally detaches the area to avoid vibration impact.

The "laboratory spine" is a rigorous, solid 150 m long, 17 m tall and 15 m wide volume with a façade with punched windows that reduces solar heat gain. The reflecting and constantly changing stainless steel cladding takes away the heaviness of this façade – it almost seems to de-materialise it. The entrance building is comparable in the sense that it appears open and inviting.

The prominent wave-figure of the office wing is enhanced by the horizontal layering of the escape balconies. It represents movement-cum-architecture and

– in conjunction with the landscape design – supports the integration of the complex into the open space of Rheinauen Park.

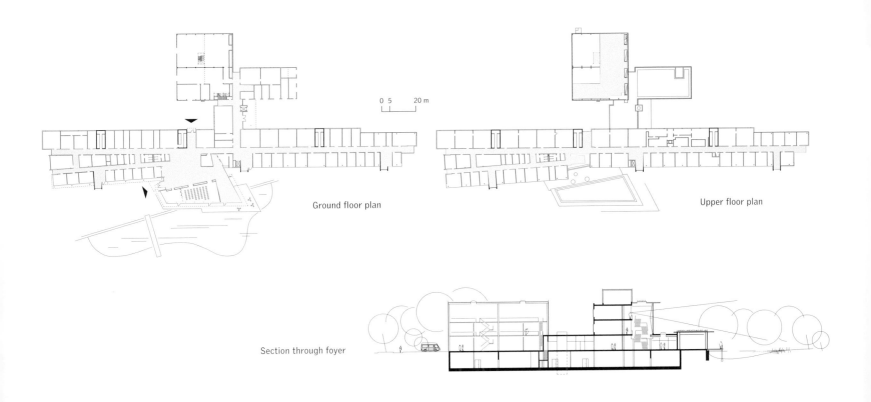

0 5 20 m

Ground floor plan

Upper floor plan

Section through foyer

Fraunhofer Institute for Applied Polymer Research

Golm near Potsdam, Germany

Client	Fraunhofer Gesellschaft
Architects	Brenner & Partner Architekten und Ingenieure Brenner-Hammes-Krause
Construction period	1998-2000
Net floor area	5,300 m²
Cubic content	46,000 m³

Together with three Max Planck Institutes, the IAP constitutes a first significant scientific cluster as part of the Science and Technology Park in the community of Golm near Potsdam. The state-of-the-art technology park was established on a 20 ha site. It provides spaces for living and working, teaching, and research in closest proximity and affords sweeping views of the meadows of the Havel River.

The design proposes a plausible solution for the arrangement of the programme in terms of building typology. The main entrance is located between the linear main edifice with the attached pilot plant hall and the adjacent secondary workshop building.

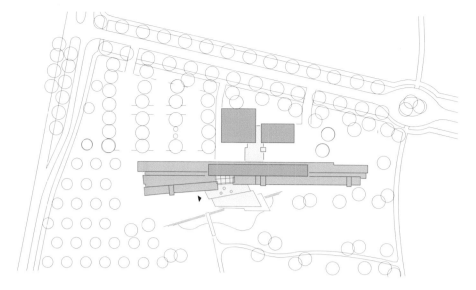

Site plan

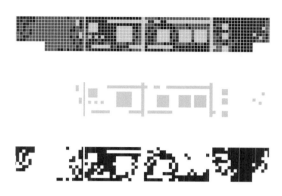

from left to right
The long linear volume with continuous strip windows and lake
in front | North façade of the pilot plant hall with graphic design
showing circles and lines that associates the chemical composition of substances

The spaces on each floor of the elongated three-storey main building are organised along one, and partly two, corridors. Offices are allocated to the respective laboratories in a conventional way. The highly equipped laboratories face north; the offices that do not comprise mechanical ventilation face south.

In the building part with two access corridors, the secondary spaces that do not require daylight are arranged in the middle zone. The required floor space was created by slightly rotating the southern row of rooms. This way, the sculptural qualities of the building are enhanced – an effect further increased by a drawer-like projecting volume that contains shared facilities.

This wing contains the communal areas. When seen from the south, the complex appears to be one single edifice. An exterior terrace and an artificial pond – as parts of the exterior landscaping – merge the building with the surrounding landscape.

In contrast to the vivid southern façade of the institute, the solid northern façade is based on a rather strict range of materials. The contrast between the two facades is further enhanced by the complex urban context. Combined, these characteristics make for an exciting metaphor for the complex requirements of the building.

The main building is a framed reinforced concrete structure. While the laboratory façade with its flush exterior window strips appears rather solid, the more generously glazed office facade open up towards he south. The fully glazed inserted volume housing the communal areas blurs the boundaries between building and landscape.

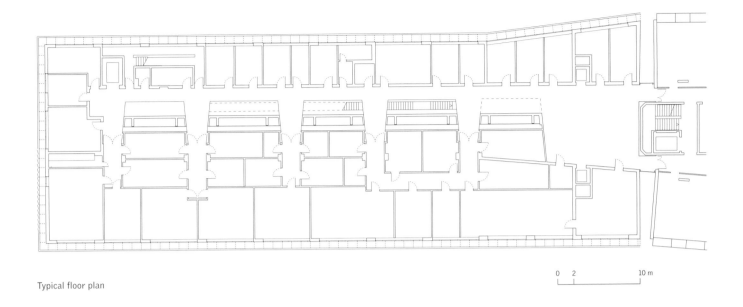

Typical floor plan

0 2   10 m

from left to right
The nearly symmetrical building occupies a narrow site | Colour takes away the rigidity of the building volume and expresses its solitary character | Open stairs and galleries with lateral light slots admit daylight into the building and assist natural ventilation at night | The colourful louvered façade provides reversible solar protection | Perspective drawing showing build-up of double-layered façade

Pharmacological Research Building, Boehringer Ingelheim Pharma KG

Biberach, Germany

Client	Boehringer Ingelheim Pharma KG
Architects	sauerbruch hutton architekten
Completion	2002
Net floor area	7,500 m²

The pharmacological research centre in Biberach is part of the research campus of Boehringer Ingelheim Pharma KG Company. Essentially, the building accommodates laboratories and offices.

The elongated seven-storey building shows a layout with a hybrid double-loaded corridor; it largely follows the shape of the given site. On the ground floor, the core zone widens into a foyer space on the side where it connects to the existing building fabric. This space functions as a structural and functional hinge linking to its neighbour on the other floors as well. Additionally, circulation routes on campus are to cross within the foyer.

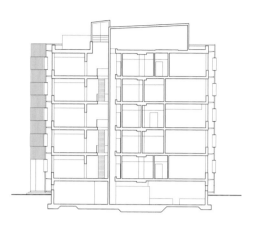

Cross section

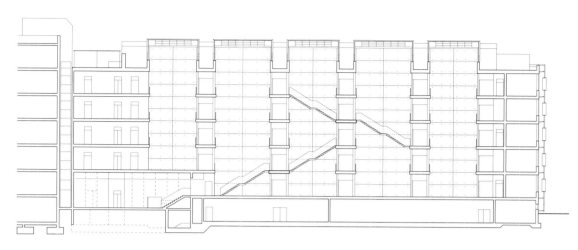

Longitudinal section

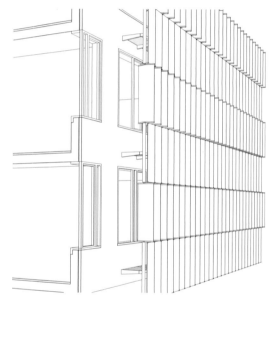

The floor plan comprises naturally ventilated offices on the west side and a highly equipped laboratory zone on the east side. As a special variation of the common research layout, equipment and measuring rooms, rooms with constant temperature, and chemical stores are directly attached to the laboratories. Between these highly air-conditioned special laboratories access corridors are located reducing the distances between the offices/think tanks and the experimental spaces.

The laboratories are 6 m, the office 4 m deep and separated by a narrow atrium space. Both zones are linked via galleries and bridges. Between the bridges, daylight can penetrate deeply into the building. Simul-taneously, thermal convection in the voids creates a stack effect assisting the natural ventilation of the offices. During summer, this building part is naturally cooled at night. The voids also accommodate an open staircase linking all levels.

The building is a reinforced concrete structure with a curtain wall façade. Glazed elements comprise integrated solar blinds, which when closed let the building appear as an austere box. The coloured louvers add a contrasting lively element. The double-skin façade also functions as a reversible solar control device and climatic buffer zone. When the blinds are fully opened, the façade cavity also functions as hot air extract and smoke extract for the supplementary escape route.

Site plan

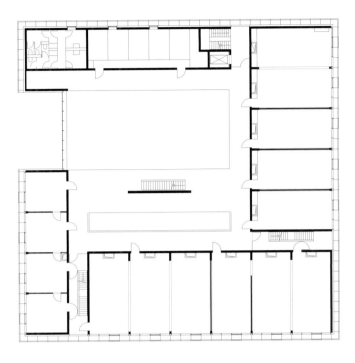

Upper floor plan

The glass façade provides the building with a coherent appearance |
Accentuation of the cores by means of printed façade elements. Opened
and closed louvers generate a vivid interplay

Centre for Energy and Technology

Rendsburg, Germany

Client	Stadt Rendsburg
Architects	Knoche Architekten
Construction period	1998-2000
Net floor area	3,400 m²
Cubic content	20,600 m³

The Centre for Energy and Technology aims to function as an "incubator" for young enterprises dealing with the generation and marketing of alternative sources of energy and the improvement of the respective technological processes. ZET addresses companies which develop system solutions for the optimisation of energy use – for instance through energy management of buildings. Both the exploitation of regenerative sources of energy and the use of fossil fuel are involved.

The building comprises four functional areas: administration (including spaces for events, training, and conferences), rented office spaces, workshops, and secondary spaces. All areas are arranged around a

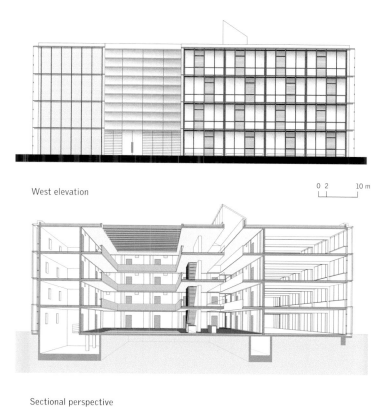

West elevation

0 2   10 m

Sectional perspective

Façade section

The common rooms benefit from transparency and brightness | The distinctive horizontal façade order of the atrium continues in the roof and is supplemented by solar blinds

four-storey atrium, which consists of a public entrance space for visitors and another hall segment that is reserved for the users. The galleries running round the atrium support communication and contact between users.

The interior design of the reinforced concrete frame structure restricts itself to a range of exposed finishes resulting from the structure itself. A monochrome environment is created that defines the architectural background for later and unforeseeable changes through the tenants. Interior walls are made of prefabricated timber elements that are mounted to the concrete structure. According to their function they have glazed or wooden panels.

The building avoids references to the bland urban situation on a peninsula in the east of the city and positions itself as a solitary volume on a square floor plan. Similar to the interior, which reacts to different functional requirements, its façades react to their respective directions. On all sides, the building received a double-layered façade creating a thermal buffer zone in winter and providing daytime-ventilation and night-time cooling during summer. The outer façade in front of the solid inner layer consists of imprinted float glass.

The areas for events, the offices, and workshops are generously glazed and have full height window elements. In this case, the outer skin consists of float glass with glass louvers for ventilation. The landscaping follows the idea of a harmonious integration into the environment, loosely arranged green spaces, and soft spatial transitions.

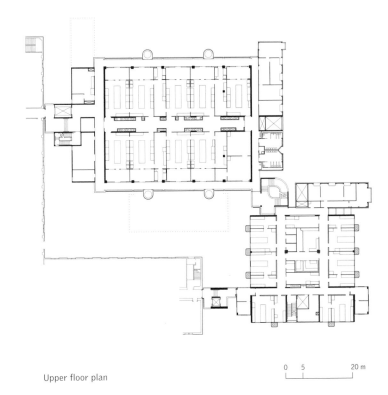

Ground floor plan

Upper floor plan

0 5   20 m

from left to right
Technical necessities define the high-tech character of the façades |
View from the south: biological laboratories are located in the western
wing (left-hand side); administration and chemical laboratories are
located in the eastern wing. Both wings combined form an L-shaped
figure forming the future entrance to the campus | Air-extracts of the
chemical laboratories are an integral part of the architectural concept |
Chemical labs are accessed via exterior walkways that also provide
solar protection

Molecular Sciences Building

Los Angeles, California, USA

Client	University of California
Architect	Anshen + Allen
Completion	1994
Total floor area	14,900 m²

A new generation of research buildings is changing
the appearance of the University of California in Los
Angeles campus. Among the projects that have been
realised since 1990, the Molecular Sciences Building
has had to meet the highest requirements in terms of
technical services. In addition to these complex and
specific requirements the building was also to serve
as "future gateway" and vivid plaza for scientific
communication.

The architects split the building into two main wings
which are connected at the corner by an expressive
cylindrical open stair tower that appears like a hinge
between the two buildings. The eastern wing is accessed via a central interior corridor and exterior

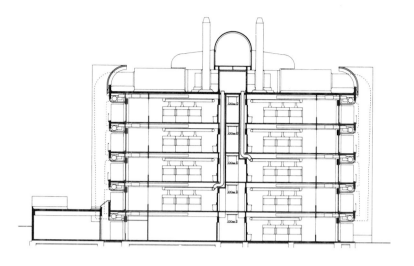

Cross section

walkways around its perimeter. Chemical laboratories are stacked on five storeys and arranged on either side of the central corridor. Study rooms are allocated behind the façade and additional offices are situated at its southern end. The west wing comprises two interior access corridors on four levels. Cold stores and rooms for technical equipment are arranged in the dark zone between the biological laboratories. Supplementary offices are positioned at its western gable end.

The main architectural features of the building are the components expressing technical services. Plant rooms are positioned on the roofs of both wings; they connect to vertical air-supply ducts that form an inte-

gral part of the façade structure. The exhaust system utilises air-extracts, double installation walls, and single shafts in the core of the chemical wing. The nearly 300 air-extracts that had to be installed inside the laboratories inspired an architecture that plays with the theme of "ventilation". The complex system of air-supply, conditioning, distribution, and extract became an integral part of the structure and the architectural language. Three square ventilation openings accentuate the entrance façade.

The use of material as well as the façade design reflecting the inner organisation of the building follow the notion of "form follows function" exactly and logically. Various concrete textures, the proportion of

open and solid areas, and the protruding and recessed elements give the chemical and biological laboratories, offices, seminar rooms, and even the sanitary spaces a very individual architectural expression.

The reinforced concrete frame structure possesses a powerful, almost monumental appearance and enhances the campus with its unique presence and high degree of individuality.

Site plan

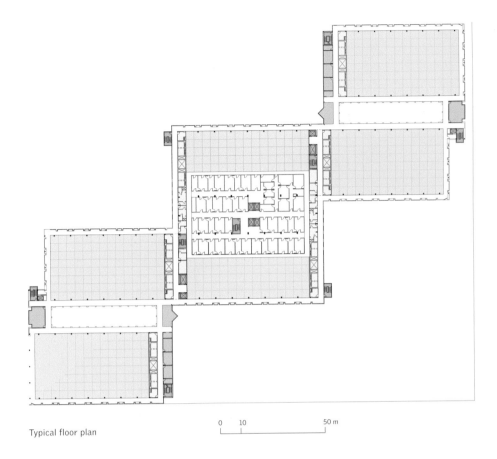

Typical floor plan

0   10   50 m

CIBA-Geigy
Life Sciences Building

Summit, New Jersey, USA

Client	Ciba Pharmaceuticals Division
Architects	Mitchell / Giurgola Architects, LLP
Construction period	1990-1994
Total floor area	40,900 m²

The renowned Swiss-based pharmaceutical company required an economical laboratory building of extremely high and sustainable flexibility to be built on a relatively tight site with unfavourable proportions. The extensive programme included a great number of biomolecular laboratories, a few special laboratories, and animal testing facilities; it led to a building highly equipped with technical services. The layout had to ensure that expected conversions resulting from frequent changes of use can be conducted efficiently and cause as few disruptions to the scientific operations as possible. At the same time, the large technical building was to maintain a communicative and friendly profile.

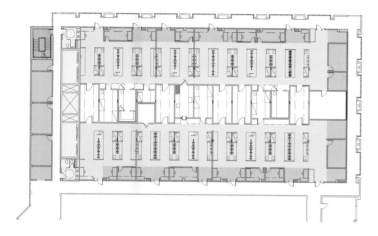

Partial floor plan showing laboratories

Cross section

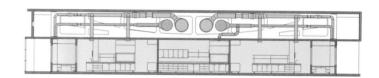

Detailed section of laboratory

from left to right
The prefabricated concrete façade elements are 6.7 m wide. Small square windows admit light to the service floors. In order to reduce the building mass, the top floor is slightly recessed | The courtyards with water features | Spaces for communication and interaction | The scientists have a laboratory area of 1,200 m² at their disposal

The architects solved the demanding task by a skilful use of the site, a structural system that provides flexibility, and an exemplary arrangement of the functional areas. Three staggered volumes break down these areas into single building parts to create a well-balanced distribution of the enormous building mass. All buildings comprise three laboratory floors, each with a service floor on top. This enables horizontal service ducts to connect to all laboratories via individual shafts; central installation cores are installed only at the gable ends. The relatively high expenditures for this layout including a large extent of mechanical services provide maximum flexibility in the event of future conversions or maintenance of services and will minimise disruptions to the operations.

The central building part with perimeter dimensions of 62 m x 73 m accommodates an animal testing laboratory and special laboratories for magnetic resonance based display systems.

Both end modules with perimeter dimensions of 55 m x 72 m respectively are split into two parts and comprise a full height, light-flooded inner hall with a water pond whose fountains are to dampen the noise coming from the laboratories. The storeys on either side of the hall are accessed via galleries and comprise five different zones. The central dark zone contains equipment and secondary spaces while the outer zones contain flexible open plan laboratories. As sufficient daylight enters the atrium, narrow zones with work

desks are positioned on the sides facing it. Seminar rooms and vertical access cores are located at the gable ends.

The prefabricated concrete structure with storey-high, 27 m long Vierendeel girders spanning the column-free laboratory areas accommodates interstitial technical floors to provide maximum flexibility with regard to building services.

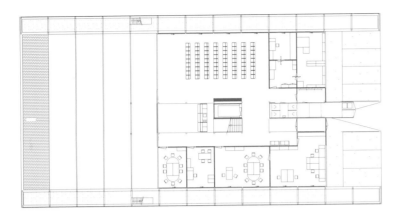

Ground floor plan

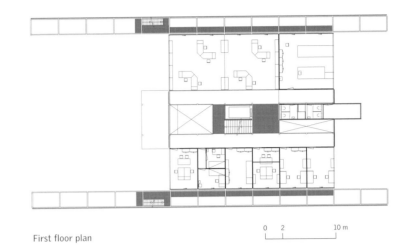

First floor plan

0   2   10 m

from left to right
The transparent wall provides privacy, yet maintains the building's contact to its environment | Perforated screens in front of the glazed main façades protect the research centre from wind and sun | The central glazed lift connecting the three storeys | The exterior transparency is also reflected in the interior

Centre for Human Drug Research

Leiden, Netherlands

Client	Foundation C.H.G. Immobilien
Architects	Architectenbureau cepezed b. v.
Construction period	1994-1995
Cubic content	13,500 m³

The client – a young expanding company – required a highly flexible and easily extendable building to accommodate unpredictable changes related to future activities and shifts in the research market for new medications. At the same time, the state-of-the-art building with a positive image was to provide an inspiring work environment supporting vivid interaction between scientists.

A feasibility study established that the common Dutch office grid of 5.4 x 1.8 x 5.4 m was not suitable. The alternative was a functional, asymmetrical building layout with two access corridors. The narrow eastern part of the building (width: 7.4 m) contains offices; the wider part (9.2 m) accommodates larger spaces

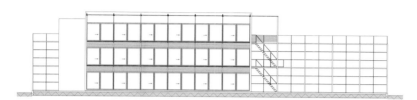

West elevation

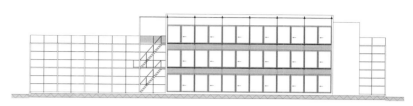

East elevation

as laboratories and conference rooms. Situated between the two parts, a generous foyer space with a vertical access core links both sides. This core also includes the mechanical core that serves both sides.

Due to the maximum building height of 10 m stipulated by the strategic master plan the building comprises three storeys. The main research areas and attached secondary spaces are located on the top floor, the large chemical laboratories and the offices on the first floor, and the spaces for visitors and management as well as archives and conference rooms on the ground floor.

The structure is based on a 3.6 m grid and consists of 2 m wide load-bearing steel frames. They receive the

loads of the steel girders supporting the floor slabs. The overall structure is composed of two independent parts. A flat roof connects both wings and distributes the wind loads.

Down to the lift shaft, the building stands out for its transparency. The two perforated steel screens lining the façades above all set the stage for the building's appearance: At night, light seeps through the façade so it looks veiled; during the day, it appears much larger than it actually is. The screens provide solar protection, security, and wind protection. Spaces with walkways behind the façade screens enable natural ventilation. In the event of fire they can also be used as escape routes, rendering other fire protection measures superfluous.

Elevation

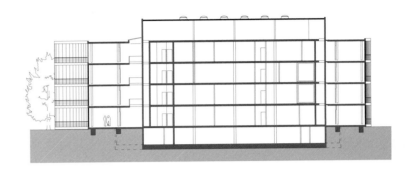

Longitudinal section

Laboratory Building for Medical Genome Research

Berlin, Germany

Client	Max-Delbrück-Centre (MDC)
Architects	Volker Staab Architekten
Completion	2004
Net floor area	3,500 m²

The building is situated at the far end of the main axis of the Biomedical Research Campus in Berlin-Buch. The prominent curve on one of its corners, which houses the main entrance, reaches out to this axis. The organically shaped envelope also reflects the adjacent forest and the little brook bordering onto the premises in the east.

The design juxtaposes a "hard" orthogonal core containing laboratories with a softly undulating envelope. The curved façades change from a glazed curtain wall in front of the office zones to a more conventional band façade in front of the laboratories.

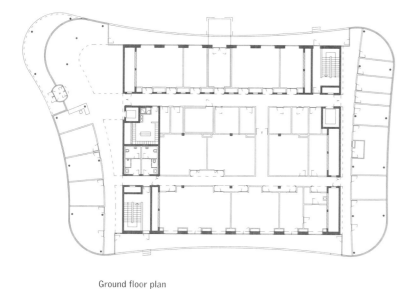

Ground floor plan

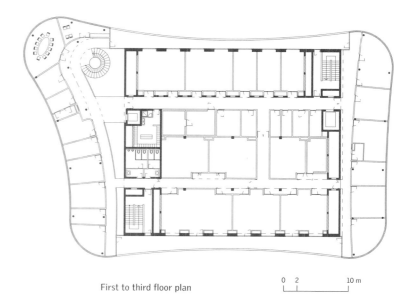

First to third floor plan

0 2   10 m

from left to right
Site plan | The organically shaped envelope takes up the scenery of the adjacent forest and little brook bordering onto the premises in the east | The central stair inside the entrance hall serves as main vertical access and focal point of social life | Access to laboratories

Offices are located east and west of the laboratory zone. The glazed curtain wall consists of transparent and solid elements that act as casement windows, spandrel panels, or solar protection devices. Raised floors in the office area contain full services for data processing that can be extended as required. Many scientists take advantage of the office equipment to control their experiments in the laboratories online.

The middle zone houses highly equipped laboratories. Façades here are recessed, making this zone recognisable. Escape balconies follow the outline of the building and prevent potential vertical fire spread. On the south side, they cantilever further than on the north side, thus contributing to solar protection.

The laboratory area is split into two zones of different character. On the north side, classical laboratories are located and serviced via service shafts located between access corridors and labs. They comprise laboratory furnishings arranged perpendicular to the façade and writing desks allocated next to the windows. The central dark zone houses rooms for equipment, cooling cells, rooms for chemicals and solvents as well as storage rooms. Laboratories on the south side have been arranged in a different way: shafts for media, gas, and water supply are part of the façade. The interior wall facing the corridor is a flexible drywall partition that allows parts of the central dark zone to be combined with the spaces to create a variety of laboratory sizes up to 350 m².

Ducts for ventilation and air-conditioning of the laboratories run in central cores that enable horizontal servicing without the intersection of ducts. This leads to relatively low ceiling heights of approx. 3.75 m.

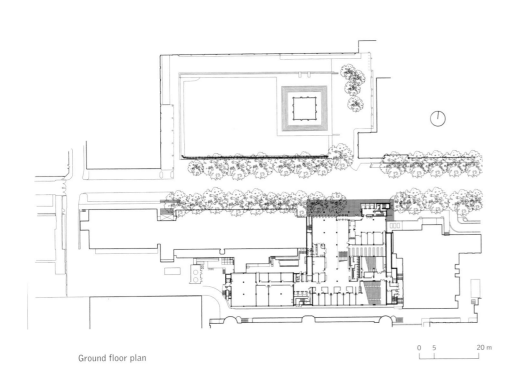

Ground floor plan

0 5   20 m

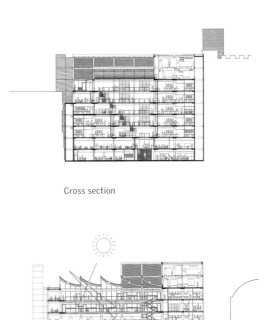

Cross section

North-south longitudinal section

Sir Alexander Fleming
Building, Imperial College

London, UK

Client	Imperial College and South Kensington Millennium Commission
Architects	Foster and Partners
Construction period	1994-1998
Total floor area	25,000 m²
Net floor area	16,000 m²

The destruction of numerous buildings of the Imperial College during World War II left the scientific campus without a clear urban layout. To ensure an integrated and coordinated future development, in the beginning of the nineties a master plan was established defining building plots and massing of the most important building projects; it also stipulated essential planning and design criteria.

The first building to be erected in accordance with this master plan is the Sir Alexander Fleming Building whose advanced architecture represents progress and the great potential of biomedical research and is to give rise to unprecedented interdisciplinary scientific exchange of ideas on a social and intellectual level.

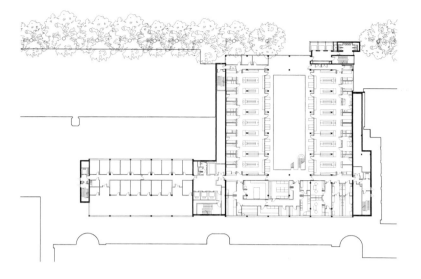

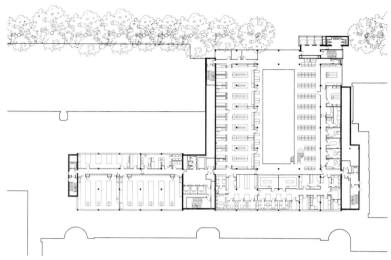

Floor plan level 3

Floor plan level 4

from left to right
Historic Queen's Tower mirrored in the glazed façade | Open galleries with work desks surround the atrium; laboratories follow | Colourful atrium wall designed by Per Arnoldi | Footbridges serve as zones for social interaction | The atrium widens from the second to fourth floor and provides terraces to be used by students

The available site was a gap between two institute buildings to the east and west. Towards the south, only a small path separates the new building from the existing Science Museum. Only towards the north the building affords relatively unrestricted views onto Queen's Law and Queen's Tower – the last remaining fragments of the original campus of 1890.

The scheme makes skilful use of the restrictive site and proposes a compact introverted building with a five-storey light-flooded communication space at its centre and research spaces arranged around it. The central space is reminiscent of an agora and gets increasingly wider and brighter towards the top as the floor areas around it get smaller. The saw-tooth roof covering the atrium provides an interesting and optimised mixed lighting scenario which is composed of indirect northern light and direct sunlight in points.

Open galleries with work desks surround the central space. Laboratories are arranged adjacent to the galleries. Their modular layout and strict service grid that includes central service shafts along the main façades ensure the required variability in terms of size and technical equipment. A service zone comprising equipment, cool storage, and special laboratories partly constitutes a dark zone that is located adjacent to the existing building or faces south and receives daylight. This U-shaped typical floor plan with various access corridors ensures short distances between related spaces and close cooperation between scientists conducting theoretical studies and scientists working in the laboratories.

The north-facing entrance area – comprising individual office cells and connecting bridges that are also used for informal meetings – with its fully glazed main façade affords attractive views of the historic part of the campus.

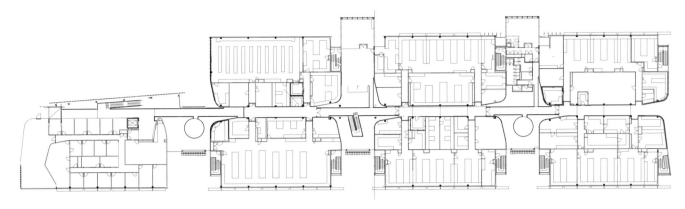

First floor plan

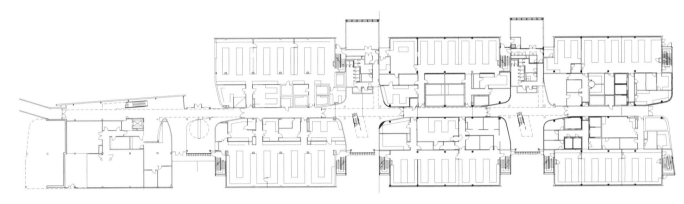

Ground floor plan

from left to right

Canopies and blinds are typical for the architecture in a country exposed to extreme solar radiation | The entrance is accentuated by an inclined glass screen. It mirrors the sky and the earth, but not approaching onlookers or the surrounding buildings | Laboratories | Communication platforms with wavy polycarbonate balustrades are suspended within the towers | Laboratory façades feature solar blinds made of timber or concrete

Biosciences Building, Bundoora West Campus, RMIT University

Melbourne, Australia

Client	RMIT University
Architects	John Wardle Architects
Construction period	1998-2001
Total floor area	10,600 m²
Net floor area	5,000 m²
Cubic content	47,800 m³

During the last years, RMIT University consistently extended its campus in Bundoora, a suburb in the northwest of Melbourne. In 2001, the new Biosciences Building was completed. The idea for the two-storey building is based on the layering and connection of landscape and research areas. The end of the linear building volume cuts into the slope with a height difference of 6 m on a length of 160 m. Hence, both floors possess its own separate entrance at ground level.

The project reflects the architect's passion for structural interpretations of architectural concepts, which shows in every detail. He describes the building as "a rope with spliced end" that could merge with the next

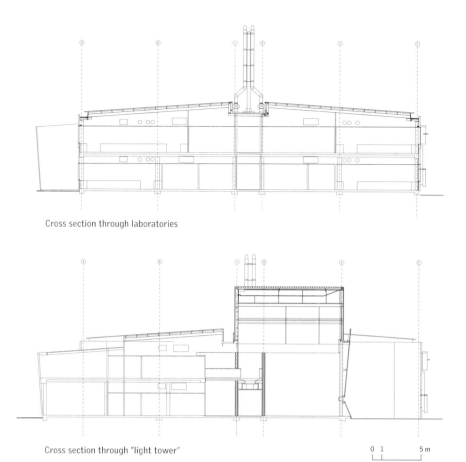

Cross section through laboratories

Cross section through "light tower"

0 1   5 m

Site plan

module. Six modular research areas follow the entrance building. Arranged on both sides of a central corridor, they accommodate large laboratories suitable for biomedical research as well as allocated deep service and equipment zones. A single-sided administration area completes the scheme.

The corridor between these modules widens into communication areas; vertically, these areas form "light towers" that are fully glazed, thereby relating to the exterior. These spaces for events and communication are conceived as cross-paths within the building that at the same time allow daylight to reach the central corridor.

The exterior appearance plausibly reflects the various functions within the building. The entrance hall across the administration wing features an inclined glass screen split in two parts mirroring the sky and the earth, but not the onlooker or other buildings. With its aluminium "visor" inspired by palisade fences the administration area clearly sets itself apart from the laboratory wings and links the whole complex to the campus centre.

The fixtures and furnishings of the laboratories are strictly functional and follow an austere and elegant line. The laboratory façades consist of horizontal strips of etched concrete and glass panels – the latter ma-

terial was chosen to achieve even, diffuse daylight conditions. T-shaped sunscreen elements are fixed in front. On the first floor, they consist of etched concrete; on the ground floor, black steel interspersed irregularly with red wood was used as a reference to the red wood trees that used to grow here.

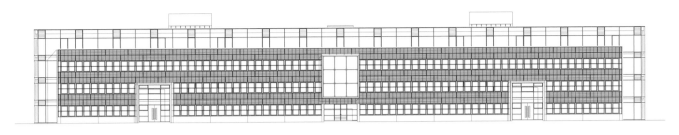

Elevation of laboratory building

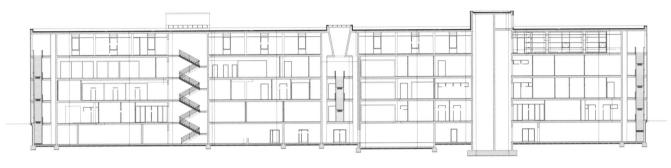

Section through laboratory building

from left to right
Laboratory building with glazed mechanical floor | Terracotta and larch contrast with steel and glass | Corridor | Above: The colour scheme accentuates certain areas: yellow is used as a guiding colour throughout the building, blue highlights "cold" materials | Bottom right: Greenhouses are arranged adjacent to the laboratory building containing application and climatic chambers

BIOSTEIN
Agrobiological Research Centre of Novartis Crop Protection AG

Stein/Aarau, Switzerland

Client	Novartis Crop Protection AG, Basel
Architects	wilhelm und partner Freie Architekten
Construction period	1996-1998
Net floor area	15,400 m²
Cubic content	89,600 m³

After the fusion of CIBA and GEIGY the corporation was owner of four research facilities for crop protection and yet another one after the fusion with Sandoz in 1996. To amend this inefficient decentralised situation the new Novartis Corporation decided to build a central agrobiological research centre.

Through the particular arrangement of the buildings, footpaths at ground level, and the successive layout of courtyards of varying sizes, the complex provides optimum functionality, orientation, and lighting. The symmetrical complex is orientated in north-south direction. In successive order, the three-storey laboratory and office building, followed by the application and climatic chambers, the greenhouses and finally

First floor plan
of laboratory building

Ground floor plan
of laboratory building

0 2   10 m

the horticulture have been arranged symmetrically. Facilities are linked via glazed passages. This linear arrangement corresponds with the research processes within the main sections Disease Control und Insect Control. All four areas are connected within these respective sections via east-west and north-south orientated paths. The zoning, which mainly follows functional considerations, is also motivated by a graded security concept for toxicological or genetic experiments.

The southern laboratory and office building framed by a glazed service floor on top and glazed staircases on both ends forms the entrance the complex. Both sections have a separate entrance. On the ground floor, the mentioned glazed passages are linked to the mid-

dle zone of the entrance building and connect it to the application and climatic chambers.

The middle zone accommodates the cores including lift, stair, sanitary rooms, and secondary spaces. This zone also contains the central shafts for the technical infrastructure. They feed horizontal lines along the corridors so that the service connections to office and laboratory areas can flexibly adapt to changes of the layout.

Escape stairs at either end and in the centre of the building split up each floor into two equally sized fire compartments.

Within clearly structured spaces, the complex offers qualities like openness, spaces for teamwork, and an inspiring research environment. Each section comprises a lounge and cafeteria on the first floor. The "intellectual centre" is the shared two-storey library at the building's centre. As do the entrances, it juts out of the façade.

Main elevation

from left to right
The scale of the massive complex was broken down by court-yards, terraces, and pergolas | Brick and stone cladding | The three-storey atrium featuring an open stair enlivens the building's | Transparent walls of the laboratories towards the corridors provide a visually open environment

Biological Sciences and Bioengineering Building, Indian Institute of Technology

Kanpur, India

Client	Indian Institute of Technology
Architects	Kanvinde Rai & Chowdhury Architects & Planners
Construction period	2002-2003
Total floor area	5,900 m²

The building is located on a rectangular, east-west orientated site. It belongs to the campus of one of the leading technology institutes of India. According to the brief it is divided into two wings – a laboratory building and a common multi-purpose zone. Thus, the different areas can be horizontally and vertically arranged according to their function and the required technical services.

The laboratory building, which consists of three modules in a row, comprises altogether 16 large laboratories with 80 m² net floor area each. Each laboratory has access to its own office space and contains writing desks along the windows. There are two interior corridors per floor; the middle zone of the two west-

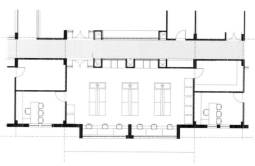

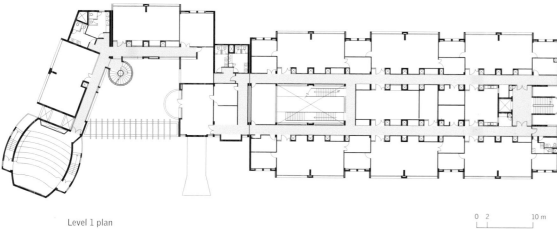

Level 1 plan

0 2   10 m

ern modules contains service areas including cold storages, zones for technical equipment, and auto-clave rooms. A building-height glass-covered atrium is located in the eastern module. It opens up the interior corridors and creates a pleasant and inviting atmosphere. This effect is added to by glazed elements between the hallways and the laboratories. The central module contains two laboratory levels; the outer modules are three storeys high. By means of this variation in height the building responds to the existing context and structures the substantial building bulk.

Plant rooms on the basement level distribute services via a dense grid of individual vertical shafts, this way providing the required flexibility for future changes of laboratory and equipment standards.

A shared building comprises a lecture hall that can also be used by neighbouring institutes. It also accommodates a number of seminar rooms, a library, and the management of the institute. These spaces are arranged around a two-storey, freely shaped fore-court that is dominated by a spiral stair reminiscent of the DNA double helix.

Other measures taken by the architects to break down the scale of the building are numerous projections and recesses in the façade as well as rhythmical changes in the material. The solid construction has façades with punched windows or horizontal strip windows clad with facing brick or stone. These materials pay reference to the immediate urban environment, which is also solidly constructed and shows brick or concrete façades, as it is customary in Kanpur.

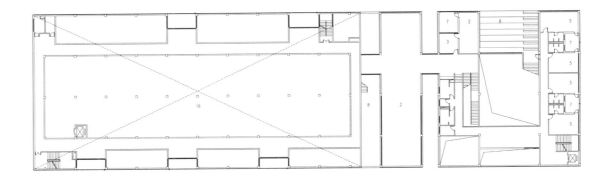

First floor plan

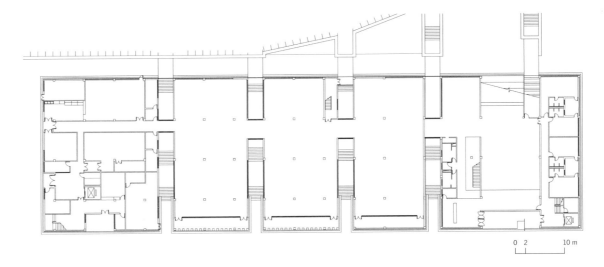

Ground floor plan

0 2   10 m

Southwest Bio-Tech Intermediate Test Base

Chongquing, China

Client	Blue Blood Sci-Tech Investment and Management Co. Ltd
Architects	Atelier Feichang Jianzhu
Construction period	2000-2001
Total floor area	8,100 m²

The research centre is located in a hilly terrain in one of the most densely populated regions of the world. To the northeast, a road with increasing traffic load flanks the institute that is set back from the south bank of the Yangtze River. The building's design is determined by this context and by a mixed programme that did not lend itself to a conventional layout.

The biomedical and biotechnological enterprise required a building providing laboratories and offices for the scientists as well as production areas, secondary and multi-purpose spaces, and apartments for the employees working in shifts.

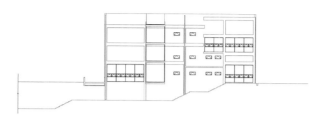

Cross section

Site plan

Longitudinal section

from left to right
The deep cuts in the façade relate to different functions behind | The façade made of grey concrete blocks does not tell that the building houses highly equipped laboratories | Towards the rear, the building affords sweeping views of the surrounding landscape | Highly equipped laboratories mainly used for biomedical research

The result is a design that organises the different functions heterogeneously both in vertical and horizontal direction. The exterior presents itself as an elongated compact building volume that unifies various groups of rooms between two oversized wall slabs. However, their differences are pronounced by individually placed openings and deep cuts in the façade, which also connect the building to the landscape and river.

The building accommodates areas of different floor heights. The northern four-storey wing contains apartments and offices and connects to the remaining building part via bridges and corridors. Three linked modules in the centre of the complex house areas for test

production; to the south, a cafeteria has access to the exterior. Hence, the ground floor can be classified into public, non-public, and semi-public zones.

Due to larger floor heights the southern part of the complex comprises only three storeys. The major part of the first floor consists of an open laboratory area including study spaces. A conference room, some laboratories, meeting rooms, and offices are located on the second floor, the offices being detached by courtyards allocated behind the cuts in the façade. Together with a palm court these areas serve as spaces for communication and regeneration and characterise the integrating general concept.

The reinforced concrete frame structure received a façade of facing hollow concrete blocks that appears rather conventional; it does not tell that highly equipped laboratories are located behind it.

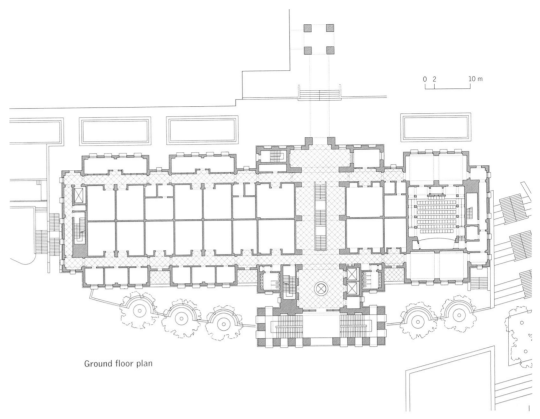

Site plan

Ground floor plan

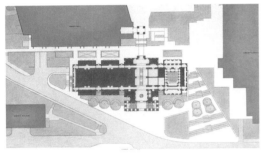

0 2   10 m

from left to right
View from the north-west: A bridge links the research area to the engineering faculty | A protruding six-storey office volume on columns marks the main entrance to the building | Copper barrel roof and oversized ventilation pipes are integral parts of the sculptural design concept | Entrance staircase to the first floor

Engineering Research Center, University of Cincinnati

Cincinnati, Ohio, USA

Client	University of Cincinnati
Architects	Michael Graves & Associates with KZF Inc.
Completion	1995
Net floor area	8,800 m²

The Engineering Research Center is centrally located on the premises of the University of Cincinnati at the end of University Avenue (the eastern main access). To the west, the site borders onto Rhodes Hall, which belongs to the engineering faculty. To the north, a representative outside staircase extends to an upper level plaza, the university library, and an auditorium.

An axis connecting University Place, the main entrance, an inner staircase, and the upper plaza runs at right angles through the building. At the end of this axis, a two-storey bridge links the centre to the main buildings of the engineering faculty.

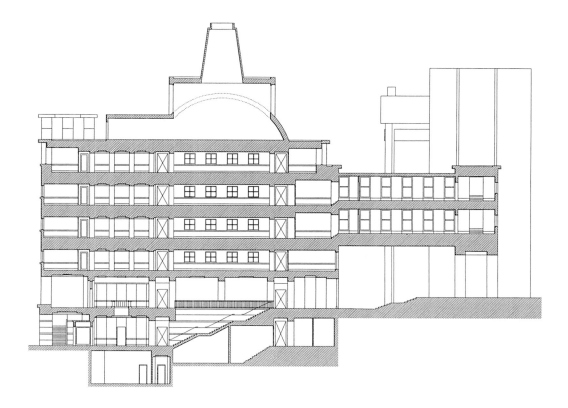

East-west section through loggia, entrance hall and bridge

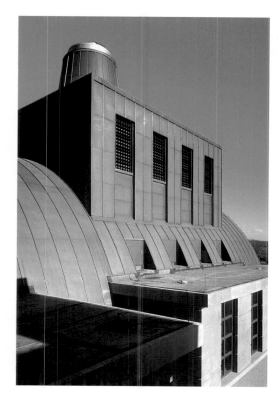

A consequent zoning and stacking of the complex' main functions in plan and elevation strictly follows economical considerations and typological criteria. The upper floors comprise a rectangular core zone with highly equipped dry and wet laboratories. Naturally lit standard offices are arranged along the main façades. Shared spaces like lecture hall and seminar rooms are located at the northern gable end. Further office and conference spaces are located near the main entrance.

The rational arrangement of the functions is combined with a poignant sculptural exterior of the building that is expressed strongest in the south and north elevations. A barrel roof with oversized exhaust pipes above the plant room dominates the façades. The main elevation to the east is characterised by the large-scale massing through building-high oriels and a protruding symmetrical six-storey volume featuring the main entrance.

The façades with punch windows received a cladding of terracotta and ochre-coloured facing brick with applications of cast stone. The partly vaulted and partly cuboid roof above the plant room – which leaves sufficient room for supplementary installations in the future – and the large air exhaust and intake "chimneys" are clad in copper.

The architectural language directly refers to the existing context on the university premises. It combines sturdy monumentality with delicate detailing in timber, brick and clinker, which gives the complex its individual character and reflects the artchitects' and the client's affiliation to historic examples.

From a science point of view, today's international and interdisciplinary character of basic research clearly leads to one conclusion: In the future, only few discoveries will be the result of individual work taking place in separate work spaces. Today, most scientific ideas arise from social and multi-disciplinary interaction of people with different backgrounds and working on different projects. Innovative results can only be achieved through active communication.

Hence, in order to accomplish sustained economical viability of a building, design concepts have to be more than a simple response to the brief. Beyond the basic requirements for experimental and theoretical work, the architecture has to create an overall atmosphere of communication. It has to provide a special "communicative quality" by offering spaces where users can meet, by chance or as part of a schedule. Globally, modern research buildings meet this requirement by a higher ratio of circulation areas and by improving the quality of circulation and lounge areas to serve as places of social interaction. These circulation areas can be used for spontaneous communication or scientific discussions, lectures, poster workshops, exhibition spaces, and for increasingly socially relevant public relation work.

Communication

168
Max Planck Institute for
Molecular Cell Biology and Genetics

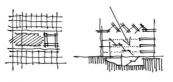

172
Donald Danforth Plant Science Center

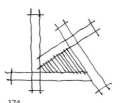

174
Graz Research Centre of the
Austrian Academy of Sciences

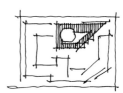

176
Naito Chemistry Building and Bauer Laboratory
Building, Harvard University

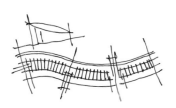

178
Gifu Research Laboratories
of Amano Enzyme Inc.

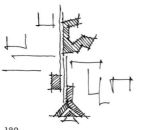

180
AstraZeneca Research and Development Centre
for Biology and Pharmacy

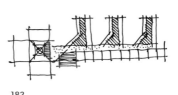

182
Max Planck Institute for Plasma Physics,
Greifswald Branch

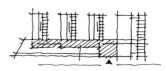

186
Max Planck Institute for Chemical Ecology

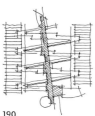

190
Faculty of Mechanical Engineering,
Technical University of Munich

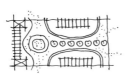

192
James H. Clark Center, Stanford University

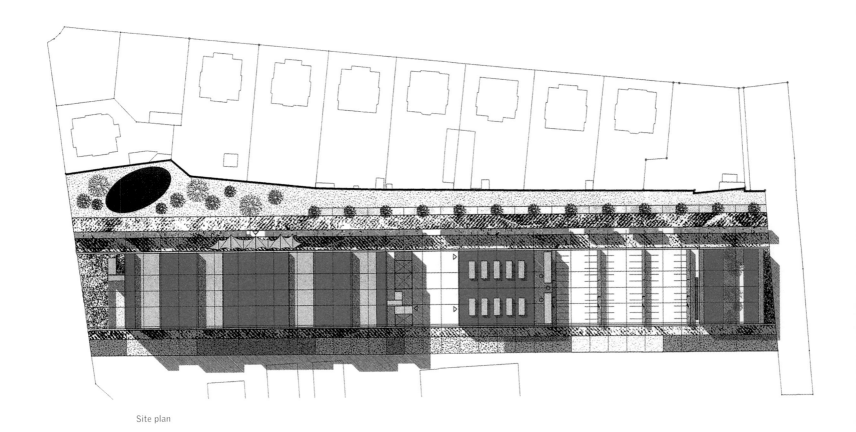

Site plan

from left to right
Access area | Main façade with top service deck | Main entrance covered by canopy | Entrance hall featuring wall installation by George Steinmann

Max Planck Institute for Molecular Cell Biology and Genetics

Dresden, Germany

Client	Max-Planck-Gesellschaft zur Förderung der Wissenschaften e.V.
Architects	Heikkinen-Komonen Architects with Henn Architekten
Construction period	1999-2000
Net floor area	9,700 m²
Cubic content	101,000 m³

The Max Planck Institute for Molecular Cell Biology and Genetics provides an example how local, regional, national, and global parameters and developments can be taken into account when planning a research building. When the institute was built, basic medical-biological research in the field of life sciences played a similar role as did physics at the beginning of the 20th century when it stood at the verge of a paradigm change. The institute was founded in Dresden in 1997 as part of the reconstruction programme of the former GDR – subsequent to the German reunification seven years earlier. The location is ideal in terms of future scientific co-operations with Central and Eastern European countries and in terms of support of potentially numerous young scientists in the region.

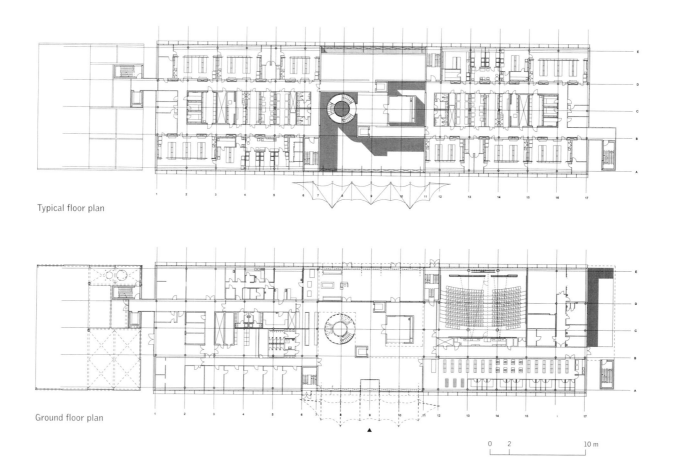

Typical floor plan

Ground floor plan

0   2   10 m

Also, the close proximity to the Clinic of Dresden Technical University promotes co-operation. In the medium term, the institute is expected to produce viable research results attracting new biotech investors and encouraging the foundation of new biotechnical businesses in its vicinity.

The architectural design strives to create a sophisticated work atmosphere fit to support the ambitious, creative work of the scientists. Apart from the required technical functionality of individual work places and apparatuses, the building was also to encourage social interaction. Corridors, shared areas, vertical circulation areas, and even the relatively large laboratory units were designed not only to support social inter-

action but to make it a downright unavoidable, essential part of everyday life.

The brief called for three functional units. Institute building, animal testing facilities, and guest apartments were arranged linearly on the site of a former tram depot 50 m in width and 270 m in length: Accordingly, the whole complex was divided into many more segments that can be associated with the barcode of a genetic fingerprint. All building volumes are linked by an access route running the entire depth of the site. On the side facing a row of turn-of-the-century villas a landscaped green space is laid out parallel to the site.

The institute building is situated in the northern part of the site and can be easily recognised from Pfotenhauerstraße. Further south follow the animal testing facility, a parking area that constitutes an area for potential future extensions, and the guest apartments including a kindergarten jointly operated with the clinic. The institute building itself consists of two separate five-storey volumes. A full height foyer space is situated in between.

The light-flooded entrance hall acts as a hub for all vertical and horizontal circulation routes. Mainly on the ground floor, it is used intensively as a place of social interaction, for communal lunches, and the exchange of scientific ideas. The large space contains a

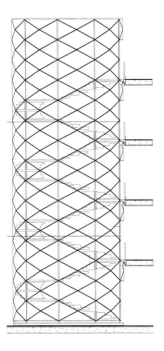

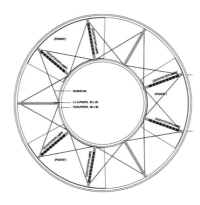

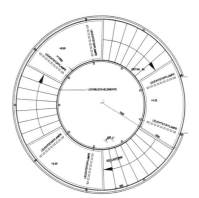

Spiral stair in central hall:
Elevation – structure – ground floor plan

number of shared facilities such as a cafeteria, restaurant, reading gallery, seminar rooms, and a spiral stair without losing its splendid spatial qualities. The foyer also provides direct access to common facilities, for example the library, auditorium, administration, kitchen, and workshops.

The typological layout of the floor plans results from the subdivision of the institute in up to 32 independent and self-sustained scientific research teams. Each team can dispose of a large laboratory space of approx. 80 m² which is equipped to suit molecular biological and partly also wet preparation works. Four such large laboratories on each floor respectively form a so-called "home base". They largely lack individual offices or studies and are instead fitted with writing desks positioned near the windows and acoustically separated from the main space by glazed partitions. This arrangement ensures constant flux between theory and experiment. Single offices have been allocated only at the northern and southern gable ends. "Think cells" within the library provide spaces for concentrated work.

The layout of interior circulation and functional zones follows the principle that new ideas and scientific success can only be achieved through a vivid, sometimes random exchange of ideas. The design attempts not to confine the scientists to secluded, isolated laboratory cells or "think cells" but to encourage active and critical exchange by means of corridors and circulation paths that support meetings. Their generous dimensions, a number of attractive views, seats and bays at crossing paths invite the users to linger and communicate.

Both building volumes comprise two access corridors on all upper floors with nearly symmetrically laid out functional areas. The central dark zone consists of common special laboratories for analysis, cell culture, and microscopy.

Altogether, the institute has a capacity of about 300 work places for scientists. The technical building comprises two storeys for animal keeping and a plant

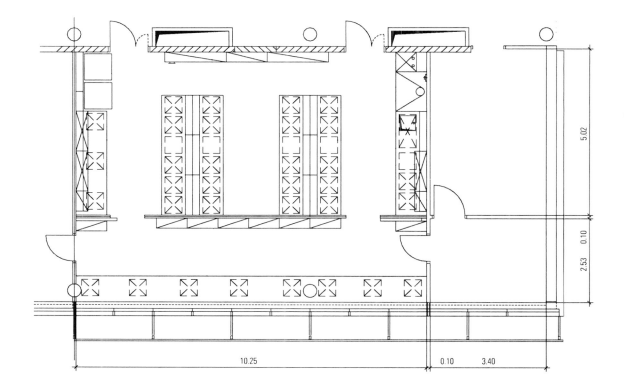

Schematic floor plan
with allocated writing desk zone

5.02

0.10

2.53

10.25

0.10

3.40

from left to right
Lounge and reading zone in central hall | Seminar rooms articulated with entrance hall as individual building volumes | Central stair case | Transition between lab benches and writing desks in open plan laboratories

room basement. Exterior walkways provide access to the 18 guest apartments that can be combined to form 2-bedroom flats.

The exterior of the complex is dominated by the structure and colour scheme of the façades. At its gable ends the reinforced concrete frame structure is clad with bright blue aluminium panels. The plant rooms at roof level form prominent sculptural volumes. The most striking feature, however, are the fixed exterior solar protection blinds consisting of a fine green aluminium mesh. Depending on the viewpoint of the onlooker, the mesh and the blue façade behind generate unique iridescent effects that stick in one's memory.

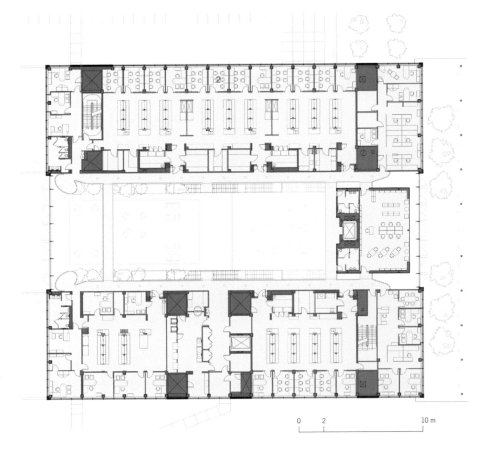

The public space in the centre is flanked by the two work zones, which are divided into workstations for theoretical and experimental activities

0   2   10 m

from left to right
Greenhouses in classic north-south direction | View from the south showing canopy shading the main entrance | The rational design concept is reflected in the layout of workstations within laboratories | Above: view of the atrium as centre of communication showing galleries, bridges and "Jacob's ladders" | Bottom right: local timber was used for the laboratory furnishings

Donald Danforth Plant Science Center

St. Louis, Missouri, USA

Client	Donald Danforth Plant Science Center
Architects	Nicholas Grimshaw & Partners
Completion	2001
Net floor area	15,500 m²
Cubic content	62,000 m³ (greenhouses not included)

The Donald Danforth Plant Science Center is an independent non-profit research facility committed to a broad scope of fundamental research in the field of plant physiology. In this function, it is part of an exemplary partnership of various private organisations and state universities. The region known as Corn Belt of the United States today hosts the "Silicon Valley" of agricultural research with St. Louis as its centre.

The centre aims at the sustained improvement of human health and nutrition standards as well as the efficiency of agricultural production, for instance by means of improved and pest-resistant seeds. The new building is situated on a 40 acre site which offers sufficient possibility for future extensions. As a cen-

Cross section facing north

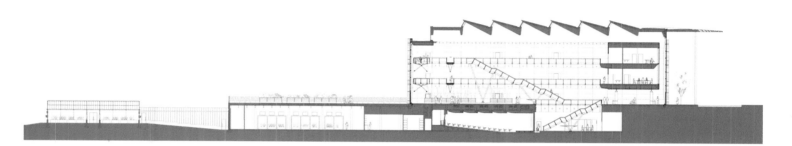

Longitudinal section with greenhouses and plant growth chambers

tre at the heart of an agro-biological region, the facilities play an important role in the communication with other leading research institutes and enterprises.

In the middle of the symmetrical complex an atrium covers the entire length and full height of the building. This space is accessible to everyone and forms the centre of internal and external communication. Offices and laboratories are arranged according to their required mechanical services to the east and west of the atrium. The variously dimensioned open plan laboratory spaces are situated between the office area oriented towards the façade and the service and specialised laboratory spaces directed towards the hall. Signalising openness and transparency, the

gable ends of the atrium are fully glazed. Additional daylight enters the atrium through a saw-tooth roof. The vertical as well as horizontal circulation system between public and research areas comprises a number of elements that structure the atrium and provide a human scale: open galleries, bridges linking both wings, and two "Jacob's ladders".

To the south, a widely cantilevering canopy highlights the main entrance. The canopy acts as a screen keeping direct sunlight off the glazed front, thus reducing solar gains inside. Combined, the saw-tooth roof, the canopy, and a reflecting water pond control the building's thermal balance.

To the north, the building makes use of the sloping site to accommodate underground growth chambers well protected from exterior climatic conditions. They received green roofs that provide further thermal insulation. Finally, classical rows of greenhouses in north-south direction complete the layout.

The building is a reinforced concrete frame structure with thermal insulation and a terracotta rain screen on an aluminium substructure. The complex is of a unified appearance that strengthens the identity of the research centre. The combination of technically advanced and traditional, natural materials will support the idea and the goals of the Center.

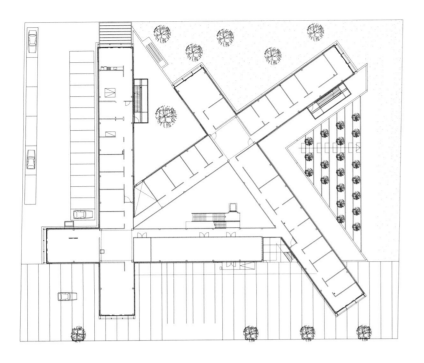

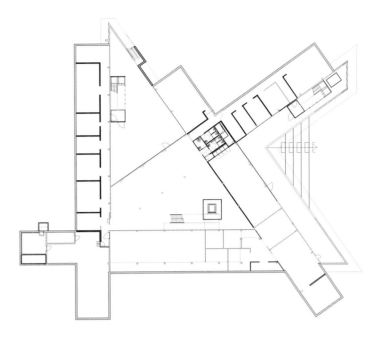

Ground floor plan

First floor plan

from left to right
The horizontal strip windows afford direct views onto the differently designed exterior courtyards and improve orientation within the building | At night, the main entrance and the glazed building ends start to shine | Exterior courtyard with glazed staircase | The atrium with the main stairway and the galleries around its perimeter

Graz Research Centre of the Austrian Academy of Sciences

Graz, Austria

Client	Österreichische Akademie der Wissenschaften
Architects	Architectenbureau cepezed b.v.
Construction period	1998-2000
Total floor area	6,000 m²
Cubic content	23,600 m³

The research centre accommodates sections of the Institute for Space Science, the Institute of Biophysics and X-ray Structure Research as well as five project teams of the humanities. Major design parameters for the design concept were different space requirements of the individual sections and a rather small site near the Mur River. The brief called for high flexibility and variable institute sizes; internal communication areas were considered to be of equal importance.

Extensive preliminary design work conducted by the architects led to a solution with two freely sited cross-shaped building volumes enclosing a central atrium. Throughout the building, single-loaded corridors provide access to the individual offices that without ex-

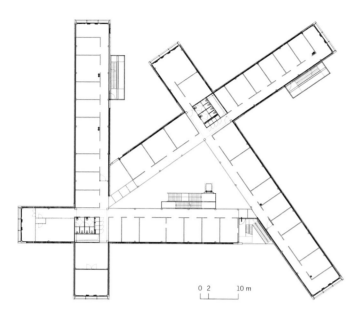

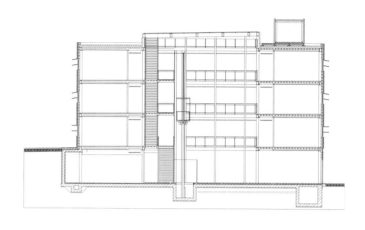

Third floor plan

0 2   10 m

Cross section

ception receive sufficient daylight. The offices themselves are largely standardised but favourably contrast with the unusual geometry and layout of the wings resulting in highly individual orientation, views, environment, and lighting. The exterior landscaping enhances these qualities.

The atrium with its surrounding galleries reinforces the importance of internal communication for the building concept. It is the central circulation node containing the main staircase that provides access to the galleries. Spaces for meetings and informal conversations are located at the end of the wings; service cores are to be found where the wings intersect. The basement below the atrium houses primarily

shared facilities, for example the library, canteen, and seminar rooms.

The façade consists of transparent and solid components: thermally insulated aluminium-clad concrete panels and glazed elements with fixed or movable aluminium panels which fulfil multiple tasks as windows, walls, or solar protection devices. In the work areas, they mostly serve as solar blinds or blacking-out panels; in the access corridors they are fixed.

For the most part, the structure consists of prefabricated elements – to some extent storey-high sandwich elements that were installed with fully completed finishes on either side. The interior atrium makes

use of the thermal stack effect for natural ventilation and allows night-cooling via ventilation louvers during summer.

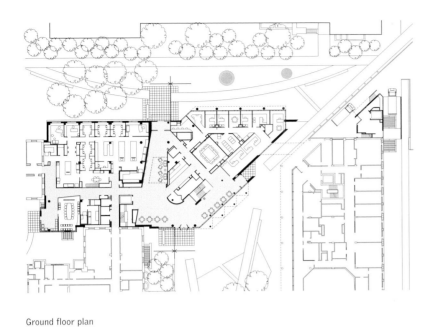

Ground floor plan

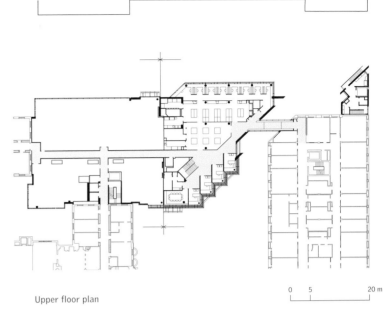

Upper floor plan

0 5 20 m

from left to right
The vivid composition of red sandstone panels and glazed elements projects an image of openness and transparency, and represents a new interpretation of the existing brick buildings | The austere outdoor space at Frisbie Place mediates between existing and new buildings | A laboratory in the Naito Building showing air extracts and exposed installations | Transparency of Bauer Institute's laboratory and entrance zones

Naito Chemistry Building and Bauer Laboratory Building, Harvard University

Cambridge, Massachusetts, USA

Client	Harvard University
Architects	Ellenzweig Associates, Inc., Architects
Completion	2000 (phase I) – 2002 (phase II)
Total floor area	11,400 m²

The new buildings located on Harvard University campus unify three existing institute buildings by completing the quadrangle of the Cabot Science Complex, thus finishing the urban plan. The new landscaping scheme provides common and recreational outdoor spaces and integrates the science complex into the general campus.

The buildings are accessed from two sides: from the north via Frisbie Square at the Peabody Museum and from the south via the Cabot Science courtyard, which serves as a circulation hub for the entire complex. The elegant landscaping design including small groups of trees, clearly defined geometrical patches of lawn, and brick footpaths mediates between old and new,

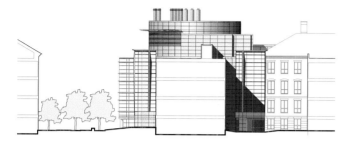

Sectional view

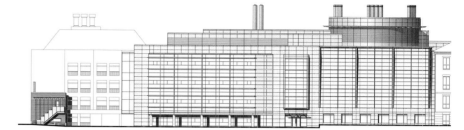

Main elevation

and creates a human scale and an almost private, intimate atmosphere.

During two construction phases, first the Naito Chemistry Building to the west and then the Bauer Laboratory and Centre for Genetic Research were built. Professors specialising in medical chemistry, biochemistry, and organic chemistry head various research teams in the Naito laboratory. The Bauer Institute, on the other hand, provides laboratories for genomics and bioinformatics that can be used by varying research teams engaged in temporary interdisciplinary co-operations.

The scheme provides communal social and conference spaces to support collegial co-operation between the scientists, a spontaneous exchange of thoughts, and the generation of ideas in casual talks or during conferences. The institutes also share a centrally located entrance hall on the ground floor, which simultaneously serves as a transit space from the forecourt to the inner courtyard. Cellular office zones along the façades and glazed inner laboratories characterise the interactive work in the Bauer Building. On the upper floors of the Naito Chemistry Building, the research teams have generous laboratories including supplementary service spaces at their disposal.

The façade design was guided by the idea of integrating the building into the existing fabric. The combination of red sandstone panels and glass elements constitutes a modern interpretation of the existing brick buildings. The institute is to set itself apart from its introvert neighbours by means of an open and transparent architecture. Generously glazed areas on the exterior and interior link the building to its environment and allow sufficient daylight to enter the deep laboratories and other interior spaces.

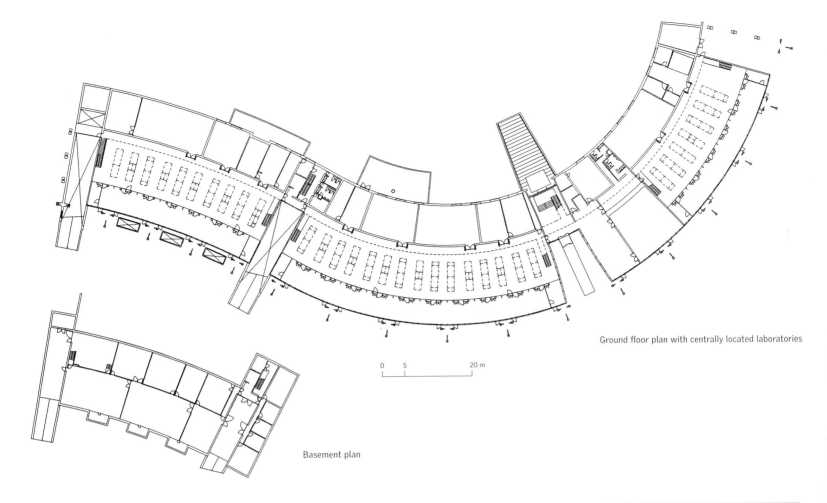

Ground floor plan with centrally located laboratories

0 5   20 m

Basement plan

from left to right
The appeal of transparency | The main entrance is clearly marked by the red steel structure | The mono-pitch roof supported by slender large-span lattice girders covers a generous open space | Above: Merging spaces and visual connections | Below: The light-flooded dining hall

Gifu Research Laboratories of Amano Enzyme Inc.

Gifu Prefecture, Japan

Client	Amano Enzyme Incorporation
Architects	Kisho Kurokawa architect & associates Richard Rogers Partnership Japan Ltd.
Construction period	1998-1999
Total floor area	6,700 m²

The basic idea for this multifunctional building was to develop a laboratory building that would encourage internal communication and discussion between the co-workers. An open building with merging functional zones was conceived that stimulates intellectual achievements by means of a light-flooded and highly transparent environment.

The building takes advantage of its location at the foot of a hill. An S-shaped structure with a mono-pitch roof traces the contour of the hill; existing trees on site were retained. The large-span exterior roof structure made of curved steel trusses supported by slender three-point columns clears the floor plans and enables continuous open laboratory zones. The

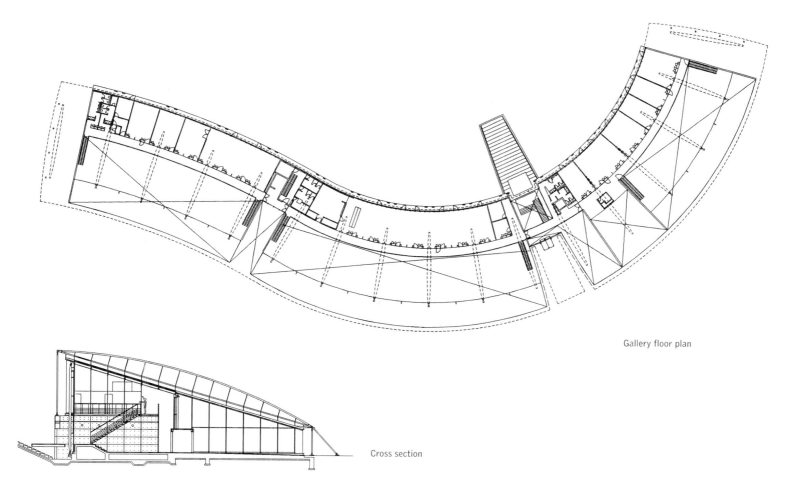

Gallery floor plan

Cross section

poignant red of the steel structure reflects its importance for the open floor plan arrangement. A fully glazed exterior skin makes the roof seem to float and almost seamlessly links the interior to the surrounding landscape. Two ramps that are required to service the basement storage areas and the accentuated main entrance rhythmically order the long edifice.

The basement is subdivided into three zones: a technical service zone at the rear that apart from storage and technical areas also contains rooms for laboratory equipment; a middle zone with laboratories which is protected from direct sunlight and benefits from a pleasant ceiling height due to the mono-pitch roof, and a south-orientated analysis and study area sepa-

rated from the laboratory desks by cupboards. At top level, conference and administrative spaces are located as well as the staff restaurant that opens up north towards the slope and the trees. A continuous gallery at this level facilitates orientation within the long building and links all laboratory areas. Frequent stair connections between gallery and ground floor prevent disturbing circulation between laboratory desks. The foyer space and a large conference hall are located adjacent to the lobby and can be reached from inside or outside without disrupting work.

Altogether, the architects designed a communicative and inspiring continuous space that is articulated in a pleasant way vertically and horizontally. It allows the

enlargement or reduction of work areas and supports interdisciplinary co-operation of different project groups.

Site plan

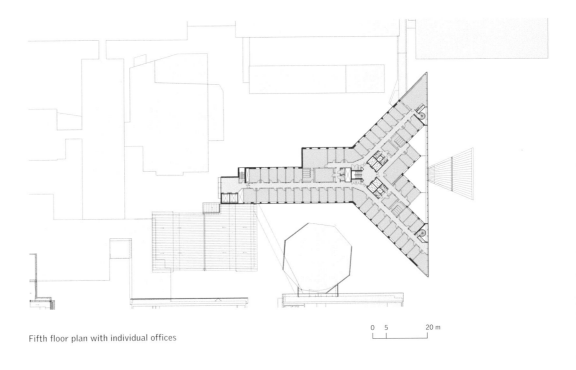

Fifth floor plan with individual offices

0   5   20 m

from left ot right
North façade showing glass curtain wall | The entwined building fabric of the Astra Hässle complex | The main access corridors are light-flooded and clearly structured | The visitor's area

AstraZeneca Research and Development Centre for Biology and Pharmacy

Gothenburg, Sweden

Client	AstraZeneca R&D Centre
Architects	Wingårdh Arkitektkontor AB
Completion	1996
Net floor area	120,000 m²

To unite the research laboratories scattered across the country, the architects were commissioned in 1989 to design an outstanding research complex as centre and home of the think tank of the important Swedish pharmacy corporation Astra Hässle. As a result of the rapid developments in fundamental research in the fields of biology and pharmacy, the centre was growing through constant alterations and expansions. Furthermore, the fusion with the British Zeneca Group made the new AstraZeneca PLC a global player in pharmaceutical research and product development.

AstraZeneca's outstanding R&D Centre provides scientists with state-of-the-art laboratories and constitutes an ideal platform of ideas for team-based re-

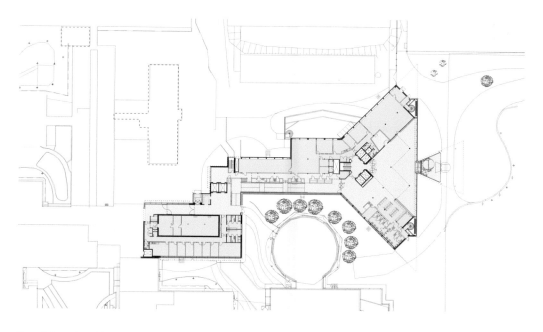

Ground floor plan with entrance hall and reception area,
and the main access corridor behind them

search. In order to promote the creativity of the employees and encourage mutual exchange, it was decided to concentrate the little "pockets of creativity" of individual laboratories in larger pools. As opposed to neutral and anonymous open plan offices, the designers opted for a new type of multi-purpose office. This Scandinavian version of the multi-purpose-principle was conceived to retain the privacy of the employees in their own "sacred" compartments yet offer larger and exceptionally well-equipped laboratory spaces for the highly specialised research teams. These shared zones and various kinds of spatially differentiated lounge areas are to encourage social interaction and exchange of ideas. The highly communicative, open and transparent workplace design,

which offers frequently changing views in and out of the building, forms the ideal backdrop for the intended effects.

The branching-out research centre comprises a net floor area of about 120,000 m². Red brick buildings of the sixties are scattered over the vast premises and combined with the new buildings to form a convincing urban and functional layout. The individually expressed building volumes based on a modular system are tied together by the use of aluminium and glass as exterior materials to form a functionally and formally consistent yet complex cluster.

The new laboratory buildings with their characteristic exterior cladding give the complex a high sense of individuality and the entire scheme a certain modular order that is pronounced by the limited range of materials. Precisely these laboratory units with their metal barrel roofs, aluminium-and-glass façades and the prominent oversized extract pipes render the building a landmark.

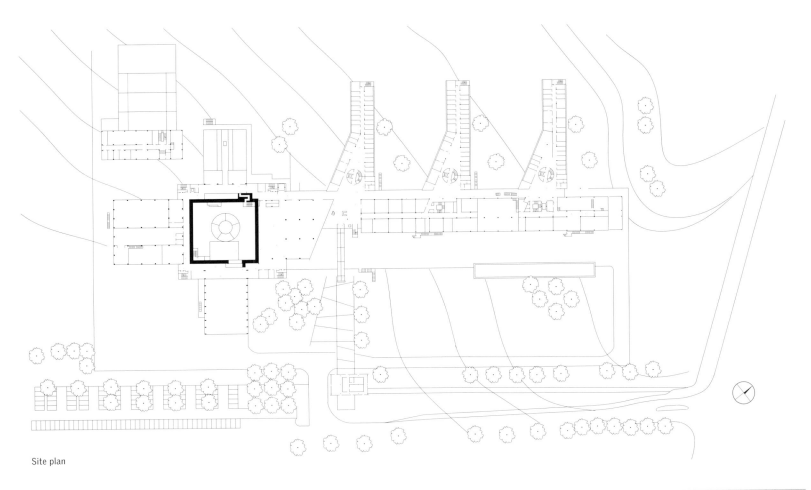

Site plan

Max Planck Institute for Plasma Physics, Greifswald Branch

Greifswald, Germany

Client	Max-Planck-Gesellschaft zur Förderung der Wissenschaften e.V.
Architects	Henn Architekten
Completion	2000
Net floor area	8,800 m²
Cubic content	245,500 m³

The Max Planck Institute for Plasma Physics (IPP) aims to establish the plasma physical fundamentals of a fusion power station that, like the sun, generates energy out of nuclear fusion. The fuel for this process is a so-called plasma, a thin ionised gas composed of the hydrogen derivatives Deuterium und Tritium. To spark the fusion process, this fuel is trapped in an annular magnetic coil and brought to a high temperature. If it can be achieved to confine the plasma particles by the magnetic forces to a sufficiently dense and thermally insulated state, it will start to "burn" above a temperature of 100 million degrees centigrade. The hydrogen nucleuses merge to Helium releasing usable energy. As resources of the basic agents Deuterium (in the sea) and Tritium (derived from

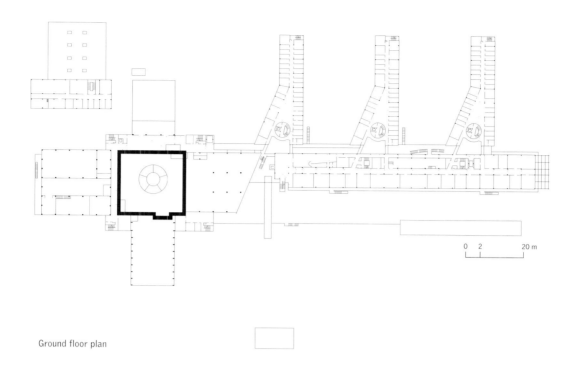

Ground floor plan

from left to right
View from the south showing the Torus building on the left, the main entrance with workshop and laboratory wing to the right, and the seminar rooms and library on the top floor, covered by a wavy roof | View towards the access spine

Lithium in the power plant) are nearly unlimited, nuclear fusion could become a key technology for future energy supply.

An experiment comprehensive as this requires the co-operation of scientists, engineers, and technical staff from all kinds of backgrounds. The institute founded in 1960 currently employs approximately 1,000 employees. For a long time, Garching near Munich was the only facility of its kind until a Plasma Diagnostics Section was opened in Berlin in 1992. The new Greifswald branch was founded in 1994 as part of the Max Planck Society's campaign to found or outsource new institutes in the former GDR and will employ up to 300 scientists. An important reason to chose Greifs-

wald as a new base was the strong existing academic and technological infrastructure in plasma physics: Both the University Institute of Physics and the Institute for Low Temperature Plasma Physics (a branch of the Leibnitz Society) are located in Greifswald.

Accordingly, the programme of the building is highly complex. All areas have to be arranged in such a way that they enable efficient multi-disciplinary co-operation between the scientists working in the laboratories as well as co-operation between scientists and analysts, technical staff, and office and administrative staff. The layout of the different areas and their interconnection according to functional criteria called for a strict zoning, yet still led to a highly communicative complex.

The scientific work at the institute is characterised by the close proximity of development and experiments. A central programme of the Greifswald centre is WENDELSTEIN 7-X. This is a fusion experiment conducted to prove the suitability of the IPP stellarator concept for industrial power generation. The core of this technology is the so-called Torus, a system of 50 non-planar supra-conductive magnetic coils that is housed in its own building. The layout of the institute was to provide shortest possible connections and good orientation between this testing facility and the offices, preferably under one roof.

The various spaces are arranged along a central access spine. It links the offices of the think-tanks,

North-east elevation

South elevation

which are stacked on three to four levels, with the workshops and the Torus building at its end. As innovative thinking and the generation of new ideas primarily depend on face-to-face communication, informal conversations are essential. Hence, the circulation axis serves communication and social interaction; at the same time it links the entrance hall and the library as well as the cafeteria and the seminar rooms on the upper floors. As a transparent structure made of steel and glass it affords visual links to the exterior environment and marries the architecture with the surrounding landscape. This connection is further enhanced by the succession of green courtyards and office wings reaching out into the environment like fingers. Furthermore, the different institute sections

Research and Development were symbolically and physically connected by a prominent and literally superimposed wavy roof.

The exterior appearance of the two building parts is a direct result of the different requirements. The Torus building as a purely technical facility is a largely solid structure nearly without windows. Its exterior walls of heavy 2 m thick concrete received a cladding of trapezoid aluminium panels. Since during the experiments inside Neutron radiation is released, Boron had to be added to the concrete. The Torus hall was built as a monolithic concrete structure for two months, 24 hours a day, under the highest safety regulations and constant supervision.

The office wings form an architectural juxtaposition to the Torus building: façades are clad with prefabricated brick panels reminiscent of traditional North German brick façades. Exterior shutters provide solar protection and casement windows provide natural ventilation. The southern front of the workshop wing incorporates little maintenance balconies for solar protection during summer. In wintertime, low sunrays fall deeply into the building resulting in desirable solar heat gains.

Ventilation of the individual building parts follows the requirements with regard to their position, use, and the extraction of heat or air. Essentially, the building was laid out in a way that allows all exterior physical

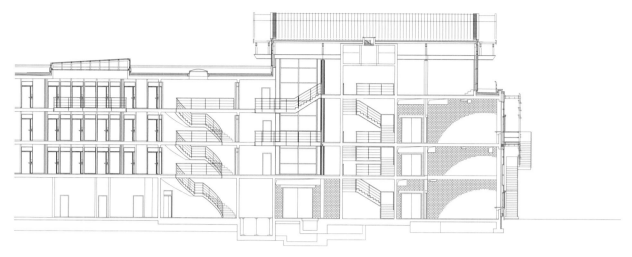

Cross section

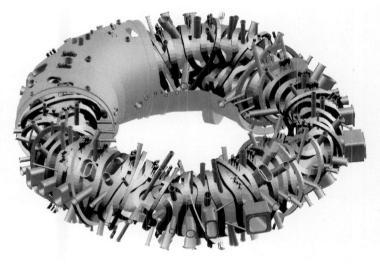

from left to right
View towards access spine with footbridges | An office wing connecting to the access spine via a stair tower to the left; the light-flooded cafeteria to the right | Test cryostat used for the nuclear fusion experiment WENDELSTEIN 7-X | Computerized visualisation of plasma container, magnetic coils, and surrounding cryostat of the nuclear fusion experiment WENDELSTEIN 7-X (stellarator concept)

laboratories, the workshops, the library, and the offices to be naturally ventilated. However, as a result of the high thermal output and critical air contamination in parts of the laboratories and workshops, supplementary mechanical ventilation was required. The seminar room, the computer pool, and the cafeteria as well as the testing area are also air-conditioned.

Tests in the Torus hall are characterised by an extreme energy use. The amounts of required electrical energy are of such an exceptional nature that they cannot simply be supplied through the local net (furthermore, experiments run in different cycles). This made a special 110 kV line necessary that was provided by a nationwide energy supplier. In order to

transform the high voltage to the respectively required wattage the institute comprises its own open-air transformer station.

Operation of the plasma burners prompts waste energy outputs of up to 40 MW per test run that have to be extracted. To provide the required cooling water of 13 degrees centigrade, it is pumped in a special cooling circuit from a 1,300 m³ water reservoir into another basin of equal dimensions. Subsequently, the water is cooled down again via heat exchangers.

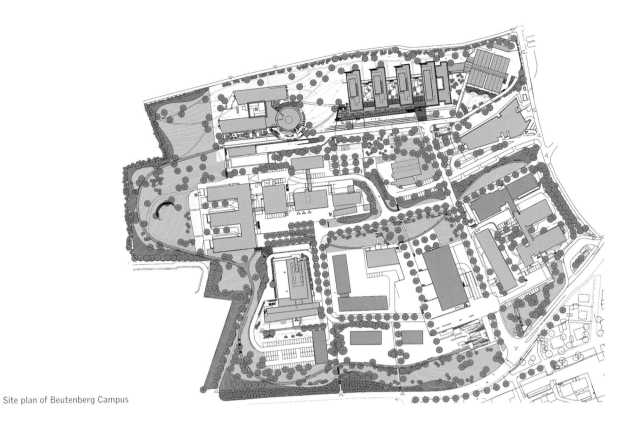

Site plan of Beutenberg Campus

from left to right
Panoramic view of the Saale River valley | The main entrance
to the southeast with adjacent glass louver façade of the hall |
The water courtyard as part of the landscaping scheme | Escape
route between glass louver façade and inner facade | Library
reading room with desks and suspended acoustic sails

Max Planck Institute
for Chemical Ecology

Jena, Germany

Client	Max-Planck-Gesellschaft zur Förderung der Wissenschaften e.V.
Architects	BMBW Architekten + Partner
Construction period	1999–2001
Net floor area	7,400 m²
Cubic content	70,100 m³

The Max Planck Institute for Chemical Ecology explores importance, variety, and properties of chemical signals controlling interrelations between organisms and their environment. The institute was established in Jena, a city with a significant scientific and industrial tradition. It is located at the northern edge of the "Am Beutenberg" natural science campus that borders onto a nature reserve. Together with the adjacent Max Planck Institute for Biogeochemistry to the west, it marks the upper end of the terrain which steeply slopes towards the southern Saale River valley.

The differentiated complex consists of four three-storey building wings aligned along the entrance hall. This way, the structure is embedded harmoniously

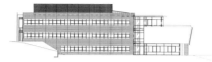

West elevation

East-west section through research wings

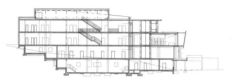

North-south section

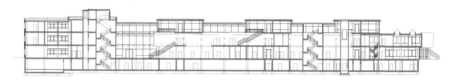

East-west section through hall

into the landscape and the sloping terrain can be experienced.

A private road takes the visitor from the entrance of the campus to the institute. Via an outside stair, which forms an integral part of the landscaped exterior, he is led to the main entrance.

The main idea of the design was to create a building supporting communication; this was achieved by providing perfectly linked work areas for multi-disciplinary research. The connecting element of the different functional areas laid out on a comb scheme is the linear, about 90 m long hall. In terms of fire regulations it was defined as "exterior space"; hence, an

economical building of great spatial and design quality could be realised that offers visual connections towards interior and exterior spaces.

On the hillside, five scientific sections are located in four parallel buildings separated by courtyards. The eastern wing accommodates two sections that closely co-operate, while the three other wings house individual sections. The three-storey wings have double-loaded corridors with laboratories on one side and theoretical studies on the other side. Additional access is provided by interior staircases that are enhanced by skylights; in terms of fire regulations, these are not required. However, they reduce horizontal and vertical distances and provide a transparent, pleasant

space that supports communication. Parallel to the hall, facing the valley, central and shared facilities such as a library, cafeteria, and seminar rooms are located. At basement level and practically concealed, areas for logistics and technical services as well as a delivery zone and further secondary spaces are to be found.

The Institute for Chemical Ecology shares facilities with the adjacent Max Planck Institute for Biogeochemistry, which creates useful synergies. The lecture hall and guest apartments for both institutes are situated in the Institute for Biogeochemistry, while the other institute accommodates a shared library.

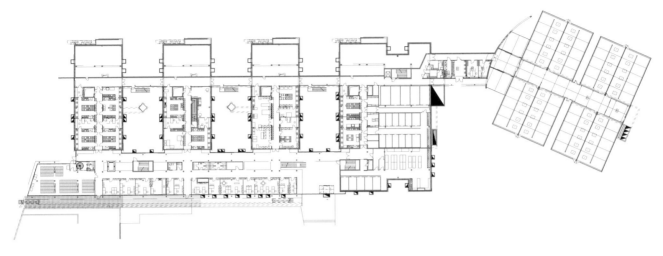

Ground floor plan

The four teeth of the comb containing the individual sections received a horizontally structured aluminium cladding. The solid appearance of these arctic-blue metal façades contrasts with the façade of the main building, which is dominated by a full height structure consisting of mechanically controlled glass louvers. This structure, which also structured horizontally, provides solar protection. Individual movable louvers have a transparent coating to create an iridescent appearance that changes from east to west from a cool blue to a warm red. In front of the main entrance, ground-recessed luminaires further reinforce this effect and highlight other components of the main façade: the glazing of the hall, and the clean architecture of the office wing.

Thoughtful use of colour on the interior of the hall gives each wing an "address". The exposed concrete walls of the individual entrances received differently coloured mineral glazing. The colours used are blue, green, yellow, and red; they were also used to accentuate particular areas throughout the interior. Otherwise, the colour pallet is rather neutral and reduced

As a result of the different requirements of the individual functional areas the building is equipped with a broad range of mechanical services. The institute sections comprise central service shafts and plant rooms on the roof and in the basement. In order to maximise flexibility and facilitate maintenance, the central service shafts are placed in the middle of the

respective laboratory zones. Mechanical ventilation and air-conditioning systems that are expensive in terms of construction and maintenance are only installed where absolutely necessary due to health and safety regulations or out of scientific considerations. All systems comprise heat exchanger and cooling. Spaces with particularly high thermal output are equipped with supplementary air circulation cooling.

The institute combines two apparently contrary research lines under one roof. In one section, organic chemical synthesis is conducted in chemical laboratories that require an extraordinary number of air-extracts. Furthermore, the use of large amounts of solvents requires safety storage cabinets, special

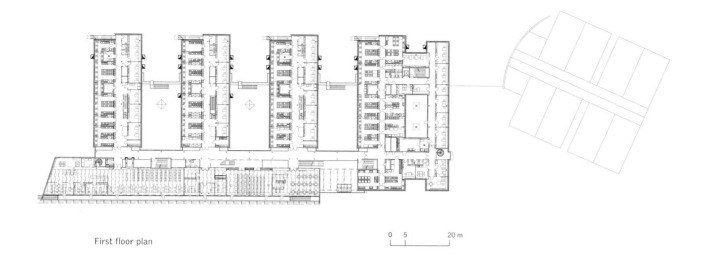

First floor plan

0 5   20 m

from left to right
Interplay of inside and outside spaces on the second floor | Open corridor spaces | The main entrance lobby is characterised by connecting galleries and the blue wall | View of the greenhouse laboratory to the east with pond in front collecting drainage water | Interior view of the greenhouse showing mobile lighting system and plant tables

rooms for re-distillation and desiccation of solvents as well as the respective technical services. In other areas, biochemical and molecular biological laboratories are equipped with only one air-extract. Since the cell cultures in these laboratories have to be protected from contamination, work is conducted on sealed clean benches.

A greenhouse laboratory with optimal orientation is located east of the institute building. The scientists can dispose of a total of 17 climatic simulation chambers for plant testing at temperatures ranging from 10 to 40 degrees centigrade and a relative humidity of 30 to 95 percent. Individual chambers allow illumination of up to 100,000 Lux. The chambers are venti-

lated via 48 units with integrated heater/cooler. In order to protect the plants, the chambers use replacement ventilation by textile hoses. Between the individual chambers pressurised security gates prevent cross-contamination of the plants.

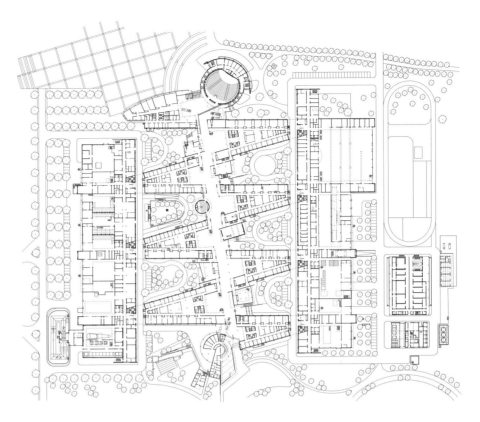

Ground floor plan with landscaping

from left to right
Aerial view of parts of the campus | Artwork in front of the buildings supports orientation towards the main axis | "Faculty street" with lounge areas on the galleries

Faculty of Mechanical Engineering, Technical University of Munich

Munich, Germany

Client	BMW AG + Freistaat Bayern
Architects	Henn Architekten
Completion	1994-1997
Net floor area	53,300 m²
Cubic content	650,000 m³

The mechanical engineering faculty on the Technical University's Garching campus near Munich is a "city of knowledge" on a 13 ha site. It houses 28 departments belonging to seven institutes with altogether 3,800 students. The campus comprises laboratories, offices, workshops and testing facilities, a number of lecture halls, seminar rooms, and computer pools, down to service buildings such as a block power station, and a kindergarten.

The large figure of the building is designed as a direct and precise expression of the idea of communicative networking. The main access route is a 220 m long axis that is fully roofed at a height of 18 m. At the ends of this "faculty street" the respective communal spaces

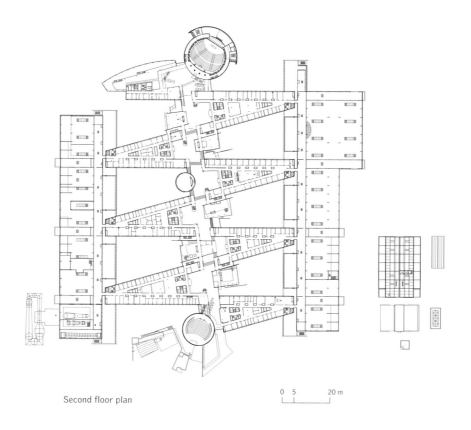

Second floor plan

0 5   20 m

are located: at the main entrance, adjacent to the underground station, the lecture halls are to be found; at the other end, the cafeteria with outdoor terrace is situated. The individual institutes are aligned like houses along the "faculty street" and interconnected. Each of the five-storey trapezoidal buildings contains an atrium space which is covered by a glazed barrel roof. These atriums rhythmically open up and enhance the space of the central axis. On their wider side, the institute buildings accommodate seminar and training rooms, drawing rooms, and computer pools. Recessed staircases ensure a smooth circulation in the highly frequented building complex. The narrower building part houses smaller offices and laboratories, which partly have been laid out as mixed open plan multi-functional office spaces.

The individual institute buildings are inserted into the testing halls at the rear like screws into a nut. They have a full basement. Individual service shafts containing the technical infrastructure ensure a large degree of flexibility.

The open spaces flexibly adapt to changing requirements. Areas can be exchanged between the individual faculties and additional spaces for joint or temporary projects can be provided at short notice.

The "engineered" exterior appeal of the building complex, whose structure is composed of a reinforced concrete frame structure and steel, is dominated by the precise use of aluminium, glass and concrete,

which are used according to their physical properties. Light-flooded interiors and triangular green courtyards with water features create an overall communicative atmosphere and a strong sense of place.

Site plan

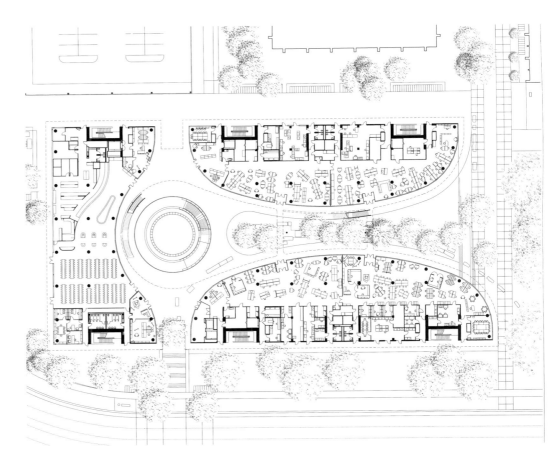

Ground floor plan

from left to right
View from the park showing the integration into the block pattern typical for the campus | Curved façades enclose the organically shaped courtyard | Open plan laboratory areas oriented towards the courtyard | Offices are acoustically and visually separated or can be integrated into the open plan labs if required

James H. Clark Center, Stanford University

Stanford, California, USA

Client	Stanford University
Architects	Foster and Partners
Construction period	1999-2003
Total floor area	16,900 m²
Net floor area	13,600 m²

The research concept of the James H. Clark Center is based on a broad scientific co-operation in the fields of medical and biological fundamental research. Natural scientists, scholars, engineers, physicians as well as scientists conducting solely experiments or theoretical analysis work together in multi-disciplinary teams. The faculties of biotechnology, biomedicine and bioscience of Stanford University participate in this joint project. It was developed as part of the "Bio-X Programme" initiated and funded by James Clark and other donators.

The architecture reflects this approach towards research; the complex is designed to encourage communication and the exchange of ideas and thoughts.

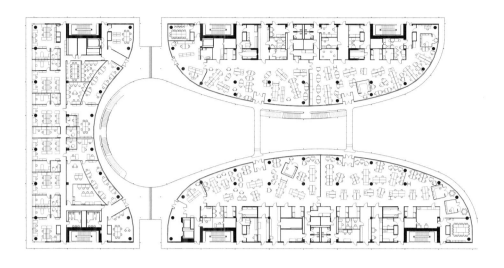

Typical floor plan

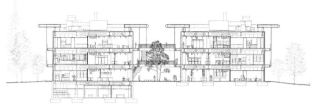

Section

0 2   10 m

Located at its very heart, the complex forms the integrating centre of campus life. Three wings with three storeys each are grouped around a central courtyard and linked via bridges. Their building lines follow the block pattern of the university campus, while the sweeping interior façades define a freely formed green space that lends itself for multiple uses and breaks.

The brief called for a mixed-use scheme, which led to an innovative layout that clearly sets itself apart from common typologies of research buildings. To a large extent, the areas in the eastern and western wing comprise large open spaces facing the courtyard. They contain individual service shafts to enable flexible layouts and can be used as wet or dry laboratories or studies. If required, individual units can be visually and acoustically separated. With a view to constantly changing research scenarios, every conceivable furnishing is possible.

The buildings' outer zones accommodate circulation areas, secondary rooms, and individual office cells. Due to their glazed interior walls they can be integrated into the large lab areas. Interior circulation areas were minimised. Connections are established via exterior walkways covered by a protruding canopy. This structure unifies the complex; it strengthens the organic shape of the interior courtyard and its spatial privacy; last not least, it conceals the plant rooms at roof level.

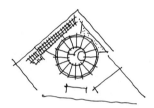

196
Berlin Electron Storage Ring BESSY II,
Adlershof Science and Technology Park

198
Nuclear Magnetic Resonant
Instrument Laboratory, Peking University

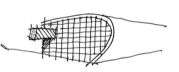

200
Panta Rhei Research Centre
for Lightweight Materials

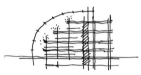

202
Degussa Construction Chemicals
Competence Centre

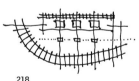

218
BASE Factory & Laboratory

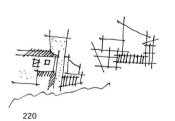

220
Research Station, University of Namibia

222
Centre for Photonics 1,
Adlershof Science and Technology Park

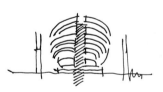

224
International Neuroscience Institute

This section comprises projects which present highly individual solutions in terms of functionality or design. Impulses may come from the urban or natural context; design approaches may be guided by different factors such as function, type of research conducted in a building, or a particular product developed within. Other structures may be characterised by an unusual formal idea or represent an outstanding structural or technical approach.

The particular characteristics of the featured projects have led to their appraisal as individual achievements that should not be filed into any category. Nevertheless, they correspond with basic typological building principles that were aptly integrated into the overall design idea.

Form

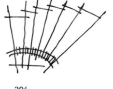

206
Mercedes-Benz Design Center

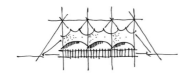

210
Schlumberger Cambridge Research Centre

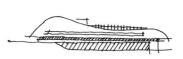

212
Semperit Research Building

214
Physics and Astronomy Laboratories, Leiden University

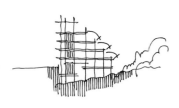

226
Van Andel Institute

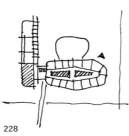

228
Research and Laboratory Building, Beiersdorf AG

BESSY II complex, summer of 1997

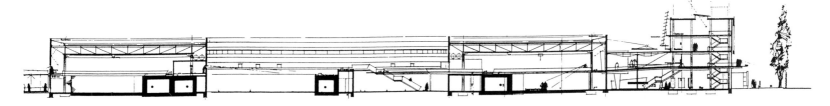

Longitudinal section

from left to right
Main entrance area linking the office and laboratory building
and the storage ring hall | Electron storage ring with aluminium
curtain wall | View into the storage ring hall showing beam
tubes and testing facilities | Above: Entrance hall of the office
and laboratory building at Einsteinstraße | Below: Storage ring
tunnel, injection area, transfer from synchrotron

Berlin Electron Storage Ring BESSY II, Adlershof Science and Technology Park

Berlin, Germany

Client	Land Berlin (Senatsverwaltung für Wissenschaft, Forschung und Kultur)
Architects	Brenner & Partner Architekten und Ingenieure Brenner-Hammes-Partner
Construction period	1992-1997
Net floor area	12,600 m²
Cubic content	148,000 m³

What used to be the largest science and engineering centre of its kind in the former GDR is being remodelled since the middle of the nineties. The area of 150 ha in the southeast of Berlin is to become a high-profile science and business park for cutting-edge enterprises and institutes. Part of this scheme is the high brilliance "light" source developed by scientists of the Berlin Electron Storage Ring Company for Synchrotron Radiation (BESSY). With this building the architects achieved an exemplary symbiosis of scientific research and architectural expression.

The building is consistently designed to reflect the technical and scientific functions therein. The architectural form follows the large-scale scientific equip-

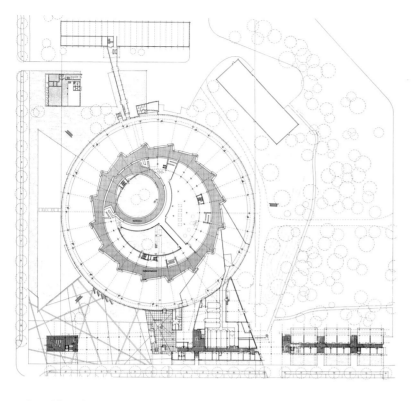

Ground floor plan

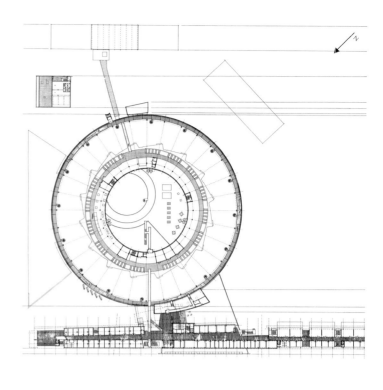

Upper floor plan

0 10   50 m

ment: a synchrotron radiation source ranging from infrared to vacuum ultra violet (VUV) light to the X-ray region that is used by more than 130 research teams worldwide. The storage ring hall with a diameter of approximately 120 m and a height of about 13 m forms the central piece of the complex. The floor plan clearly reveals its function: by means of circular acceleration, light from the off-centred radiation source (the synchrotron) can be diverted into tangential beam tubes and "shot" into different testing facilities in the hall.

A physically decoupled, 3 m wide exterior walkway around the perimeter contains the required technical services. Occasional strip windows in an otherwise solid façade connect the storage ring hall with the

environment. The roof structure consisting of steel trusses spans 27 m across the storage ring tunnel and test areas below. Machines and test facilities are also decoupled and supported by a continuous 60 cm thick floor slab absorbing vibrations. The synchrotron and storage ring are enclosed with an in-situ concrete shell that is up to 1 m thick.

Offices of the operator, the BESSY GmbH, and office and laboratory areas for the users of the storage ring are located in a building on Albert-Einstein-Straße. Its height complies with the regulations of the master plan that stipulate four-storey buildings on an urban block pattern. It is linked to the storage ring hall by a glazed two-storey hall.

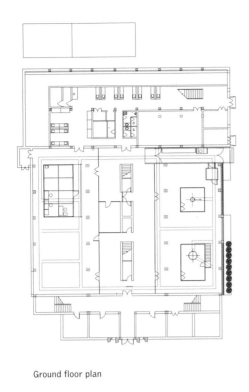

Ground floor plan

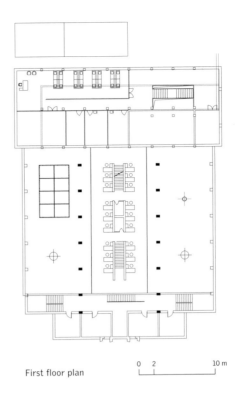

First floor plan

0 2   10 m

from left to right
Glass walls make the cubes reveal their interior | The clean room area within the central hall follows the "house-in-house" principle | New and old elements in the former power station hall | View of the central stair flight between two load-bearing exposed concrete walls

Nuclear Magnetic Resonant Instrument Laboratory, Peking University

Beijing, China

Client	Bejing Nuclear Magnetic Center
Architects	Atelier Feichang Jianzhu
Construction period	2001-2002
Total floor area	1,200 m²

Following detailed planning studies it was decided to refurbish the obsolete power station of Peking University and fit it out for innovative use rather than demolish it. It now accommodates facilities for magnetic resonance research. This discipline calls for high expenditures on equipment and apparatuses. Particular care is extended to air-filtering and conditioning as a basic requirement for an efficient and successful operation. The cubic content of the former power station was able to accommodate the required large spaces which house the complicated mechanical ventilation system that provides clean room air quality.

Despite these specific scientific requirements and the resulting complex mechanical infrastructure,

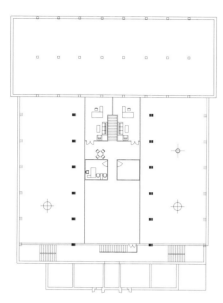

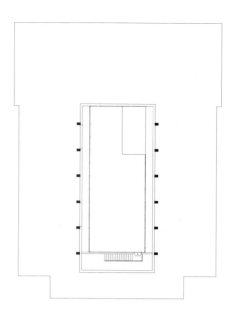

Second floor plan   Third floor plan

the architects managed to incorporate the entire programme into the existing structure with its various
large spaces. Following the "house-in-house" principle
the clean room area and the work places of the scientists are located in an independent pod structure. It
was inserted into the central hall that bears resemblance to a basilica. Hence, the interior spatial quality
of the former power station could be retained. The independent, transparent pod structure impresses through
its rigorous sculptural design. On three floors, it accommodates the NMR laboratories that are seismically,
electro-magnetically, and acoustically screened by a
perimeter zone consisting of access cores, offices, work
desks, and service areas.

The aisles of the hall contain service areas and plant
rooms, in particular the air-conditioning equipment
with high-power filters for the clean rooms. The large
existing building volume did not pose any restrictions
for the installation of an efficient and flexible system
of service lines.

Access to the NMR structure is provided from the exterior by staircases positioned on its sides and inter-
nally by a central single flight stair located between
two load-bearing exposed concrete walls.

The new statically independent structure consists
of reinforced concrete and steel. In contrast to the
existing solid structure the main materials used for

the interior fit-out are timber, steel, and, above all,
glass. As a result, the new cubes do not appear as
introvert, or even "alien" volumes, but as modern
transparent work places for scientists. An atmosphere of interaction and co-operation within this
high-tech research facility prevails.

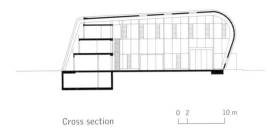

Cross section

0 2   10 m

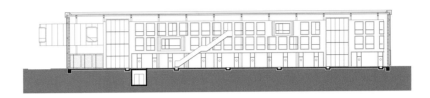

Elevation of integrated office volume

from left to right
A large curved roof and an office wing placed under it form a clear and compact basic structure | The distinctive cantilevering seminar room – a red box – accentuates the entrance which is oriented towards the main campus walk | Experiments and theoretical work are carried out next to each other: the hall houses machinery, the long structure accommodates offices and laboratories | Communication zone in the office wing | Interior view of the office wing

Panta Rhei Research Centre for Lightweight Materials

Cottbus, Germany

Client	Panta Rhei GmbH
Architects	kleyer.koblitz.architekten
Construction period	2001-2002
Net floor area	4,000 m²
Cubic content	41,000 m³

Four professorial chairs of the Faculty for Mechanical Engineering and Electronics of Cottbus University do research in the field of lightweight materials for innovative application in the automotive and aviation industry. Since the university wants to combine academic teaching with hands-on practice and work experience, students of architecture and their teachers established a non-profit planning company to work on refurbishment projects and extensions on campus. The research centre is their first completed project.

The brief called for a building offering spaces for research and development propelled by communication and teamwork; it was also to reflect the innovative research concept with cutting-edge architecture.

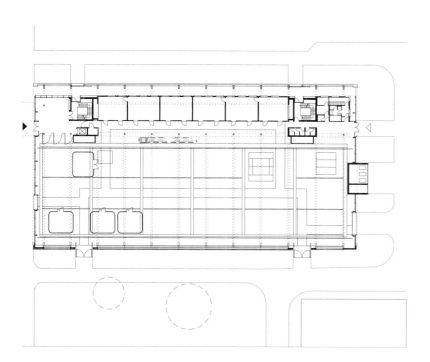

Ground floor plan

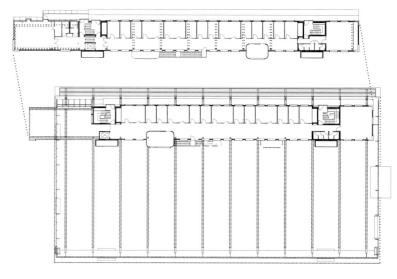

Second floor plan

The priority objective of the participating chairs is to establish synergies between university and companies of the industry to bridge the gap between theory and practice.

Panta Rhei is classical Greek and can be translated with "all things are in constant flux". The term stands for the high flexibility and variability the project is to provide for future developments. The most suitable form to achieve this goal is a single large space with an open plan arrangement.

The design idea is simple: A long building volume is placed into a hall covered by a curved roof. These elements form a clear and compact large structure.

The mono-curved roof clad with perforated sheet metal covers all laboratory and study rooms on an area of 72 x 38 m. Following a "house-in-house" scheme, an elongated three-storey structure is arranged on one long side of the hall. On the ground floor, it houses the laboratories, and mixed-use offices and meeting rooms on the two upper floors. Highly flexible areas for experiments are located in the hall and visually linked to all rooms within the building.

Curved steel girders constitute the form of the hall building. Its gable ends are fully glazed. On its south side, the cantilevering seminar room marks the entrance which is oriented towards the axis of the campus walk. The lightweight building envelope encourages onlookers to have associations with the research field of the building: the development of applications for magnesium (besides aluminium) in order to reduce weight and thus energy consumption.

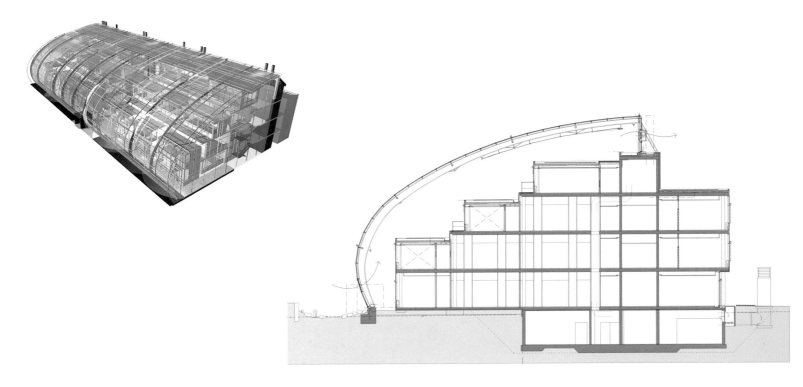

Section through the "house-in-house" structure

Degussa Construction Chemicals Competence Centre

Trostberg, Germany

Client	Degussa Construction Chemicals GmbH
Architects	Raupach + Schurk Architekten
Construction period	2001-2002
Total floor area	9,500 m²
Cubic content	50,500 m³

A changed environmental awareness and a new public understanding of sustainable consumption of energy for producing building material has triggered innovative research and developments in the field of construction chemicals and has opened up new possibilities for architects to realise their ideas and visions. In co-operation with engineers of different disciplines, Degussa Construction Chemicals GmbH has developed products for a more environmentally sound, energy efficient, and economical building practice. Under the slogan "sustainability goes mainstream" this development increasingly becomes commonplace.

Trostberg in Upper Bavaria was chosen as the R&D hub of the company. The centre is located in close

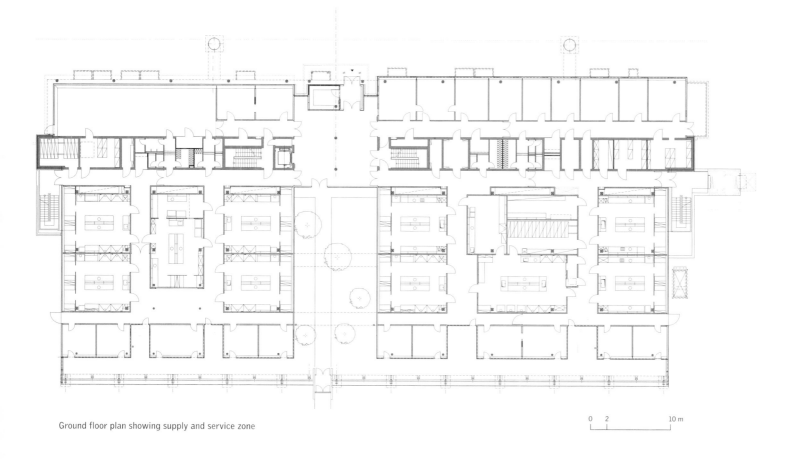

Ground floor plan showing supply and service zone

0   2   10 m

proximity to the Technical University Munich, which prompted the company to seek co-operation and to sponsor the university's Chair for Construction Chemicals. The northern wing of the centre accommodates the facilities of this chair; the southern wing houses research areas of Degussa Construction Chemicals GmbH. The centre reinforces the position of the Trostberg location, creates attractive jobs, and strengthens the image of the corporation through its unconventional architecture. The exceptional shape of the centre creates a sense of identity and place which positively supports Degussa's marketing strategy and corporate identity.

The research centre is located on the old Degussa premises south of Trostberg. The site is framed by the gardens of the former director's building and the rail tracks along the little Alz River. The historic town centre borders onto the opposite side of the river. The architects wanted to retain the pleasant green space of the existing garden and positioned the new building at the northern edge of the premises. It stretches along the rail tracks and its orientation and façade design strongly relate to the historic town centre and the surrounding green spaces.

The building consists of a steel structure spanning 30 m; it is based on a primary structural grid of 7.2 m and an interior fit-out grid of 1.2 m. It received a highly

insulating, fully glazed double-layered building skin with a u-value of 1.0. Under the skin, a "research landscape" breaks new grounds both in terms of concept and architectural realisation. At its core is a multi-storey stepped structure that accommodates laboratories, offices, and secondary spaces. The decreasing levels allow optimal daylight and afford attractive views of the surrounding landscape and the town.

The building envelope enables a nearly Mediterranean indoor climate and green terraces with different plant themes on each level. On the higher levels, vegetation grows increasingly sparse, finally making way for an artificial desert. In contrast, the lower levels have been planted with Mediterranean and East Asian

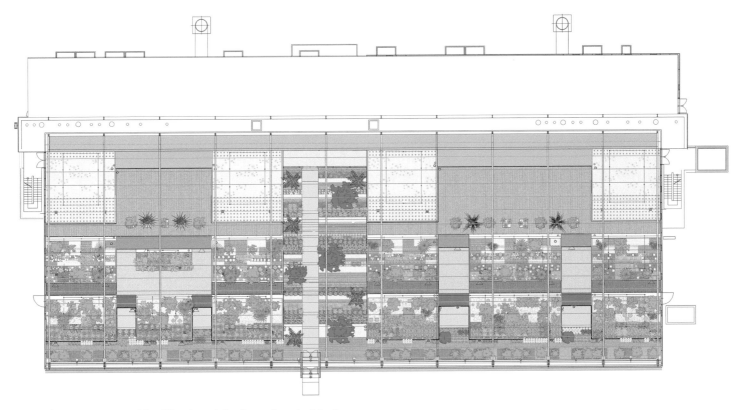

Planting concept comprising different vegetation themes throughout the floors

trees and shrubs. All year round, employees benefit from a pleasant indoor climate offering much daylight, ventilation, and transparency. The idea of green laboratory terraces is transferred to the outside and supplemented there through landscaped areas.

The building is accessed via two entrances on either side. Both entrances connect to a central foyer space, from which two corridors lead into each main direction. Two central stairs and a lift core provide vertical access; an additional escape route is presented through exterior escape stairs at the gable ends. This circulation system creates a clear plan layout that provides good orientation and reduces distances between the individual spaces.

A central, linear service zone clearly divides the building into two halves, a laboratory and a management area. The laboratories and service rooms are serviced via double installation walls connected to the plant rooms in the basement and on the top floors.

The sustainable concept of the premises is reflected in the mechanical engineering of the building. Openings at the lowest and highest level provide natural ventilation. The indoor vegetation positively affects the energy and moisture balance and reduces thermal gains and energy consumption. The terrace structure admits daylight into nearly all laboratory and office spaces. The building makes use of core cooling through building masses, fed by a buried duct. Overall energy

consumption is reduced by heat exchangers and the use of passive energies such as wind, water, and light. Drain water is collected in troughs feeding a little "creek" in front of the façade.

On the east façade, the solid central structure of the building turns into a lightweight post-and-beam façade with external solar protection. Exposed air exhaust ducts hint on the position of plant rooms and chemical laboratories. A two-storey box that juts out of the solid core marks the entrance on this side.

The composition of the façades of the gable ends reveals the interior layout. The interplay of views out of and into the building, the juxtaposition of introverted

Vegetation theme Macchia on the second and third floor terraces

Exterior vegetation and entrance area with examples of plants in the bud

from left to right
The exterior landscaping extends the interior vegetation themes by means of a "creek" | The entrance hall showing both "house-in-house" volumes | The glass-covered "research landscape" | Standard laboratory showing the exposed services and the transparancy of the spaces

and extroverted spaces, the almost Mediterranean interior and the foothills of the Bavarian Alps outside create a singular place that regularly sets the stage for cultural events.

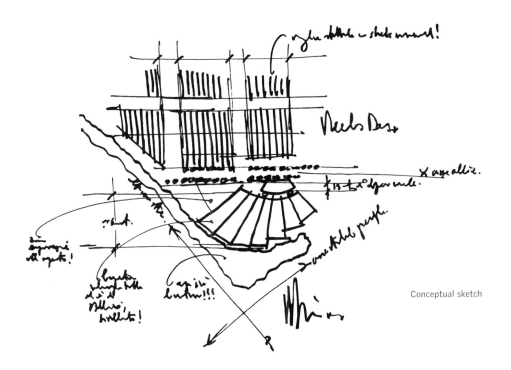

Conceptual sketch

Mercedes-Benz
Design Center

Sindelfingen, Germany

Client	Mercedes-Benz AG
Architects	Renzo Piano Building Workshop with C. Kohlbecker
Construction period	1993-1998

The Mercedes-Benz design team is internationally renowned for its product design, which is based on ever-shorter development cycles and the close co-operation of all involved parties. To bundle all forces, the corporation closed all 18 centres in Germany and established a new central research and development centre in Sindelfingen.

The brief called for a work environment that would best suit the team-orientated design processes of a variety of vehicle types. These processes are based on communication and the exchange of ideas. Following these requirements, the architects conceived a building which is at the same time extraordinary and pro-totypical. The open and light-flooded interior provides

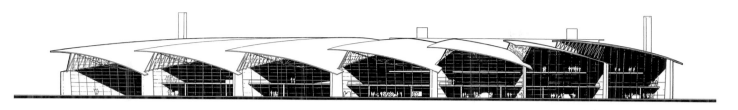

West elevation

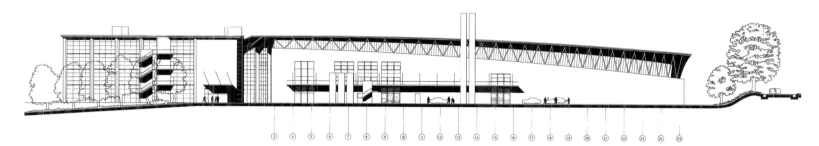

North elevation

from left to right
Aerial view of the complex during construction | West façade of the design area showing the large cantilevers of the roofs above the lateral skylights | View at night

an inspiring work environment, which is nonetheless closed off from the exterior to prevent disruption and, last not least, industrial espionage. The participants in the design process – designers, model makers, and prototype developers – are electronically and spatially linked.

Bruno Sacco, Mercedes-Benz chief designer, was impressed by the openness and transparency of architect Renzo Piano's own Building Workshop. He asked Piano to create a similar atmosphere for the design centre in Sindelfingen. The difference was that the building had to serve for a few hundred employees, not only a few dozen. Hence, the desired work atmosphere had to be transferred to a much larger scale.

The building is located at the south-western tip of the overall premises of the research and development centre. It is based on the existing master plan that proposes an orthogonal grid organising the engineering offices and production halls to be positioned at right angles. At the intersections of the grid, shared courtyards with an almost private atmosphere are placed encouraging communication between engineers and designers.

The design centre was the first building of the master plan to be completed; it is protected by vegetation on one side. It forms the final part of the master plan and juxtaposes its perpendicular grid. The building shape follows the triangular site but is also motivated

by the call for an unconventional building that presents the design team as a self-contained unit of the company without creating the image of a privileged elite.

The design is reminiscent of a fan whose individual segments house different functions such as design, model making, prototype development etc. Several "fingers" radiate around a central point at a constant angle of nine degrees and get longer from south to north. Three-dimensionally curved saw-tooth roofs cover the seven industrial halls. The fanning-out, individual roofs create a dynamic form that seems to be generated by centrifugal forces. Light bands provide daylight that is necessary to control prototypes; solid

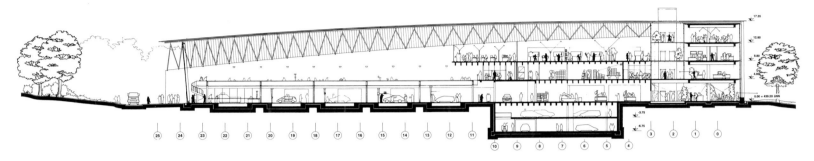

Cross section through hall

from left to right
Different lighting scenarios in the presentation hall: The lower area is painted black to avoid reflections of the photographers on the shiny bodywork of the cars | Solar glazing above presentation hall | Louvers react to changing light conditions | Workshop on the ground floor | The spiral stair at the end of the section links the workshop area to the offices grouped around the atrium

external walls below afford visual protection. The geometry of the roof surfaces is derived from sections of a torus. Their surfaces are not perpendicular to the walls but inclined. Hence, the skylight strips get narrower at the ends and reinforce the impression of "floating" roofs.

In close proximity to the design centre, a four-storey administration building including an entrance hall and foyer is located. The linear office building forms the architectural hinge between the free form of the design centre and the perpendicular organised engineering offices and production halls further east. Two hall segments protrude beyond the administration building forming a triangular forecourt as main access to

both buildings. The presentation hall is positioned roughly perpendicular to the five shorter segments of the main building. In the west, the gable ends of the halls face onto a common garden that is enclosed by a dense hedge satisfying concerns of privacy and security.

The constant interaction between the employees called for an architectural concept that links all interior levels in a complex and efficient way. This has been achieved by means of vertical accesses and visual links between the design offices on the second floor, storage on the first floor, and workshops on the ground floor. Each "finger" incorporates a central atrium where car models are exhibited; this way, employees can check them any time. Offices have been

arranged in a U-shape around these atriums and provide direct visual contact to the workshops.

The centre comprises a presentation hall for completed prototypes. It was created by eliminating the end sections of two radial walls and bridging the gap with steel tube trusses. To simulate various light conditions, skylights consist of a super-fine plastic mesh sandwiched between two insulating glass panes that follow the curve of the roofs.

The design centre receives its particular architectural charm from the large dimensions of the spaces, the merging of different work zones, and the elegant interior detailing. Partitions are rendered and painted

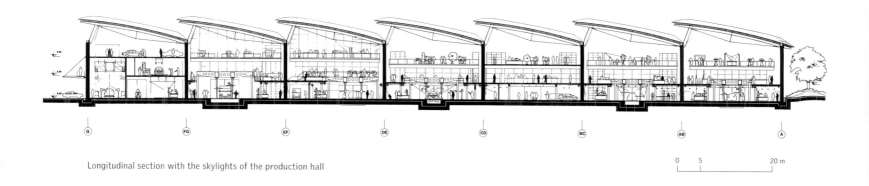

Longitudinal section with the skylights of the production hall

0	5		20 m

white. The curved roof surfaces consist of inclined parallel parabolic louvers with reinforcing crossbars that form a grid of tiny north-orientated skylights. They solely allow north light to enter the building and diffuse direct sunlight.

To the exterior, the building presents itself in almost monochrome tones of grey and silver. The façades received a cladding of tall and narrow Alucarbon panels, which were also used on the roof and provide a mat silver finish. According to Renzo Piano, he wanted to create a monolithic building that looks like a singular piece of cast aluminium. The wafer-thin exterior envelope elegantly wraps the enormous cubic content of the building.

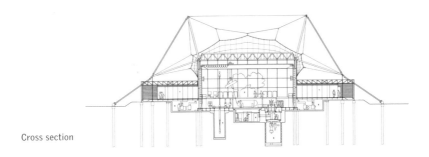

Cross section

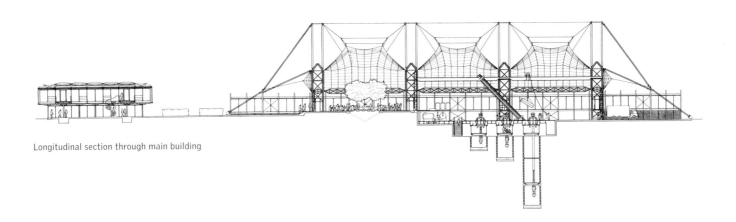

Longitudinal section through main building

from left to right
View at night | Overall view of complex | Detail of tensioned cable structure of a load-bearing exterior steel roof truss | Coffered ceiling of the first floor with exposed structural elements shading the ground floor | The second phase entrance hall with its translucent roof membrane links the identical pavilions

Schlumberger Cambridge Research Centre

Cambridge, UK

Client	Schlumberger Cambridge Research Ltd.
Architects	Michael Hopkins & Partners
Construction period	1985-1988 (phase I) 1990-1992 (phase II)

The Schlumberger Development Centre represents one of the most interesting architectural examples for the extensive use of Teflon-coated fibreglass. The complex was erected in two phases: during the first phase, a test drilling station and a general area were built; they are covered by a translucent space truss reminiscent of a marquee. This structure is flanked by one-storey wings, housing offices and laboratories. During the second phase, two freestanding pavilions were built, which accommodate offices, laboratories, and computer rooms. They are linked by a shared entrance hall that is likewise covered by a translucent roof.

The special shape of the building reacts to the functional requirements of the brief and also meets the

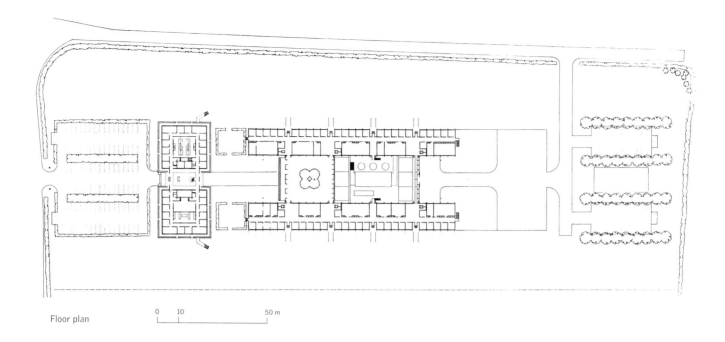

Floor plan

clients wish for vivid social interaction between the scientists. The prominent space truss with a translucent membrane protects the oil-drilling platform and a winter garden from the elements. Three fields measuring 24 x 18 m are located in the centre of the complex; the southern field houses the winter garden and a canteen and library. The mentioned five low-rise office wings are positioned on either side to the east and west. The gaps between the volumes form the entrances that are highlighted by tensioned cables of steel trusses supporting the roof membrane.

The laboratories of the first building phase face the test areas and the general zone, while the offices are orientated towards the surrounding landscape. At the

planning stage of the second building phase, the majority of scientific test procedures were to be replaced by computer simulations. Instead of providing large central test areas as did the first phase, the central zone of the second phase now contains laboratories and shared areas.

Each of the five office/laboratory wings of the first phase consists of five structural bays with steel trusses at 3.6 m centres from which the roof build-up is suspended. Except for the foundations the entire building was assembled using prefabricated elements.

The translucent Teflon-coated fibreglass roof membrane is expected to last more than twenty years. It

is suspended from the exterior steel frame structure with cables. Primary structural elements are framework towers spaced at 19.2 m. They are connected by inclined trusses and tensioned members and fixed to the ground with guy cables.

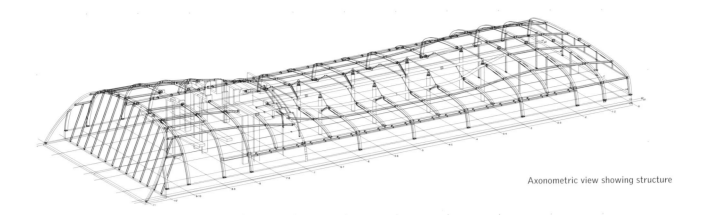

Axonometric view showing structure

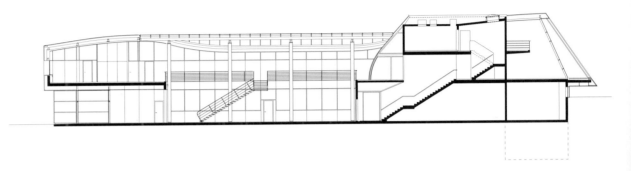

Longitudinal section

Aluminium tube

Semperit
Research Building

Wimpassing, Austria

Client	Semperit
Architects	Najjar & Najjar Architekten
Completion	2002
Total floor area	2,400 m²
Net floor area	1,500 m²
Cubic content	10,900 m³

In 1999, the Semperit Company held a competition calling for a landmark building reflecting the corporate identity. It was to provide space for the research section, which is mainly concerned with the testing of rubber products – above all rubber gloves.

The dynamic two-storey high-tech "tube" represents the international position and innovative potential of the company. At the gable end facing a federal highway it received an inclined two-storey glazed façade that may cause different associations such as "a large mouth, car grill, or air-intake" and affords views into the workspaces of the technicians.

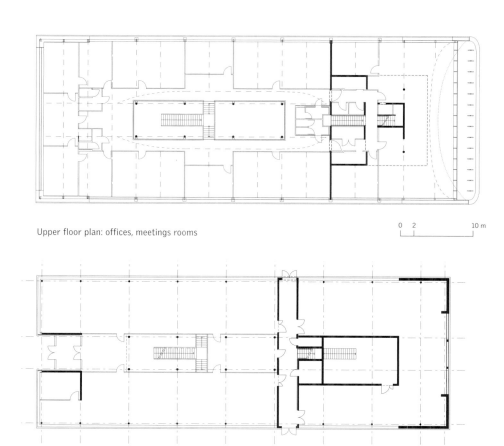

Upper floor plan: offices, meetings rooms

0 2 10 m

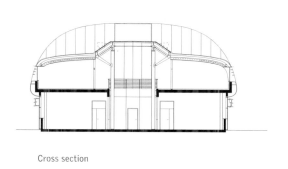

Cross section

Ground floor plan: laboratories

Atrium covered by skylights

The silvery aluminium tube rests on a mainly glazed rectangular base housing laboratories. An atrium with orthogonally arranged rooms around it is located within the tube. The atrium also serves as access zone for the laboratory areas on the ground floor. An open stainless steel stair reminiscent of a gangway leads up to the administration and executive offices and meeting rooms on the first floor.

The construction of the aluminium tube posed a big challenge: the most difficult part was to design an aluminium envelope that would wrap around the curvature of the building as precisely as a car chassis. What is common in the automotive industry still is pioneer work in architecture. Apart from the three-dimensional curvature and the homogeneity of the building skin thermal expansion of the aluminium was crucial.

To construct the aluminium envelope the builders had to resort to smoothing techniques common in shipbuilding. Essentially, the building was constructed like a ship hull turned upside down. Reinforced concrete columns of the glazed ground floor support the upper floor slab, which carries steel ribs consisting of curved box profile segments. This steel structure has infillings made of trapezoid sheet metal; an insulating layer and another layer of trapezoid sheet metal cover the structure.

This outer layer provides drainage and supports the exterior aluminium envelope. The envelope itself consists of 7 cm thick and 6.5 m long extruded aluminium sections that were lengthwise mounted like ship planking. Only in this way was it possible to construct the amorphous form. The tube appears as if tailored out of a single piece.

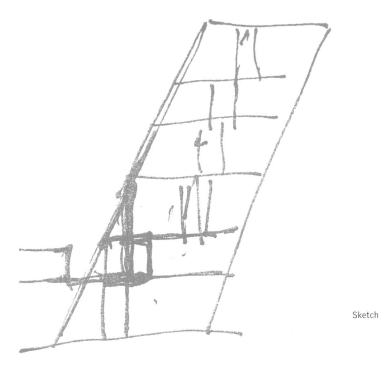

Sketch

Physics and Astronomy Laboratories, Leiden University

Leiden, Netherlands

Client	Leiden University
Architects	(EEA) Erick van Egeraat associated architects
Construction period	1995-1997
Net floor area	6,700 m²

The laboratory and office building is situated on the western outskirts of Leiden on a green university campus whose urban layout and character is determined by buildings of the sixties and seventies. The dynamical sculptural qualities of the new building can thrive within this context and render it a symbol for Leiden as a visionary place of science.

Physicist Heike Kamerlingh Onnes was active in Leiden and was able to determine the temperature of absolute zero at -273,1 degrees Celsius in the late 19th century. At this temperature, movement of all particles comes to a complete stop. This discovery continues to be the scientific base for the experimental and theoretical research conducted in the new

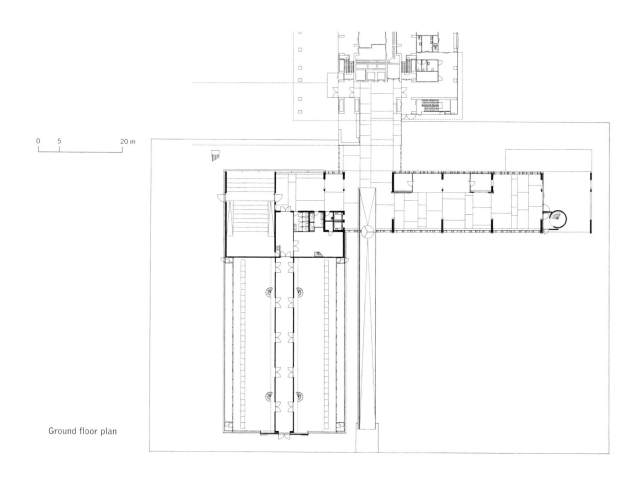

0 5 20 m

Ground floor plan

from left to right
View from the west: the laboratory wing containing the auditorium pushed under the office wing | The office wing inclined by ten degrees increases the space between the existing and the new building | Industrial exterior escape stair at the gable end of the office wing | The glazed footbridge links the existing and the new building on six floors

building. For the scientific experiments, breadboard constructions, laboratory equipment, and scientific gear are required that only deliver reliable and optimised results under high vacuum and intercepted vibration conditions. These conditions can only be established by the use of complicated technical installations, considerable structural efforts, and sound detailing under consideration of all internal and external seismic, electro-magnetic, and acoustic factors.

The complex is composed of three architectural elements: the glazed transparent ground floor, a solid, vertically inclined office building, and the slightly pitched laboratory hall building that is pushed under the office building. The complex is linked to the exist-

ing Christian Huygens Laboratory – an eleven-storey functional building – via footbridges on all floors.

Materials like glass and light beech welcome employees and visitors with a bright and friendly atmosphere on the ground floor of the office wing. The auditorium and the canteen are located here. For the auditorium seating 150 students, a wavy ceiling made of Oregon pine was designed to improve acoustics.

The office wing is inclined towards the visitor at an angle of ten degrees. This architectural twist creates the distinctive character of the building, rendering it a major landmark within its context. Above all, a particular genius loci is created by the western elevation

– with the low, curved laboratory hall building, the inclined volume, and the attached escape stair – that forms the backdrop of a water pond. The structure's inclination that gradually increases the distance towards the existing opposite building improves the daylight conditions within as well as views to the outside. In terms of planning regulations, the increasing spacing between the buildings also prevents the spread of fire. Horizontal strip windows structuring the façade are cut into the zinc cladding and afford panoramic views of the surrounding pastures especially from the higher floors.

According to the programme the five office floors have a traditional layout with a central corridor. A

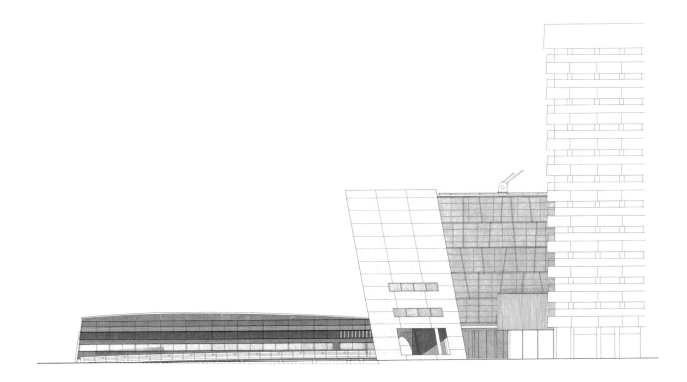

West elevation

continuous horizontal strip of glass just below the ceiling creates a bright, transparent atmosphere in the corridor, yet sustains the employees' privacy.

The entire structural system of the laboratory wing was designed to keep the formation and effects of seismic vibrations at bay: This is reflected in the detailing of the main works and interiors and the layout of the building's technical infrastructure. The result is a simple hall whose interior is characterised by a clearly structured and economically dimensioned steel structure. The transparent façade of screen-printed overlapping panes affords views into the building as to reveal the secrets of the long tradition

of scientific instrument making on which the international reputation of the university is partly based on.

The open ground floor plan of the laboratory wing provides maximum flexibility for future breadboards and installations that can be rearranged during research operations on predefined supplementary foundations located on a dynamic grid. Along both lengths of the laboratories the technical infrastructure runs in linear raised floor service ducts that can be refitted to suit future requirements. Here, the extremely powerful vacuum pumps are also located, which ensure that experiments can be conducted under the required technical conditions at a temperature around absolute zero.

The wide central corridor on the ground floor of the laboratory hall building also serves as storage and additional installation area for surplus gear and supplementary breadboards. In this area, also the distribution panels, manifolds etc. for water, electro, and gas supply have been installed visibly. On the first floor, workplaces for students are located above the glazed central corridor. They offer spaces for quiet, concentrated use of computer workstations while maintaining a visual contact with the experiments.

The overall building complex, which is characterised by the inclined office wing and the laboratory hall with its curved roof, narrates the architectural approach as a formally – or formalistically – motivated

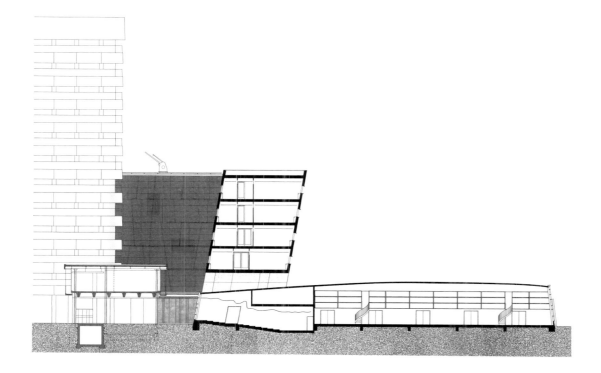

Longitudinal section

from left to right
The lightweight steel structure of the footbridge varies in its vertical position from floor to floor | Laboratory hall and gallery containing student workplaces | The centre of the laboratory space is characterised by maximum flexibility | A continuous strip of glass brings light into the corridor and endows it with an atmosphere of transparancy

dynamic idea that might be interpreted as a contrast to the building's function and the scientific significance of "absolute zero" respectively. However, at closer inspection, this superficial and formal interpretation has to be revised and it becomes apparent that the design was rather motivated by practical i.e. legal, technical, and functional aspects. These aspects have resulted in a building which impresses mainly on the inside through the choice of materials and the deliberately imperfect fit-out; this way it adequately reflects the experimental nature of research facilities.

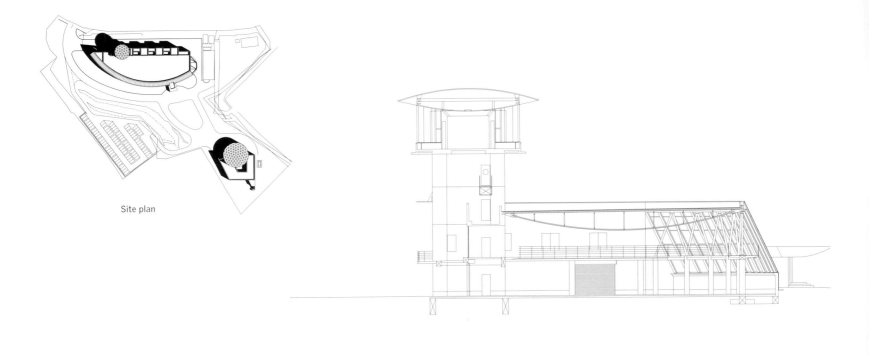

Site plan

Section

from left to right
Contemporary architecture is juxtaposed with traditional gardens | Curtain wall façade | Production hall | View into production hall showing walkway

BASE
Factory & Laboratory

Nagoya, Japan

Client	Osada Electric Co. Ltd.
Architects	Architect 5 Partnership
Construction period	1991-1992
Total floor area	14,300 m²
Net floor area	4,200 m²

The research and production building for medical and dental instruments of Osada Electric Co. Ltd. in Nagoya, Japan, provides a net floor area of 4,200 m² accommodating research laboratories, offices, administration, and production.

The project's particular quality is generated through the merging of Hoigaku (the Japanese version of Chinese Feng Shui) with high-tech architecture. The traditional rules of Hoigaku, which is used to ensure the safety and durability of structures, fell into oblivion more and more, especially in the field of modern town planning. Lately Hoigaku has been rediscovered and is assigned certain significance, last not least as it suits Japan's cultural heritage. The big challenge according

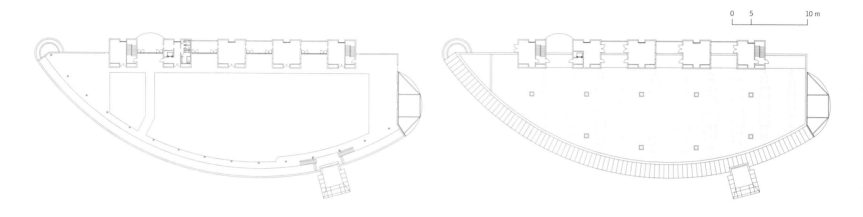

Second floor plan   Third floor plan

to Hoigaku is to "read" the genius loci of a place to retain harmony with nature. This way, the architecture will "breathe" and create an inspiring and human environment.

In keeping with Hoigaku, the architects tried to integrate into their concept the landscape, the existing building fabric, local characteristics, and the people that will work in the factory. The resulting scheme is in balance with the surrounding landscape and draws its inspiration from this fact. All facilities are arranged around a central courtyard, which links the two buildings and determines the premises.

The curved complex with an aluminium curtain wall façade shields noise and heat. Work and production areas are located on the south side. The quiet north side is flanked by rows of representative cherry trees and a pond. On this side, the key areas of the complex including offices as well as meeting and conference rooms are concentrated, but also plant rooms, lifts, and sanitary areas. Lounge zones are allocated in between. The two different functional areas of the complex represent the opposite poles of yin and yang: movement and calm, introverted and extroverted.

The large light-flooded production hall supports inspiration; the roof span of 25 m creates a column-free space allowing all kinds of furnishings and a highly

flexible use of the hall. Both the central laboratories and the observatory have lentil-shaped roofs that seem to be suspended in mid-air and which create a special sense of place and identity of the factory. The architects have called their project BASE, hoping the architecture is deeply rooted in the soil it is built on and is enhanced and supported by the positive energy that the site radiates.

Ground floor plan
of laboratory building

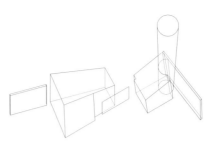

Isometric view
(components of entrance tower)

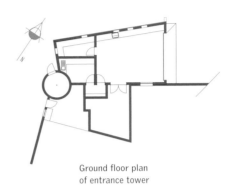

Ground floor plan
of entrance tower

Research Station,
University of Namibia

Henties Bay, Namibia

Client	University of Namibia
Architects	Erhard Roxin Architects
Completion	1999
Total floor area	1,000 m²

The design for the research station of the University of Namibia in Henties Bay goes beyond common spatial and aesthetical boundaries. The architects designed an innovative research centre that evokes associations with the playful and diverse aspects of scientific life and work. The complex strikingly explores the contrast between the architecture of a civilisation striving for knowledge and the barren, spacious and sparsely inhabited desert that surrounds the buildings.

Three buildings were erected during the first phase: a multi-purpose hall, a laboratory building, and a resource centre. The client envisages an extension of the premises if the Namibian government should

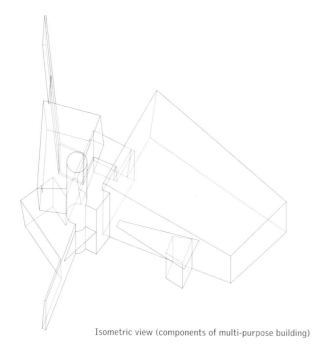

Isometric view (components of multi-purpose building)

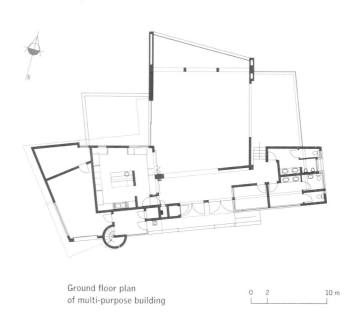

Ground floor plan
of multi-purpose building

0 2   10 m

from left to right
The barren landscape of the desert contrasts with the colourful asymmetrical forms of the research station; the entrance tower exemplifies the idea of the complex | The lightness and variety of the architecture also reflects the spirit of the young research team | The range of materials and colours define the character and sense of place | Interiors are also dominated by a variety of shapes and colours

decide to increase its measures for building training and research facilities in the country.

The extreme climate of the Namibian coastal region substantially influenced the design of the research station. Big day/night and summer/winter differences in temperature and frequent storms called for unconventional design strategies. In order to avoid direct exposure of the main façades to morning and evening sun the new buildings run in east-west direction. The largest window openings are on the north façade (which is the sunny side in the southern hemisphere) to admit sufficient daylight into the building. Exterior spaces such as balconies and terraces also face north, thus turning away from the wind.

Namibian architecture typically features thick massive brick walls – mainly because they have positive effects on the interior climate and the material is easily available. The research station is no exception and was built for the main part of local sand-cement-bricks to reduce the energy consumption of the building, control the interior climate night and day, and meet structural requirements.

The sustainable vernacular design approach meets the basic standards of the Zero Emission Research Initiative (ZERI), which were developed in conjunction with United Nations University (UNU).

All buildings comprise a central, architecturally distinctive service tower. Among other things, it thermally exhausts hot air and serves as a water tower. It enables the installation of future technologies such as systems for the use of fog, wind power stations, and modern communication technology.

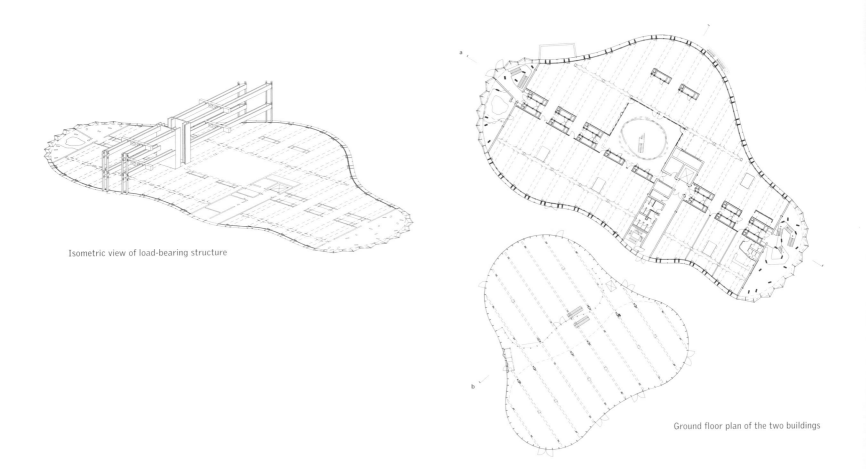

Isometric view of load-bearing structure

Ground floor plan of the two buildings

from left to right
The Amoeba-shaped perimeter and vivid colour scheme | The assembly and testing hall with a load-bearing steel structure next to a three-storey reinforced concrete building | Round openings in the colourfully glazed concrete balustrades in combination with suspended steel stairs dominate the central access space of the laboratory building | Differently coloured solar protection louvers

Centre for Photonics 1, Adlershof Science and Technology Park

Berlin, Germany

Client	WISTA-Management GmbH
Architects	sauerbruch hutton architekten
Construction period	1996 -1998
Total floor area	10,900 m²
Net floor area	6,500 m²

The business and innovation centre for optics, opto-electronics, and laser technology consists of two organically shaped building volumes: a single-storey experimental hall and a three-storey laboratory building. Their outstanding amorphous architecture strikingly contrasts with the rigorous rectangular block pattern of the Adlershof Technology Park. The shape and colour scheme of the buildings create an identity and a unique sense of place which respond to the difficult site.

Photonics are a scientific key topic with a broad range of potential applications in fields such as laser, medicine and display technology, and x-ray analytics. The brief called for multi-functional areas providing flexibility in terms of size, layout, and technical equipment

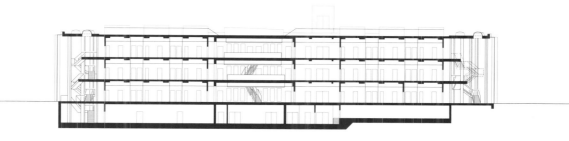

Longitudinal section

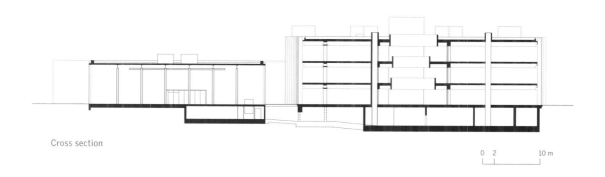

Cross section

0 2   10 m

in order to accommodate the many different work and research scenarios and requirements of changing tenants. The organic shape of the buildings was partly motivated by the different sizes of required work areas ranging from 100 m² to 1,000 m².

Minimised circulation areas and the need for large laboratories that can be blacked out led to a relatively deep floor plan which is organised along a central service and access route. The functional areas are arranged at right angles to this route. Based on a perpendicular structural and infrastructural grid the building allows any spot to be connected to all kinds of services.

The three-storey main building has a glazed double-layered façade providing maximum transparency in combination with an increased thermal insulation and natural ventilation. The 7.5 m tall experimental hall for large-scale tests is a simple steel structure with fully glazed exterior walls. Both buildings were fitted with coloured solar blinds. Additionally, the columns of the multi-storey building received a vivid colour treatment. The lively colour scheme reflects the colour spectrum of light and reinforces the organic undulating appearance of the building exterior. Shape, colour, light, and transparency create a dynamic building volume that smartly juxtaposes the restored neighbour buildings.

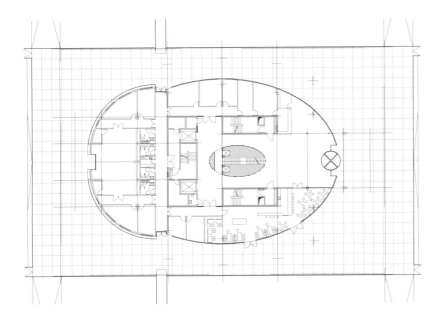

Ground floor plan

Fifth floor plan (surgery area)

from left to right
The building shape reflecting a human cerebrum is accentuated
by the lighting | The elliptical plan with floors of different sizes
determines the exterior | Interplay of shapes and light | Two
glazed lifts within the generous atrium space link all levels of
the building

International
Neuroscience
Institute

Hannover, Germany

Client	INI – International-Neuroscience Institute Hannover GmbH
Architects	SIAT GmbH
Construction period	1998-2000
Total floor area	19,000 m²
Net floor area	8,400 m²
Cubic content	86,500 m³

The institute, a specialised hospital with state-of-the art
medical equipment, integrates departments for neuro-
surgery, neuro radiosurgery, and neuro radiology. It
is to become a global leader as a "Centre of Excellence"
for research and treatment of neurological diseases.

In order to represent medical competence and innovation the clients looked for a unique architectural concept with a great sense of identity. The result is a 38 m
tall, nine-storey sculptural building modelled after a
human head or cerebrum respectively.

The building forms part of the Hanover Medical Park in
the northeast of the city and is located adjacent to the
Medical College and further non-academic research fa-

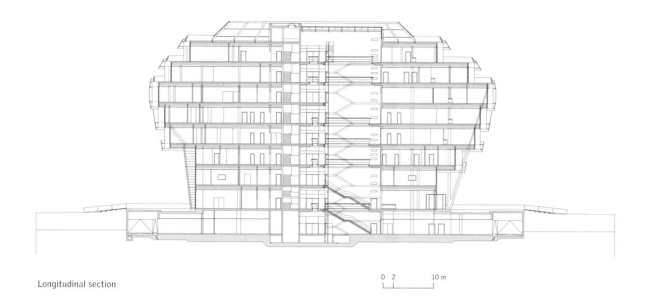

Longitudinal section

0 2 10 m

cilities. The landscaping of the 27,000 m² site is split into four areas. A large open stair to the east provides access to the building. To the north, there is staff parking; to the south, parking for visitors is located. A generously laid out hospital park stretches towards the west.

In contrast to what one might expect when looking at the curved exterior, the interior of the institute is based on a clearly structured layout. At the centre of the elliptical plan is an oval glazed atrium around which all spaces are arranged on a strictly orthogonal grid. On the ground floor, the cafeteria and reception are situated, on the first floor the neuro radiological clinic, on the second to fourth floor the patients rooms, on the fifth floor the surgery area with intensive care unit, and on

the sixth and seventh floor therapy and doctors areas. The layout and central vertical access provide optimal orientation.

The façade consists of three glazed layers. The inner layer is composed of a post-and-beam structure. The outer layer consists of alternating transparent, translucent, white, coloured, or screen-printed panels. Inclined glazed balustrades of the exterior maintenance walkways form the third layer. The different glazing finishes and the layered arrangement create a lively pattern of shadows, reflections, and distortion effects.

The printed glazing in front of the post-and-beam structure blurs the position of the storeys and symbolises the

texture of the cerebrum. The cerebellum is visualised by a curved concrete wall with an aluminium curtain wall without openings that contrasts with the rest of the building.

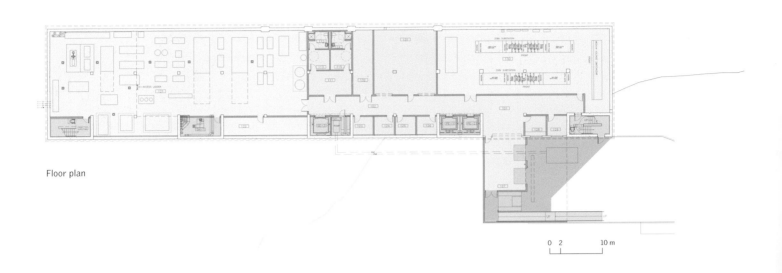

Floor plan

0 2   10 m

from left to right
The office and meeting room zone forms the backbone of the
building | Rectangular volume to the west and attached cascading
"waterfall" façade consisting of convex glass panes | Insulating
glass façade of the laboratory area | Laboratories

Van Andel Institute

Grand Rapids, Michigan, USA

Client	The Van Andel Institute
Architects	Rafael Viñoly Architects PC
Construction period	1997-2000
Total floor area	40,500 m²

The cancer research centre is located on a steep slope
near the city centre. With its stepped convex glazed
roofs it evokes associations with the rapids of the
Grand River. The individual sculptural appearance of
the building is derived from practical requirements.
It is also designed as a research building that supports social interaction between the scientists and
provides spatial and functional flexibility of the laboratory areas.

As the exterior of the building suggests, the interior
is arranged in three zones. In the eastern part underneath the glazed cascades, office areas are laid out
as large open spaces with flexible laboratory furnishings. The translucent roof structure above the step-

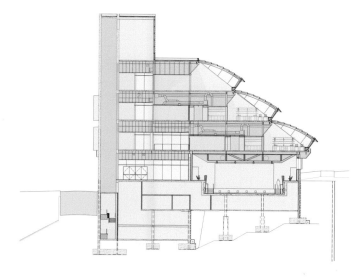

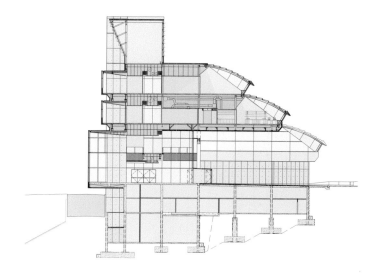

Cross sections

ped levels admits intensive daylight, thus creating a unique atmosphere in which communication and social interaction can thrive and new ideas can be born while conducting experiments.

According to the brief, modular work benches and worktops are standardised and can be easily rearranged with regard to their technical equipment and spatial layout. Horizontal service lines support flexibility since they enable a number of defined spots of the floor plan to connect to the technical infrastructure. Transparency enhances the open plan character of the laboratories.

In contrast to the transparent "cascades" the western wing adjacent to the "rapids" provides solid sculptural qualities. It houses the theoretical studies and meeting rooms. The access areas at the gable ends of the building are fully glazed and admit daylight into generous circulation zones that are also designed to encourage social interaction. Like the technical and service rooms located in the central dark zone the studies and meeting rooms cannot be rearranged easily. The auditorium and laboratories that require no or little daylight are located in the core zone which follows the sloped site.

A proposed building west of the existing institute would triple the current floor areas if required. It is envisaged to be a similar but mirrored and bigger version of the existing one and would create an open courtyard between the two buildings.

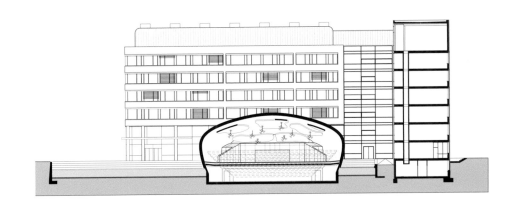

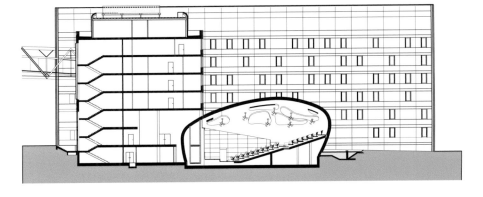

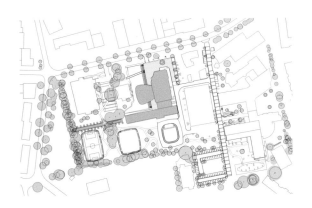

Site plan

Cross sections

from left to right
A bridge with a clear span of 70 m links the new research building to the existing neighbour buildings | Interior and exterior are linked symbolically by a lecture hall situated in an exterior pond | Inviting open lounge zones at the intersections of circulation paths | Above: Cloud-shaped acoustic panels in the lecture hall | Below: Open plan design of the laboratory level

Research and Laboratory Building, Beiersdorf AG

Hamburg, Germany

Client	Beiersdorf AG, Hamburg
Architects	HHS Planer + Architekten AG
Construction period	2002-2004
Total floor area	16,000 m²
Cubic content	60,000 m³

The design concept for the new laboratory building – an extension of the "Werk 005" research and development centre of Beiersdorf AG in the central Hamburg district of Eimsbüttel – takes up the theme of the building skin as a metaphor of one of the company's main product lines: cosmetics and skin care. The rounded corners of the building, a blob-shaped lecture hall, and plant rooms with curved roofs encourage onlookers to attribute elastic qualities to the building envelope.

Two six-storey volumes are linked by access and communication areas on each level to form an L-shaped building. On the fourth and fifth floor, a 70 m long glass tube suspended from steel trusses connects the

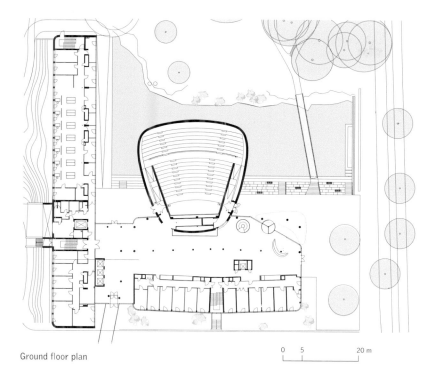

Ground floor plan

0   5   20 m

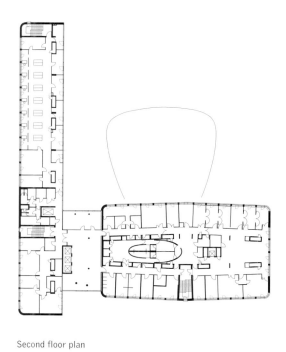

Second floor plan

respective access areas with existing buildings. The lecture hall seating 500 is covered by a shell structure clad with stainless steel. Adjacent to the lecture hall, the main entrance from the north leads into a two-storey public entrance hall. The lecture hall is situated in the centre of a large water basin while penetrating the main building. A suspenseful contrast is established between organic and geometrical, engineered and free building forms.

From the second to fifth floor, the main building is arranged along two interior corridors per floor. The external zones contain open plan laboratories with writing desks positioned next to the façades. Individual office and meeting rooms have been allocated to

these laboratories. The central dark zone houses special equipment laboratories and service zones. Technical services run in decentralised individual shafts feeding exposed horizontal service ducts. Therefore, no suspended ceilings were required and relatively low ceiling heights could be achieved. The resulting total building height is below the high-rise limit, making planning requirements in terms of fire protection and escape routes easier to fulfil.

The long southern wing accommodates large laboratory areas. Little office units are located behind the fully glazed north façade. The units' interior partitions, which face the central laboratory and meeting area, are also glazed. Open plan work desks for scien-

tific analysis are allocated near the south façade. Single wet chemical laboratories supplement the general open plan arrangement. The building structure with large ceiling spans, single service shafts, and low ceiling heights provides maximum flexibility as it allows the refurbishment of lab floors into office floors.

PROJECT DATA

AstraZeneca Research and Development Centre for Biology and Pharmacy

Architects
Wingårdh Arkitektkontor AB
Kungsgatan 10 A
SE-411 Gothenburg
www.wingardhs.se

Construction management
Ake Larson Bygg, NCC Vast
AB, Platzer A
Gothenburg

Barcelona Botanical Institute

Architects
Carlos Ferrater, Joan
Guibernau, Elena Mateu
Balmes, 145 Bajos
08008 Barcelona
www.ferrater.com

Mechanical services
P.G.I.

Laboratory planning
Dr. Josep Montserrat

BASE Factory & Laboratory

Architects
Architect 5 Partnership
5-2 Kamiyama-Cho,
Shibuya-Ku
Tokyo
www.architect5.co.jp

Construction management
Kajima Corporation, Nagoya
E & M design ES Associates

Umezawa
Structural Engineers

Belfer Building for Molecular Genetics and Cancer Research, Weizmann Campus

Architects
Moshe Zur Architects
Urbanists & Town Planners
323 Hayarkon St.
Tel-Aviv 63504

Berlin Electron Storage Ring Bessy II, Adlershof Science and Technology Park

Architects
Brenner & Partner,
Architekten und Ingenieure,
Brenner-Hammes-Krause
Marienstraße 37
70178 Stuttgart
www.brenner-partner-stuttgart.de

Mechanical services
*HVAC and
sanitary engineering*
Jaeger, Mornhinweg
+Partner, Stuttgart;
Electrical engineer
Klaus Engelhardt & Partner,
Berlin

Biological Sciences and Bioengineering Building, Indian Institute of Technology

Architects
Kanvinde Rai & Chowdhury
Architect Planners
14-F Middle Circle Connaught
Place
New Delhi 110 001

Mechanical services
*HVAC and
sanitary engineering*
Gupta Consultants, New Delhi
Electrical engineer
Kaanwar Krishen &
Associates P. Ltd., New Delhi
Sanitary installation
S.G. Deolalikar, New Delhi

Centre for Cellular and Biomolecular Research

Architects
Behnisch, Behnisch & Partner
Architekten
Christophstraße 6
70178 Stuttgart
www.behnisch.com

In collaboration with
architectsAlliance, Toronto

Laboratory planning
Flad & Associates, Madison,
Wisconsin

Mechanical services
H.H. Angus & Associates,
Don Mills

Centre for Energy and Technology

Architects
Knoche Architekten BDA
Rothebühlstraße 89 / 2
70178 Stuttgart

Construction management
Uwe Schüler, Rendsburg

Mechanical services
Paul + Sampe, Esslingen

Centre for Human Drug Research

Architect
Architectenbureau cepezed b.v.
Phoenixstraat 60b
Postbus 3068
2601 DB Delft
www.cepezed.nl

Engineers
Eccs bv, Hoofddorp

Centre for Information and Media Technology, Adlershof Science and Technology Park

Architects
Architectenbureau cepezed b.v.
Phoenixstraat 60b
Postbus 3068
2601 DB Delft
www.cepezed.nl

In collaboration with
DGI Bauwerk, Berlin

Centre for Photonics 1, Adlershof Science and Technology Park

Architects
sauerbruch hutton
architekten partnerschaft
Lehrter Straße 57
10557 Berlin
www.sauerbruchhutton.de

Mechanical services
Zibell, Willner und Partner,
Berlin/Cologne

Façade consultant
Ingenieurbüro Michael Lange,
Berlin/Hanover

CIBA-Geigy Life Sciences Building

Architects
Mitchell/Giurgola Architects,
LLP
170 West 97th Street
New York, NY 10025
www.mitchellgiurgola.com

Mechanical services
Earl Walls Associates

Fraunhofer Institute for Manufacturing and Advanced Materials

Architects
Brenner & Partner,
Architekten und Ingenieure,
Brenner-Hammes-Krause
Marienstraße 37
70178 Stuttgart
www.brenner-partner-stuttgart.de

Laboratory planning
Dipl.-Ing. H. Eickhoff,
Lilienthal

Mechanical services
Bruns & Partner GmbH,
Bremen

Fred Hutchinson Cancer Research Center

Architects
Zimmer Gunsul Frasca
Partnership
320 SW Oak St. Suite 500
Portland, OR 972043115
www.zgf.com

Laboratory planning
McLellan & Copenhagen

Mechanical services
Affiliated Engineers

Gifu Research Laboratories of Amano Enzyme Inc.

Architects
Kisho Kurokawa
architect & associates
11th Floor Aoyama Building,
1-2-3 Kita Aoyama, Minato-ku,
Tokyo 107-0061
www.kisho.co.jp

In collaboration with
Richard Rogers Partnership
Japan Ltd.

Mechanical services
Inuzuka Engineering
Consultants

Graz Research Centre of the Austrian Academy of Sciences

Architects
Architectenbureau cepezed
b.v.
Phoenixstraat 60b
Postbus 3068
2601 DB Delft
www.cepezed.nl

In collaboration with
Architekturbüro Herfried
Peyker, Graz; Ingenieurbüro
Wendl, Graz

Mechanical services
TB Pickl, Graz

Headquarters of NeuroSearch A/S

Architects
Henning Larsens Tegnestue
A/S
Vesterbrogade 76
1620 Kopenhagen
www.hlt.dk

Institute for Chemistry and Lecture Building for Chemistry and Physics, Humboldt University of Berlin, Adlershof Campus

Architects
Volker Staab Architekten
BDA
Schlesische Straße 20
10997 Berlin
www.staab-architekten.com

Construction management
Ingenieur- und
Planungsgesellschaft mbH
Kappes Scholz

Mechanical services
ITC Ing. Gemeinschaft
Chemieinstitut Scheller-
Dauphin-Desz-Falk-Hosang

Biosciences Building, Bundoora Campus, RMIT University

Architects
John Wardle Architects
and Design Inc.
Level 10, 180 Russel Street
Melbourne Victoria 3000
www.johnwardle.com

Structural engineer
Connell Mott MacDonald

Biosciences Building, University of Liverpool

Architects
David Morley Architects
18 Hatton Place
London EC1N 8RU
www.davidmorleyarchitects.
co.uk

BIOSTEIN Agrobiological Research Centre of Novartis Crop Protection AG

Architects
wilhelm und partner
Freie Architekten
Am Unteren Sonnenrain 4
79539 Lörrach

Mechanical services
Suiselectra
Ingenieurunternehmung AG,
Basle

Bourns Hall, Engineering Science Building, University of California

Architects
Anshen + Allen
5055 Wilshire Boulevard
Los Angeles, California 90036
www.anshenla.com

Center for Biotechnology and Bioengineering

Architects
Bohlin Cywinski Jackson
Suite 1300
307 Fourth Avenue
Pittsburgh, PA 15222
www.bcj.com

Laboratory planning
BBN

Mechanical services
P. L. Frank, Caplan
Engineering Company

Center of Advanced European Studies and Research (CAESAR)

Architects
BMBW Architekten BDA +
Partner, Bachmann, Marx,
Brechensbauer, Weinhart,
Werner, Pietsch
Gustav-Heinemann-Ring 121
81739 Munich
www.bmbw.de

Laboratory planning
Dr. Heinekamp Labor und
Institutsplanung GmbH,
Karlsfeld/München

Mechanical services
*HVAC and
sanitary engineering*
Jaeger, Mornhinweg +
Partner, Stuttgart
Electrical engineer
Müller & Bleher,
Sindelfingen/Radolfzell
CBP Cronauer Beratung
Planung, Munich

Computer Science and Electrical Engineering Institutes, Graz University of Technology

Architects
Riegler Riewe Architekten
ZT-Ges.m.b.H.
Griesgasse 10
8020 Graz
www.rieglerriewe.co.at

Mechanical services
Ingenieurbüro Hammer
Electrical engineer
Friebe und Korp. OEG

Degussa Construction Chemicals Competence Centre

Architects
Raupach + Schurk
Architekten
Bauerstraße 19
80796 Munich

Laboratory planning
Dr. Heinekamp Labor und
Institutsplanung GmbH,
Karlsfeld/Munich

Mechanical services
Ebert Ingenieure, Munich

Landscaping
Landschaftsarchitektin Dipl.-
Ing. Irene Burkhardt, Freising

Donald Danforth Plant Science Center

Architects
Nicholas Grimshaw
& Partners Ltd.
1 Conway Street
Fitzroy Square
London W1T 6LR
www.grimshaw-
architects.com

In collaboration with
HOK, Hellmuth,
Obata & Kassabaum

Laboratory planning,
mechanical services
HOK, Hellmuth,
Obata & Kassabaum

Greenhouse planning
Agritechnove

Engineering Research Center der University of Cincinnati

Architects
Michael Graves & Associates
341 Nassau Street
Princeton, New Jersey 08540
www.michaelgraves.com

In collaboration with
KZF Inc., Cincinnati

Laboratory planning
Smith Hinchman & Grylls,
Detroit

Faculty of Mechanical Engineering, Technical University of Munich

Architects
Henn Architekten
Augustenstraße 54
80333 Munich
www.henn.com

Mechanical services
Kuehn Bauer Partner,
Halbermoss with
PRO-Elektroplan GmbH,
Ottobrunn-Riemerling;
Bartenbach LichtLabor GmbH,
Aldrans/Innsbruck

Fraunhofer Institute for Applied Polymer Research

Architects
Brenner & Partner,
Architekten und Ingenieure,
Brenner-Hammes-Krause
Marienstraße 37
70178 Stuttgart
www.brenner-partner-
stuttgart.de

Laboratory planning,
mechanical services
Plarewa GmbH, Berlin

Institute of Physics, Humboldt University of Berlin, Adlershof Campus

Architects
Augustin und Frank
Architekten
Schlesische Straße 29-30
10997 Berlin

Mechanical services
Ingenieurgesellschaft
Kannewischer mbH, Berlin

Institutes and Lecture Hall for Biology and Chemistry, University of Rostock

Architects
Volker Staab Architekten BDA
Schlesische Straße 20
10997 Berlin
www.staab-architekten.com

In collaboration with
A. Nieuwenhuizen

Laboratory planning
Horst Hosang GmbH,
Hensch-Stedt-Ulzburg

Mechanical services
HVAC engineering
Ingenieurbüro Scheller,
Heroldsberg
Sanitary engineering
Ingenieurbüro Dauphin,
Nürnberg
Electrical engineer
Ingenieurbüro Desz-Falk
GmbH, Nürnberg

International Neuroscience Institute

Architects
SIAT GmbH
Rosenheimer Straße 145
81671 Munich
www.siat.de

Mechanical services
Siemens Gebäudetechnik
Nord GmbH & Co. oHG,
Laatzen

James H. Clark Center, Stanford University

Architects
Foster and Partners
architects and designers
Riverside Three
22 Hester Road
London SW11 4AN
www.fosterandpartners.com

In collaboration with/
Laboratory planning
MBT Architecture

Mechanical services
Alfa Tech, Santa Clara;
Cupertino Electric, Cupertino;
Therma, San Jose;
Claude Engle, Washington, DC

La Ruche, Technocentre Renault

Architects
Valode & Pistre Architectes
115, rue du Bac
75007 Paris
www.valode-et-pistre.com

Mechanical services
SGTE, Paris; Georges Berne

Laboratory Building for Medical Genome Research

Architects
Volker Staab Architekten
BDA
Schlesische Straße 20
10997 Berlin
www.staab-architekten.com

Laboratory planning
LCI mbH, Berlin

Mechanical services
Scholze Ingenieurgesellschaft
mbH, Berlin

Laboratory Building of Cologne University Hospital

Architects
Heinrich Wörner +
stegepartner GmbH & Co. KG
Architekten und
Generalplaner BDA
Rheinische Straße 169-171
44147 Dortmund
www.stegepartner.de

Laboratory planning
Ingenieurbüro Christoffel,
Bonn

Mechanical services
Zibell Willner & Partner,
Cologne

Life Sciences Complex, Ben Gurion University

Architects
Ada Karmi-Melamede
& Partners
17 Kaplan Street
Tel-Aviv 64734

Laboratory planning
Arch. Zadok Sherman

Maersk McKinney Møller Institute for Production Technologies

Architects
Henning Larsens Tegnestue
A/S
Vesterbrogade 76
1620 Kopenhagen
www.hlt.dk

Male Urological Cancer Research Centre

Architects
Copping Lindsay Architects
14 Methley Street Kennington
London SE 11 4AJ
http://home.btconnect.com/
coppinglindsay

Max Bergmann Centre of Biomaterials

Architects
Brenner & Partner
Architekten und Ingenieure,
Brenner-Hammes-Krause
Marienstraße 37
70178 Stuttgart
www.brenner-partner-
stuttgart.de

Laboratory planning,
mechanical services
Rentschler + Riedesser GmbH,
Stuttgart
Electrical engineer
Müller & Bleher, Filderstadt

Max Planck Campus Tübingen

Architects
Fritsch + Tschaidse
Architekten
Gabelsbergerstraße 15
80333 Munich
www.fritsch-tschaidse.de

Construction management
Schmitt & Bessey Freie
Architekten, Tübingen

Laboratory planning
Dr. Heinekamp Labor und
Institutsplanung GmbH,
Karlsfeld/Munich

Mechanical services
*HVAC and
sanitary engineering*
Jaeger, Mornhinweg +
Partner, Stuttgart
Electrical engineer
Müller & Bleher,
Sindelfingen/Radolfzell

Mercedes-Benz Design Center

Architects
Renzo Piano Building
Workshop s.r.l.
via P. P. Rubens, 29
16158 Genoa

In collaboration with
C. Kohlbecker

Engineering consultants
Ove Arup and Partners; IBF
Dr. Braschel & Partner GmbH

Lighting designer
Arup & Partners

Molecular Sciences Building

Architects
Anshen + Allen
5055 Wilshire Boulevard
Los Angeles,
California 90036
www.anshenla.com

Mechanical services
Ove Arup & Partners

Naito Chemistry Building and Bauer Laboratory Building, Harvard University

Architects
Ellenzweig Associates, Inc.,
Architects
1280 Massachusetts Avenue
Cambridge, Massachusetts
02138
www.ellenzweig.com

Mechanical services
BR+A Consulting Engineers,
Boston

Nokia Research Center

Architects
Tuomo Siitonen
and Esko Valkama,
Helin & Siitonen Architects
Veneentekijäntie 12
00210 Helsinki
www.tsi.fi

Construction management
LCC Finnland Ltd.
HVAC engineering
Olof Granlund Ltd.
Electrical engineer
Lausamo Ltd.

Nuclear Magnetic Resonant Instrument Laboratory, Peking University

Architects
Atelier Feichang Jianzhu
Jing Chun Yuan,
No.79 Jia Peking University
Beijing, P.R. China, 100871
www.fcjz.com

Panta Rhei Research Centre for Lightweight Materials

Architects
kleyer.koblitz.architekten
Urbanstraße 116
10967 Berlin
www.kleyerkoblitz.de

Laboratory planning
Freischladt + Assmann,
Haiger

Mechanical services
HVAC engineering
Siegert und Krah, Cottbus
Electrical engineer
Wernicke, Cottbus

Semperit Research Building

Architects
Najjar & Najjar Architekten
Mariahilferstraße 101 St.2/22
1060 Vienna
www.najjar-najjar.com

Mechanical services
*HVAC and
sanitary engineering*
Scholze, Stuttgart;
Boll & Partner, Stuttgart

Schlumberger Cambridge Research Centre

Architects
Michael Hopkins & Partners
27 Broadley Terrace
London NW1 6LG
www.hopkins.co.uk

Sciences Institute

Architects
Heinle, Wischer und Partner
Freie Architekten
Villastraße 1
70190 Stuttgart

In collaboration with
Krebs und Kiefer
International

Sir Alexander Fleming Building, Imperial College

Architects
Foster and Partners
architects and designers
Riverside Three
22 Hester Road
London SW11 4AN
www.fosterandpartners.com

Laboratory planning
Research Facilities Design
Electrical engineer
Claude Engle

Southwest Bio-Tech Intermediate Test Base

Architects
Atelier Feichang Jianzhu
Jing Chun Yuan,
No.79 Jia Peking University
Beijing, P.R. China, 100871
www.fcjz.com

Structural engineer
Sun Fangchui, Yu Zhixiong,
Bejing

State Office for Chemical Investigations

Architects
Dipl.-Ing. Michael Weindel
Freier Architekt BDA
Im Ermilsgrund 16
76337 Waldbronn/Karlsruhe
www.weindel.com

Laboratory planning,
mechanical services
Giller + Weltecke, Stuttgart

Max Planck Institute for Chemical Ecology

Architects
BMBW Architekten BDA +
Partner, Bachmann, Marx,
Brechensbauer, Weinhart,
Werner, Pietsch
Gustav-Heinemann-Ring 121
81739 Munich
www.bmbw.de

Laboratory planning
Dr. Heinekamp Labor und
Institutsplanung GmbH,
Karlsfeld/Munich

Mechanical services
*HVAC and
sanitary engineering*
Jaeger, Mornhinweg +
Partner, Stuttgart
Electrical engineer
Ingenieurbüro IBA, Bau und
Ausrüstungen GmbH, Jena
Greenhouse planning
APK Kamphausen + Partner,
Willich

Max Planck Institute for Evolutionary Anthropology

Architects
SSP Architekten Schmidt-
Schicketanz und Partner
GmbH
Osterwaldstraße 10
80805 Munich

Laboratory planning
Ingenieurbüro Hans
Christoffel, Bonn

Mechanical services
*HVAC and
sanitary engineering*
Ing. Gem. Hensel + Sedlmayr,
Nuremberg
Electrical engineer
Ingenieurbüro G. Loy &
Partner GmbH, Hamburg

Max Planck Institute for Infection Biology and German Arthritis Research Centre

Architects
Deubzer König Architekten
Knesebeckstraße 77
10623 Berlin

Construction management
Deubzer König + Döpping
Widell with Lamberg +
Spital, Berlin

Laboratory planning
Dr. Heinekamp Labor und
Institutsplanung GmbH,
Karlsfeld/Munich

Mechanical services
Kuehn Bauer Partner,
Halbergmoos

Max Planck Institute for Molecular Cell Biology and Genetics

Architects
Heikkinen-Komonen
Architects
Kristianinkatu 11-13
00170 Helsinki

Henn Architekten
Augustenstraße 54
80333 Munich
www.henn.com

Laboratory planning
Dr. Heinekamp Labor und
Institutsplanung GmbH
Karlsfeld/Munich

Mechanical services
*HVAC and
sanitary engineering*
Jaeger, Mornhinweg +
Partner
Electrical engineer
Müller & Bleher

Max Planck Institute for Plasma Physics, Greifswald Branch

Architects
Henn Architekten
Augustenstraße 54
80333 Munich
www.henn.com

Mechanical services
*HVAC and
sanitary engineering*
Jaeger, Mornhinweg +
Partner, Stuttgart
Electrical engineer
Müller & Bleher,
Sindelfingen/Radolfzell

Max Planck Institute of Biophysics

Architects
Auer + Weber + Architekten
Georgenstraße 22
80799 Munich
www.auer-weber.de

Construction management
Doranth Post Architekten,
Munich

Laboratory planning
Ingenieurbüro Hans
Christoffel, Bonn

Mechanical services
*HVAC and
sanitary engineering*
HL-Technik, Munich
Electrical engineer
Hildebrand + Hau, Munich

Parque Tecnológico IMPIVA

Architects
Carlos Ferrater, Carlos Bento,
Jaime Sanahuja Balmes,
145 Bajos
08008 Barcelona
www.ferrater.com

Structural engineer
Agroman, S.A.

Pharmacological Research Building, Boehringer Ingelheim Pharma KG

Architects
sauerbruch hutton
architekten partnerschaft
Lehrter Straße 57
10557 Berlin
www.sauerbruchhutton.de

Construction management
Zibell, Willner und Partner,
Cologne

Physics and Astronomy Laboratories, Leiden University

Architects
(EEA) Erick van Egeraat
associated architects
Calandstraat 23
3016 CA Rotterdam
www.eea-architects.com

Mechanical engineer
Sweegers & de Bruijn

Research and Laboratory Building, Beiersdorf AG

Architects
HHS Planer + Architekten AG
Habichtswalderstr.19
34119 Kassel
www.hhs-architekten.de

Master planning
EUROLABORS, Kassel

Research Station, University of Namibia

Architects
Erhard Roxin Architect
11 Daniel Tjongarero Street
Swakopmund

Structural engineer
Bicon Namibia

Saitama Prefectural University

Architects
Riken Yamamoto
Takamisawa Bld. 7F,
2-7-10 Kitasaiwai
Nishi-ku, Yokohama

Technology Centre, Rhine-Elbe Science Park

Architects
Kiessler + Partner
Architekten GmbH
Mauerkircherstraße 41
81679 Munich
www.kiessler.de

Mechanical services
*HVAC and
sanitary engineering*
Ingenieurbüro Trumpp,
Munich
Electrical engineer
Ingenieurbüro Zerull, Munich
Energy consultant
Fraunhofer-Institut, Freiburg

Van Andel Institute

Architects
Rafael Viñoly Architects PC
50 Vandam ST
New York, NY 10012
www.rvapc.com

Laboratory planning
GPR Planners Collaborative
Inc., Purchase New York

Mechanical services
Burt Hill Kosar Rittelmann
Associates, Butler
Pennsylvania

ILLUSTRATION CREDITS

The authors and the publisher thank the following photographers, architects and organizations for the kind permission to reproduce the photographs in this book.

Principles of Research and Technology Buildings

13
H. G. Esch,
Hennef-Stadt Blankenberg

15
Photographs:
Katrin Bergmann

16
Archiv Lehrstuhl für
Raumkunst und
Lichtgestaltung, Munich
Technical University

17 above
Archiv Bayerisches
Nationalmuseum
17 below, 18
Archiv Lehrstuhl
für Raumkunst und
Lichtgestaltung, Munich
Technical University

20
Ezra Stoller © Esto

21 above
Johnson Wax
21 below
Klaus-Peter Gast

22 above
Archiv Philip Johnson
22 center
Klaus-Peter Gast
22 below
Bruno Suner

24, 25, 26
from: Reinhold Martin,
The Organizational Complex,
MIT Press 2003

24 below, 26 above
Oswald W. Grube

34 above
Universitätsbauamt
34 above center
Laaser
34 below center
Max-Planck-Gesellschaft
34 below
Krase

36
from: T. D. Brock, M. T.
Madigan, J. M. Martinko and
J. Parker, Biology of
Microorganisms, 7th edition,
Englewook Cliffs, New Jersey
1994, p. 676.

38 below, 39 above
Dr. Heinekamp Laborplanung,
Munich / Berlin

56 above
Bayerisches Staatsministe-
rium für Wirtschaft, Verkehr
und Technologie

57
from: Heike Kluttig,
Andreas Dirscherl,
Hans Erhorn:
Energieverbräuche von
Bildungsgebäuden in
Deutschland.
In: Gesundheitsingenieur,
vol. 122 (2001), no. 5,
p. 221-268

Selection of Projects

66-67
Torben Eskerod

68-69
Timothy Hursley

70-71
Werner Huthmacher, Berlin

72, 73 left
Manfred Grohe,
Kirchentellinsfurt
73 right
Fritsch + Tschaidse
Architekten, Munich

74-75
Werner Huthmacher, Berlin

76 left
J. Housel
76 right, 77
Strode Eckert
77 left
Eckert & Eckert

78-81
Amit Geron

82-83
Heinrich Wörner +
stegepartner GmbH & Co. KG
Architekten und
Generalplaner BDA

84-85
Behnisch, Behnisch & Partner
Architekten, Stuttgart

86-87
Peter Durant

88-89
Morley von Sternberg

90-91
Hélène Binet

92-93
Michael Krüger
Architekturfotografie, Berlin

94-95
Lluis Casals, Barcelona

96-97
Karl A. Backus

98-99
H. G. Esch, Hennef-Stadt
Blankenberg

100-101
Frank Speckhals, Leipzig

102-103
Ulrich Schwarz, Berlin

104-105
Alejo Baguè, Barcelona

108-111
Paul Ott, Graz

112, 113 right
Tomio Ohashi
113 left
Shigeru Ohno

114-115
Ralph Richter, Düsseldorf

116-117
Georges Fessy

120-121
Jens Lindhe

122-123
Werner Huthmacher, Berlin

124-125
Heinle, Wischer und Partner
Freie Architekten

126 left
Voitto Niemelä
126 right
Jussi Tiainen
127 right
Kari Uusiheimala

128-129
Ivan Nemec, Berlin

130-133
E-Eins Eicken/Ott, Mühltal

134-135
Lukas Roth, Cologne

136-139
Christian Richters, Münster

140-141
H. G. Esch, Hennef-Stadt
Blankenberg

142-143
Gerrit Engel Fotografie, Berlin

144-145
Dietmar Träupmann,
Augustusburg

146-147
Timothy Hursley, Assassi
Productions/Farshid Assaddi

148-149
Jeff Goldberg, Esto
Photographics, Mamaroneck,
New York

150-151
Peter de Ruig, The Hague

152-153
Volker Staab Architekten,
Berlin

154-155
Nigel Young

156-157
Trevor Mein, Clifton Hill,
Victoria

158-159
Thomas Dix, Grenzach-Wyhlen

160-161
Mahatta Photography,
New Delhi

162-163
Fu Xing

164-165
Steven Brooke Studios

168-171
Jussi Tiainen, Helsinki

172-173
Timothy Hursley,
Little Rock, AR

174-175
Helmut Tezak, Graz

176
Sam Gray
176 right
Edward Jacoby
177 left
Steve Rosenthal

178-179
Koji Kobayashi

180 left
Björn Breitholz
180 right
Nils-Olof Sjöden
181
Bengt Ericksson

182, 183 left
Fetzi Bauer, Filderstadt
183 right, 184
H. Bauer
185
IPP Garching

186-189
Massimo Fiorito, Munich

190-191
Stefan Müller-Naumann,
Munich

192-193
Robert Canfield,
San Rafael, CA

196 right, 197 above right
H. G. Esch, Hennef-Stadt
Blankenberg
197 left, below right
Uwe Rau, Berlin

198-199
Cao Yang

200-201
Christian Richters, Münster

202-205
Jens Weber, Munich

206
Renzo Piano Building
Workshop
207 left, 208 left, 209
P. Horn
207 right
G. Berengo Gardin
208 right
Sawnji Istuda

210-211
Dennis Gilbert, London

212-213
Manfred Seidl, Vienna

214-217
Christian Richters, Münster

218-219
Osamu Murai, Shinkenchiku

220-221
Erhard Roxin

222-223
Bitter + Bredt Fotografie,
Berlin

224-225
Palladium Photodesign
Barbara Burg, Oliver Schuh,
Cologne

226-227
Jeff Goldberg, Esto
Photographics, Mamaroneck,
New York

228-229
Constantin Meyer, Cologne

Every effort has been made
to trace the copyright holders, architecs and designers
and we apologize in advance
for any unintentional omission
and would be pleased to insert
the appropriate acknowledge-
ment in any subsequent edition.

AUTHORS

CONTRIBUTORS

Professor Dr.-Ing. Hardo Braun
Architect BDA, *1941

until 1968
studied architecture
at Munich Technical University
1969-1971
trainee at the Bavarian Building
Administration Authority
1971
Government Master Builder
1972
municipal councillor for building
for the state capital of Munich
1972-1978
employed at the Bavarian Building
Administration Authority
1978-2000
employed at the building department (general
administration) of the Max Planck Society
for the Advancement of Science, Munich
1987
PhD at Munich Technical University
Subject: The development of research
buildings using the example of the
Kaiser Wilhelm/Max Planck Society
1991-2000
head of the building department of the
Max Planck Society for the Advancement
of Science, Munich
since 1998
chairman of EUROLABORS AG
Integrated Laboratory Planning, Kassel
since 1999
guest lecturer at Stuttgart University
since 2001
vice-secretary general of the Max Planck
Society for the Advancement of Science,
Munich
since 2005
Honorary Professor at Stuttgart University,
Department 1, Architecture and Urban
Planning

Dipl.-Ing. Dieter Grömling
Architect, *1955

until 1982
studied architecture at Darmstadt
Technical University
1985-1987
trainee at the Deutsche Bundespost
(Federal Mail), Munich/Bonn
1982-1985
work for the architectural firm
Grellman & Leitl, Würzburg
1987-1991
employed at the building department of the
Deutsche Bundespost, Regensburg/Munich
since 1991
employed at the building department of the
Max Planck Society for the Advancement
of Science, Munich
since 2001
head of the building department of the
Max Planck Society for the Advancement
of Science, Munich

Dipl.-Ing. (FH) Helmut Bleher
Electrical engineer, *1959

until 1985
studied power engineering at Esslingen
Technical College
1985-1989
employed at the technical department of a
large energy corporation
since 1989
managing partner of Müller & Bleher (practice
for electrical engineering, lighting design, and
materials handling) in Filderstadt, Radolfzell,
and Munich

**Univ.-Professor Dipl.-Ing.
Hannelore Deubzer**
Architect, *1954

1978
diploma at Berlin Technical University
1978-1983
work for the architectural firm Bangert,
Jansen, Schultes, Scholz
1984-1985
work for the architectural firm James Stirling
since 1988
partnership with Jürgen König
(Deubzer König Architekten)
1991
scholarship of Villa Massimo, Rome
since 1997
professor at Munich Technical University
since 1998
member of numerous design panels:
München–Riem (1998-2002);
Regensburg (2000–2004); DLR (since 2001);
Halle a. d. Saale (since 2003);
Linz (since 2004); Salzburg (since 2004)

Dipl.-Ing. Jürgen Eichler
Architect, *1939

1959-1965
studied architecture at
Darmstadt Technical University
1965-1966
co-operation with Professor E. Neufert
1968-1970
co-operation with Professor M. Guther
1970-2004
employed at the building department of
the Max Planck Society for the Advancement
of Science

Dipl.-Ing. (Univ.) Oswald W. Grube
Retired Director of Building,
senior member of BDA, DWB, *1936

until 1962
studied architecture at Munich Technical
University; further studies with post-graduate
DAAD grant at the University of British
Columbia, Vancouver B.C.
1965-1969
co-operation with Professor Horst Linde and at
the Building Authority of Stuttgart University
1969-1971
work for the architectural firm Skidmore,
Owings & Merrill (SOM), Chicago/Illinois
1973-1976
exhibition "100 Years of Architecture in
Chicago", Munich and Chicago/Illinois
1972-1991
head of department of the Building Authority
of Munich Technical University, responsible for
the Garching university and research campus
1972-1996
honorary head of the district council and building official in charge of Herrsching district;
1992-1996
deputy mayor of Herrsching

1978-1996
member of the Starnberg district assembly
1991-2001
official of the Government of Upper Bavaria,
responsible for hospital building
since 2001
consulting firm for hospital and institute
building in Herrsching
since 2002
lectures and seminars in the field of American
Urbanism at the Bauhaus University Weimar

Professor Dr.-Ing. Gerhard Hausladen
Mechanical engineer, *1947

until 1972
studied mechanical engineering at Munich
Technical University
1973-1980
assistant lecturer at Munich Technical
University and PhD thesis
1980-1985
technical manager of a medium-sized
supplier of heating technology
1986
founded his own mechanical engineering and
building physics practice in Kirchheim near
Munich
1992-2001
professor of Technical Building Service
Systems at Kassel University
since 1998
executive of the Centre for Sustainable
Ecological Building at Kassel University
since 2001
professor of Building Climatology and
Technical Building Service Systems at
Munich Technical University

Professor Manfred Hegger
Dipl.-Ing. M.Sc.Econ Architect BDA, *1946

1967-1974
studied in Ulm, Stuttgart (Dipl.-Ing.)
and London (M.Sc.Econ)
1974-1990
partner of the task group
"Research of Utilisation"
1980
founded the architectural firm Hegger Hegger
Schleiff HHS Planer + Architekten
since 1991
honorary professor at Hanover University
since 1995
spokesperson of BDA (German Institute of
Architects) in the working group "Co-operation of BDA, German Federation of Housing
Enterprises, and German Association of
Towns and Cities"
1998
founded EUROLABORS AG Integrated
Laboratory Planning
since 1998
director of UIA Work Programme „Sustainable
Architecture of the Future"
since 2001
professor of Architectural Design and Energy
Efficient Building at Darmstadt Technical
University

Professor Dr.-Ing. Gunter Henn
Architect, *1947

1967-1971
studied civil engineering at Munich Technical
University and Berlin Technical University
1972
graduated from Berlin Technical University
1972-1975
studied architecture at
Munich Technical University
1975
phD awarded by Munich Technical University

since 1979
Henn Architekten, Munich, Berlin
since 2000
professor for Building Theory and Design
at Dresden Technical University
since 2002
guest professor at the Massachusetts Institute
of Technology, Cambridge
member of the Bavarian Chamber of
Architects
member of the Federation of German
Architects

Dipl.-Ing. Hans-U. Jaeger
Mechanical engineer, *1943

until 1969
studied mechanical engineering at Stuttgart
Technical University
1969
work for The Trane Comp.
(centre for continued professional development), La Crosse/Wisconsin; project engineer
at J. E. Sirrine & Comp. Architects and
Engineers Greenville, South Carolina
1970-1975
project engineer at Ingenieurbüro Hans Jaeger
1975-1982
managing partner of Hans und
Hans-U. Jaeger GbR
1982-1992
managing partner of JMP GbR
1992-2002
spokesperson of JMP Ingenieurgesellschaft mbH
currently
Ingenieur-Beratung Jaeger
(engineering consultancy)

Dipl.-Ing. Hana Meindl
*1975

until 2003
studied architecture at Munich Technical
University
since 2003
assistant lecturer at Munich Technical
University

Professor Dr. Svante Pääbo
Professor of Genetics and Evolutionary
Biology, *1955

until 1986
studies and PhD in Uppsala
1986-1990
fellowships in Zurich, London, and Berkeley
1990-1998
professor of General Biology, Munich
since 1997
director at the Max Planck Institute for
Evolutionary Anthropology in Leipzig

Professor Dr. Kai Simons
*1938

1964
MD University of Helsinki
1965-67
studies at Rockefeller University, New York
1971-79
professor at University of Helsinki
1975-2000
team leader at EMBL, Heidelberg
1982-98
co-ordinator of the Cell Biology Programme,
EMBL Heidelberg
since 1998
managing director of the Max Planck Institute
for Molecular Cell Biology and Genetics,
Dresden

INDEX OF ARCHITECTS

INDEX OF BUILDINGS

INDEX OF PLACES

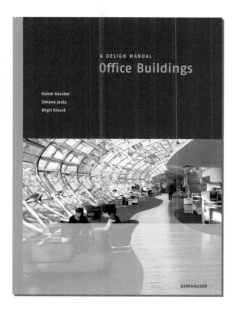
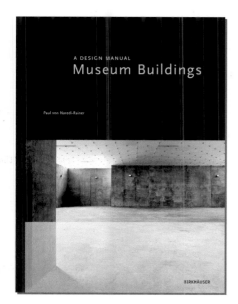
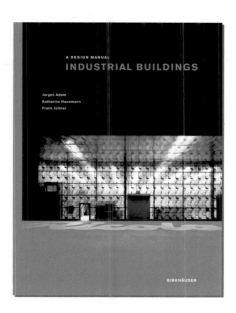

PRAIRIE STYLE

WE OF THE MIDDLE WEST ARE LIVING ON THE PRAIRIE.

THE PRAIRIE HAS A BEAUTY OF ITS OWN,

AND WE SHOULD RECOGNIZE AND ACCENTUATE

THIS NATURAL BEAUTY, ITS QUIET LEVEL.

FRANK LLOYD WRIGHT, 1908

PRAIRIE STYLE

STEWART, TABORI & CHANG

NEW YORK

HOUSES AND GARDENS BY

FRANK LLOYD WRIGHT

AND THE PRAIRIE SCHOOL

TEXT BY DIXIE LEGLER

PHOTOGRAPHS BY CHRISTIAN KORAB

AN ARCHETYPE PRESS BOOK

AT HOME ON

THE PRAIRIE

The typical American house at the outset of the twentieth century "lied about everything," contended Frank Lloyd Wright. It had no sense of unity or purpose, no understanding of nature or comfort. It was nothing more than a "bedeviled box with a fussy lid," an insult to the landscape. Looking to the horizon of his native Midwest, Wright found in the prairie the perfect metaphor to redefine the American home. ■ Born in the heartland, in suburban Chicago around 1900, the Prairie style revolutionized home design. The movement became known as the Prairie School, and although Wright emerged as its leader, he was just one of about twenty idealistic young architects who rewrote the rules of domestic architecture. Prairie School architects rejected the day's ornate Victorian and classical revival styles, believing that these stylistically derivative, claustrophobic "boxes" were not appropriate for the citizens of a democracy. Americans deserved something better, they thought, houses that reflected their own culture and time. Their solution was the Prairie house, a style that expressed America's democratic spirit by echoing one of its most distinctive landscapes. ■ With its refreshingly open interiors and strong horizontal lines, the Prairie house clearly evoked the freedom and sweep of the limitless midwestern landscape. Deep, sheltering eaves and low terrace walls reached out to nature; broad bands of casement windows let it come inside. Stationary interior walls were transformed into head-high screens that allowed air and light to flow

As Wright described it in the *Ladies' Home Journal* in 1901, his prototype Prairie house clearly "recognizes the influence of the prairie" with ground-hugging lines, wide expanses of windows, and broad, sheltering roofs.

easily. Boxlike formal rooms gave way to open plans with built-in furnishings that freed up floor space. Nature's colors—golds, rusts, yellows, greens—reinvigorated interiors. Gardens planted with native trees, wildflowers, and grasses brought the prairie right up to the door. ▪ Each new house grew naturally and honestly from the needs of the people who would live in it and from the landscape, rather than from an inflexible design formula from the past. Prairie School architects added custom-designed furnishings, art glass, integrated lighting, and landscaping, lending harmony and integrity to the whole. Although these innovative houses often shocked the neighbors, their unconventional appearance was deceiving. The form, while revolutionary, was merely a fresh interpretation of exalted conservative themes—the family, the home, time, and place. ▪ The term *Prairie School* to describe the architects working in this style was not suggested until the 1930s. Most of Wright's colleagues believed that they were creating a progressive new American style, not just a style for the prairie. Connecting a house to the landscape was simply a means of stressing the regionalism, horizontality, and repose important to them. In fact, most of the Prairie-style houses were built not on the prairie but on suburban or city lots. Today, *Prairie style* commonly refers to the work of Wright and his contemporaries from about 1900 to 1915. The style took shape in many other building types—churches, schools, factories, stores, office buildings, and banks—but

Massive, richly carved furniture, such as the dining set for George Maher's 1897 Farson House in Oak Park, Illinois, was the norm until the Prairie style took firm hold. Then furnishings became simpler and more rectilinear—more modern.

its most successful application was in the American home. ■ The Prairie style did not materialize overnight, nor did it evolve in a vacuum. Much of the initial thought was contributed by the Chicago architect Louis Sullivan, who encouraged new building forms that rejected historical designs. The Prairie architects also felt a kinship with the Arts and Crafts movement's plea for honest craftsmanship and natural materials. A national "back to nature" crusade inspired greater interest in country living. And Japanese art and architecture introduced simplicity of design. The Prairie architects also embraced new machine technology that made possible the crisp, linear designs they preferred. Wright and his colleagues built on these concepts, carefully crafting them into a set of principles that focused on beauty and comfort instead of outdated ideas from the past. ■ The new house style held great appeal for a cadre of confident, often young, upper-middle-class midwesterners. Impatient with the pretenses of the conservative eastern elite and its preoccupation with styles from the past, these practical homeowners welcomed the Prairie houses, which were regularly featured in new home magazines such as *House Beautiful* and the *Ladies' Home Journal*. Many women of the day wanted not only the vote but also simpler homes with less clutter. A reform mood was in the air, and the Midwest was on the cutting edge. ■ As suburbs grew, so did interest in the Prairie style. But its appeal was short-lived. When World War I began, a wave of nostalgia struck the country, and American taste shifted back to the colonial and historical revival styles. Those architects

Prairie architects favored geometric forms—cubes, circles, squares, and triangles—over classical motifs to unite their designs. Maher summoned all these shapes in art glass for the Farson House, enhancing them with intense color.

who championed the cause of a new architecture found themselves either out of work or forced to adapt to change. ■ The Prairie style left its most significant imprint on the Midwest, particularly Illinois, Wisconsin, Iowa, and Minnesota. But Prairie houses were also built in places far removed from the prairie, such as the Louisiana flatlands, the Massachusetts seashore, a Seattle hilltop, and even Puerto Rico and Australia. Based on adaptable principles rather than on a rigid formula, they looked at home in almost any location. ■ Many Prairie houses are nearly a century old now, yet they still seem astonishingly innovative. They possess an authenticity, timelessness, and warmth lacking in modern and postmodern architecture. The Prairie houses' natural materials and ground-loving forms seem more permanent and honest. Their graceful lines and open spaces are pleasing to the eye and to the soul. Prairie houses speak to something deep within all of us: rooted in the land, they fill our need to put down roots. ■ Now, at the threshold of a new century, interest in the Prairie style is reviving. New houses embracing Prairie-style principles are taking shape across the country. Most encouraging of all, the works of Wright's contemporaries are at last being given the attention they deserve. Wright's buildings have long been a focus of preservation efforts, but now the once-neglected masterpieces of his colleagues are also being restored, their walls shored up, chimneys tuck-pointed, and furnishings rebuilt. Slowly these works of art are taking their rightful place in our architectural lexicon as treasures to learn from, live in, and admire.

When nineteen-year-old Frank Lloyd Wright stepped off the train in Chicago in 1887 from his home in Wisconsin, the city was bursting with creative energy and architectural promise. In the aftermath of the destructive fire of 1871, a massive construction boom was under way. Suburbs were expanding, and a fresh crop of businesspeople was finding success in the Midwest's thriving economy. ■ Against this hopeful backdrop, Wright's architectural career unfolded in tandem with the rise of the Prairie School. Wright became the movement's chief practitioner and most dynamic spokesman. Yet all across the city, young architects were reexamining American home design. Like Wright, they produced an exceptional body of work. But unlike Wright—still the world's most famous architect long after his death—they have remained in relative obscurity, their buildings, furnishings, art glass, and ornament routinely mistaken for his. Only recently has the work of George Grant Elmslie, William Gray Purcell, Walter Burley Griffin, Marion Mahony, Robert Spencer, Barry Byrne, William Drummond, John Van Bergen, Vernon Watson, Thomas E. Tallmadge, George Maher, and others emerged from Wright's long shadow. ■ The visionary Chicago architect Louis Sullivan inspired a generation of these young designers with his ideas about nature and design, urging them to seek an indigenous architecture that grew as naturally and logically from the soil as a plant

emerges from a seed. Sullivan applied these concepts to that great midwestern symbol of progress, the skyscraper, but it was Wright—his employee for nearly six years and his most illustrious protégé—who led the search for a new form for the American home. After breaking with Sullivan in 1893, Wright took an office in Chicago, eventually moving to Steinway Hall, where the architects Dwight Perkins, Robert Spencer, and Myron Hunt also worked. At the age of twenty-six, Wright made a gigantic leap toward reinventing the traditional house with his first independent commission: the 1893 Winslow House in River Forest, Illinois. Its simple facade and honest treatment of materials represented a rejection of standard nineteenth-century building methods. The design was so unusual that William Winslow, claimed Wright, had to sneak out to the train station to avoid his neighbors' derision. ▪ Emerging as the group's natural leader, Wright built a studio alongside his Oak Park, Illinois, home in 1898 and invited some of the brightest young talent to join him there. The new studio, although informal and congenial, was no democracy. Wright

Intimacy with nature was vital. At Rock Crest–Rock Glen in Mason City, Iowa, depicted in Marion Mahony's exquisite drawing on satin, Walter Burley Griffin nestled houses into the landscape along a picturesque bend in the river.

Griffin's Melson House in Rock Crest–Rock Glen, as envisioned by Mahony, erupts from a rocky cliff (left). Concrete and limestone bring her delicate drawing to life. Lanterns cast in concrete (right) reinforce the house's bold design.

was the architect; all the others were employees. The core group that coalesced included Mahony, Drummond, Griffin, Byrne, and eventually Van Bergen. ■ In 1901 Wright made another breakthrough with two model house designs published in the *Ladies' Home Journal*: "A Home in a Prairie Town" and "A Small House with 'Lots of Room in It.'" These unprecedented designs broke even further with the past, embodying concepts that would form the basis of nearly every Prairie house. Immediately putting theory into practice, Wright a year later produced the Willits House in Highland Park, Illinois, regarded as the first great Prairie house. With its outreaching wings, sweeping banks of windows, and long terrace walls, it clearly belonged to the prairie. It also signaled a stunning change in the arrangement of interior space: rooms were not boxes bound by corners but were spaces that interpenetrated and merged. This seemingly simple yet critical idea may be the Prairie School's most important contribution to modern architecture. ■ Dozens of commissions followed for Wright, resulting in a glittering constellation of new designs, amazing in their variety. None of this was accomplished alone. Mahony, Griffin, Drummond, Byrne, Van Bergen, and others were critical participants, contributing design ideas, developing specifications, preparing renderings, and supervising construction. To ensure that his houses were cohesive works of art from lighting to landscaping, Wright collaborated with other artists and design professionals. George Mann

Giant keystones crown art glass windows, energizing the solid walls of the Melson House. Wood mullions hold glass pieces in place and strengthen the simple, abstract shapes. The walls are clad in thick limestone over clay tile.

Niedecken supervised many of Wright's furnishings and interior appointments, as he did for other Prairie architects as they came into their own. Artists such as Orlando Giannini and the sculptors Richard Bock and Alfonso Iannelli collaborated on larger commissions. ■ Wright's studio was clearly the locus of the Prairie School movement, but other architects not trained by him were developing their own means of expressing this new style. Tallmadge and Watson formed a partnership in 1905, developing a distinctive gabled Prairie house with a highly articulated facade of rough plaster and wood banding. Purcell, an Oak Park native, joined with his Cornell classmate George Feick in Minneapolis to forge new ground in Minnesota. And George Maher, an early associate of Wright's, was having considerable success with his own new American style. Although more formal than Wright's work, it was still a clear departure from Victorian thinking. ■ Landscape architects, too, began looking to the prairie for inspiration. Jens Jensen and Ossian Cole Simonds, both based in Chicago, advocated a Prairie style of landscape design, pioneering the use of native plants and prairie landscape features in their urban parks and large private estates. Jensen collaborated with Wright on a number of occasions and later with Maher, Van Bergen, and Spencer, although several Prairie School architects developed their own landscape plans. The relatively new concept of community planning inspired Griffin, Drummond, and Wright to explore methods of integrating

Firmly wedded to the earth, the Willits House in Highland Park, Illinois, embodies the peace of the prairie, as Wright planned. Outstretching wings and wood banding underscore the horizontal, while vertical lines add visual rhythm.

communities of Prairie School architecture with the natural features of the landscape. ■ In the fall of 1909, the Prairie School movement took an unexpected turn when Wright departed abruptly for Europe with the wife of a client to oversee a German publication of his work. Attempting without success to persuade Purcell, Byrne, and then Mahony to take over his practice, he finally left it in the hands of a non–Prairie School designer, Hermann von Holst. Working with von Holst, Mahony completed several of Wright's commissions with minimal input from Wright or von Holst. This brought to a close Wright's full-time involvement with the Prairie School. ■ Although Wright liked to propagate the notion that the Prairie School perished without him, it flourished as never before. Architects trained by Wright were released to forge their own expressions of the style, while others continued to make their contribution. Griffin, on his own since 1906, built about sixty Prairie houses before leaving the United States in 1914 to design Australia's new capital city, Canberra. Mahony produced several houses and a church before she married Griffin and joined him in Australia, where they practiced together. Drummond and Van Bergen went on to establish independent and rewarding careers centered in suburban Chicago. Elmslie, who had served as Sullivan's chief draftsman after Wright's departure, joined Purcell in Minneapolis, where they produced dozens of exceptional works, finding success both in residential design and in a series of elegant small-town banks and commercial structures. Tallmadge and Watson continued their work, primarily in the Oak Park,

In the doorway of the 1912 Parker House in Minneapolis, George Grant Elmslie synthesized geometry and flowing plantlike forms. The ornamental fan of sawn wood contrasts with the linear casement windows to balance the facade.

River Forest, and Evanston neighborhoods. In 1908 Byrne joined Andrew Willatsen in Seattle, carrying the Prairie School to the Northwest. Maher had more than three hundred commissions. This small band of extraordinary artists pursued the new, democratic architecture with a missionary zeal. Putting Americans in houses that were honest, simple, free, and open to nature was not just a profession; it was a calling. Changing American tastes, not the absence of Wright, proved fatal. By the beginning of World War I, midwesterners who once embraced the Prairie style lost their independent spirit and turned back to reassuring revival styles. Home magazines withdrew their support, offering readers stories on pretty colonial houses, English rose gardens, and chintz-covered tea caddies. *House Beautiful* published its last Prairie house in 1914. By the time the postwar buildup began in the 1920s, the concept of an indigenous American architecture was all but forgotten. The basic tenets of Prairie design—simplicity, open planning, respect for natural materials, and integrated interiors—would resurface again, championed by Wright himself. He never abandoned these principles. Using modern technology and recognizing changes in contemporary lifestyles, over the next four decades Wright incorporated Prairie principles into new houses for a new day, making them the basis of his "organic architecture." The buildings he left behind are powerful reminders of his lifelong effort to give America its own architecture, a quest that began on the prairie.

Generous horizontal wood bands lead the eye from room to room, seamlessly merging living and dining areas in Wright and Mahony's Irving House in Decatur, Illinois. On the structural square piers, vertical wood banding conceals radiators.

THE PRAIRIE

STYLE

When the architectural excesses of the Victorian age prompted calls for reform, Frank Lloyd Wright and his colleagues led the way with a new American look for walls, roofs, porches, windows, and everything in between. Colors drawn from the prairie, honest materials, and clean, geometric lines resulted in simple, natural houses that seemed to grow from the land. The Prairie house was forged from ideals still highly valued today: love of nature, respect for democratic freedoms, and a renewed focus on home and family. These principles gave birth to the grouped windows and open terraces that connected a house with nature, the open floor plan that promoted free movement, and the large and warming fireplace where the family could gather. The goal was a completely integrated design—unity of every individual element in the house.

Bradley House. Louis Sullivan. Madison, Wisconsin

THE NEW LOOK

Low and broad like the prairie itself, Prairie houses celebrate the flatness of the midwestern landscape with strong horizontal lines and outstretched wings that actively engage the house with the earth. Frank Lloyd Wright advocated "gently sloping roofs" to make a house "appear to grow easily from its site." Whether hipped, gabled, or even flat, Prairie roofs tend to be low and broad, with deep, generous eaves that sail well beyond the walls. They offer protection, both symbolic and real, as well as a sense of well-being. ■ A wide, low chimney, rather than a tall, narrow one, helps keep proportions low. A strong base anchors the house "firmly in its socket in the earth," as Wright liked. Garden walls, terraces, and side porches further extend the lateral thrust. The result was simplicity, repose, and a strong connection to the site. Yet sometimes a sense of mystery was encouraged, particularly at the entrance. Off center and cleverly concealed beneath the sweep of a porch or a porte cochere (a covered entrance extension for people alighting from carriages or cars), hidden entryways encouraged visitors to interact with a house and appreciate its intricacies. ■ Prairie architects treated outside walls not as solid barriers but as opportunities to blur the distinction between interior and exterior space. Windows and doors were no longer

mere holes punched into walls; instead, they were grouped into sweeping bands of light that figuratively break down the wall, forming uninterrupted views. Set snugly beneath deep eaves, they could be kept open even in a vigorous rainstorm, heightening the experience of nature and refreshing the house with cooling breezes. Rough-sawn wood trim and stringcourses organized walls and windows into strong geometric planes, emphasizing horizontality and conveying a sense of order. If a site was cramped, a Prairie house might take a vertical turn, as seen in Walter Burley Griffin's work, especially after 1910, and that of Barry Byrne. As their designs became more cubic, abstract, and massive, they left behind the deep, solid overhangs and lower proportions, developing their own vision of the modern house. Yet every Prairie house was alike in eliminating references to the past. Gone were the elaborate gingerbread and fanciful turrets of the Victorian era—all replaced by simple lines, flat wall planes, and clean geometric forms.

Everything about the Prairie house seemed lower, longer, and more attuned to the earth. The Irving House's low-pitched roof, sweeping windows, and long horizontal lines pin it to the prairie, as do its wide brick piers and low chimney.

Wright wrapped bands of stained wood around windows and stucco walls, all treated naturally at the Stockman House (left).

Unadorned, tawny-hued brick and richly carved stone welcome visitors to Robert Spencer's McCready House (center).

The jagged limestone walls of Griffin's Melson House (right) appear to be hewn directly from the cliff.

Honesty was the watchword for building materials among the Prairie architects just as it was for their Arts and Crafts counterparts. Wood should look like wood, brick like brick, they reasoned. Each material was respected for its inherent qualities, its unique beauty and poetry. At a time when wood was painted, bricks were covered with plaster, and concrete was hidden in embarrassment, this was a revolutionary attitude. Equally innovative was the Prairie architects' interest in new materials and modern technology, which allowed them to use glass, wood, concrete, and steel in exciting, new ways. ■ For exterior surfaces, stucco and wood were popular choices. Crisp wall planes of stucco, accented with rough-sawn strips of wood, emphasized a house's horizontal geometry. Some board and batten can be found, but masonry was preferred when budgets allowed. Long, narrow Roman bricks, the mortar raked deeply in the horizontal joints but left flat in the vertical joints, created thin, ribbonlike courses that echoed the continuous sweep of the prairie. ■ Reinforced concrete, valued for its fireproof qualities, also made an appearance on the prairie. Frank Lloyd Wright used it first in his 1904 design for Unity Temple in Oak Park, Illinois, and specified it for a 1907 plan in the *Ladies' Home Journal* entitled "A Fire-

HONEST MATERIALS

proof House for $5,000." But Walter Burley Griffin was the greatest champion of concrete's highly plastic qualities, which were well suited to his monolithic designs. ■ Most Prairie architects preferred regional woods for their innate richness and as a means to further connect the house to its place. Quartersawn oak, revered for its sumptuous graining, was perfect for flooring, millwork, and furnishings and became the wood of choice for the completely integrated house. Birch and pine were chosen for out-of-the-way spaces such as upstairs bedrooms and kitchens. Gumwood, with its amber overtones, was used on occasion. Wright was fond of the light, honey-colored tones of oak. Griffin favored darker stains for the heavier trim and millwork in his houses. Walnut, mahogany, and rosewood, all popular during the Victorian era, were rarely selected by Prairie architects. ■ In keeping with the pursuit of simplicity, wood was never forced into fancy, unnatural shapes—neither scrolled, nor turned, nor bent. Straightforward planes, broad bands, and squared spindles were the norm. Staining and waxing—not painting—allowed the wood's texture and grain to shine through.

The real revolution created by Prairie houses was inside, in the handling of space. Today's informal lifestyles at home are directly linked to the open plans promoted by the Prairie architects. They regarded space as almost palpable, something real to be shaped, extended, and released. To Frank Lloyd Wright, the space within a building was more important than the walls that defined it. In his view, Victorian houses were nothing but boxes within boxes: rigid, claustrophobic compartments that confined space and sequestered family members from each other and from nature. Wright took the lead in dismantling "the box" by eliminating unnecessary walls, opening his houses inside and out, dissolving the corners, and compressing and releasing space. ■ Changes in ceiling heights and floor levels, and even the artful placement of a sculpture or plant on a low wall, define areas for dining, reading, and living without the need for solid barriers. Interior walls stop short of the ceiling or are eliminated altogether, permitting air and light to flow freely. Built-in furnishings and freestanding pieces visually separate space. Broad bands of

casement windows and French doors further erase boundaries, extending space beyond the house into nature. Windows joined at right angles make corners disappear. Continuous strips of wood trim, placed just below the ceiling and along window and door tops, lead the eye horizontally from space to space. Views are open from room to room, conveying a sense of freedom and movement. ▪ Credit for the Prairie house's L-shaped plan, which joined the living room and dining area generally around a central hearth, probably goes to Walter Burley Griffin. Wright himself rarely used the concept in his early houses, but it became popular with other Prairie architects and builders. Since the 1940s this simple way of molding space has transformed the shape of nearly every modern American house.

Purcell and Elmslie broke open boxlike Victorian rooms with free-flowing spaces. Living and dining areas blend together in Purcell's own home in Minneapolis, separated only by a slight shift in floor level up to the dining room.

CUSTOM FURNISHINGS

Most ready-made furniture was incompatible with Prairie architecture. Much of what was available, lamented Frank Lloyd Wright, was "senselessly ornate," and it pained him to see clients drag offensive, poorly constructed furniture into his houses. So Prairie architects designed their own, striving for graceful, simple pieces suitable for informal living. Each element, from a built-in cabinet or window seat to a light fixture or chair, was conceived as an integral part of the overall design—an extension of the house itself. Using the same materials and ornamental detailing for both house and furnishings lent integrity to the whole and guaranteed artistic harmony. ■ Prairie furnishings, like the architecture, were carefully crafted to emphasize a tranquil, horizontal line. Tabletops and other horizontal planes were cantilevered beyond their supports and often rested on massive legs, creating the illusion that the furnishings, like the house itself, were grounded to the site. Squared spindles were incorporated into banisters and used in screen-like room dividers and chair backs. Art glass patterns in built-in sideboards and bookcases related to window patterns. Chairs, sofas, and other furnishings often followed a theme based on a geometric shape,

A built-in bench frees up space in William Drummond's Yelland House (left) in Mason City, Iowa, while its end posts hide the radiators. Use of the same woods on windows, trim, and floors ensured harmony. Not far away, Griffin built cabinets into each corner of his Rule House (right), whose square shape is underscored by geometric art glass.

generally rectilinear, found in the floor plan. ■ Textiles were of natural materials such as linen, cotton, and wool, all in plain weaves. Some were embellished with simple embroidery—the Prairie house was a model of restraint and harmony. ■ Much Prairie-style furniture was created under the supervision of the designer George Mann Niedecken through his studio in Milwaukee. From concepts supplied by the architects, he would prepare working drawings, guide color selection, oversee manufacture, supervise installation, and occasionally design furniture as well. ■ When clients could not afford custom designs, the Mission and Craftsman-style furniture of Gustav Stickley and other Arts and Crafts pieces would do. Their unadorned surfaces and clean geometric lines suited the Prairie house well. Except for Wright's work, only a few original Prairie furnishings, primarily built-in cabinets, bookcases, and light fixtures, still exist. Some freestanding pieces by Niedecken, Walter Burley Griffin, Marion Mahony, Purcell and Elmslie, George Maher, Barry Byrne, and others remain but are rarely in their original settings. Many Prairie house owners today choose either vintage Mission pieces or recent reproductions to furnish their homes.

To the Prairie School architects, the home was a sacred place and the hearth its perfect symbol. Here the family gathered around the warming fire, safe and secure. The fireplace, suggested Frank Lloyd Wright, should be "a substantial thing of beauty . . . solidly incorporated" into the building. He situated nearly all his fireplaces at the heart of the house as an anchor from which rooms, inglenooks, and screenlike walls radiated. Built there, instead of on an outside wall, it provided additional structural support and allowed the architect to eliminate unnecessary walls. With fewer walls, one large fireplace could warm the entire floor. ■ Most Prairie fireplaces were brick or tile, rarely stone. Some were simple, with unadorned brick and plain concrete or wood mantels; others were more complex and decorative, with sweeping arches of tapered brick or mosaics of opalescent glass and tile. Often a built-in seat was situated perpendicular to the hearth or a mural was placed above, enhancing the area as the room's focal point. ■ Wright and William Drummond preferred long Roman brick with deeply raked horizontal joints to emphasize the sweep of the prairie. Walter Burley Griffin also favored brick, sometimes with a double, prow-shaped

FIREPLACES

hearth that opened on two sides to warm both living and dining areas. ■ Often found in Griffin's houses are Marion Mahony's decorative fireplace designs, which confirm her brilliant grasp of color and detail. Occasionally flat to the wall, their decorative patterns seem almost woven. Many of George Maher's fireplace designs reflect his trademark style: heavy, sloping walls and an arched top. William Gray Purcell and George Grant Elmslie were fond of raised hearths and generally incorporated a mural and inglenook next to the fireplace to ensure its prominence. Whatever the final form, the fireplace was an integral part of the Prairie house, evoking permanence, comfort, and security.

Inspired by nature and influenced by Asian art, a glass mosaic anoints the library fireplace in Louis Sullivan's Bradley House (left).

Alternating bands of light and dark brick stress the horizontal in Marion Mahony's house for Adolph Mueller (center).

Proportions are low, but the hearth is raised in this comforting bedroom fireplace in William Purcell's house (right).

NATURAL COLORS

"Go to the woods and fields for color schemes," Frank Lloyd Wright urged. "Use the soft, warm, optimistic tones of earths and autumn leaves." Earthy browns and rusts, autumnal reds and golds, leafy greens, and the warm tans and beiges of natural stone—transferred to walls, fabrics, and carpets—brought the calm, restful tone of the prairie into the house and further unified the design. The prevailing Victorian mode of dark brocades and gaudy floral prints was considered overwrought, depressing, and completely dishonest. ■ Often the materials of the house itself—such as unadorned golden oak or brick, then available in many shades—supplied the major source of color inside. Natural oak woodwork with a tan plaster wall and a reddish brick fireplace produced a pleasing glow as rich as a sunset. Metallics such as gold leaf were used sparingly to add a note of brilliance and luxury. ■ Wright often favored monochromatic schemes to unclutter a house, using several shades of the same color. Walter Burley Griffin

The rich hues of golden oak and unadorned brick blend with prairie colors to infuse Wright's Willits House with warmth (opposite). Autumnal plants—goldenrod and flame-red sumac—inspired Mahony's palette for art glass in the Adolph Mueller House (above). Red pillows and chairs pick up tiny spots of color in the winglike ceiling lights.

recommended a smooth untinted coat of plaster to achieve a "lovely, grey tone" on which transparent glazes or stains were layered one over another. Often glazes and stains were rubbed or "scumbled" with a rag to blend the tones, creating a complex, saturated color with a rich patina. ■ Purcell and Elmslie preferred more varied colors, choosing greens, reds, and lavenders for stencil designs and art glass. A sojourn in Italy in 1906 made Purcell "enthusiastic to get the joy of color into our buildings." Marion Mahony, too, was liberal with color, selecting shades of violet, turquoise, rose, orange, and brown for glass and tile mosaics. But the designers who deviated most from the Prairie palette were Barry Byrne and his collaborator Alfonso Iannelli, whose intense, saturated reds, blues, blacks, and whites echo the Dutch de Stijl movement's embrace of pure primary hues.

A dazzling array of art glass graced nearly all Prairie houses, embellishing cabinets, French doors, sky-lights, and wall sconces. But the jewel-like prisms of glass danced most brilliantly in windows grouped into sweeping bands of pattern and light. Casement windows were the perfect vehicle for art glass, Frank Lloyd Wright argued. When closed they formed a field of shimmering ornament. When open, they swung free of the wall plane, like paintings of light reaching for nature. ■ Art glass was one more step toward unity. Following Wright's lead, Prairie architects often selected a motif—a geometric element from the house or an abstraction of a prairie plant—and then repeated variations of that design in glass throughout the house. In Wright's hands, the prairie sumac became a rhythmic interlocking of green and gold chevrons. Clean, straight lines, Wright believed, were more fitting for his modern houses and more suit-able to the nature of glass than the undulating Art Nouveau glass then in vogue. His pioneering geometric compositions were so popular with Chicago glass manufacturers that they made similar designs available by the square foot. ■ Most other Prairie architects produced comparable straight-edged designs. Marion Mahony created many exquisite art glass patterns during the years she spent in Wright's Oak Park studio.

Mahony's geometric art glass echoes the gabled roofline and pitched ceilings of the Adolph Mueller House (left).

In Robert Spencer's McCready House (right), a simple abstract motif unites the art glass with other design elements.

Wright would present a motif or a suggestion to Mahony, who would then develop it into glass designs using her bold color palette. Walter Burley Griffin used little art glass in his windows, saving it for cabinet and bookcase fronts. ■ George Grant Elmslie, influenced by Sullivan's flowing, efflorescent designs, often produced intricate art glass patterns in shapely curves and swirls. George Maher generally selected a signature botanical element—a poppy, tulip, or thistle—but reproduced it in a more representational manner than Wright might have approved. Yet both Elmslie and Maher placed their curvilinear designs on fields of linear, geometric glass. ■ Intricately patterned art glass often eliminated the need for curtains. When the view was prominent, the center of the window was left clear. When privacy was important, complex designs filled the window with almost solid color, creating an intimate, subdued lighting effect. Each window was a complex design composed of hundreds of pieces of glass held in place by zinc or lead bars. Simple and geometric, sparkling with flashes of color, they welcomed sunlight into a room in a way that no ordinary window could.

Simple, linear glass in the Irving House (left) by Wright and Mahony frames views without competing with nature.

Purcell and Elmslie's colored and patterned window diffuses the light in this corner of the Purcell-Cutts House (right).

INTEGRAL ORNAMENT

Ornament was part of the fabric of a Prairie house, "wrought in the warp and woof of the structure," as Frank Lloyd Wright wanted it. Louis Sullivan, the master of fluid, nature-based ornament, encouraged this holistic approach. His curvilinear terra-cotta designs influenced Wright and then George Grant Elmslie to produce equally sumptuous ornament. ■ To highlight an entrance or a fireplace inglenook, Elmslie added florid terra-cotta panels or an intricate fret-sawn wood screen; to reinforce the flow of space, he encircled a room with stencils in delightful shapes and colors. Although Wright's earlier work often incorporated similar designs, he later took a more abstract and subtle approach, believing that the textures, rhythms, and patterns of wood and brick were ornament enough. ■ Pictures were generally discouraged. Instead, murals might be incorporated directly into the walls, reinforcing the palette or a decorative theme. The fireplace of the Purcell-Cutts House in Minneapolis comes alive with Charles

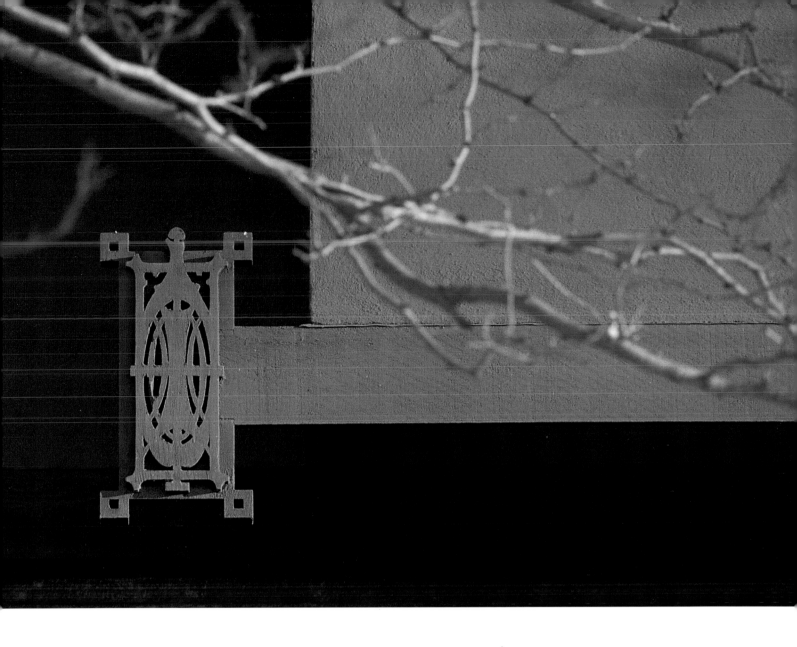

A champion of efflorescent Sullivanesque ornament, Elmslie exploited the plastic possibilities of terra cotta when he festooned the Powers House fireplace (opposite) in Minneapolis with a swirl of oak leaves, berries, and arabesques. The beam ends of his firm's Hoyt House (above) in nearby Red Wing received a more abstract flourish in another oval shield.

Livingston Bull's mural of an ethereal pond and marsh that plays on the house's watery theme. ▪ Art glass was the most consistent ornament, but colorful Teco tiles were also valued for their decorative qualities. Marion Mahony was especially skilled at creating mosaic designs with them. Often nature itself would be the primary ornament. Dried weeds, tree branches, or simple floral arrangements placed in metal holders and pottery vases or draped over high ledges brought the outside in. ▪ Occasionally sculptors such as Richard Bock and Alfonso Iannelli were commissioned to create specific pieces. Bock produced sculpture in collaboration with Sullivan, Wright, Purcell and Elmslie, Dwight Perkins, and Robert Spencer. Iannelli, who worked closely with Wright, Purcell and Elmslie, and Barry Byrne, was especially in tune with the notion of integrated ornament. Sculpture, he said, "should grow from the structure itself, being so much a part of the plan, that were the sculpture eliminated, the building would be incomplete."

Prairie houses seemed to bloom from their sites—paragons of the era's "back to nature" movement stressing the healthful and spiritual benefits of outdoor life. Giant geometric urns spilled over with colorful floral displays, while terraces, pergolas, and garden walls reached out to gather nature close. Such intimacy encouraged easy movement between house and landscape, a hallmark of the Prairie style. ■ Formal European gardens were rejected in favor of a more rustic, more natural, and more American approach, using plants that were either indigenous to the prairie or adapted to its harsh realities. Frank Lloyd Wright chose flowers and trees that grew well in the Midwest—lilacs, hollyhocks, daylilies, ferns, oaks, maples, and elms—but planted them in ways that related to the architecture, placing flowers in planters or along garden walls that were part of the building itself. ■ Walter Burley Griffin also saw landscapes as another unifying element in a house's overall conception, but unlike the self-taught Wright, he was trained in landscape design. His gardens tended to be more ordered and geometric than Wright's, and he was particularly fond of rooftop gardens. Wright entrusted several landscape plans to him. ■ Sparked

LANDSCAPES

by the same love of the prairie, the Chicago landscape architects Jens Jensen and Ossian Cole Simonds advocated a natural approach for their urban parks and large estate plans. Horizontal specimens were favored, particularly midwestern trees such as hawthorn and crabapple, with their distinctive outward branching, paired with flat limestone rockwork set out in stratified layers. Like Frederick Law Olmsted and Andrew Jackson Downing, Jensen and Simonds preserved the natural terrain and sequenced views so that a walk through a garden flowed without interruption from open meadow to mysterious wooded glen, from light to shadow. In their Prairie gardens, curved pathways, horizontal rockwork, prairie rivers, sunny meadows, and sylvan "outdoor rooms" were ringed with native bushes, wildflowers, and trees.

Vines dangle from high planters at Griffin's Blythe House (left) in Rock Crest–Rock Glen, softening the limestone facade.

Flowers spring up around the rugged limestone walls of Wright's Taliesin (center) as they might have grown in the wild.

Wood trellises filter sunlight into the dining and living rooms of Griffin's Rule House (right) in Rock Crest–Rock Glen.

PRAIRIE
HOU

The American home "will be a product of our time, spiritually and physically," predicted Frank Lloyd Wright in 1896. "It will be a great work of art, respected the world over." With the Prairie style, he fulfilled that vision. Instead of turrets and towers, he gave us houses that melted into the landscape. Instead of cramped, boxlike rooms, he shaped open interiors. Instead of look-alike plans, he created designs as varied as the people for whom they were designed. He changed houses forever. Wright seemed to know instinctively that a family's home should fit its surroundings and its residents—a completely new idea. He was an innovator, unafraid to test the limits of new thinking or new technology, arguing that the machine was a perfect tool for creating simplified designs. From masterworks such as the Willits House to more modest homes such as the Stockman House, Wright ensured the Prairie style's distinction as one of the great creative moments in American architectural history.

Roberts House. Frank Lloyd Wright. River Forest, Illinois

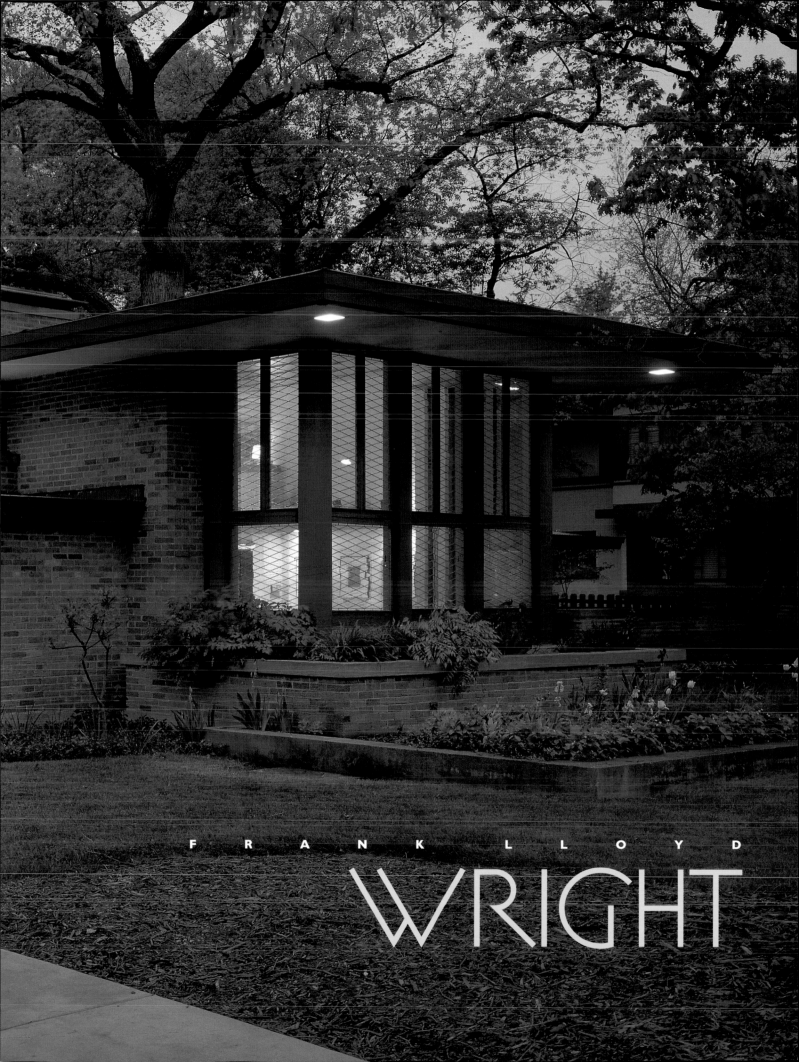

FRANK LLOYD

WRIGHT

WILLITS HOUSE

"It's a very noble place," says Sylvie Robinson, who with her husband, Milton, now owns Frank Lloyd Wright's Willits House in Highland Park, Illinois. "Everything is so serene and soothing. It's such a contrast to the clutter of the outside world." This residence for Ward and Cecelia Willits marked a turning point in Wright's career and the history of home design. Today, a century after it was designed in 1902, it still has the power to thrill. Historians and Wright both agree: the Willits House is the first great Prairie house. ■ Even in this early house, Wright, just thirty-five years old, had already perfected the idea of the hidden entry, setting it off to one side beneath the porte cochere. The reward for finding it is an explosion of vertical space, a reception area that soars a full two stories before culminating in a

shimmering skylight high above. There seem to be no interior walls at all. Rooms unfold from the entry like a maze, while square-spindled screens allow glimpses of spaces just beyond, beckoning exploration. ▪ Based on a cruciform, or cross, plan, the house projects in four wings that extend from a central hearth. Each wing contains a separate function: the entry and dining room are at the sides, the living room is in front, and the kitchen, pantry, and former servants' quarters are in the rear. The bedrooms and a library are above. Around the central fireplace wall, space flows freely, and rooms spiral off to each wing.

An icon of the Prairie style, the Willits House spreads horizontally beneath sheltering eaves, reflecting the midwestern landscape Wright loved. Even the planter is as flat as the prairie. The entrance hides behind the porte cochere.

A substantial fireplace of rich brick anchors the house to its core. Unifying horizontal lines lend order and harmony, while vertical spindled screens and chairs testify to Wright's love of Japanese art and architecture.

The house's serene atmosphere and screenlike walls may owe something to Wright's love of Japanese art and architecture, a design aesthetic that helped shape the Prairie style. The Willitses shared this love and traveled with the Wrights to Japan in 1905, a sojourn that kept the busy architect away from his office for nearly three months and that frayed their friendship. Two of Wright's souvenirs from this trip, a copper lantern and a Japanese print, are owned by the Robinsons. Wright also designed much of the furniture for the house. Unfortunately all his pieces were sold at a yard sale in the 1950s. Treasures such as high-back dining chairs were priced at $2 apiece. Thirty years later one of those dining chairs sold at auction for $198,000, a record price for a twentieth-century chair. Most of the furniture is now in private collections, but the Robinsons worked with the restoration architect John Eifler to locate original pieces from which to make measured drawings. With permission from the Frank Lloyd Wright Foundation, a reproduction was made of the dining set, as well as elements such as cabinets and a

Encircled in glass, Wright's favorite material, the dining room (left) stretches toward the horizon. Walls and ceilings glow with the colors of autumn: deep mustard yellows, greens, and rusts. Overhead a forest of oak beams merges with an ethereal light fixture of woven white-and-gold glass. Crystalline bays, like vitrines, project the room into the landscape (center and right), breaking down walls and blurring the distinction between inside and outside.

window seat that were part of the original design but had never been built. ▪ The Robinsons have spent several years restoring the house—analyzing wall colors, stripping varnish from dozens of squared spindles, and searching for the perfect Stickley and Limbert pieces to complement Wright's furnishings. Now, the colors of the prairie move uninterruptedly from room to room, smooth golden oak glides along window tops, and clean-lined furnishings add a sense of repose, together conveying the inner harmony Wright strived to attain.

The entrance (opposite, top left and center) soars the full height of the house toward a shimmering skylight above. Rotated forty-five degrees, it foreshadows the twists and turns to come. Upstairs, the colors of the prairie wash over the master bedroom (opposite, top right), where smooth golden oak frames a luxurious bed.

A wall of art glass in simple, linear shapes "plays the effect the jewel plays," as Wright planned, bathing the master bedroom in changing natural light (below). Owner Milton Robinson designed the bed, taking his cues from the architect.

Frank Lloyd Wright. Mason City, Iowa. 1908

Mason City, Iowa, was a small prairie town with big city dreams when it coaxed Frank Lloyd Wright into giving architectural expression to its emerging eminence. Nothing but the best was good enough for this ambitious, prosperous young community of brickyards and cement plants. Other small midwestern towns—Cedar Rapids, Owatonna, Winona, Sioux City—also looked to the Prairie School architects to freshen their image and became a second focus of the movement as it spread outward from its suburban Chicago roots. ■ While in town to discuss the design of a bank and hotel in 1908 "right here in River City" (the model for *The Music Man*), Wright turned his attention to a modern update of the classic American foursquare. For Dr. George Stockman and his wife, Eleanor, Wright adapted his "Fireproof House for $5,000," published the year before in the *Ladies' Home Journal*. The plan inspired countless imitations among Prairie architects, and even speculative builders liked this new interpretation of a familiar form. ■ Deep, sheltering eaves, one-story wings that extend the house horizontally, windows grouped in bands, and the elimination of unnecessary interior walls transformed what might have been a typical

STOCKMAN H O U S E

suburban house. The change was most dramatic inside, where the dining and living rooms are combined into an ell that pinwheels as one continuous space around the central hearth. Both rooms open onto the projecting side porch through a wall of French doors, bringing fresh air and more light into the free-flowing plan. ▪ Wright's abrupt departure for Europe in 1909 with the wife of a client and the ensuing scandal were too much for little Mason City to endure. Developers passed over him in favor of Walter Burley Griffin, his former assistant, to design an enclave of houses for a spectacular riverside site. In 1990 the Stockman House, which had slumped into disrepair, inspired a citywide grassroots movement to save it from demolition. Moved to a new site near Griffin's Rock Crest–Rock Glen, now a National Historic District, it is operated and opened to the public by the River City Society for Historic Preservation.

Wright turned the typical American foursquare into a Prairie classic by stretching the boxy shape into a horizontal form that fit more comfortably into the landscape. Giving it a low, hipped roof, he outlined the stucco finish in dark wood.

With its rows of narrow Roman brick and a low, elongated hearth, a central wall becomes a fireplace that recalls the prairie's flatness (this page). Paired ceiling moldings of quartersawn oak pass from dining to living room, both opening onto a porch (opposite, top). Arts and Crafts and reproduction Wright furnishings fill a bedroom (opposite, bottom).

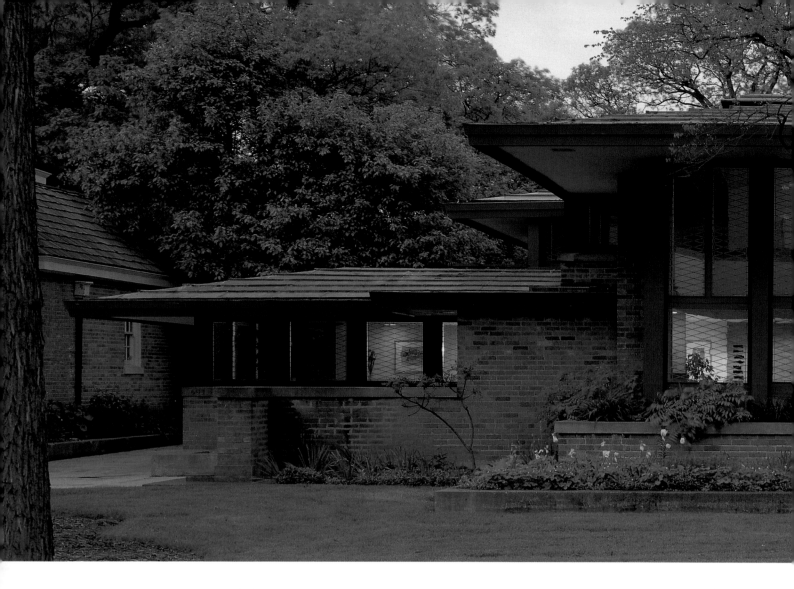

ROBERTS H O U S E

The quiet lines of the prairie resonate in the River Forest house that Wright designed for his bookkeeper. One-story
side wings holding the porch and the dining room pull the house to the ground, and even the tall central section seems
suppressed by its broad overhanging roof. Originally stucco and wood, the house was refaced with brick in the 1920s.

William and Carol Pollak were not in the market for a Prairie house when they took a drive to River Forest,
Illinois, to meet a real estate agent in 1989. "We just thought it would be a nice way to spend a Saturday
morning," William said. But what they saw changed their minds. "We came into the house, and we were
stunned. The whole first floor was like a sculpture of space." Frank Lloyd Wright was forty-one in 1908
when he designed this house for Isabel Roberts, the bookkeeper in his Oak Park studio whom he called
his "faithful secretary." A microcosm of fifty years of Wright's evolving design ideas, it is pure Prairie style
on the outside, with a low-slung roof, layered parallel planes, and bands of casement windows. On the
inside it is classic Usonian, a style Wright pioneered later in his career. In 1955, at the age of eighty-eight,

Frank Lloyd Wright. River Forest, Illinois. 1908, 1955

the ever-resilient Wright returned to update it. ■ The house projects in four wings, much like the earlier Willits House. But here the living room soars a full two stories, an unusually grand statement for such a small house. Floor-to-ceiling casement windows wrap around corners to form a cathedral-like bay adorned with a diamond-shaped pattern in clear glass. Although simpler than Wright's other art glass of the period, the diamond pattern screens the room for privacy and works well with the contemporary interior. Opposite the glass bay, Wright tucked a broad, deep fireplace beneath a cantilevered balcony, creating a sheltered inglenook below and a lavish open space above. ■ Interior space flows with unusual ease. Rooms weave together on multiple levels. Walls never quite meet, corners disappear, and ceilings change from low to high and back to low again. ■ Wright created an equally compelling composition on the exterior, with low side wings extending from a tall central mass. By emphasizing the horizontal instead of the vertical, Wright made the house seem lower and longer than it actually is. From its central two stories, it gradually steps down until it embraces the earth with great care.

Loath to cut down even a single tree, Wright planned the house around an English elm that grows inside the porch and erupts through the ceiling. The roof has been rebuilt twice to make room for the one-hundred-year-old tree.

Sculptural forms intensify on the second floor, where built-in cabinets conserve space and ledges hold plants and pottery. Lapped Philippine mahogany boards, added by Wright in 1955, gleam overhead in the pitched ceilings.

Wrapping around three sides of the living room (opposite, top left and right) is an airy balcony, underneath which Wright tucked a massive brick fireplace with a low concrete mantel. Art glass glistens everywhere, in the dining room and even the bedrooms (opposite, bottom left and right). The mahogany cabinets were added in the remodeling.

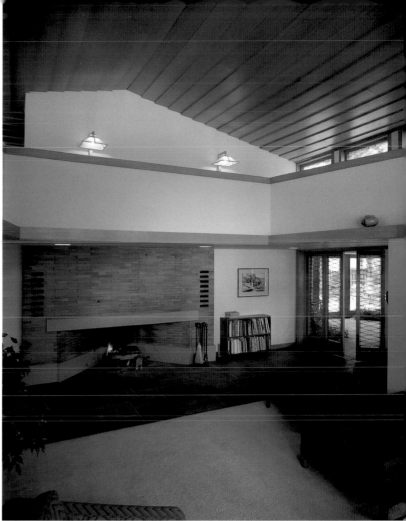

Frank Lloyd Wright. Oak Park, Illinois. 1909

Not far from his own Oak Park home, Frank Lloyd Wright swept away all notions of Victorian fussiness with this compact treasure. Streamlined and angular, from its flat roof to its drawerlike balconies, it was, Wright said later, "the progenitor of Fallingwater," his famous cantilevered house of 1935 set above a waterfall in western Pennsylvania. Commissioned by Laura Gale, this stucco-and-wood house looked amazingly avant-garde when it was built in 1909. Still surrounded by Victorian neighbors, it seems just as forward-looking today. ■ The carefully composed exterior reflects Wright's increasing regard for geometric abstraction and simplified forms. The horizontal slab roof and dramatic cantilevered balconies reach from the house like outstretched arms, shading open porches and offering a strong sense of seclusion and privacy. Piers rise alongside, adding structural support and vertical interplay. ■ The rooms are not large but, extending onto open porches, impart a sense of spaciousness and comfort. The living room, which has an imposing central fireplace and high wood molding, is open on two sides. One looks toward a projecting porch and the other toward the dining room, whose raised floor creates the effect of a clois-

GALE

H O U S E

Forceful horizontal planes and sturdy vertical piers suggest the precision of pure geometry in the modern-looking Gale House (left). Wright, who liked to see a "fire burning deep in the solid masonry of the house," gave Laura Gale a large brick fireplace (center) with a low hearth and, for balance, a wood deck that serves as a high mantel and a roost for family treasures. Art glass windows and French doors in the bedrooms swing open to a treetop balcony (right).

tered retreat. Extensive amounts of glass, primarily at the corners, opens these small spaces to the outdoors. ■ Henry-Russell Hitchcock, a noted architectural historian, called the Gale House "a small masterpiece" and suggested that its highly disciplined, abstract forms anticipated the development of the International Style in the 1920s. Wright no doubt would have been pleased with the "masterpiece" part of this analysis, but he regarded the International Style as sterile and repetitive. Wright worked all his life to create individualized designs—houses with natural materials that suited the specific place, time, culture, and people, such as Laura Gale, for whom they were built.

The dining room at the back of the Gale House is "a bright, cozy, cheerful place," as Wright maintained dining rooms should be. It shares a common ceiling with the living room but seems more intimate because the floor is raised two steps, compressing the space. In place of a solid wall, Wright used freestanding cabinets like pillars to separate rooms.

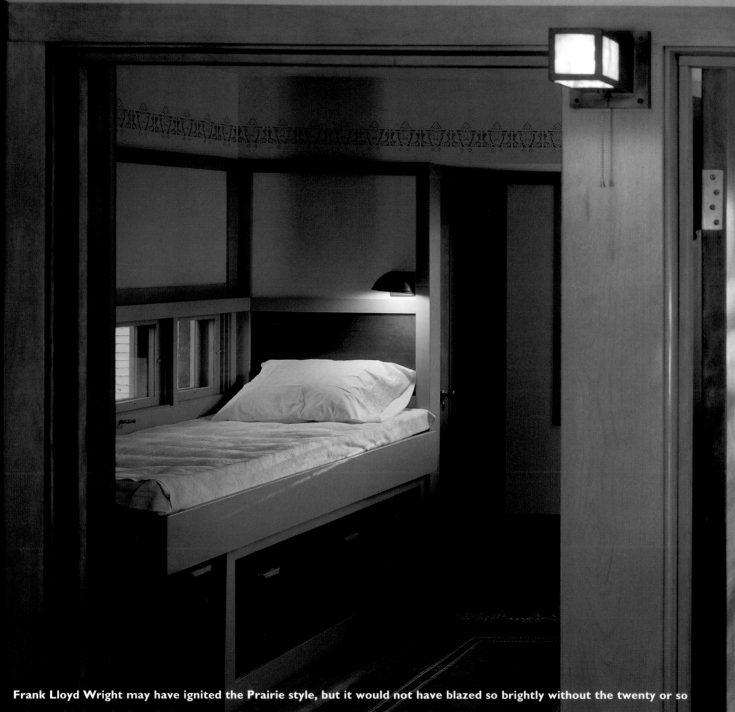

Frank Lloyd Wright may have ignited the Prairie style, but it would not have blazed so brightly without the twenty or so other architects who lent their genius to the movement. Young, talented, and bursting with creative energy, they each made valuable contributions. Most apprenticed with Louis Sullivan or Wright, but others, such as George Maher and Robert Spencer, took independent although parallel paths. Walter Burley Griffin produced work so advanced that Australians eventually hailed him as the father of their modern architecture. Marion Mahony, the only woman Prairie designer, is renowned for her exquisite architectural renderings. George Grant Elmslie's efflorescent decorative designs are unmatched by his colleagues. From William Drummond's airy and spacious Baker House to Purcell and Elmslie's magnificent home for Purcell, these young pioneers created hundreds of exceptional works that graced the prairie with pride.

PRAIRIE
COLLEAGUES

Vernon Watson. Oak Park, Illinois. 1904

Watson shared Wright's fondness for the broad midwestern prairie, as his design for the cottagelike Andrews House (above) indicates. A comfortable porch (opposite) sweeps across the front, extending the living space out-of-doors.

When the Andrews House in Oak Park, Illinois, came on the market several years ago, its charms were not immediately obvious, even to Karen and Don Rosenwinkel, who had owned one historic house and were looking for another. "The entire house was stained flat black, right down to the foundation," remembers Karen. "The porch was screened in. The detail was completely hidden." But the part-bungalow, part-Prairie cottage, designed by Vernon Watson for the Barrett Andrews family in 1904, grew

ANDREWS HOUSE

on them. Two years and much effort later, guided by old photographs and advice from the Oak Park restoration architect John Thorpe, they had restored the house to its original form. ▪ Its spreading profile, open floor plan, wood exterior, and unpretentious nature are classic American bungalow features. But the sweeping porch that stretches the entire width of the house, the forceful horizontality, the casement windows, and the broad foundation clearly say Prairie style. Separated only by posts and partial walls, the entrance hall, living room, and dining room are arranged as if they were one large space. A complex array of wood bands flows around window tops and across the ceiling, reinforcing the connection. In the living room a red brick fireplace flanked by built-in bookcases dominates an outside

Stalwart beams and oak banding in clear, straight lines define the Andrews House's fluid, open spaces. Mottled walls demonstrate Prairie-style techniques for enriching color by using several hues or glazes to add unusual depth.

wall, unlike Frank Lloyd Wright's usual placement of the fireplace in the center of the house. In typical Prairie style, the entire first floor, including the floors and trim, is finished in oak. ■ Not the usual stucco or brick, the house is covered with narrow cedar weatherboarding. The boards—black no more—are now a rich brown that closely simulates the original color. An addition spanning the entire rear of the house mirrors the interior plan of the living and dining area at the front, with the same arrangement of piers and oak trim separating and defining spaces. The new fireplace, designed by Don Rosenwinkel, is a massive Richardsonian Romanesque arch, similar to those used by Wright and William Drummond. ■ The Andrews House was under construction when Watson joined forces with Thomas Tallmadge in a

partnership that continued until the mid-1930s. Although the firm rarely designed such horizontal houses again, this commission was admired by *Architectural Review* in 1907 for its close association with the prairie. "Certainly it is true that much work designed by the architects of Chicago has this strongly horizontal feeling, and after all it is a keenly appreciative trait," it observed. "This feeling of broad, flat masses was strong in the architect when he designed this house."

A family room addition in the back synchronizes perfectly with the Prairie spirit, from its glass doors to its built-in cabinets. The fireplace was designed by owner Don Rosenwinkel, who handcut the brick to fit the arch's curve.

Simple Mission-style furniture harmonizes with beams and oak banding. Electric lights, relatively new when Prairie houses were built, took the form here of bare bulbs fastened to hammered-brass plates stamped in an organic leaf pattern (opposite). The sconces in the music and family rooms (this page) are reproductions by Don Rosenwinkel.

Ralph Gerbie has always been drawn to the work of the Prairie School architects. Because of his six-foot, three-inch height, however, he never felt comfortable in Frank Lloyd Wright's houses. But those designed by Robert Spencer are another matter. "Spencer was a taller man than Wright and built his homes to a scale that felt right for me," Gerbie explains. The McCready House in Oak Park, Illinois, built in 1908, is the second Spencer-designed home Ralph and Jodie Gerbie have owned. ■ Some Prairie houses are decidedly more formal than others, and this—with its prominent entrance and forthright facade—is certainly one. Stretching wide and rising high on a corner lot, the house sets a gracious tone with its richly ornamented doorway and dignified central pavilion. Yet it possesses clear Prairie-style elements: art glass windows grouped in bands, long honey-colored Roman brick in pronounced horizontal rows, and a prominent hipped roof. Designed for the businessman Edward W. McCready and his wife, Caroline, the house is characteristic of the more stately interpretation of the Prairie style favored by Spencer, whose writings helped proselytize its attributes. The massing and form, developed during his partnership with

Horace Powers, echo Spencer's own modest home nearby in River Forest. ■ Behind the entry pavilion, a narrow vestibule gives way to an immense hallway leading to the living room and a raised dining room. These rooms do not share corners or interpenetrate as in many Prairie houses, yet they are open and filled with light. Accessible from both these rooms is an enclosed porch set at the back of the house. An attached three-car garage, one of the earliest in a Prairie-style house, is connected by a covered breezeway. ■ The Gerbies and their three children enjoy the open, circular flow of space. "It's not only functional. It's also a great place for hide-and-seek for the kids," Ralph Gerbie explains. "For such a formal and elegant design, it lends itself to very comfortable living."

A close friend of Wright's, Spencer was not, however, a close follower of his work. In his beautifully proportioned McCready House, he created an asymmetrical entrance but balanced it with a row of vertical casement windows (opposite). In the living room (below), white plaster ceiling beams stand in for more customary wood bands.

A featured space in every Prairie house, the dining room encouraged a sense of ceremony and family unity. An art glass fixture (this page) illuminates the table, and a long row of windows opens the room to nature. Even in the pantry (right top), Spencer did not stint on art glass. Above the kitchen stove (right bottom), probably original, new tiles echo the decorative motif of the carved stone doorway, beams, and art glass found throughout the house.

BRADLEY HOUSE

When opened, the Bradley House's art glass windows (left) transform solid dark walls into three-dimensional flashes of color and light. Massive steel beams sheathed in wood with elaborate decorative finials support the porches (right).

Unlike other Prairie houses that rest gently on the earth, Louis Sullivan's Bradley House towers majestically over the Madison, Wisconsin, landscape, its bold, second-story porches thrusting high into the air. Massive and imposing, the powerful form of this house invites thoughts of mystery. Sullivan, the philosophical leader of the Prairie School, designed only a handful of residences, making the Bradley House—the only one that survives—rare indeed. ■ Sullivan's strengths were tall commercial buildings and brilliant, fluid ornament, but in 1909, with little other work, he agreed to design a house for a favorite client, Charles Crane, a wealthy Chicago industrialist. The house was a wedding gift from Crane to his daughter Josephine and her husband, Harold Bradley, a professor at the University of Wisconsin. It would be the first of three great Prairie houses the family would build. ■ Although Sullivan's residential work—the Prairie style's focus—was limited, his influence was absolute. He laid the groundwork, teaching Frank

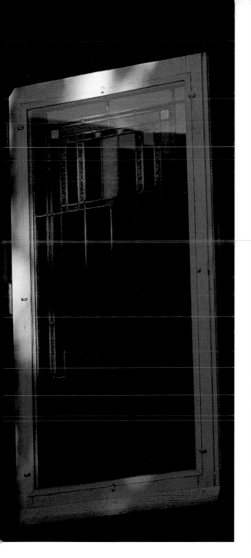

Lloyd Wright, George Grant Elmslie, and the others that logical thought and close observation of nature were the ways to build an organized, functional building. In the Bradley House, rooms unfold organically from the center, branching out in great arms before spilling onto open porches. The interior is expressed directly on the outside in the forceful balconies and spreading wings that give the house its great drama.

While the massing and form of the house rest squarely with Sullivan, Elmslie, his chief draftsman after Wright's departure, was responsible for the interiors. The art glass windows, pendant light fixtures, mosaic tile fireplaces, fret-sawn decorations, and original furnishings (most now gone) bear his unmistakable imprint. Elmslie spent nearly twenty years with Sullivan, but this would be their last project together. The Bradleys apparently felt uncomfortable in such a large house. Just four years after moving in, they turned to Elmslie, by then working with Purcell and Feick, for a new design. The couple sold their Sullivan house to the university's Sigma Phi fraternity, which has occupied it ever since. In 1972 an electrical fire destroyed much of the second-floor interior, but alumni raised $762,000 to restore the house to its 1909 appearance, including replicating many art glass windows that had been lost over the years.

The vigor of Sullivan's design comes inside with heavy oak beams and wood trim that convey permanence (this page).

A large round table fit for a fraternity fills the room where the Bradleys once dined. Elmslie's imprint is visible in

the house's light fixtures and art glass (right top). In the library (right bottom), a built-in bench curves with the wall.

Although many Prairie houses are recognized by their low, hipped roofs, some clients such as Purcell's father favored a gabled roof for its ability to shed rain and the heavy snows of the Midwest. A fret-sawn screen ornaments the porch gable (left). The garage (right), which has its own pitched roof, deep soffits, and decorative molding, is a miniature of the house.

"William Purcell must have loved his father very much to design such a house," conclude the current owners of this residence in River Forest, Illinois, which the architect created for Charles A. Purcell in 1909. Frequent visitors to Japan, the owners were drawn to the exquisite glass patterns and Japanese feel of the house, particularly the tranquillity of its living spaces. Their response is not coincidental, as many of the Prairie architects were influenced by the serenity of Japanese architecture, with its sweeping gabled roofs and airy rooms. ■ For William Gray Purcell, as for all the Prairie School architects, the roof was a powerful symbol. Wright called it the "ultimate feature" of a house, the element that gave shelter a sense of dignity. This elegantly proportioned three-story house features several lovely gables: a bold one covering the entire house, as well as smaller gables sheltering porches, entryways, and dormers.

CELL HOUSE

William Gray Purcell. River Forest, Illinois. 1909

Beneath the sweep of these roof planes, broad bands of stucco cover the upper two floors, punctuated by windows in unusual configurations. ■ Inside the house, walls edged in rich warm wood, built-in cabinets, integrated lighting, and coordinated art glass suggest the harmony of a perfectly unified plan. To maintain a flow of space, Purcell placed the living room and dining area side by side, connected by a wide opening. At one end of the living room is a cozy inglenook with a tile-faced fireplace, a bench seat, and a hand-painted mural; at the other end French doors open onto the house's most exquisite feature: a jewel-like smoking room completely encircled in art glass. Light pours in all around, but privacy is maintained by the green-and-gold leaded glass, which also softens the direct sun. ■ The house was under construction when George Grant Elmslie joined Purcell's practice. At that time or shortly thereafter Elmslie added his own touch, designing fret-sawn wood screens for the porch and inglenook and many art glass windows. Purcell too designed a few windows, but his art glass was purely geometric, while Elmslie's was more flowing and complex, with exuberant curves and swirls set into fields of linear glass. Side by side, they make a fascinating study of the partners' compatible yet diverse styles.

Art glass in the stair hall (left) and the handsome fret-sawn screen in the inglenook (this page) are believed to be Elmslie's

contributions. A low bench, a warming fire, and a hand-painted mural evoking a pastoral scene invite quiet moments.

The most delightful space in the Purcell House, the jewel-like smoking room pairs Elmslie's artistry—the distinctive
V-shaped art glass in the windows and French doors—with Purcell's triangular tympanum of glass in the gable.

Purcell, Feick, and Elmslie. Minneapolis, Minnesota. 1910

Growing up in a Prairie house is, for devotees, the experience of a lifetime, but it can have one unexpected drawback: it sets an uncommonly high standard. Edward and Maureen Labenski lived in this house in Minneapolis for twenty years, raising their family and enjoying the myriad details of Purcell, Feick, and Elmslie's design—unrestrained ornament and plenty of porches, built-in cabinets, and closets. "It spoiled the kids," says Ed Labenski. "After they grew up and moved away, they were very fussy about where they lived." ■ The Powers House, designed in 1910, was the firm's first large-scale commission after Elmslie joined the Minneapolis practice, and his touch is evident throughout. Initially the layout of the house posed a problem. Although the property had a backyard view of Lake of the Isles and the project's budget was ample, the lot was narrow, only fifty feet wide. In an ingenious scheme, the architects turned the house to the side and then elevated all the major living spaces in the rear toward the sunny, southern exposure and pastoral lake views. William Gray Purcell later wrote that situating the living room in the rear "was a revolutionary procedure. Up to this time, parlors were in front and kitchens in the rear . . .

POWERS HOUSE

The Powers House does not appear to express the horizontality of the Prairie style—it was turned sideways

to fit a narrow lot—but the distinctive two-story tower with a flared roof gives it streetside prominence (left).

Inside, the tower's curves are repeated at the back in the living room's bank of windows and built-in bench (right).

and that was that." ■ In the living room the architects created a comfortable semicircular window seat to enjoy nature's show, balanced by an intimate inglenook near the fireplace. Like Wright, they were keenly aware of the need to open up the house with large windows while providing quiet zones around the fireplace for the family. ■ More than any of the other Prairie architects, George Grant Elmslie had a passion for ornament. As Louis Sullivan's employee for twenty years, he became so adept at the master's efflorescent ornamentation that historians now debate the true authorship of some early designs. In this house Elmslie pulled out all the stops, designing lush terra-cotta tiles, elaborately incised oak doors, and delicately filigreed art glass. Clearly Sullivan would have been proud—or perhaps envious.

Purcell and Elmslie carefully controlled the design so that every space and feature harmonized. In the dining room, framed by linear bands of dark wood (this page), the sideboard and the polychrome stencils incorporate an inverted triangle, which also appears in the doors. A profusion of terra-cotta tiles strengthens the side entrance (right top), setting the stage for more ornament inside, including an oak door incised with the same motif (right bottom).

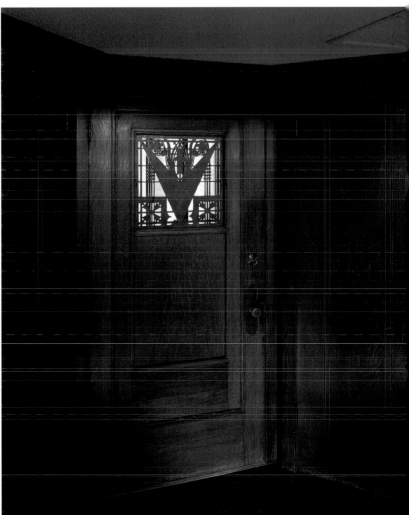

Deep inside the house a lavish terra-cotta frieze crowns the austere gray brick fireplace with a burst of color. Two built-in benches embrace this masterpiece, the room's focal point. The hearth is raised, as Purcell and Elmslie liked.

ELLIOTT H O U S E

Located just two blocks from Louis Sullivan's Bradley House and next door to Frank Lloyd Wright's Gilmore House in Madison, Wisconsin, George Maher's Elliott House is in excellent company. This charming residence in the University Heights neighborhood, less ornate than some of Maher's larger commissions, was designed in 1910 to suit the budget of Edward Elliott, a university professor. Owners Patricia and Robert Wood were drawn to its views, open interior spaces, light quality, and overall simplicity. ■ Deceptively simple, in fact, this emphatically symmetrical house perfectly illustrates Maher's unique ability to synthesize contrasting styles. The arch over the doorway (a Maher trademark) and the slightly sloping corners reflect the work of contemporary Viennese designers, while the house's

shape and massing call to mind a rustic English cottage. Maher merged these attributes with Prairie-style features—horizontal trim, a low roof, and sheltering eaves—to form his own progressive American style. "He borrowed from a lot of genres," explains Robert Wood, "and applied his own sensibility to them." The facade, dignified and straightforward, is dominated by a central entrance with matching pairs of

Simple, straightforward, and symmetrical, the Elliott House (left)—a large stucco-and-wood rectangle with a jaunty hipped roof—draws from both Prairie and European design sources. The thin segmental arch over the doorway (right) is a signature Maher element, one he carried inside as well; the flower box above it echoes the shape of the roof.

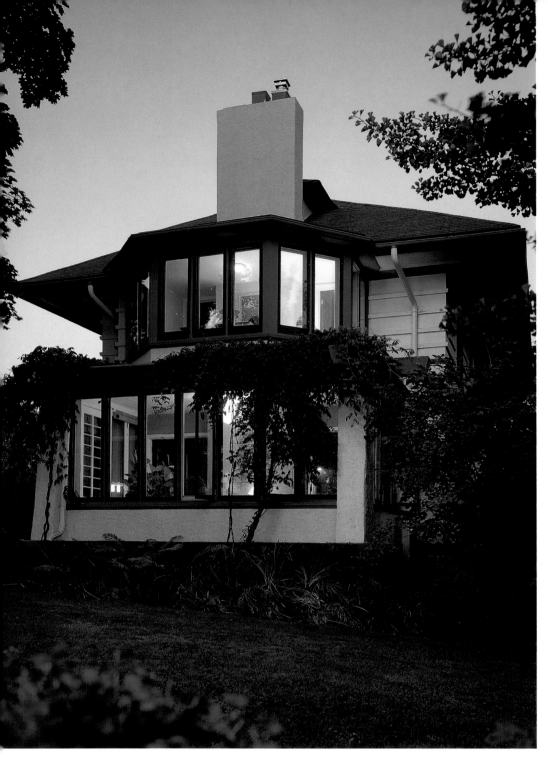

casement windows for balance. An elegant coppery green-and-gold hollyhock motif adorns the art glass windows, including the entrance sidelights. Although Maher could be heavy-handed with decoration, here he used it sparingly to maintain simplicity and clarity. ■ With its vaulted ceiling and pendant light fixture, the entrance hall is a beautiful introduction to the house. It divides the first floor into a plan more typical of a colonial house: dining room on the right and living room on the left. But wide openings between rooms, large casement windows, and a double set of French doors that lead to an expansive porch give the house a comfortable, airy feeling. ■ The tall, imposing brick fireplace, with its signature Maher arch, is often a focal point for gatherings, but Patricia Wood did not initially appreciate its beauty.

Intrinsically Prairie in its airiness, the house reaches out to embrace nature with porches of various configurations (left)—a rectangle below and a pentagon, probably added in the 1920s, above. Banks of windows in the downstairs porch (center) draw the outside in. From the dining room, similar French doors swing open to the hall and living room (right), while others beckon beyond. The owners' contemporary furniture works well in Maher's simplified settings.

"My first thought was to drywall over it," she admits. "Now it's my favorite element." The couple believe that Maher's simplified design permits them more flexibility than a typical Prairie house. "It has allowed us to add our own colors and furniture. Maher doesn't pin you to a style."

The entrance's sloping walls and segmental arch find their mirror image in the living room's imposing brick fireplace (opposite). Another telltale Maher feature, the tripartite balustrade (this page) leads upstairs, where hollyhock-patterned art glass adorns the windows, the delicate motif a perfect complement to the house's uncluttered design.

Walter Burley Griffin. Winnetka, Illinois. 1912

The moment she walked through the door of Walter Burley Griffin's Mess House in Winnetka, Illinois, Catherine Stika knew it was going to be home. "I've always wanted to live in a house that looked like this," she explained, gazing at the splendid detailing and extensive woodwork that gives this house its great warmth. A giant cube of concrete and hollow tile embellished with wooden trellises, this 1912 design for Harry M. Mess, a schoolteacher, represents Griffin's radical concept of the Prairie style. Initially, influenced by his employer, Frank Lloyd Wright, Griffin produced the ground-hugging, horizontal lines most associated with the movement. But around 1910 his work began to evolve into something far more abstract and cubic. ■ The front of the house, bereft of wooden trellises, is especially austere. Yet the exterior is deceptive. Inside, the richness of natural materials and the warmth Stika was seeking radiates from wall to wall. Heavy wooden beams and trim boards dominate walls and ceilings, crossing vertically and horizontally in a geometric ballet. The windows are simple casements with wooden mullions in a square design. Griffin preferred these mullions to leaded art glass, asserting that they conveyed a sturdiness that complemented his strong, blocky designs. ■ The house's focal point is undoubtedly the fire-

MESS

H O U S E

Elaborate wooden trellises extending from flat roofs (opposite) add color and dimension to the garden side of the Mess House, which reflects Griffin's evolving style and growing fondness for cubic and vertical forms. Mahony's fireplace of irregular glazed tiles (above) recalls the Japanese-style architectural renderings for which she is so famous.

place. Composed by Griffin's wife, Marion Mahony, of hand-painted Teco tiles in muted shades of green and brown, it forms a hauntingly beautiful scene of billowing trees and twisted grapevines. Mahony is known for her complex Teco tile designs, but none are as sinuous and irregular as this. "Most of the tiles are four-by-four shapes, until you move to the right," explains Stika. "The entire third on the right side are oddly shaped, with grout in the curves creating an impression of grapevines." ▪ The original living room, library, dining room, kitchen, four bedrooms, and two baths were augmented by a family room and master bath added to the back of the house by a previous owner. The scale is small for a Prairie house, but that suits Stika, her husband, James Kaufman, and their young son just fine. "Other Prairie houses seem so grandiose, big and sprawling," she says. "This is a really cozy house."

Griffin's imprimatur can be seen in the bookcases set into corners and clear-paned, wood-mullioned windows, whose square shape reflects that of the house. As on the exterior, vertical and horizontal elements converge in a lively mix.

Built-in pieces such as this oak cabinet, which takes up most of a wall and seems part of the house's structure, allowed the Prairie architects more design control. Using only one type of wood throughout produced a soothing harmony.

HOYT HOUSE

Reaching for the sky, the Hoyt House in Red Wing, Minnesota, seems to be straining for a better view of the Mississippi River to the northwest. Modern looking even today, it must have been shocking to the residents of this staid river town in 1913. The Hoyts, according to William Gray Purcell, codesigner of the house with George Grant Elmslie and George Feick, "rather enjoyed the new excitement of being pioneers in art." The neighbors, unschooled in the beauties of the Prairie style, referred to it as "that Chinese house." ■ Walls of dark red brick recede beneath planes of crimson plaster, a bold color scheme for a Prairie house. Even the mortar is tinted reddish pink to match. Although two stories high, with ribbon windows set below deep eaves and a low, hipped roof, the house gives a decidedly horizontal impression. To take maximum advantage of the view, Purcell placed the living and dining rooms side by side facing the river. Upstairs, two bedrooms, a sitting room, a den, and a porch also share the view. The second story, partially cantilevered over the first and resting on wood-faced beams, recalls Louis Sullivan's Bradley House in Madison, Wisconsin, another design in which Elmslie was a critical participant. ■ Jean Chesley

and her late husband, Frank, purchased the house in the 1970s from Hazel Hoyt, the daughter of the original client, and made few alterations. "In many ways," Chesley muses, "the house seems to have been planned to accept different lifestyles." As with most Purcell, Feick, and Elmslie houses, the detailing is exquisite, from the glittering glass mosaic above the fireplace to the coordinated light standards. Linking the living and dining spaces is a wall of diamond-patterned casement windows that open onto grand, extended views. "The sun shines in these windows almost all day long," says Chesley. "Yet their size and arrangement give me a feeling of privacy. They are a constant source of beauty and pleasure."

Bands of windows and sweeping lines accentuate horizontality, while vivid color imparts an oriental sensibility (left).

An elaborate fret-sawn wood screen (right) introduces the house's major decorative theme—the diamond— a favorite motif of Elmslie's. Situated in a covered breezeway, the screen gracefully links the house with the garage.

Art glass sparkles throughout the house, and diamond shapes abound. In the hall (this page), French doors throw patterned light across the floor. An unusual interior clerestory (opposite, top) borrows daylight from the next room to brighten a dark stairway. In the living room (opposite, bottom), a screen of glass breaks down the wall, yet the window's rich pattern shields the interior from the street. Original built-in light standards provide additional illumination.

The diamond motif comes into play as a unifying theme throughout the Hoyt House. In the dining room (below), miniature diamond shapes embellish the built-in cabinets (the kitchen can be glimpsed between them), while a child's bedroom gets its own art glass nook (bottom). By turning the corner, the windows further open up the wall.

In the comfortable and spacious open plan, views unfold from room to room. The central hearth casually divides the living and dining areas, a connection reinforced by the ceiling trim and wood banding. Above the fireplace a mosaic in opalescent and iridescent glass—its theme the moon—adds a note of serenity to the already tranquil space.

PURCELL-

In the house he designed for himself, Purcell favored geometry's clean-edged lines. Assertive flat roofs float over walls of dazzling art glass, while brilliant blue and orange stencils ring the upper story, showcasing his love of color.

"On summer evenings I have seen the orange red squares of the sun sending ribbons of light down the whole length of the . . . living room," said William Gray Purcell about his own home in Minneapolis, remembering "shadow and sunlight basking against the lavender light of evening." What architects build for themselves is always instructive. Purcell's house is a jewel that glitters with eighty art glass

CUTTS

H O U S E ☐ **Purcell and Elmslie. Minneapolis, Minnesota. 1913**

windows. Natural light, streaming in from the east through a floor-to-ceiling wall of glass, fills the corners. High windows at the sides bring additional daylight into the living room through prisms of colored art glass. The effect is breathtaking. ■ Purcell and Elmslie were masters at conceiving total interior environments—the level of detail they achieved in Purcell's 1913 home rivals that of Frank Lloyd Wright. It neatly combined Purcell's talents for layouts with Elmslie's flair for decorative details, and it expressed in very personal terms the importance of the home as a setting in which to nurture the family. Years later Purcell called it "brilliantly successful . . . the most complete dwelling we ever did together."

The artist Charles Livingston Bull worked within Elmslie's arched and linear wood bands above the living room fireplace to produce a mural of Louisiana herons in a misty landscape. Delicate pendant lights shimmer like half-moons.

A writing nook (left) carved out of the living room has a low window at just the right level for the chair's occupant.

Richard Bock's sculpture *Nils on the Goose* (right) graces the cabinet-filled prow of the dining room on the next level.

The Victorian box of a house is gone. In its place, multipurpose spaces are ingeniously divided by partial walls, screens, and floor levels. The entrance, living room, and dining area sweep from the front to the rear on three separate planes. From the entry, steps descend into a sunken living room, which stretches across the front; more steps rise one-half story to a prow-shaped dining room. The result is a rare combination of freedom and intimacy, flawlessly composed. ■ From Louis Sullivan, Purcell and Elmslie each inherited a love of color and displayed it in nearly all their works. Stencils in lavender, green, teal, orange, and red encircle the upper interior walls, while outside, above the windows, stencils in intense blue and orange pick up the refrain. Despite these colorful accents, the overall interior scheme is subdued and mellow, with light wood tones and mottled beige walls that Purcell called "rose chamois." This almost feminine quality is a clear departure from the darker wood tones and wall colors found in

The dining set (left), designed for another client, could be moved through the French doors onto the porch.

The no-nonsense kitchen (right) has been preserved and restored as it was when Purcell's house was built in 1913.

most Prairie houses. ■ Unexpected pleasures await in playful details and in the furnishings (faithful replicas of the originals). A delightful pair of "surprise point" side chairs, their elongated backs like subtle exclamation points, could be a variation on Wright's famous tall-back chairs. They contrast nicely with more sober built-in desks and bookcases, spindled armchairs, a fern stand, and pendant and standing light fixtures. The "peek-a-boo" windows at the front door and a Pullman-style child's bed (see page 70) led Elmslie to dub the house "The Little Joker." ■ The Purcells lived here for only four years before moving to Philadelphia. Anson B. Cutts purchased the house from Purcell in 1919, and it remained in his family until 1985, when his son, Anson B. Cutts Jr., bequeathed it to the Minneapolis Institute of Arts. Restored to its appearance in Purcell's time, the house is open to the public one weekend a month.

Light fixtures throughout the Purcell-Cutts House (top row) show the Prairie School architects' fondness for pure geometric forms. The spheres could have come straight from the designer's compass, the cubes from his T square. Stencils in soft lavender, green, teal, orange, and red tones ring many of the upper walls.

A cluster of glowing spheres illuminates the stair landing, backed up by a flood of natural light (bottom).

Narrow wood pillars frame sheets of delicate art glass (left) as they support the projecting roof. Sunlight bounces from a reflecting pool at the base of the pillars up to the deep eaves and into the house in a colorful display.

Glass at the front door of "The Little Joker" (right) shows that the architects enjoyed their work. Such whimsical details were antidotes to the prevailing stuffiness of Victorian houses.

In a second-floor bedroom (this page), simply furnished with a wooden bed and another "surprise point" chair, corners dissolve into glass, a trick Wright often used to destroy a wall's typical sense of confinement. At the top of the open stairway (right top), the master bedroom is separated from a child's room by a Japanese-style folding screen covered in grass cloth. Art glass windows and stencils bring key design themes even into the bathroom (right bottom).

No natural woodwork, no earth tones, no feeling of heaviness or mass can be found inside this residence by Frank Lloyd Wright's former chief draftsman—only light and air and an exhilarating sense of space. William Drummond's Baker House in Wilmette, Illinois, presents a most un-Wrightian aspect to the street: balance just short of symmetry, which is characteristic of many Drummond designs. The main entrance on the right side is balanced by a mirror-image window on the left; twin porches flank the second-floor clerestory windows; and walled terraces of equal size and shape skirt the projecting front veranda. Designed in 1914 during his three-year partnership with Louis Guenzel, the house is one of the most sophisticated of Drummond's career and, with its abstract, cubic forms, bears a striking exterior resemblance to his own home in nearby River Forest, which proudly proclaims itself "Drummond Country." ■ Inside, Drummond's light touch is evident everywhere—in the woodwork painted in shades of ivory and white and in the amazing breadth and height of the living room, which soars to two stories and vanishes into a wall of glass. Bands of clear glass sweep across a full-height clerestory and

BAKER HOUSE

around corners at the front of the house, offering views into the treetops just outside. A cantilevered balcony encircles the rest of the living room, providing entry points for second-story bedrooms and eliminating unnecessary corridors. Panels of art glass, bejeweled in shimmering squares of leaf green and opalescent white, provide contrast back at ground level. Balancing all this lightness is an immense arched fireplace set into the masonry core at the center of the house. ■ Keeping in mind the needs of their family of six, owners Jim and Liz McNair have made some adaptations. They use the dining room, with its close access to the kitchen, as a family room and the enclosed front veranda as a formal dining space. Here, surrounded by walls of glass and with a nod to Drummond's mentor, diners sit in new tall-back chairs like the classic designs Wright made for his Robie House in Chicago.

Flat roofs and geometric simplicity make the Baker House seem astonishingly modern. Bands of dark wood outlining the crisp stucco walls underscore its well-balanced symmetry (left) and delineate the entrance (right).

Two stories of windows fill the living room with light, in effect eliminating the wall (this page). Beyond, an enclosed porch, encircled in glass, serves as an almost-alfresco dining space. The semicircular geometry of the fireplace (opposite) offers a refreshing counterpoint to the house's rectilinear forms, reiterated by the second-floor balcony along three walls.

Drummond's penchant for symmetry is obvious in the dining room sideboard, painted in a faux-wood finish. Early photographs indicate that he broke with Prairie-style principles by painting interior woodwork, not leaving it natural.

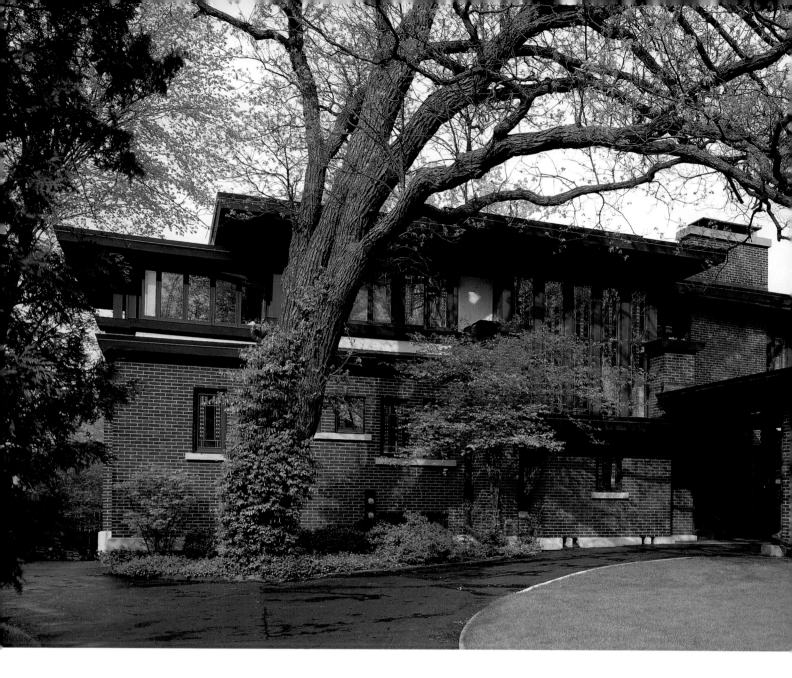

BERSBACH

Van Bergen's mentors and colleagues clearly influenced the Bersbach House (left), which reflects Wright's sense of repose, Griffin's muscularity, and Drummond's abstraction. As humble and shy as Wright was flamboyant, Van Bergen came the closest to imitating his work. A Purcell and Elmslie ceiling light illuminates the library (right).

In 1993, when Kimberlee Kepper spied the "For Sale" sign on the lawn of the Bersbach House in Wilmette, Illinois, high above the sand dunes along Lake Michigan's western shore, she was not looking for a Prairie-style house. And this one appeared dark and uncomfortable. But once inside, she was smitten: "It was so light and open, and the windows reminded me of a church. It seemed like a more elevated place to live

than an ordinary house." ■ Earthbound and complex, this elegant house on its spectacular lakefront site traces a complex horizontal line. Flat roofs extend in sweeping planes that step down in ever-widening tiers. Yet a lively mix of vertical elements—masonry piers, tall casement windows, and a bold chimney— breaks up the flatness like a stand of trees on the open prairie. From a low, compressed entrance the reception hall and stairwell expand dizzyingly upward, and light pours in from all sides. The architect, John Van Bergen, like Frank Lloyd Wright, understood that the simple act of entering a house should be an experience. Here it is almost reverential. ■ In this 1914 house for Alfred Bersbach, a wealthy lawyer, and his wife, Van Bergen elevated the major living spaces—dining room, living room, and covered porch—at the rear, toward the lake. Windows grouped in bands offer a panoramic vista of sky, sand dunes, and water. The dining room is almost completely sheathed in glass; in the living room, windows open up the eastern and southern walls and surround the masonry fireplace. ■ At first Kepper's husband, Randy Randazzo, saw only the repairs that the house required. The seventeen roof planes covering the main residence and the nearby coach house, battered for years by punishing winds and the storms that march across Lake Michigan, all needed replacement. More than one hundred art glass windows, each composed

of 115 tiny pieces of glass, had to be recemented and partially releaded. Maintenance is an ongoing concern, but Randazzo is now as fascinated as his wife with the house. ■ Leaving colonial furniture behind in the couple's previous Georgian-style house, Kepper began collecting Stickley, Prairie, and Mission pieces. Her choices suit the house's fine proportions and add to the feeling of unity and repose.

Art glass windows in the living room frame views of Lake Michigan and open to a porch. Clear glass in the center allows unobstructed views, while green and gold pieces along the edges recall the wheatlike beach grass just outside.

Rich mahogany reaches around the living room fireplace (left top), linking it with the windows. Spindled furnishings harmonize with the screened stairway. The dining set, cabinet, and chandelier (left bottom) are Prairie antiques from a Milwaukee home. With its newel post light and art glass windows, the stairway (this page) is a focal point of the house.

James Frederick Clarke, a doctor in Fairfield, Iowa, was a visionary drawn to the work of the Prairie School. His wife, Melinda, was not. When their family home burned, she had her heart set on a traditional American colonial to replace it. Claiming that a colonial house would cost far more than they could afford, Dr. Clarke commissioned Barry Byrne to design their new house and then hid the construction bills. To his great relief, Melinda Clarke was thrilled with the results. ■ The Clarkes' house, built in 1915, could hardly be further from a colonial design. Stark and bold with vast, unbroken wall planes of rich red brick, it pushes the Prairie style in an abstract direction, combining the free-flowing space of a typical Prairie house with a sculptural facade spun from pure geometry: a triangular gable, a cube-shaped balcony, and a half-circle window. Austere but incorporating a provocative use of color, the house represents Byrne's independence from his mentor, Frank Lloyd Wright. Byrne's interior collaborator, the sculptor and artist Alfonso Iannelli, intended to unite the design through color—

Sturdy red brick walls, befitting a solid midwestern house, lend stability and permanence to Byrne's Clarke House.

white walls, a wood floor stained black, silver-gray woodwork, and rugs and upholstery in vivid reds and blues—rather than with a repeated geometric motif, and so the same colors are found on the exterior as well. ■ Owners in the 1980s undertook an extensive restoration, tracking down the dining room chairs and table in the local Presbyterian church. Original furnishings still with the house included a blue rug and light fixtures, discovered in the basement. A few furnishings were re-created. As a result, this Prairie house remains one of the most complete still in private hands. ■ The current owners, Bruce and Sherry Kendell, found themselves drawn to the house in ways they did not expect. "When we were looking for a house to buy in the neighborhood, this one caught my eye," Bruce explained. "I'd go in and sit down and not want to leave. It's a wonderful house, comfortable and functional. The more I live here, the more I develop a respect for Barry Byrne."

Lessons in simplicity from Wright and bold, heavy massing learned from Griffin shaped Byrne's personal style: edgy and abstract. The color choices—brilliant blue for the balcony and white and black for the gable—came from Iannelli.

White, black, red, and blue—all original colors—replaced the customary Prairie palette inside and out. Above the living room fireplace (opposite), a theatrical poster by Iannelli from about 1910 offers clues to his design approach. The front window's circular theme (top left) is repeated in the round dining table (top right), while its gold stencils reappear in a stair hall (bottom left), adding luster to the white scheme. The simplified sideboard (bottom right) eliminates clutter.

PRAIRIE

GARDENS AND

Just as the prairie inspired a new way of building, it also stimulated a new concept of landscape design. At a time when formal gardens filled with exotic foreign plants were seen as proof of prosperity, the Chicago landscape architects Jens Jensen and Ossian Cole Simonds proposed a bold move: why not look to the prairie for what grows best in the garden? Horizontal forms so important to the Prairie architects showed themselves in hawthorn trees, daylilies, goldenrod, violets, sumac, and other hardy native plants. Coming directly from the midwestern soil, they seemed more democratic than showy foreign specimens. Prairie architects were equally passionate about naturalistic landscapes. They all paid heed to the elements that made the Prairie style so successful: the needs of the client, the natural features of the site, and a respect for native materials.

LANDSCAPES

Taliesin. Frank Lloyd Wright. Spring Green, Wisconsin

Frank Lloyd Wright and Walter Burley Griffin. Oak Park, Illinois. 1909   W   I   L

Bursting forth from their geometric enclosures, antique roses, lush dahlias, and purple asters pay homage to the picturesque garden that once stood beyond the William Martin House in Oak Park, Illinois, a three-story Prairie house designed by Frank Lloyd Wright in 1902. In 1908 Martin purchased the lot next door and the following year commissioned Wright to fill it with gardens, an ornamental pool, bridges, and a trellis-covered pergola. When the extra lot was sold and a small house built there in 1951, the garden was destroyed. ■ The house's current owners, Laura and Rick Talaske, decided to replicate the original garden in a more compact form. "We wanted to put the house back into context, to re-create some of the magic that had been lost," Laura explains. Historic photographs show a wildly romantic setting with exuberant

LIAM MARTIN GARDEN

Wright and Griffin liked to place flowers along terrace walls to make them seem to bloom from the architecture itself. The house's abstract forms are the perfect backdrop for nature's randomness—asters, false indigo, and blue stem (left).

Ash and honey locust trees shade the garden (right) and provide anchors for 'Annabelle' hydrangeas and peonies.

masses of greenery tumbling from low concrete beds, a vine-covered pergola, and walkways leading to a fish pond and built-in benches. A charming statue by Richard Bock of a little boy gazing at a frog once stood guard over all. ■ Walter Burley Griffin probably supervised the garden's installation during Wright's trip to Europe in 1909. Griffin took credit for it in a 1914 letter to Wilhelm Miller, who first used the term *Prairie style* in referring to architecture and landscape design. The plan was typical of both Wright and Griffin, who loved to see flowers growing naturally but liked to control them within the confines of geometric planting beds and garden walls. ■ Under the guidance of John Thorpe, an Oak Park architect,

An outdoor lantern (left top), re-created from a Wright sketch, illuminates a gateway, its form mimicking the column that holds it. Geometric planters flanking a built-in bench (left center) will serve as footings for the new pergola. Water lilies, arrowhead, and yellow flag iris bloom around the reconstructed pond (left bottom), home to thirty large goldfish.

the ornamental fish pond and the concrete bridges have been rebuilt at one-third scale. The original thirty-three-foot-square pond was reduced to eleven feet with small bridges spanning it. The Talaskes also plan to replace the trellis-covered stucco piers that formed the pergola and are on the lookout for a statue to replicate Bock's little boy. Slowly the garden is coming back "in a small way," says Laura Talaske.

Neither Wright nor Griffin restricted himself to prairie species, so owner Laura Talaske mixes native plants with those common to the period. The original pergola and garden extended into the lot beyond the trellis.

TALIESIN

G A R D E N

When Wright envisioned the house he would build for himself on family land near Spring Green, Wisconsin, in 1911, he gave almost as much thought to the gardens and landscape as to the architecture. He saw masses of apple trees, their boughs "bending to the ground with red and white and yellow spheres." He saw plum trees, "fragrant drifts of snow-white in spring," that in summer would scatter blue and red fruit over the ground. He saw rows of berry bushes, necklaces of pink and green gooseberries, and pendant clusters of red currants hanging like "tassels in the dark leaves." "I saw it all and I planted it all," he said without exaggeration. ■ But Wright did more than plant a garden at Taliesin. Over the five decades he lived there, he transformed the entire landscape into his ideal of a bucolic country estate, weaving a seamless tapestry of buildings, gardens, and landscape. Earlier Prairie houses may have

Frank Lloyd Wright. Spring Green, Wisconsin. 1911–59

embraced the landscape, but Taliesin revered it. Its rough limestone walls, wings, and courtyards reach across the ground like the tendrils of a vine. Set into a hill, just below the crown, Taliesin ("shining brow" in Welsh) is part Italian hill village, part Prairie house, and part English country estate—a rambling composition of studio, farm, house, workshop, gardens, orchards, and fields. ▪ Wright created three major landscape experiences at Taliesin: intimate gardens close to the house, the larger landscape that was farmed or left in meadow, and the most spectacular feature of all—the water garden. ▪ At the rear,

Masses of blooms envelop Taliesin in color, fragrance, and texture as a Chinese Kuan Yin looks on serenely. Wright disliked regimented, formal gardens, considering them completely inappropriate for his natural houses.

At one time the water poured over Taliesin's dam with enough force to power a hydraulic ram that pumped water back up the hill to nourish gardens and fill ponds. Wright's Prairie-style hydro house, which sat on the far ledge, eventually washed away, but the trees he planted years ago at his Wisconsin home remain, now grown tall and strong.

house meets hill in a cloistered garden as beautiful as any of Taliesin's interior rooms. Three wings wrap around this space, opening onto a secluded outdoor world. A raised ornamental pool, a suite of low flower beds brimming with color, and shallow stone steps lead up to the hill, where a curved limestone wall encloses a picturesque garden seat, the setting for Wright's ritual of afternoon tea. ■ The landscape

beyond the hill garden is every bit as planned. In earlier years the terrain ran wild with long grasses and native flowers, but today the gently sloping ground meets cultivated fields, the remnants of Wright's apple orchard, and a stand of grapevines. An early champion of contour plowing, Wright planted oats, barley, potatoes, and corn in colorful, sweeping bands of green. ▪ Striving for the sense of completeness that water adds to a landscape, the architect dammed a winding stream below the house in two places, creating a wide, languid lake. A waterfall he engineered plunges over the lower dam, dancing and swirling around limestone projections set carefully into place. Stretching out at the foot of the hill, the lake reflects the sky and clouds all the way back up to Taliesin.

The terrace outside his bedroom afforded Wright a spectacular view of the forested hills and broad valleys settled by his Welsh ancestors (opposite). Rustic limestone garden walls advertise his services (top left) and serve as foils for plants (top right). Trellises of Cherokee red pipes (bottom left) support clusters of blooms and provide year-round color. A low pond with limestone ledges on which to set Asian artifacts adds a serene beauty to the site (bottom right).

Attributed to Jens Jensen. River Forest, Illinois. mid-1920s

All the poetry of a true Prairie-style garden was just waiting to be discovered when Carol Pollak began digging around the backyard of her Wright-designed house (pages 60–65) in River Forest, Illinois. A previous owner told her that the garden was a Japanese design, but the stratified rockwork, council ring, limestone walkway, and stand of hawthorn trees made her doubtful. Pollak thought that they all pointed to the work of one man—Jens Jensen, the father of Prairie landscaping. ▪ To assist in researching and restoring the garden, Carol and William Pollak called on Carol Yetken, an Oak Park landscape architect. She concurred that the garden was in Jensen's style, although no plans have surfaced. They believe that it was

ROBERTS

G A R D E N

A profusion of carefully laid rockwork at Wright's Roberts House indicates that Jensen may have designed the garden. Peeking over the stone are leaves of his favorite tree, the hawthorn, whose spreading branches echo the prairie.

designed in the mid-1920s and speculate that Jensen's involvement might have come through his association with William Drummond, the Prairie School architect whose own home is right next door. ■ The most telltale Jensen imprint, according to Carol Pollak and Yetken, is the extensive limestone rockwork. Arranged in horizontal layers outside the rear veranda, it forms a narrow walkway through the backyard, where it blooms into a council ring, a low, circular stone bench. Jensen was also fond of water features, and this garden once had two small pools, each bordered by stratified stonework. An extensive channeling system led from the larger pool near the veranda to the smaller "bird pool" at the back of the property, an indication of an elaborate and carefully conceived plan. Another Jensen link is his favorite plant, the relic hawthorn trees dotting the edges of a "clearing," the term he used to designate open, sunlit spaces. ■

Combining his own Danish folk traditions with Native American customs, Jensen created in many of his gardens stone council rings where people could gather to tell stories or contemplate nature, warmed by a fire in the center.

Pollak has excavated the stonework and with Yetken's guidance has replaced many of the plantings with those Jensen might have used: viburnum, bottle-brush buckeye, and a burr oak tree. Around the rockwork near the house she added other shade-loving species to the trillium, jack-in-the-pulpit, and may apples already there. In the sunny opening at the center of the garden are typical prairie plants—Queen Anne's lace, goldenrod, and asters. In the fall the back fence, like the prairie itself, is ablaze with flame-red sumac.

Shade-loving plants thrive amid the rockwork near the Roberts House. "There is a remarkable nobility in rocks," Jensen once noted, explaining his fondness for native stone. "Rocks, like trees, have a character all their own."

BECKER

From the wide avenues of Highland Park, Illinois, lined with fine old Georgian and Tudor mansions, a narrow road curves away into a wooded glen. American lindens, hawthorns, sugar maples, and other native Illinois trees spread their leafy branches as the road winds further on, eventually culminating in a grassy meadow. Reminiscent of the open prairie, the meadow rests back from the bluff, high above the sparkling waters of Lake Michigan far below. It is the centerpiece of a seventeen-acre sylvan sanctuary created in 1926 by Jens Jensen, the master of Prairie landscape design. Designed for A. G. Becker to complement his early 1920s Tudor house by Howard Van Doren Shaw, this landscape of woods, water, and native plants appears so subtle and natural, yet Jensen painstakingly planned every tree, bush, and plant.

"Peace was my uppermost thought" when planning the Becker estate, Jensen later wrote. Abstract sculpture now finds a home in the placid meadow he carved from the woods of native burr oaks (left). Curving paths and soft edges delighted Jensen, who maintained that "straight lines have nothing to do with nature." A curved bench mirrors the bend in the path (center), while flat rocks set in layered curves embrace hostas close to the house (right).

■ This spectacular site offered Jensen an abundance of nature's riches, with all the elements he regarded as critical to compose a shrine to the out-of-doors: "the mystery of the forest, the joy and peace of a sunlit meadow . . . the perfume of flowers, the song of birds, the symphony of colors in trees and shrubs." To the left of the house, in a low, damp depression, Jensen shaped a prairie waterscape, a pond edged by a stand of tall cedars. He situated the trees so perfectly that their looming forms cast deep, mysterious shadows as the moon swept across the darkened southern sky. Native grasses, narrow-leafed cattails, and other water plants filled out his plan. Toward the house he planted phlox and other flowering plants that "sang of the prairies." ■ Time and nature have wrought many changes on the Becker estate. To restore the original splendor the current owner, working with Stephen Christy, a landscape architect and Jensen expert, has planted ten thousand wildflowers and several hundred trees and shrubs along the curving roadway. The bluff has been returned to prairie, a rustic bridge rebuilt over a ravine, and much of Jensen's original rockwork in walkways and stone borders has been restored. Now the garden looks so natural and unplanned that it is difficult to see just what Jensen did. That, of course, was his genius.

Gardens—even more than buildings—are subject to change, but an ancient arborvitae that Jensen himself planted

shades a limestone path and a rustic bridge spanning a ravine on the Becker estate north of Chicago (opposite). Near

the bluff along Lake Michigan's edge, young cottonwoods rise and native black oaks send up new volunteers (this page).

At the beginning of the twentieth century, the dream of a home in the country prompted the rapid growth of suburbs and the development of planned communities. Such planning intensely interested Prairie architects because it perfectly fit their goal of a completely integrated environment: houses placed to take maximum advantage of the site's natural features and best views; unified design of street lamps, terrace walls, gates, and bridges to establish neighborhood identity; and gardens integrated with open space. Today, old-fashioned neighborhoods are growing more popular as people long for the sense of community they lost to suburban sprawl. The New Urbanism movement, with its message of smaller lots, pedestrian-friendly streets, and houses that encourage neighborhood interaction, seeks to improve even on the century-old Prairie-era ideals.

Rock Crest–Rock Glen. Planned by Walter Burley Griffin. Mason City, Iowa

PRAIRIE

COMMUNITIES

Robust masonry masses are interposed with ethereal sweeps of glass in the Irving House, which Wright sketched and Mahony completed. Its weighty presence and strong horizontal lines clearly convey Wright's confident mature style.

Millikin Place is a very short street in the center of a small town in the heart of the Illinois plains, but it is a showcase for the work of the Prairie School's only woman architect. Also an exceptional artist, known for her architectural drawings composed in the style of Japanese prints, Marion Mahony worked for Frank Lloyd Wright off and on for fourteen years. His abrupt exodus for Europe in 1909 opened a world of possibilities for her. She rejected her employer's request to take over his unfinished commissions but agreed to work as chief designer for the architect who did, Hermann von Holst. In no time she set about finishing the three houses on Millikin Place in Decatur, Illinois, that had originally been Wright's commissions. ■ Mahony supervised completion of the Irving House, designed by Wright in 1909. She added her own imprint, however, changing Wright's original stucco exterior to brick and adding exquisite

MILLIKIN

P L A C E

Mahony's gateway of sturdy brick piers topped by geometric lanterns establishes Millikin Place as a distinctive community (including one non-Prairie house). Griffin landscaped it as an idealized prairie park.

tile mosaics at the back of the house. Its symmetrical layout was an anomaly for Wright—the living room is placed in the exact center, flanked by the dining room and library. ▪ The other two houses, designed in 1910 for the brothers Adolph and Robert Mueller, are more clearly Mahony's designs, although Walter Burley Griffin may have had some input. Long, tranquil horizontals blend with snug verticals to form the core of both. Adolph Mueller's home, the largest of the Millikin Place houses and the last to be built, has a pinwheel plan, typical of Mahony's designs during this period. The main living areas spread out with no visual interruption from porch to living room, through the entrance hall and dining room, and on into a second porch at the opposite end of the house. Such a continuous sweep of space along a single axis is characteristic of Mahony but not Wright, who probably would have broken these long vistas with partial barriers to evoke a sense of mystery. But there is still great drama here, particularly in the sunken living room, with its tented ceiling and six enormous, sloping art glass panels in prairie reds and golds. ■ The Robert Mueller House is purely Mahony's. Composed of variegated blue-and-gray brick with a low, hipped roof, it shows her unusual color palette. Instead of the prairie's muted shades, she chose deep violets, glittering blues, and bright reds for art glass windows, light fixtures, and the five-part geometric tile mosaic on the facade. ■ To unify the miniature neighborhood, which also includes one non-Prairie house, Mahony designed brick-and-wrought-iron street lamps and a pair of entrance gates for

the cul-de-sac. Griffin, who became her husband in 1911 after a whirlwind courtship, provided a natural-istic landscape that defined the communal space as a Prairie-style enclave yet gave each house its own elaborate garden setting. Mahony later confided that she was swept off her feet by Griffin's accomplish-ments, which she regarded as superior to Wright's.

The Prairie architects' love of the horizontal comes inside the Irving House with banding above a wide, low fireplace recalling the balcony treatment outside. Prairie flower murals by George Mann Niedecken once adorned this wall.

Niedecken, under Mahony's direction, created the custom furnishings and textiles for the Irving House—

silk and wool curtains, Austrian hand-tufted carpets, and goat's-hair upholstery fabric; only a few built-in pieces remain.

In the library (this page) and dining area (opposite), simple, linear art glass embellishes windows and cabinets.

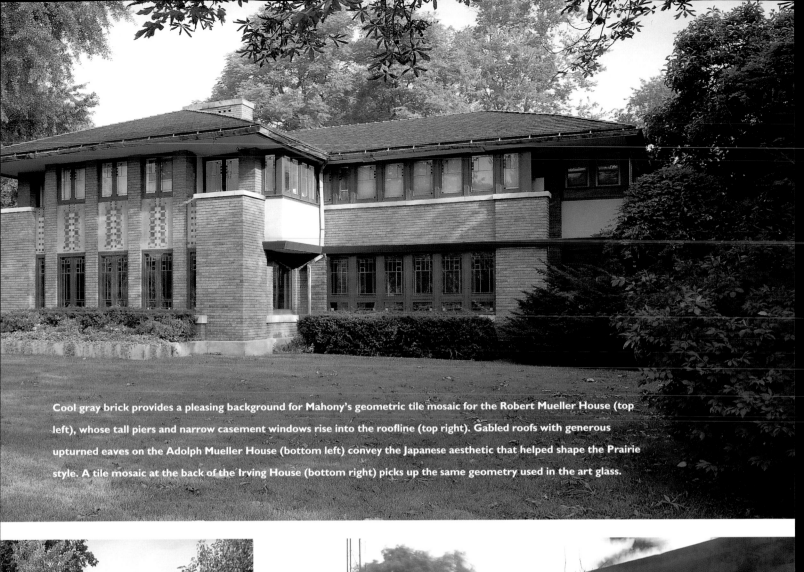

Cool gray brick provides a pleasing background for Mahony's geometric tile mosaic for the Robert Mueller House (top left), whose tall piers and narrow casement windows rise into the roofline (top right). Gabled roofs with generous upturned eaves on the Adolph Mueller House (bottom left) convey the Japanese aesthetic that helped shape the Prairie style. A tile mosaic at the back of the Irving House (bottom right) picks up the same geometry used in the art glass.

In Mahony's house for Adolph Mueller, wood banding zigs in and out, pulling rooms together. Her skill with art glass turned a simple stair hall (opposite, top left and right) into a sculpture of light. The one hundred art glass windows, including those in the dining room and entrance hall (opposite, bottom left and right), were inspired by native prairie plants and their colors. Tented ceilings and sloping panels of glass (this page) echo the exterior's angular quality.

Daringly poised at the edge of a bluff, fifty feet above Willow Creek, the jagged limestone walls of the Melson House merge so completely with the rocky site that it is difficult to tell where the cliff ends and the house begins. Crowned with giant keystones and devoid of the customary sweeping roofline and deep eaves, this exotic fortress appears at odds with the Prairie-style vocabulary. Yet all the key elements are present: the sensitive use of natural materials, an open floor plan, and a strong sense of place. The place just happens to be the vertical face of a cliff rather than the flat prairie. A house so perfectly suited to its natural setting recalls Frank Lloyd Wright's spectacular merging of nature and architecture in Falling-water (1935). But Walter Burley Griffin did it here in Mason City, Iowa, a quarter of a century earlier. ∎ The house he designed for Joshua and Minnie Melson in 1912 is part of Rock Crest–Rock Glen, a Prairie-style community three blocks from downtown. Divided by a meandering curve in the creek, half of the eighteen-acre property hugs a steep limestone cliff known as Rock Crest, while the other half spans a meadow and woods called Rock Glen. Planned by Griffin in 1912, it includes eight Prairie houses—six by

Griffin, one by Barry Byrne, and one by the local architect Einar Broaten. ▪ The rugged Rock Crest site was regarded as unbuildable when the town was plotted in the mid-nineteenth century, but Melson, a local businessman, saw only its great possibilities in purchasing the tract in 1903. Wright, whose Stockman House (pages 56–59), a bank, and a hotel were under construction in Mason City, seemed the logical choice to develop the plan for this model community, but after his scandalous retreat to Europe in 1909 his work in Mason City was over. Melson turned to Wright's former employee Marion Mahony, who demurred to her new husband, preferring to promote his career. Griffin, also an alumnus of Wright's studio, quickly prepared a scheme for the site that, along with Mahony's elegant drawing, was impressive enough to win him the commission to design all the houses. ▪ Griffin proposed that nine houses be

Many Prairie architects—Wright, Griffin, Mahony, Drummond, and Byrne—left their imprint on Mason City, but Griffin had the greatest impact. With designs such as the Blythe House, he skillfully wedded architecture to nature.

Mahony's touch in the Blythe House is evident in decorative elements such as her Italian-tile fireplace, which, flat to the wall with no mantel, radiates a luminescent glow (this page). The pre-Columbian motif on the tripartite concrete panels and terrace walls outside (right top) is re-created in the bow-tie shapes on the windows (right bottom).

placed on the cliff edge overlooking the water and nine in the glen, leaving the grassy creekside meadow free as a park. (Of the houses built, only the Melson House was sited on the cliff; seven were placed in the glen.) Building in harmony with nature in this riverbank setting did not call for the low, horizontal response that suited the prairie. Taking his cues from the stratified limestone cliff on the creek's south side, Griffin keyed the houses to the cliff's upward thrust and used its materials to thematically link the structures. Solid and dense, with a clear vertical momentum, all but one of the houses rise from a base of ashlar-cut limestone, bearing Griffin's trademark heavy corner piers and windows with wood mullions. ▪ Griffin's first two designs for Rock Crest, both built earlier in 1912, were the Page House, a tall struc- ture of reinforced concrete with a broad, upturned gabled roof and deep eaves, and the Rule House, a square, symmetrical building of stucco and wood reminiscent of Wright's 1907 "Fireproof House for $5,000." (This famous design may have originated in an L-shaped floor plan Griffin developed in 1906. Some historians now believe that the "Fireproof House" should be regarded as a joint effort by Wright and Griffin, with some input from Mahony, who prepared the drawing.) In 1913–14 came the Blythe House, which recalls a Mayan temple. Its ornament and the details of several other houses may be the work of Mahony, who collaborated extensively with her husband on Rock Crest–Rock Glen. ▪ While Griffin was

Willow Creek snakes through Mason City, slicing into limestone bluffs—Rock Crest—on one bank and a gentle slope of woods and meadows—Rock Glen—on the other. The site's rugged beauty offered Griffin endless possibilities.

immersed in his work in Mason City, word came that he had won the international competition to design Australia's new federal capital, Canberra. Griffin turned over his practice to Barry Byrne, and in February 1914 he and Mahony sailed for Australia, where they took up permanent residence. ■ Byrne supervised the completion of Griffin's Schneider House in 1915 (changing a few details), modified Griffin's Gilmore House in 1915, and two years later designed the Franke House. Both the Gilmore and Franke Houses have narrow eaves, unadorned wall surfaces of stucco, and plain, square-mullioned windows, characteristic of Byrne's more abstract style. The last Prairie house in Rock Crest–Rock Glen, the 1914–16 Drake House, was designed by Broaten, who was retained when Drake and Byrne failed to agree on a design. ■ Although Rock Crest–Rock Glen fell short of its projected eighteen houses, the ones that were built offer clear proof of the Prairie style's versatility. Its principles of a site-specific, uniquely American architecture work well here, in a setting far different from the prairie. Griffin considered himself as much a land planner as an architect and had developed several Prairie community plans. But only at Rock Crest–Rock Glen and a later project in Australia, Castlecrag, did he come close to so beautifully realizing his objectives.

The Melson House's rough limestone walls seem to complete the sheer cliff as they rise above the precipice, erupting into huge bursts of stone. Instead of a porch, Griffin created a "secret afternoon-tea terrace" (opposite) and a treetop balcony (top and bottom left) facing the creek. The two-car garage (bottom right) can be driven straight through.

When the Melson House was restored by Peggy and Roger Bang, a new kitchen with Prairie-style woodwork was added (left). The massive fireplace between the living and dining rooms (this page) captures the exterior's monumental nature, although the stonework is more refined inside. Keystones around the opening echo the window treatment

Griffin's symmetrical Rule House (opposite and top left) is built on a square plan, reflected in its golden French doors. With its flared eaves and narrow piers, his T-shaped Page House (top right) recalls Mahony's designs for Millikin Place. Just outside Rock Crest, the Yelland House (bottom left) was designed by Drummond while supervising completion of Wright's bank and hotel. The Schneider House (bottom right) rests partly below grade on a limestone base.

8

Local architects emulated Prairie-style features they had seen in magazines or observed directly. In the Drake House in Rock Crest–Rock Glen, Einar Broaten captured the key elements: a low pitched roof, casement windows, and deep eaves.

Frank Lloyd Wright. Glencoe, Illinois. 1915

Nestled snugly in the woods, Ravine Bluffs in Glencoe, Illinois, north of Chicago, was to be the setting for twenty-three moderate-cost houses designed by Frank Lloyd Wright. The intent was to create the illusion of rural life in a romantic landscape—through curving streets and houses carefully placed in the pastoral, eight-acre site—yet all the homes would be within walking distance of the commuter railway station. Although the 1915 plan for this community developed by Sherman M. Booth II of Chicago fell short of projections, five Prairie-style houses, a bridge, and two lighted concrete planters were built, as well as Booth's own large house. Ravine Bluffs offered Wright his first opportunity to explore community planning ideas along with his interest in affordable housing. Jens Jensen, the noted Prairie landscape

RAVINE

B L U F F S

The sophisticated geometry of Wright's home for Sherman Booth (left) betrays no hint of its humble origin. The central addition's elegant proportions and flat roof convey his increasing interest in abstraction, yet the older sections' hipped roofs are classic Prairie style. Voluptuous concrete orbs mark the boundaries of Ravine Bluffs (right).

architect, was engaged to carry out the landscaping. ■ Booth, who was Wright's client, friend, and attorney, saw himself as a gentleman farmer and commissioned Wright in 1912 to design a garage and a stable. He rejected Wright's elaborate design for a house to go with them, deciding in 1915 to simply remodel the existing structures. In a typical flash of brilliance, Wright converted the stable into a kitchen and dining room wing and the garage and its caretaker apartment into a bedroom wing. In between he inserted a four-story cube containing a large living room and an open porch at ground level, bedrooms and a balcony on the second floor, a sleeping porch on the third, and a tower on the fourth.

■ When the current owners, Ted and Sonia Bloch, bought the house in 1966, they were told it might be a Wright design. After moving in, they found out that they did indeed have a Wright design—a remodeled garage and stable! "We told them this had to be wrong," recalls Sonia. "Then they sent us a set of plans and explained the situation." ■ Wright's 1907 plan for "A Fireproof House for $5,000" became the blueprint for the small community's other five houses, all designed in 1915. A far cry from the unimaginative, boxy structures typical of the day's low-cost housing, these homes featured extensive windows, spacious interiors, and a strong link with nature through a veranda called a "living porch." Living and

dining rooms shared corners in an L-shaped plan pivoting around a central fireplace. Natural materials—stucco and wood—bonded houses to their woodland sites. Varying roofs, from hipped to flat to gabled, set them apart. ■ Abstract, geometric forms—particularly circles and spires—had begun to permeate Wright's work at this time, a fascination obvious in the reinforced concrete bridge. The one-lane passage features vertical light pylons, planters as flat as platters, and a five-sided seating bench. A pedestrian pathway is supported by a graceful arch of poured concrete. The whole composition is part sculpture, part architecture—robustly three-dimensional like all of Wright's work.

A Wright fireplace on an outside wall is rare (left), but in the Booth House it may be the result of restrictions from adding onto an existing structure. The wood-mullioned windows and wide expanses of clear glass on the porch (right), also part of the addition, cast an eye to the future, as do the graceful light standards. Gumwood is used throughout.

Wright carefully positioned the Ravine Bluff houses to ensure maximum privacy in the secluded woodland setting. With its gabled roof and flared eaves, the Perry House (opposite, top) imparts a Japanese sensibility, in contrast to the Kier House (opposite, bottom), with its more traditional hipped roof. Clean lines and flat roofs distinguish the Kissim House (top) and Root House (bottom). Low porches help blend these two-story houses into the landscape.

MIDDLETON HILLS

The choice of Prairie-style houses for Middleton Hills, a new community outside Madison, Wisconsin, that will eventually include 320 residences, is particularly apt: they are historically authentic to the region, and the developer, Marshall Erdman, worked closely with Frank Lloyd Wright on several of his 1940s and 1950s designs. In 1995 Erdman hired the eminent New Urbanist architects Andres Duany and Elizabeth Plater-Zyberk to bring to life his dream of an old-fashioned neighborhood. In concept their plan for Middleton Hills resembles William Drummond's 1915 scheme for suburban Chicago, which linked

The attention lavished on homes a century ago has come to Middleton Hills, a neighborhood of new Prairie-style houses and bungalows in Wisconsin. Simplicity, natural materials, and a feeling for the land attract community residents.

houses and public buildings while respecting the natural features of the landscape. ▪ Although the community includes some new bungalows, the Prairie house's open floor plan appeals to many buyers today. One house designed by the Madison architect E. Edward Linville, a two-story, board-and-batten cedar structure for Robin Gates and Jan Fulwiler, has features that recall Wright's grouped windows, Mahony's tile fireplaces, and Purcell and Elmslie's tented ceilings and sense of color. Linville also designed the house for Amy Glynn and Doug Johnson's young family, complete with corner windows, a banister with squared

Rough cedar walls rise up to meet casement windows set beneath deep eaves in E. Edward Linville's Gates-Fulwiler House. The main living areas in the cross-shaped plan are elevated on the second floor, creating a private refuge.

The fireplace (above) is the focal point of the Gates-Fulwiler living room, which boasts such Prairie-style elements as built-in bookshelves, oak pillars, and an inglenook set off to the side. The pitched ceiling reinforces a sense of shelter. An upstairs hall (opposite), outfitted with cabinets, eventually spills out right and left into dining and living areas.

spindles, and an elegant tile fireplace. ■ Linville, who has designed twelve houses in Middleton Hills and forty Prairie houses elsewhere, says that his clients are drawn to the strength and permanence of the style: "It has a sense of belonging, a sense of place and permanence that people find comforting. Yet, the

flow of rooms, the open planning, supports modern living." Linville grew up in Iowa and was attracted to the Prairie houses in neighboring towns. "There was an emotional response that I tried to figure out in later years, some power that tugged at me," he says. "It had a feeling of adventure and romance and most of all rebellion that excited me. I still get thrilled by it." ■ Once Middleton Hills (now overseen by Erdman's son Tim) is completed, stores, workplaces, schools, theaters, and parks will all be within walking distance of each residence—bringing full circle the dream of a home in a Prairie town first expressed nearly a century ago.

Jane Williams drew up a cruciform design based on Purcell and Feick's Stevens House in her hometown of Eau Claire, Wisconsin, and then turned to the Minneapolis firm Mulfinger and Susanka to develop it (top). Inside (bottom left and right), the raised hearth, a classic Purcell and Elmslie element, joins Arts and Crafts furnishings to create a period feel.

The architect E. Edward Linville persuaded Amy Glynn and Doug Johnson—professed architectural novices unsure about Prairie houses—to try a popular foursquare design (top). The new home's welcoming hearth brings the family together (bottom left), and Wright-inspired pillars divide living areas without bottling up space (bottom right).

Richard Bock (1865–1949), sculptor. A native of Germany, Bock studied in Berlin and Paris before emigrating with his family to Chicago, where he trained as a cabinetmaker and woodcarver and set up a studio in 1891. Much of his early work was neoclassical, but his later designs were influenced by Wright and the Prairie School. He designed sculpture and developed decorative designs for Sullivan, Wright, Perkins, Spencer, Purcell and Elmslie, and Drummond.

Francis Barry Byrne (1883–1967), architect. Byrne joined Wright's practice in 1902 with no formal training. Although committed to Wright's vision of a new American architecture, after six years he moved on to Griffin's studio and then to Seattle to form a partnership with another studio employee, Andrew Willatsen (1876–1974). Byrne took over Griffin's practice in 1914 and formed his own office in Chicago in 1917, later specializing in church designs. Byrne's work is characterized by clean lines, severe masses, and solid, boxy forms; his mature ecclesiastical designs were intricately decorated.

William Drummond (1876–1946), architect. The son of a carpenter, Drummond worked for Sullivan before joining Wright's studio in 1899. He remained there off and on until 1909, when he formed his own practice. Between 1912 and 1915 he was a partner with Louis Guenzel (1860–1956). Drummond, who also designed landscapes and city plans, showed a preference for clean, uncluttered facades with symmetrical window placement and crisp, angular forms. Much of his architecture is in River Forest, Illinois.

George Grant Elmslie (1871–1952), architect. Scottish by birth, Elmslie apprenticed with Joseph Lyman Silsbee in 1887, alongside Wright and Maher, and followed Wright to Adler and Sullivan's office in 1889; he succeeded Wright as chief draftsman. In 1909 he joined the partnership of Purcell and Feick in Minneapolis. After Feick left in 1913, the firm continued as Purcell and Elmslie, becoming the most productive of all the Prairie School partnerships. In 1922 the partnership was dissolved, and Elmslie established his own office in Chicago. His work is noted for its intricate terra-cotta and fret-sawn wooden ornament.

Orlando Giannini (1861–1928), artist, sculptor, art glass–maker. In 1894, after a five-year apprenticeship in Cincinnati, Giannini began work as a designer for Adams and Westlake, a brass and bronze foundry in Chicago. The following year he executed four murals for Frank Lloyd Wright, and in 1899 he formed a partnership with the glassmaker Fritz Hilgart (1869–1942). The firm executed art glass and glass mosaics for Wright, Maher, and Howard Van Doren Shaw. Giannini later designed art glass lamp shades for Teco Ware.

Walter Burley Griffin (1876–1937), architect. After graduation from the University of Illinois in 1899, Griffin worked as a draftsman for Dwight Perkins in Chicago's Steinway Hall and then was an integral part of Wright's studio from 1901 to 1905. The following year he opened his own practice, specializing in residences, city planning, and landscape design. In 1912 he won the competition to design Canberra, the new capital of Australia, where he won many other commissions. Before taking up work in Australia in 1914, he had produced approximately 130 designs, about half of which were built. His work falls into two styles: one influenced by Wright's ideas and one focused on severe abstract forms and the plastic possibilities of reinforced concrete. Houses of his mature style were closed cubes with flat roofs, few overhanging eaves, and strong corners. He spread Prairie School principles as far as India, where he died of peritonitis.

Myron Hunt (1868–1952), architect. One of the early members of the Steinway Hall group in Chicago, Hunt had studied at Northwestern University and the Massachusetts Institute of Technology.

Alfonso Iannelli (1888–1965), artist and sculptor. A native of Italy, Iannelli was apprenticed to Gutzon Borglum, the sculptor of Mount Rushmore, and later specialized in sculpture, poster design, industrial design, and graphic arts. In 1910 he traveled to California, where his work gained the attention of Byrne and Wright's son John Lloyd Wright, who persuaded his father to hire the sculptor for Midway Gardens (1913) in Chicago. Iannelli also collaborated with Byrne as well as Purcell and Elmslie.

Jens Jensen (1860–1951), landscape architect. Jensen emigrated from Denmark in 1884 and began his career in Chicago's West Side park system two years later. In 1900 he opened a private practice, designing landscapes for large country estates as well as subdivisions, resorts, parks, schools, and businesses. Along with Simonds, he was a founder of the Prairie style of landscape design and an active conservationist. His trademarks include extensive use of hawthorn and other native prairie plants, stratified rockwork, open spaces ("clearings"), and council rings. He worked with Sullivan, Wright, Maher, and Spencer.

George Washington Maher (1864–1926), architect. Maher began his architectural apprenticeship at the age of thirteen in Chicago. He later apprenticed in Joseph Lyman Silsbee's office alongside Wright and Elmslie and in 1888 began his own practice, specializing in residential work. Influenced more by the Vienna Secessionists and C. F. A. Voysey than by Sullivan or Wright, his work was often more formal, solid, and formulaic than that of others in the Prairie School. He developed a rhythm motif theory, in which all decorative details are designed to harmonize with a guiding motif drawn from the prairie, such as a poppy, thistle, or lily.

Marion Mahony (1871–1962), architect. The second woman to graduate from the Massachusetts Institute of Technology's School of Architecture, Mahony worked for her cousin Dwight Perkins in Steinway Hall before joining Wright's practice in 1895. She is known for her exquisite architectural drawings and her decorative patterns and details. After Wright's departure for Europe in 1909, she was hired by von Holst to carry out Wright's uncompleted commissions. In 1911 she married Griffin, later traveling with him to Australia and India. In her house designs she showed a preference for tight, narrow verticals and pinwheel floor plans.

George Mann Niedecken (1878–1945), interior architect. Trained in Chicago, Berlin, and Paris, Niedecken worked with several Prairie School designers supervising construction of furniture and textiles, color selection, and installation. He also designed pieces of his own. As a muralist, he developed a technique of translating trees and flowers into conventionalized flat-pattern designs, as seen in Wright's Dana House (1902) in Springfield, Illinois. In 1907 he formed the Niedecken-Walbridge decorating firm in Milwaukee (the firm continued under a different name into the mid-1970s). Niedecken worked with Wright, Purcell and Elmslie, Tallmadge and Watson, Drummond, and Spencer.

Dwight Perkins (1867–1941), architect. A graduate of the Massachusetts Institute of Technology, Perkins moved to Chicago to work with the architects Burnham and Root. In about 1895 he formed his own practice and the following year produced his first major work, Steinway Hall. Here he rented a top-floor office and invited others, including Spencer, Hunt, and Wright, to join him. A cousin of Mahony's, he hired her after her graduation from MIT.

William Gray Purcell (1880–1965), architect. Raised in Oak Park, Illinois, primarily by his grandparents, Purcell spent many hours as a teenager observing Wright's work, although he never studied with him. He was drawn more to the work of Louis Sullivan and apprenticed with him for a few months in 1903. In 1907 he formed a partnership with George Feick (1881–1945), a Cornell University classmate, in Minneapolis. Two years later Elmslie joined the practice, and in 1913 Feick departed. In addition to its residential work, the firm designed churches, service stations, stores, public buildings, and many small-town banks. In 1916, while still practicing architecture, Purcell became advertising manager for a leather belting company in Philadelphia. In 1919 he moved to Portland, Oregon, and later to Pasadena, California, where he continued to design as well as write.

Ossian Cole Simonds (1855–1931), landscape architect. After studying architecture and civil engineering at the University of Michigan, Simonds first worked for William LeBaron Jenney in Chicago and in 1880 formed the firm Holabird and Simonds. He soon became interested in landscape design and was named superintendent of Graceland Cemetery in 1881, which he landscaped in a naturalistic style. A founding practitioner of the Prairie style of landscape design, he designed parks, cemeteries, large estates, and campus plans and was one of the first landscape designers to use native plants in man-made settings. His fame in Chicago prompted Griffin, then still in high school, to consult him about a career in landscape architecture; ironically, Simonds advised him to pursue architecture.

Robert Clossen Spencer (1864–1953), architect. Along with Wright, Hunt, and Perkins, Spencer was one of the original Steinway Hall group that coalesced in the late 1890s. In 1895 he established an independent practice, which Horace Powers (1872–1928) joined in 1905. Inspired by Louis Sullivan and contemporary English architects who were translating medieval architecture for modern-day needs, he developed a conservative, formal version of the Prairie style with rectangular details and a suggestion of medieval half-timbering. Spencer spread the word of the Prairie style through dozens of articles for architectural journals and home magazines, helping popularize the work of the Prairie School architects; he wrote the first major study of Wright's work, which appeared in *Architectural Review* in 1900.

Louis Sullivan (1856–1924), architect. The philosophy of architecture that formed the basis of the Prairie School was laid down by Sullivan, who believed that each style of architecture should arise from the intellectual and social forces of its own time. Often called the father of the American skyscraper, he is also known for his elegant, efflorescent ornament conceived as part of the structure. He was in partnership with Dankmar Adler in Chicago from 1883 to 1895, and his later apprentices included Wright, Elmslie, Purcell, and Drummond. He was one of the few influences that Wright ever acknowledged.

Thomas Eddy Tallmadge (1876–1940), architect. A draftsman for Daniel Burnham in Chicago until 1904, Tallmadge formed a partnership with Watson the following year, specializing in residential and ecclesiastical architecture, which lasted until about 1936. Tallmadge coined the term *Chicago School* to describe the commercial work of Chicago architects around the turn of the twentieth century and wrote several books on architectural history.

John S. Van Bergen (1885–1969), architect. Van Bergen, who apprenticed with Griffin in 1907–8, was the last of the notable Prairie School architects to join Wright's studio in 1909. He later worked with Drummond and then opened his own office in Oak Park in 1911, moving it ten years later to Highland Park, north of Chicago. His work became more rustic and natural, although he was still able to carry on the Prairie School idiom well into the 1930s. A master of space in the small house with an elegant sense of proportion, he came closer than anyone else to imitating Wright.

Hermann von Holst (1874–1955), architect. Although a classical rather than a Prairie School designer, von Holst became involved in the Prairie movement in 1909, when he assumed Wright's architectural practice and hired Mahony to handle design. The author of a book on Prairie-style houses, he maintained offices in Steinway Hall.

Vernon Watson (1878–1950), architect. After training at the Art Institute of Chicago and Armour Institute, Watson apprenticed with Daniel Burnham. In 1905 he formed a partnership with Tallmadge and guided the firm's movement toward Prairie architecture. They developed many variations of engaged vertical piers rising into gabled roofs for about twenty houses in the River Forest–Oak Park neighborhoods. After World War II their work turned toward classical revival styles.

Frank Lloyd Wright (1867–1959), architect. America's most prolific and famous architect, Wright designed more than one thousand structures in a seven-decade career. After apprenticing with Joseph Lyman Silsbee in Chicago and working for Adler and Sullivan for nearly six years, he struck out on his own. At his Oak Park, Illinois, studio, which became the birthplace and prime training ground for the Prairie School after 1898, Wright pioneered the use of low proportions, grouped windows, deep eaves, and a flow of space meant to be reflective of the prairie. In 1909 Wright abruptly closed the studio, traveling to Europe to work on a monograph of his architecture. After his return in 1910, he built Taliesin, his second home and studio near Spring Green, Wisconsin, where he continued to practice architecture based on Prairie School principles.

FURTHER READING

Brooks, H. Allen. *The Prairie School: Frank Lloyd Wright and His Midwest Contemporaries.* Toronto: University of Toronto Press, 1972.

Conforti, Michael, ed. *Minnesota 1900: Art and Life on the Upper Mississippi, 1890–1915.* London and Toronto: Associated University Press and the Minneapolis Institute of Arts, 1994.

Grese, Robert E. *Jens Jensen: Maker of Natural Parks and Gardens.* Baltimore: Johns Hopkins University Press, 1992.

Hanks, David A. *The Decorative Designs of Frank Lloyd Wright.* New York: E. P. Dutton, 1979.

Hitchcock, Henry-Russell. *In the Nature of Materials: The Buildings of Frank Lloyd Wright, 1887–1941.* 1942. Reprint, New York: Da Capo Press, 1973.

Hoffmann, Donald. *Frank Lloyd Wright: Architecture and Nature.* New York: Dover Publications, 1986.

———. *Understanding Frank Lloyd Wright's Architecture.* New York: Dover Publications, 1995.

Jensen, Jens. *Siftings.* 1939. Reprint, Baltimore: Johns Hopkins University Press, 1990.

Kruty, Paul, and Mati Maldre. *Walter Burley Griffin in America.* Urbana: University of Illinois Press, 1996.

Lind, Carla. *The Wright Style: Recreating the Spirit of Frank Lloyd Wright.* New York: Simon and Schuster, 1992.

Manson, Grant Carpenter. *Frank Lloyd Wright to 1910: The First Golden Age.* New York: Van Nostrand Reinhold, 1958.

Peisch, Mark L. *The Chicago School of Architecture: Early Followers of Sullivan and Wright.* New York: Random House, 1964.

Pfeiffer, Bruce Brooks, ed. *Frank Lloyd Wright: Collected Writings.* Vol. 1. New York: Rizzoli International Publications, 1992.

Robertson, Cheryl. *Frank Lloyd Wright and George Mann Niedecken: Prairie School Collaborators.* Lexington, Mass.: Milwaukee Art Museum and Museum of Our National Heritage, 1999.

Secrest, Meryle. *Frank Lloyd Wright: A Biography.* New York: Alfred A. Knopf, 1992.

Sittenfeld, Michael, ed. *The Prairie School: Design Vision for the Midwest.* Chicago: Art Institute of Chicago, 1995.

Twombly, Robert C. *Louis Sullivan: His Life and Work.* Chicago: University of Chicago Press, 1986.

Van Zanten, David T. *Walter Burley Griffin: Selected Designs.* Palos Park, Ill.: Prairie School Press, 1970.

von Holst, Hermann Valentin. *Country and Suburban Homes of the Prairie School Period.* 1913. Reprint, New York: Dover Publications, 1982.

Watson, Anne, ed. *Beyond Architecture: Marion Mahony and Walter Burley Griffin in America, Australia, and India.* Sydney: Powerhouse Publishing, Museum of Applied Arts and Sciences, 1998.

CREDITS
AND ACKNOWLEDGMENTS

This book would not have been possible without the kindness and hospitality of the many homeowners who generously opened their doors to us. Their enthusiasm for the architects who created their houses and gardens is truly inspiring. I am also deeply grateful for the assistance and advice of the Oak Park architect John Thorpe and for the scholarship of historians such as H. Allen Brooks and Paul Kruty, who have contributed greatly to the understanding of Frank Lloyd Wright and his early associates. A special thanks goes to Susan Benjamin, Donald Hallmark, Robert McCoy, and Jennifer Komar Olivarez, as well as to Diane Maddex, president of Archetype Press, who conceived the idea for this book, and her staff, especially Gretchen Smith Mui for her patience and Robert Wiser for his beautiful design. Christian Korab deserves particular praise for his exquisite photography. ▪ In addition, the following individuals offered invaluable assistance: Nancy and Peter Albrecht; Rolf Anderson; Donald Aucutt; Roger and Peggy Bang; Suzanne M. Barrow, Pleasant Home Foundation; Mr. and Mrs. Lyle Bergo; Barbara Bezat, Northwest Architectural Archives; Ted and Sonia Bloch; Harold and Doris Blumenthal; Sarah Ann Briggs, Frank Lloyd Wright Building Conservancy; Greg and Alice Brock; Paul Brunsell; Max Burger; Jean Chesley; Stephen Christy; John and Jackie Conway; Bill Dring; John Eifler; Jeanette Fields; Henry and Frances Fogel; Hans Friedman; Jan Fulwiler and Robin Gates; Ralph and Jodie Gerbie; Amy Glynn and Doug Johnson; Jane Grabowski-Miller; Robert E. Grese; Kort Gustafson; Martin Hackl; Beverly Hackney, Decatur Public Library; Jerry and Jo Kolpek; Edward and Maureen Labenski; E. Edward Linville; Jonathan Lipman; Frank Lipo, Oak Park Historical Society; Maya Moran Manny; Jean Marinos; Fran Martone, Ross Elfline, and Jean Guarino, Frank Lloyd Wright Home and Studio Foundation; Terrence Marvel, Milwaukee Art Museum; Bonnie McCoy; Mary McCray; Jim and Liz McNair; Tim Mullins; David and Julie Nelsen; Frances Nemtin, Bruce Brooks Pfeiffer, Penny Fowler, Oscar Muñoz, and Margo Stipe, The Frank Lloyd Wright Foundation; William and Carol Pollak; Randy Randazzo and Kimberlee Kepper; Milton and Sylvie Robinson; Donald and Karen Rosenwinkel; John and Patricia Scribner; Michael Segal; Jay and Carmen Shriver; Sigma Phi Fraternity; Julia Sniderman; Kelly Steele, Julie Goodman, and Beth Mylander, Taliesin Preservation Commission; Catherine Stika; Rick and Laura Talaske; Kristin Visser; Babe Voertman; Ed Walker; Dr. and Mrs. J. Stephen Westly; Jane Williams; Robert and Patricia Wood; Carol Yetken; and Scot Zimmerman. Finally, I am most grateful for the encouragement of John Legler and Pedro E. Guerrero, to whom I dedicate this book.

DIXIE LEGLER

I wish to acknowledge my two dear friends Jeff Krueger and David Graeve for their participation and photography assistance, my father for his encouragement and tutelage over the years, and certainly all the homeowners for their enthusiastic cooperation.

CHRISTIAN KORAB

INDEX

Published in 1999 by

Stewart, Tabori & Chang

A division of U.S. Media Holdings, Inc.

115 West 18th Street

New York, NY 10011

Distributed in Canada by

General Publishing Company Ltd.

30 Lesmill Road

Don Mills, Ontario, Canada M3B 2T6

Library of Congress Cataloging-in-Publication Data

Legler, Dixie.

Prairie style : houses and gardens by Frank Lloyd Wright
and the Prairie School / Dixie Legler, Christian Korab.

p.   cm.

Includes bibliographical references and index.

ISBN 1-55670-931-5

1. Architecture, Domestic—Middle West.

2. Prairie School (Architecture). 3. Wright, Frank Lloyd, 1867–1959.

I. Korab, Christian. II. Wright, Frank Lloyd, 1867–1959. III. Title.

NA7218.L44   1999   99-15471

728'.37'09730904—dc21   CIP

Produced by

Archetype Press, Inc., Washington, D.C.

Project Director: Diane Maddex

Editor: Gretchen Smith Mui

Editorial Assistant: John Hovanec

Designer: Robert L. Wiser

Printed in Hong Kong

10   9   8   7   6   5   4   3   2   1

First Printing

The prairie flora pictured on the endleaves and on pages 1–9, 22–23, and 44–45
were photographed by Christian Korab at the Ladd Arboretum in Evanston,
Illinois, and the University of Wisconsin Arboretum in Madison, Wisconsin.

A Note on the Typography

The display typeface used in *Prairie Style* was designed by Robert L. Wiser of Archetype Press. It captures the spirit of early-twentieth-century typographers who created alphabets from pure geometric forms. Frank Lloyd Wright was fascinated by such letterforms and sought ways to create them with a minimum of strokes, reducing their angles and shapes. He used these ideas in creating geometric alphabets for his own presentation drawings. Aries, used for the text, and Gill Sans, used for the captions, were both designed by Eric Gill. Aries, a decorative Roman font, was commissioned in 1932 by Fairfax Hall of the Stourton Press for use in a privately printed catalogue of Chinese pottery collected by Sir Percival David. Gill Sans was created in 1927–30 for the Monotype Corporation and modeled after Edward Johnston's type for the London Underground Railway. With its clear geometric construction, Johnston's 1916 type was much more legible than earlier sans-serif forms.